BLAKE, SEXUALITY AND BOURGEOIS POLITENESS

Recent criticism has often overlooked William Blake's relationship
to the bourgeois culture of sentimentalism, focusing instead on his
association with the radical London underworld of revolutionaries,
artisans and plebeian dissenters. By removing Blake from their
company and reading him instead through the polite world he knew
well, Susan Matthews sets out to give us a new Blake, as well as a new
angle on the conflicted development of a bourgeois culture in the
late eighteenth century which was in the process of redefining the
role and meaning of sexuality. With imaginative use of personalities,
texts and images taken from an original range of archival material,
Matthews returns to the Age of Sensibility and finds within its
changing landscape answers to some of the crucial questions that
remain about an artist and writer whose work continues to challenge
scholars and critics today.

SUSAN MATTHEWS is Senior Lecturer in English Literature at
Roehampton University.

T0371518

CAMBRIDGE STUDIES IN ROMANTICISM

This series aims to foster the best new work in one of the most challenging fields within English literary studies. From the early 1780s to the early 1830s a formidable array of talented men and women took to literary composition, not just in poetry, which some of them famously transformed, but in many modes of writing. The expansion of publishing created new opportunities for writers, and the political stakes of what they wrote were raised again by what Wordsworth called those 'great national events' that were 'almost daily taking place': the French Revolution, the Napoleonic and American wars, urbanisation, industrialisation, religious revival, an expanded empire abroad and the reform movement at home. This was an enormous ambition, even when it pretended otherwise. The relations between science, philosophy, religion and literature were reworked in texts such as *Frankenstein* and *Biographia Literaria*; gender relations in *A Vindication of the Rights of Woman* and *Don Juan*; journalism by Cobbett and Hazlitt; poetic form, content and style by the Lake School and the Cockney School. Outside Shakespeare studies, probably no body of writing has produced such a wealth of comment or done so much to shape the responses of modern criticism. This indeed is the period that saw the emergence of those notions of 'literature' and of literary history, especially national literary history, on which modern scholarship in English has been founded.

The categories produced by Romanticism have also been challenged by recent historicist arguments. The task of the series is to engage both with a challenging corpus of Romantic writings and with the changing field of criticism they have helped to shape. As with other literary series published by Cambridge, this one will represent the work of both younger and more established scholars, on either side of the Atlantic and elsewhere.

For a complete list of titles published, see end of book.

BLAKE, SEXUALITY AND BOURGEOIS POLITENESS

SUSAN MATTHEWS

CAMBRIDGE
UNIVERSITY PRESS

CAMBRIDGE
UNIVERSITY PRESS

University Printing House, Cambridge CB2 8BS, United Kingdom

Cambridge University Press is part of the University of Cambridge.

It furthers the University's mission by disseminating knowledge in the pursuit of education, learning and research at the highest international levels of excellence.

www.cambridge.org
Information on this title: www.cambridge.org/9781107449138

First published 2011
First paperback edition 2014

A catalogue record for this publication is available from the British Library

Library of Congress Cataloguing in Publication data
Matthews, Susan, 1955–
Blake, Sexuality and Bourgeois Politeness / Susan Matthews.
p.   cm. – (Cambridge Studies in Romanticism)
Includes bibliographical references and index.
ISBN 978-0-521-51357-9 (Hardback)
1. Blake, William, 1757–1827–History and criticism.   2. Sex in literature.   3. Sex role in literature.   4. Sentimentalism in literature.   5. Blake, William, 1757–1827–Contemporaries. 6. Art and literature–England–History–18th century.   7. Art and literature–England–History– 19th century.   8. Literature and society–England–History–18th century.   9. Literature and society–England–History–19th century.   I. Title.   II. Series.
PR4148.S48M38 2011
821'.7–dc22

2010042531

ISBN 978-0-521-51357-9 Hardback
ISBN 978-1-107-44913-8 Paperback

Contents

List of illustrations   *page* vi
Acknowledgements   viii
Abbreviations   x

Introduction: the birth of sexuality   1

1   'Happy copulation': visual enthusiasm and the sexual gaze   16

2   Fuseli and the 'female dream' of *Europe*   30

3   A history of softness: William Hayley and *The Triumphs of Temper*   56

4   The *Essay on Old Maids* and the learned lady   82

5   Cowper's fear: nature, population, apocalypse   110

6   Blake reads Richardson: anthologies, annotation and cultures of reading   141

7   A 'blank in Nature': Blake and cultures of mourning   169

8   Wollstonecraft and the adulterous woman   188

Notes   211
Bibliography   247
Index   265

Illustrations

1 *Visions of the Daughters of Albion*, copy A, plate 9, 1793.
   © The Trustees of the British Museum.   *page* 22
2 William Hogarth, *Enthusiasm Delineated*, from John
   Ireland, *Hogarth Illustrated Vol III and last*, March 1798,
   John Boydell. © The British Library Board (131b7).   23
3 Henry Fuseli, *Titania and Bottom c.* 1790. © Tate,
   London, 2010.   43
4 *The Fertilization of Egypt* from Erasmus Darwin, *The Botanic
   Garden*, 1791. © The Trustees of the British Museum.   46
5 William Blake, *Oberon, Titania and Puck with Fairies Dancing*,
   c. 1786. © Tate, London, 2010.   48
6 Henry Fuseli, eng. William Blake, *Allegory of a Dream
   of Love c.* 1790. © The Trustees of the British Museum.   50
7 William Blake, *The Temple of Mirth*, after Thomas Stothard, 1784.
   © Tate, London, 2010 (first version).   68
8 Henry Fuseli, *The Mighty Mother Sails Through the Air* from
   The Temple of Folly, 1787. © The British Library Board (1346146). 70
9 William Blake, *As if an angel dropped down from the clouds*, 1809.
   © The Trustees of the British Museum.   76
10 William Blake, *The Whore of Babylon*, 1809. Pen and black
   ink and watercolour. © The Trustees of the British Museum.   94
11 William Blake, *The Poems of Thomas Gray*, design 22,
   A Long Story, 1797–1798. Watercolour with pen and black
   ink and graphite. © Yale Center for British Art, Paul
   Mellon Collection.   114
12 William Blake, *The Marriage of Heaven and Hell*, copy H,
   plate 1. © Fitzwilliam Museum.   124
13 Anon, *The Tree of Life*. Published by Bowles and Carver,
   undated. © The Trustees of the British Museum.   126

14 William Blake, *The Marriage of Heaven and Hell*, copy H,
    plate 3. © Fitzwilliam Museum.   127
15 William Blake, *Winter*. © Tate, London, 2010.   130
16 Henry Fuseli, *The Poet's Vision* (unused design), 1807.
    © The Trustees of the British Museum.   138
17 Henry Fuseli, *The Poet's Vision*, engr. Abraham Raimbach,
    pub. J. Johnson, London, 1 March 1807. © The Trustees
    of the British Museum.   139
18 William Blake, *Europe a Prophecy*, copy D, plate 5.
    © The Trustees of the British Museum.   159
19 Edward Bysshe, *The Art of English Poetry*, 2 vols., 1762, vol. 1,
    pp. 194–5. © The British Library Board (11603cc18).   162
20 William Blake, *The Meeting of a Family in Heaven* from
    Robert Blair, *The Grave*, 1808. © The British Library
    Board (c142e11).   177
21 William Blake, *The Reunion of the Soul and the Body* from
    Robert Blair, *The Grave*, 1808. © The British Library Board
    (c142e11).   179
22 James Barry, from A Series of Etchings by James Barry,
    Esq. from his Original and Justly Celebrated Paintings,
    in the Great Room of the Society of Arts, *Jupiter and Juno
    on Mount Ida*, c. 1804–5. © Tate, London, 2010.   181
23 William Blake, *The Spiritual Form of Nelson Guiding
    Leviathan*. © Tate, London, 2010.   186
24 William Blake, *The Penance of Jane Shore in St Paul's
    Church*, 1793. © Tate, London, 2010.   199
25 James Barry, *The Thames, or the Triumph of Navigation*,
    etching, published 1792 (1 May 1791). © National Portrait
    Gallery, London.   200

Acknowledgements

This long project has incurred a long list of debts, far more than I could remember or list. I would like to thank my colleagues at Roehampton University for continuing support and encouragement. Mark Knight tipped me off about the book of Enoch; Cathy Wells Cole, Nicki Humble, Ian Haywood and Simon Edwards read and commented on early drafts; Martin Priestman made me feel that an interest in Darwin, Cowper and Hayley was not odd; John Seed offered invaluable leads on Malkin's dissenting background; Kate Teltscher and Zach Leader read my original proposal. Above all I am grateful for the enthusiasm and insights of my students particularly those on my Blake and the Twentieth Century course.

Outside Roehampton, an army of muses, gnomes and fairies have encouraged, supported, nagged, cajoled and inspired this book out into the world. John Whale commissioned my first essay on Blake a very long time ago (and even then did not think it old historicism). I am grateful to Steve Clark for demanding a series of essays and for inviting me to the 2000 Blake conference at the Tate without which I would never have thought of writing again. Jon Mee not only invited me to speak to the Oxford Romantic Realignments seminar but spotted a book in my overlong paper. Helen Bruder and Tristanne Connolly provoked, inspired and commissioned an essay for *Queer Blake* as well as organising a conference that propelled the last changes in my book. It was a pleasure to meet some names familiar from my footnotes. Luisa Calè read an early draft of my first chapter and her work on Blake and Fuseli has been as important as her friendship. I learnt a great deal from Sarah Haggarty's patient editing of my essay in *Blake and Conflict*. Thanks also to David Fallon, Mark Crosby and Angus Whitehead for help and advice. I am lucky to have found a friend and supporter in Anne Janowitz. Martin Myrone's restaging of Blake's 1809 exhibition shaped my thinking about the end of the book and Philippa Simpson supplied the best of my pictures at the last moment: thank you to both. Perhaps my greatest debt is to those whose ideas I argue with and whose generosity and rigour is a model to follow. All Blake critics claim that 'opposition is true friendship' and I could not have formed my own argument without the work of those critics who have made Blake's visual and verbal texts a rich repository of enthusiasms and insights.

I am very grateful for the patience and continuing support of James Chandler, Linda Bree and Elizabeth Hanlon at Cambridge University Press and to the anonymous readers who helped me to firm up my argument.

Blake knew that 'Four Mighty Ones are in every Man' but did not realise that their names are Alfie, Frankie, George and Agnes. My Zoas understand intellectual war and have contributed to this project more than they know. My husband, the Lambeth writer and artist Matthew Meadows, has endured the presence of another Lambeth writer and artist for too long. Even if he has not enjoyed the process, I am glad that he has endured.

Abbreviations

Unless otherwise indicated, Blake's text is cited from *The Complete Poetry and Prose of William Blake*, edited by David E. Erdman, revised edition (New York: Doubleday, 1988), indicated by the page number preceded by E. In some cases I also give plate and line number. Blake's *Milton* is identified by *M* and *Jerusalem* as *J*. G. E. Bentley, Jr, *Blake Records*, second edition (New Haven and London: Yale University Press, 2004) is identified as BR. W refers to D. H. Weinglass, *Prints and Engraved Illustrations By and After Henry Fuseli* (Aldershot, Scolar Press, 2000).

Introduction: the birth of sexuality

The aim of this book is to trace Blake's relationship to a pro-sex culture that seemed under threat at the end of the eighteenth century and the beginning of the nineteenth. Although I expect 'Blake and sexuality' to seem a familiar topic, 'Blake and bourgeois politeness' may appear to some readers to be either counter-intuitive or plain misguided. If this is so, it is the result of decades of powerful and convincing scholarship that have established both the extent to which Blake draws on antinomian, enthusiastic and other subcultural movements and the ways in which these cultures are fascinated by sexual freedom.

Yet while Blake has stood for a prophet of sexual freedom in popular culture in the latter part of the twentieth century (and for some before this), his verbal and (to a lesser extent) visual representations of both women and sexuality have long been seen as characterised by ambiguity at best, ambivalence, contradiction and even misogyny at worst. In the wake of a decade of feminist critique, the only consensus that Robert Essick could report was that 'Blake was deeply ambivalent about female sexuality'. Not only did 'attitudes that we now tend to label feminist and anti-feminist jostle together disconcertingly in his writings' but in the later work, Essick concluded, 'the evidence for misogyny increases'.[1] Blake is typically seen not only as turning against women but as moving towards a mythic system in which 'sexuality' must ultimately be discarded. Since Blake's invented land of 'Beulah', the 'married land' of Isaiah 52, is a place where the sexes are separate, S. Foster Damon assumed that this land was also the place of 'sexual pleasure'.[2] Eternity, where 'Humanity is far above sexual organization' (E236), is a place which transcends sex. Blake's underlying model is easily read as a version of epic myth in which a male world of energetic conflict, of 'War & Hunting' (E135), is ultimately superior to a feminine pastoral idyll that offers the hero not only a vacation but also the dangerous distraction of a slide into sensual pleasure (a version of the familiar story of Dido and Aeneas). 'In Eternity they

I

neither marry nor are given in marriage' (E176), Albion tells Vala in
Jerusalem, and this is no surprise to readers familiar with an idea of an
asexual Christian heaven. After all, this line, which Wollstonecraft also
echoes, comes from the New Testament: in Matthew we are told 'For in
the resurrection they neither marry, nor are given in marriage, but are as
the angels of God in heaven.' Blake's eternity, we assume, is a place
without sex, a place to which we must all (with whatever regrets) aspire
as we give up the pleasures of the body.

Such a reading is a perfectly understandable extrapolation of the
evidence. Blake's poem *Milton*, inspired and dictated by the 'Daughters
of Beulah', records

> the journey of immortal Milton thro' your Realms
> Of terror & mild moony lustre, in soft sexual delusions
> Of varied beauty, to delight the wanderer and repose
> His burning thirst & freezing hunger!   (E96)

Here is Milton the epic hero, travelling through a delusive sexual land. In
the land of Beulah, 'the Three Classes of Men take their Sexual texture
Woven/ The Sexual is Threefold: the Human is Fourfold' (E97). In
the crucial confrontation at the end of the poem, Milton sternly warns
the virgin Ololon of a fundamental change. In order that 'the Children of
Jerusalem may be saved from slavery' she/they/the nation/the world must
cast off 'the Sexual Garments, the Abomination of Desolation/ Hiding
the Human lineaments as with an Ark & Curtains' (E142). The stark
choice is between the 'sexual' and the 'human', a choice that terrifies
Ololon, who admits that 'Altho' our Human Power can sustain the severe
contentions/ Of Friendship, our Sexual cannot' (E143). The apocalyptic
change that ends the poem follows swiftly as the lark mounts and the
smell of the wild thyme rises from Wimbledon's 'green & impurpled
Hills' (E143). It is not coincidental that my short paragraph not only
quotes every one of the five uses of the word 'sexual' in *Milton* but that it
also constructs a brief narrative which leads the reader through one of
Blake's most complex and rich poems.

If the rejection of the 'sexual' is the key to the transformation that
Blake's prophecy urgently imagines, the difficulty of aligning Milton's
clarion call with Oothoon's cry 'Love! Love! Love! happy happy Love!
free as the mountain wind!' (E50) is a central problem for the reader of
Blake's work, a problem that can be solved through chronology (Blake
changes, Blake gets older) or the favourite devices of the academic critic,
ambiguity (for the new critic), ambivalence (for those with psychoanalytic

preferences) or their more sophisticated children (aporia, multiplying meanings, complexity) to produce a playful, troubled or conflicted Blake. The production of such complexity is the professional expertise of the critic. My study will propose that such devices are themselves the tools of Beulah, the intellectual means to quiet conflict, to reduce art to a safe form of play. The complexity of Blake's work lies, I suggest, instead in the fierceness of its argument and the way it engages with hostile contexts. I aim to show that Blake's work presents a surprisingly consistent and coherent view of what we call sexuality, the 'quality of being sexual or possessing sex', a meaning that the *Oxford English Dictionary* (OED) shows as being used for the first time in 1797 in a reference to the Linnaean system and the 'sexuality of plants'.

The key to my argument lies in the newness of the word 'sexuality' in Blake's time. This word occurs only once in Blake's writing and the fact that he uses the word in *Milton* is probably a product of his contact with circles for whom Erasmus Darwin and Cowper (one of the first to use the word 'sexuality') were the key writers of the period. In Blake's surviving writing, the word 'sexual' appears exclusively in *Milton*, *Jerusalem* and 'For The Sexes/ THE GATES of PARADISE', a late reissue of the 1793 emblem book originally called 'For Children'. The change of title, according to Erdman, is certainly later than 1806.[3] It seems safe to conclude, therefore, that 'sexes', 'sexual' and 'sexuality' are words that Blake uses only after the three years from 1800 to 1803 he spent in Felpham, the small village in Sussex where he lived close to, and worked with, the popular poet William Hayley, a friend both of Erasmus Darwin and William Cowper. This period was the only one in which Blake lived outside London and it brought him into close and sustained contact with a significantly different culture from that which he is likely to have known in London.

At its appearance at the end of the eighteenth century, the word 'sexuality' is still strongly marked by an older meaning of 'sex' (closer to our modern sense of gender) to mean 'either of the two main categories (male and female) into which humans and many other living things are divided on the basis of their reproductive functions', a sense which the OED dates from Wycliff and which continues to the present day. In the eighteenth century the 'sex' is also the female sex. The word 'sex' refers to a category (closer but not identical to our understanding of gender) rather than to bodily 'acts'. The first use of the word 'sex' to refer to 'Physical contact between individuals involving sexual stimulation; sexual activity or behaviour, spec. sexual intercourse, copulation' is listed by the current OED in 1900. Typical of the shift in the meaning of 'sex' and cognate words is the difficulty that modern readers experience in understanding the title of Polwhele's 1798 poem, *The Unsex'd Females*. Attacking Wollstonecraft in the wake of the scandal caused by Godwin's memoir, Polwhele is of course not complaining that Wollstonecraft was insufficiently sexy, or even (in anticipation of Cora Kaplan's influential argument) that her writing produced a desexualised version of femininity. For Polwhele, to be 'Unsex'd' is for a woman (specifically) to fail to conform to the requirements of 'the sex', so to behave like a man and thus to demonstrate the kind of specifically masculine sexual drive that is inappropriate to a women. Polwhele's poem is the product of a view of gender which assumes that women *should be* unsexual (a view on its way in at the end of the eighteenth century) but uses 'sex'd' in a way that would be more familiar in the earlier period to describe a gendered category. The sharpest discussion of this issue is Katherine Binhammer's 2002 essay, 'Thinking gender with sexuality in 1790s' feminist thought', which quotes Claudia Johnson to explicate Polwhele's title: 'For Polwhele, "unsexed" women are "oversexed."... What being an unsexed female entails ... is indulging in unbounded heterosexual activity without the heterosexual sentiment.'[4]

For Cowper too, the word 'sexuality' carries a sense of behaviour appropriate to the sexes. His use of the word in 1800 is in a reference to Erasmus Darwin for whom, whether or not one female flower dallies with four males, sexuality is necessarily driven by contact between the opposite sexes. 'Sexuality', for Darwin, is inextricably associated with 'the instinct to propagate the species'; it is inevitably heterosexual. Blake's characteristically negative use of the word 'sexual' and cognates derives both from Polwhele's (and Wollstonecraft's) assumption that the sexual is that which represents the proprieties of a particular (female) gender, and from Darwin's account of sexuality as the patterned behaviour that leads to generation. To be 'Mortal & Vegetable in Sexuality' (E135) is to be assigned to a fixed category.

An early twenty-first-century academic book with the word 'sexuality' in its title necessarily sets up a different set of assumptions in the reader. In 2000 Bruce R. Smith calculated that the Modern Language Association online bibliography contained over three thousand items containing the word 'sexuality' written since 1981, of which 'at least ten per cent' were 'concerned with texts written before 1800'.[5] The boom in titles containing the word 'sexuality' derives from Foucault's claim that sexuality has a history that begins in the early nineteenth century. But Darwin's (and

Cowper's) use of the word 'sexuality' is very different from our modern (post-Freudian) understanding that sexuality refers to a complex cluster of psychological and behavioural meanings. Writers now tend to distinguish between writing on sex and writing on sexuality. Thus Gail Bederman in 2008: ' "Sexuality" refers to the ways that acts, pleasures, beliefs, and moralities are constructed in particular times or places. "Sex" refers to specific bodily acts, regardless of culture or context.'[6] Bederman's Foucauldian understanding of 'sexuality' is not Cowper's, or Darwin's, or Blake's.

The necessarily binary structure within the word 'sexuality' as used around 1800 rules out the possibility that 'sexuality' can describe homosexual desire. This is not to claim, as Foucault does, that same-sex desire or subjectivity could not exist in the early nineteenth century.[7] It is to claim that the words 'sexual' and 'sexuality' for Blake exclude the possibility of same-sex desire. It is no accident that much of the finest recent writing on Blake and sexuality derives from critics who use ideas of camp and queer theory: Helen Bruder, Christopher Hobson and Andrew Elfenbein are among those who have demonstrated that Blake offers positive images of same-sex desire, particularly in writing after 1803.[8] Christopher Hobson was also instrumental in making possible a reading of the end of *Visions of the Daughters of Albion* which side-steps a generation of compulsory condemnation.[9] As Katherine Binhammer points out, queer studies has become 'the institutional and methodological location for both the history and theory of sexuality' reflecting 'the desire of some lesbian theorists to break away from a particular strain of Second Wave Feminism'.[10] In this study I hope to contribute to the project of reclaiming sexuality for feminism, a project with many important predecessors.

Criticism that derived from Second Wave feminism in Britain and America has often been critical of Blake's representations of gender and sexuality. In 1998 Anne Mellor attacked the tendency of Blake's readers to see him 'as he might have liked to be seen: as an artist deeply at odds with his culture and times', insisting on the recognition that he was 'complicit in the racist and sexist ideologies of his culture'.[11] Mellor's trajectory is indicative of Blake's changing reception among feminist readers: whereas her first academic book in 1974 was *Blake's Human Form Divine*, her major work of 2000, *Mothers of the Nation: Women's Political Writing in England, 1780–1820*, celebrates the influence of the evangelical writer Hannah More. Whereas Blake's standing has slipped for many feminist scholars, work on bluestocking culture and other women writers has reshaped our understanding of the Romantic period, demonstrating the cultural power of women within the public sphere.

My study argues that Blake's work demonstrates a remarkable consistency in its defence of female sexuality, a defence that draws on a specific pro-sex discourse within the bourgeois world with which he had most contact, deriving from Milton's view of Protestant sexuality.[12] (In order to accommodate the reader of an isolated chapter, I will use the words sex and sexuality in a modern sense unless clearly signalled.) In the view of friends and contacts like Cumberland, Fuseli and Hayley, female sexuality was under attack from an attempt to redraw public culture, and this attack on the sexualisation of culture was believed to threaten the vigour of culture and the arts. If the 'sexual' in Blake's use after 1800 derives both from the now obsolete sense of the 'sex' to mean 'feminine' and from a focus on that which is appropriate to each gender, it can carry a meaning almost diametrically opposed to the modern 'sexual'. The OED cites Wollstonecraft's claim from the 1792 *Vindication of the Rights of Woman* that '[a] mistaken education, a narrow uncultivated mind, and many sexual prejudices, tend to make women more constant than men'. 'Sexual prejudices', in other words, limit women within a gendered idea of constancy.[13] Read in this sense, some crucial passages in Blake's work look different. If the 'soft sexual delusions' offered by the Daughters of Beulah in the opening of *Milton* use 'sexual' in the same way as Wollstonecraft to mean 'feminine', then Blake's Beulah becomes an account of contemporary constructions of gender rather than (what we call) sexuality. Rather than describing the delusive power of the erotic, 'sexual delusions' are 'soft' because they are the product of polite bourgeois codes of gender which use passivity manipulatively.

Second Wave feminism is in some ways a product of the new model of sexual difference that was the product of Blake's lifetime. The end of the eighteenth century witnessed the consolidation of a model of sexual difference in which women were no longer lesser or imperfect men but came instead to be seen as complementary to but essentially different from men. In the process, this two-sex model separated the word 'man' from the word 'human' turning it into a gender specific category. As Binhammer argues, it was this new idea of sexual difference that created the idea of 'Woman, in all her particularities and essential specificities . . . as a separate and proper object of study'.[14] Plate 3 of *Milton* signals Blake's concern with the new two-sex model of gender difference in its image of two figures, male and female, splitting outwards from the same root; as a poem about Beulah, *Milton* is necessarily concerned with the separation of male from female which is fundamental to the period. To the dismay of many recent readers, Blake's eternity does not include 'woman' as a gender-specific entity. There has been much discussion of what is seen as the limitations of androgyny in Blake's utopian vision of Eternity. According to Tristanne Connolly, 'the vision in question is not really androgynous' because 'the gender-neutral word "Humanity" disappears and the nominal character of this concession is revealed as Los goes on to bewail not being able to "be united as Man with Man" and enjoy the mingling and joining of souls "thro all the Fibres of Brotherhood" '.[15] A central project of feminist criticism at the end of the twentieth century was to separate 'man' from 'human' to show how 'man' could never be gender neutral and could not include 'woman'. To a modern reader, educated within a modern two-sex system, the word 'human' is a delusive slip, replicated by Los, for the gendered 'man'. Identity politics are unthinkable without the categories that Dror Wahrman sees as under construction at the end of the eighteenth century, but for Blake these categories themselves are deeply flawed.

Much of the most productive recent criticism has investigated Blake via the categories of gender and sexuality that postdate his period. But at times the labour that Blake's critics experience in sexing his figures (rather like sexing kittens) may point to the possibility that we are asking the wrong questions.[16] Moving, as Nicholas Williams has argued, between ideology and utopia, Blake's language is unstable and there are contexts in which strategic considerations are paramount.[17] This is particularly the case, I will argue, in some annotations and notebook entries. Confronted by a language which is not his own, Blake's strategy is shifting and often hard to read. Frequently Blake adopts and then subverts the categories of discourses that he rejects. In place of categories of class, gender, sexuality, race that have become established since the end of the eighteenth century I assume in this study that culture is the result of a system of minute (but cumulatively significant) differences.

The philosopher Alain Badiou offers an attack on the categories of cultural criticism as 'a tourist's fascination for the diversity of morals, customs and beliefs. And in particular, for the irreducible medley of imaginary formations (religions, sexual representations, incarnations of authority…).'[18] Badiou's model is surprisingly like that of Blake's first engraved work, *All Religions are One*, which states: 'As all men are alike in outward form, So (and with the same infinite variety) all are alike in the Poetic Genius' (E1). The crucial question in this statement is the relationship between being 'alike' and 'infinite variety'. The discourse of identity born in Blake's lifetime claims to protect the individuality of the subject. Blake's language seems at times to deny that individuality. His work shows little interest in character or in the integrity of individual identity. Nevertheless, Blake suggests that his time sets up categories of identity such as 'the female' which reduce 'infinite variety' under the banner of a binomial system founded on an idea of the 'other'. From the male point of view, the female is one example of the 'other', yet some forms of feminism merely invert this pattern to turn the 'male' into another example of the other. If my study seems to give too much time to the voices of writers such as Madan or Hayley this is because I am interested in the potential for utopian thought in many different positions.

Both Saree Makdisi and Jon Mee cite Blake's 1827 letter to Cumberland which claims that the bourgeois concept of the individual masks a rejection of 'infinite variety':

For a Line or Lineament is not formed by Chance a Line is a Line in its Minutest Subdivision[s] Strait or Crooked It is Itself & Not Intermeasurable with or by any Thing Else Such is Job but since the French Revolution Englishmen are all Intermeasurable One by Another Certainly a happy state of Agreement to which I for One do not Agree. (E783)[19]

Setting up a false model of individuality, Blake suggests, masks a reduction to categories of gender, race or nation. My focus, then, is on the 'infinite variety' which marks those with whom Blake comes into contact. As a reader and viewer I also wish to be free of the constraints of an approved 'female' eroticism.

Blake's focus on the 'Female' can be read (as Nicholas Williams has suggested) in relation to Wollstonecraft's attack on the ideology of femininity.[20] Blake writes at a historical moment in which ideas of the female and of a specifically female form of sexuality were under construction and debate. In this debate Richardson played a key role, creating a powerful image (in E. J. Clery's words) of 'the category of woman ... abstracted from biological sex' and it is for this reason that I discuss how Blake read Richardson.[21] Richardson's idealisation of a non-biological femininity prepares for what Thomas Laqueur sees as a fundamental shift in the understanding of the place of sexual pleasure in conception. Whereas female orgasm was seen as necessary to conception in the mid-eighteenth century, according to Laqueur by the early nineteenth century it came to be seen as a functionless accident.[22] Since pleasure (to some degree) is necessarily part of the male role in conception, the way is opened for the belief that the sexes experience sex differently. Under the heading 'Some Questions Answered', a verse in Blake's notebook rejects the idea that female desire is essentially different from male:

> What is it men in women do require
> The lineaments of Gratified Desire
> What is it women do in men require
> The lineaments of Gratified Desire. (E474–5)

The near parallel between lines one and three (only the verb 'do' alters the pattern) and the repetition of the answer in lines two and four assert that men and women desire the same thing, that is, the sight of their partner's pleasure. Sexuality, here, is defined in terms of visual pleasure as 'lineaments' that can be seen, and is an experience which is assumed to be the same for each sex.

It is because the new definition of 'sexuality' emerges first in writing by and about Erasmus Darwin and William Cowper that this study places Blake within what can only be described as a bourgeois world. To do so challenges some of the key beliefs and discoveries of the best recent work on Blake. In the work of E. P. Thompson, David Worrall and Saree Makdisi, Blake emerges from a variety of radical underground cultures which provided a vehicle for counter-hegemonic traditions surviving through the eighteenth century from the civil war period.[23] In Makdisi's words, Blake's work allows access to 'the language of radical antinomian enthusiasm, which he, like others, inherited from older currents of thought and modified for the exigencies of his own time'.[24] In recent work by David Worrall, Marsha Keith Schuchard and Keri Davies, Blake is shown to draw on the cultures of spiritualised sexuality preserved among Swedenborgians, Moravians and other religious groups. Marsha Keith Schuchard in particular has described the radical sexual experimentation of the Moravian 'sifting time' of 1743–53 as one example of secret sexual cultures that may have influenced the Blake family culture and been transmitted to William by his mother.[25] The contribution to our modern understanding of Blake's work by these scholars is immeasurable.

Nevertheless, I differ in my understanding of the implications of their extraordinary research, particularly in so far as I use their discoveries to understand Blake's verbal and visual texts. Whereas Worrall, Davies and Schuchard believe that Blake's works are written for particular faith communities and identify Blake as seeking out patrons with affiliations to Swedenborgian and Moravian groups, I suggest that Blake's work is addressed to 'the Public', even where he does not succeed in communicating in any effective way with his intended audience. Blake repeatedly addresses the 'Public': in a 1793 prospectus offering his illuminated books for sale in October 1793 (E692–693), in the *Descriptive Catalogue* written to accompany his 1809 exhibition and in the defaced plate 3 of *Jerusalem*. As Jon Mee points out, it cannot be assumed that the limited circulation of the illuminated books 'was Blake's desired goal merely because it was what he finally achieved'.[26] Nor do I assume that the illuminated books are the centrepiece of Blake's *oeuvre*. Blake critics are disappointed by work that does not discuss *enough* of Blake's large and difficult corpus, whereas the non-Blakean critic is often put off by the density of reference assumed by writing on Blake. Nevertheless, Blake criticism often observes a set of unspoken boundaries, placing the illuminated books at the centre of a corpus which need not acknowledge Blake's commercial work as an engraver or his illustrations to the work of other writers. Art historians have often been more willing than literary critics to see Blake as an aspiring, if ultimately failed, member of the public sphere.[27] Not only do I reject the assumption that Blake's work addresses an exclusive or even dispersed subculture but I also argue that the subject of Blake's work is the culture of the nation and even the world.

Marsha Keith Schuchard's research into Moravian and Swedenborgian traditions of spiritualised sexuality shows that Blake or his family were in contact with groups for whom sexuality was part of a regulated private spiritual practice, a route to vision.[28] But Schuchard's account of sexual secrets, handed down through closed religious communities, reads oddly in relation to Blake's attacks on secrecy, mystery and ritual. Her account of a phallic religion whose sexual techniques demand a wearying compliance from Catherine Blake seems at odds with the images of ecstatic females that decorate many of the 1790s' illuminated books. As Peter Otto argues, the phallus is associated with Urizen as a figure of authority, as 'the paradoxical symbol and product of Urizen's disavowal of the flesh'.[29] Blake's work, I suggest, critiques not only the dominant culture of his time but also its subcultures.

In this study I trace Blake's critique of dominant cultural forms, ideological constructions which Blake, I believe, often identifies with some astuteness. Northrop Frye saw Blake as a product of 'the age, in poetry, of Collins, Percy, Gray, Cowper, Smart, Chatterton, Burns, Ossian and the Wartons', authors whom Blake knew and in some cases illustrated. Nevertheless Frye was puzzled by Blake's association with William Hayley and considered the time in Felpham 'an ordeal by fire, a temptation in a wilderness of fashionable smugness'.[30] William Hayley plays a key role in this study, not so much because I wish to rehabilitate him as because I aim to investigate the tensions in Blake's relationship to fashionable, bourgeois and commercial culture. In particular, I argue that contact with Hayley enabled Blake to identify the twists and turns of the new culture of sexuality with a new precision, for Hayley was a high priest of the 'sexual' culture of his time.

Doubts remain about the extent to which Blake ever really belonged within the circles to which he gave or sold his work. Saree Makdisi argues that Blake was fundamentally opposed to the assumptions of the 'hegemonic radicals' of the Joseph Johnson circle for whom Blake's enthusiastic rhetoric marked him as an outsider.[31] Jon Mee suggests that Blake was viewed as 'a tradesman, albeit an eccentric and gifted one' in the Johnson circle.[32] I do not necessarily challenge these conclusions. Although it was Blake's bourgeois friends who kept his letters, the disproportionate survival of correspondence with Hayley may distort the evidence. Nevertheless, Blake's work found a niche within a supportive if limited bourgeois circle. For my study, Blake's excitement at reading George Cumberland's unpublished 1798 novel, *The Captive of the Castle of Sennaar*, is significant since the novel describes a sexual utopia with parallels in Blake's own writing. Blake writes to Cumberland in September 1800: 'Your vision of the Happy Sophis I have devourd. O most delicious book how canst thou Expect any thing but Envy in Londons accursed walls.'[33] Arriving in Felpham in 1800, Blake seems to value a group which is distinct from the radical intellectual milieu of the Dissenting public sphere. Blake's bourgeois friends and contacts form a surprisingly cohesive group which is distinct from that of the Johnson circle even as it touches on it: George Cumberland knew Thomas Johnes, the collector to whom Benjamin Heath Malkin gave a copy of *Songs of Innocence*, both Cumberland and Malkin knew Horne Tooke, and Malkin may well have known or met Wollstonecraft, who was central to the Johnson circle and a friend of Fuseli. Blake's most successful publication in the nineteenth century was the illustrated edition of Blair's *Grave* which was promoted by Malkin and Fuseli and was one of the few works by Blake that Hayley owned. Recent criticism has productively explored parallels with the work of women writers such as Ann Batten Cristall.[34] Martin Myrone suggests that even though the 'very idea of a "bourgeois Blake" may be disconcerting; ... what made Blake possible was a loophole within the cultural logic of a specifically bourgeois society that was taking shape around him'.[35] Even though the bourgeois world with which Blake was in contact offered its own critique of the 'Hirelings in the Camp, the

Court & the University' (E95), Blake's complex relationship to this culture has not yet, I suggest, been fully explored.

In Northrop Frye's *Fearful Symmetry*, this world was the Age of Sensibility. But because Frye's account was weighted towards male writers and readers he could not see the extent to which the Age of Sensibility was shaped by the contribution of women as writers, artists, readers and viewers. Hayley's two notable successes as an author were works for women or about women. In the (more than six) decades since Frye's work, the work of feminist scholars has made possible a view of a feminised public sphere in which Hayley seems less comical. But the embarrassment of Hayley is nevertheless key to just those areas that have proved most resistant to the work of Blake's many critics, in particular, representations of sexuality and violence, of the 'Female Will', of what seems like rape, of voyeurism and misogyny. Just as the relationship between Blake and Hayley is incomprehensible to most readers so there are still parts of Blake's work that are resistant to recuperation: the end of *Visions*; the Preludium to *America* and to *Europe*; the words spoken by the 'Divine Voice' in *Milton*; some of the jottings in the notebook. It is striking how often these passages are concerned with sexuality.

In approaching these passages and poems I am minded of Anna Clark's idea of 'sexual desire' as 'trangressing and dissolving conventional boundaries of society, as a metaphor for all that is destabilizing and polluting'.[36] Some of the passages of Blake's work that have worried readers can be seen in terms of 'twilight moments', a term that Clark coins to describe 'sexual activities or desires which people are not supposed to engage in, but they do'.[37] These passages are not acts but representations of desire and imagination which engage with the representation of sexuality in Blake's time. I am not so much concerned to discover what Blake did in the bedroom (fascinating though such speculation is) as to understand the public meanings of sexuality, meanings which are always potentially implicated in politics and history. Angela Carter was right, I think, when she argued that

[a]lthough the erotic relationship may seem to exist freely, on its own terms, among the distorted social relationships of a bourgeois society, it is, in fact, the most self-conscious of all human relationships, a direct confrontation of two beings whose actions in the bed are wholly determined by their acts when they are out of it.[38]

The period I cover, from the 1780s to the early 1800s, is characterised by a series of moral panics over the role of sexuality from the polygamy debate of the early 1780s to the adultery panic of the end of the 1790s. As Katherine Binhammer suggests, the sex panic of the 1790s 'facilitated the redefinition of female sexuality required by late eighteenth-century domestic ideology'.[39] Yet as Anna Clark argues, 'moral panics do not instigate the repression of sex; sex is regulated in societies before moral panics, and when they subside, regulation continues'.[40] My study presents Blake as a consistent critic of the new domestic ideology and as a defender of sexual pleasure. Blake's marginal position, in contact with quite different, but interwoven, cultures and discourses means that his work voices and echoes many of the debates of his time. His relative failure, however, allows us to detect the boundaries of the acceptable in his culture: if Blake's work lies on the boundary of the legitimate in his time, then it can also reveal the limits that culture places on itself.

Blake's function in my study is therefore twofold. Blake's continuing cultural power in the twenty-first century makes the study of his work necessarily always a study of reception, which opens into an account of the assumptions of our own time. Studying Blake reveals a hidden story of our own fears and views on sexuality. Robert Essick laments what he sees as the failure to distinguish between text and context in historicist Blake criticism and the shift of focus from 'that singular individual, William Blake, as the sole origin of works bearing his name' in so far as this leads to readings in which 'the meanings of Blake's texts are subsumed to their presence in a network of other texts'.[41] In this study, however, I am interested precisely in the 'network of other texts' to which Blake's work leads. Rather than chapters devoted to a succession of (verbal) texts by Blake, my chapters address significant encounters between Blake and his contemporaries, whether these are visual artists like Fuseli or writers like Cowper. They are not necessarily people that Blake knew: I am as interested in Blake's meeting with Richardson through reading *Clarissa* as with his meeting with Hayley. In some cases I am interested in the role of a discourse or a culture (mourning) as much as in a person (Malkin). In each case I go deep into what is sometimes enemy territory before returning to Blake's work to see whether now familiar work appears in a new light. Each of my chapters therefore investigates a triangular relationship between Blake, a figure more fully assimilated into the polite world, and discourses of sexuality. Blake offers a way to understand differential constructions of sexuality in the work of writers and artists such as Fuseli, Hayley, Cowper, Malkin and Hannah More. To study Hannah More alongside Blake is not just to juxtapose the little-known and the culturally influential, reversing the valuation of older literary criticism. It is also to trace one trajectory of the feminine revolution produced by the work of eighteenth-century women. Blake's marginality, his location at the limit of what this culture found acceptable, helps to identify the gaps and the exclusions of a cultural movement that has been celebrated in recent scholarship. When Fuseli writes that Blake's illustrations to Blair's *Grave* 'play on the very Verge of legitimate invention', he identifies in Blake the boundary of the acceptable. Blake's relative failure, then, is revealing.

Jon Mee has identified Blake's liminal position in terms of the discourse on 'enthusiasm'. Here I investigate how 'enthusiasm' was recuperated via the work of women into polite culture. 'How wide the Gulf & Unpassable! between Simplicity & Insipidity', Blake writes in *Milton* on a plate that describes the mythical land of Beulah. This plate, unusually, is framed: floating or flying angels or muses form a border that encloses the lines of writing (E125). With its outspoken commitment to intellectual war, Blake's work tends to produce either passionate advocacy or sweeping criticism. Here I do not wish to use those cultures that Blake rejects (and that ultimately reject or contain his work) merely as a backdrop for Blake's visionary brilliance. My aim is to respect the complexity of a period which offered to reshape culture according to models of sympathy and altruism, offering a voice to women and giving to them a key role in remodelling culture.[42] At the same time, however, I want to challenge the limits of this world, making possible a study of the cultures of sexuality that became inadmissible within feminised polite society.

The poem 'To Tirzah', added to some copies of the *Songs* which date from after 1803, has been taken as evidence both of Blake's misogyny and of his hostility to the body. According to Alicia Ostriker it is 'a furious repudiation of female sexuality in its maternal aspect as that which encloses and divides man from Eternity'.[43] Tristanne Connolly takes this poem as symptomatic of Blake's ambivalence towards the body. But in this *Song of Experience* meanings can be shifted by reading the statements dramatically rather than doctrinally. The speaker of 'To Tirzah' assumes a series of divisions: between body and spirit, between male and female, and between the Old Testament and the New; when he announces that 'The Death of Jesus set me free' he claims a freedom from the Old Testament, from the body and from death. The speaker of 'To Tirzah' belongs to the world of the 'Sexes', a word which for Blake carries the older sense of division. In this world, male and female, body and spirit, Old and New Testament are seen as opposites. The lines written on the illustration 'It is Raised a Spiritual Body' suggest the impossibility of separating body and spirit and of assigning gender. Both 'To Tirzah' and the poem 'William Bond' (from the Pickering manuscript, dating from the Felpham years) end with the same line: 'Then what have I to do with thee?' (E30, E497). This question raises the hidden assumptions of the categories within which Blake's world works, the categories of 'sexuality'. For if male is different from female, or Western from Oriental, sympathy is the means to leap over the gap which divides the 'Other'. Alain Badiou argues that sympathy for the other in the ethical system that derives from eighteenth-century sentimentalism enters the unspoken proviso that the other must be a 'good' other, or fundamentally like us.[44]

Blake's *Milton*, one of the central texts for my discussion of Blake's critique of bourgeois culture, is centred around a series of meetings: Milton's descent leads to a meeting with 'his own Shadow' (E108), with Albion (E109), with Blake (E110), with Los (E111), with Urizen (E112), with Blake (E115). Blake also meets Los (E117). But none of these meetings follows the pattern of the meetings of the sentimental traveller (from *The Man of Feeling* to 'Resolution and Independence') whose feelings of pity are predicated on an acknowledgement both of the otherness of the other and of his fundamental conformity to the self; as Badiou points out, '[t]he eighteenth-century theoreticians had already made pity – identification with the suffering of a living being – the mainspring of the relation with the other'.[45] Instead, these meetings are confrontations that result in the transformation of one identity into another. I do not argue that Blake's writing is valuable *despite* the language that he uses. It is not that Blake writes positively about women while using the 'female as metaphor' negatively, as Susan Fox influentially argued.[46] Language is a 'stubborn structure' for Los in *Jerusalem*. But verbal language is placed against a visual language which necessarily embodies and sexualises thought. If we as readers have failed to understand the fundamental difference of the categories that Blake uses, it may be because we feared that Blake was not a good 'other'. But Blake offers a way into a world which is not ours, even while its infinite variety presents the multiple ways in which sexuality, born in this period through a process of regulation, is part of culture.[47]

CHAPTER I

'Happy copulation': visual enthusiasm and the sexual gaze

When Oothoon at the end of *Visions of the Daughters of Albion* refers to 'happy copulation' she does not seem to be talking about sex but about a kind of ecstatic looking. In Oothoon's speech the word 'copulation' regains its now obsolete non-sexual meaning as the 'action of coupling or linking two things together, or condition of being coupled' that the OED lists for the last time in 1752, the year in which Johnson in the *Rambler* defined Wit as 'the unexpected copulation of ideas'. A related sense is still present in the 'copula' verb, the name for the verb 'to be' and this verb has a special role in Blake's poetic language. Statements which take the form '*a* is *b*', statements which change meanings, appear on the engraving of the *Laocoon* that Blake worked on the year before he died: 'Prayer is the Study of Art', 'Praise is the Practise of Art', 'Fasting &c. all relate to Art'. The meaning of the category of 'art' is radically changed.[1] The word 'copulation' seems, in Oothoon's speech, to describe a visual experience which transforms meaning, altering an experience of oppression to one of joy.

In an early study of Blake's poetic vocabulary, Josephine Miles claimed that 'the primary action performed in Blake's poetry is "seeing" or "beholding".[2] There can be few more striking examples than Oothoon's 'happy copulation' where looking gives birth to new meanings. Oothoon describes herself as:

> a virgin fill'd with virgin fancies
> Open to joy and to delight where ever beauty appears
> If in the morning sun I find it: there my eyes are fix'd
> In happy copulation: if in evening mild. wearied with work;
> Sit on a bank and draw the pleasures of this free born joy. (E50)

The 'evening mild. wearied with work' seems to recall the description of evening in the unfallen Eden in *Paradise Lost* IV, a celebrated passage chosen to illustrate the headings 'Evening' and 'Moon' by Edward Bysshe in a volume that Blake owned, the *Art of English Poetry*.[3] Looking at the morning sun, Oothoon enacts the visionary looking that Blake describes in his 1799 letter to Dr Trusler. If it stopped here, Oothoon's speech could be filed safely under the heading 'addresses to the sun, after Milton'.

Yet 'copulation' is already a sexual word in Blake's time; even if it still tends to need the modifier 'carnal', 'copulation' is the standard term for intercourse in popular medical texts like *Aristotle's Masterpiece*, in dictionaries and in trials for adultery. Blake's use is already anachronistic and the decision to give the phrase 'happy copulation' to Oothoon in this poem (which deals with sexual experience) insists on breaking down the category of sexuality itself. The poem, confusingly, is both about and not about sexuality. The phrases 'happy copulation' and 'lovely copulation' seem to be unique to Blake, oddly joining a technical word with adjectives of affect ('happy') and the beautiful ('lovely').[4] And while 'happy copulation' returns to the obsolete non-sexual meaning, 'lovely copulation' a few lines later is clearly sexual. Writing to Blake's friend George Cumberland in 1798, Thomas Taylor ('the Platonist') contrasts copulation with looking, which he sees as 'more incorporeal' and so more poetic: 'I consider the delight which lovers experience, when in poetic language they drink large draughts of love thro' the eyes, as far superior to that arising from copulation, because the union is more incorporeal.'[5] Blake's double use of 'copulation' in *Visions of the Daughters of Albion* blurs Taylor's distinction between the corporeal and the incorporeal and questions the opposition of the poetic and the bodily. The proximity of the two uses means that the later sexual meaning marks the earlier one, confusing meanings that other writers separate.

As a text about sexuality, the ending of *Visions* is probably the most contentious passage in Blake's illuminated texts. Oothoon's celebration of 'happy' and 'lovely copulation' and her offer to Theotormon to catch 'girls of mild silver, or of furious gold' conflict disturbingly for many readers with her earlier identity as (it is assumed) the victim of a sexual assault. I will return to the issue of rape later but I want here to focus on Oothoon's offer, which seems not unlike the action of Matilda in Lewis's later *The Monk* (a work that Catherine Blake illustrated). The difference, however, is important: whereas the rejected Matilda both encourages Ambrosio to drug and to rape Antonia and acts to make 'real' her fantasy, what Oothoon's words offer is a shared imagination. No actions follow from her words in a poem which largely evades coherent narrative and ends shortly after this speech. Moreover, Oothoon's words are ambiguous, in part because of the odd switches between first and third person. In her speech, she is both 'Oothoon' and 'I'; her lover both 'thee' and 'Theotormon':

> But silken nets and traps of adamant will Oothoon spread,
> And catch for thee girls of mild silver, or of furious gold;
> I'll lie beside thee on a bank & view their wanton play
> In lovely copulation bliss on bliss with Theotormon: (E50)

When Oothoon says 'I'll lie beside thee on a bank & view their wanton play', it is not clear whether she imagines herself lying beside Theotormon as they both watch the 'wanton play' of the girls or whether 'their wanton play' is the erotic encounter of Theotormon with the girls which Oothoon will watch alone. In Helen Bruder's influential reading, Oothoon's offer to Theotormon is an act of compliance with male sexual fantasy, evidence that Oothoon is corrupted by an internalised ideology. This solution, however, requires a significant ellipsis:

> I'll lie beside thee on a bank & view their wanton play ... nor e'er
> with jealous cloud
> Come in the heaven of generous love; nor selfish blightings bring.   (E50)

Bruder sees this passage as a 'harem fantasy' with Oothoon taking the role of procuress in a reference to 'the endemic prostitution of the late eighteenth century'.[6] But even based on this selective quotation, 'the heaven of generous love' seems an odd description of paid sex. The lines that fill the ellipsis make it even harder to see the passage as a critique of sexual ideology:

> In lovely copulation bliss on bliss with Theotormon:
> Red as the rosy morning, lustful as the first born beam,
> Oothoon shall view his dear delight   (E50)

Not only is it unclear who is watching and who is acting, these lines do not specify whose 'bliss' they describe. It is not clear whether 'his ... delight' is 'dear' to Oothoon or to Theotormon, or whether it is Theotormon or Oothoon who is 'Red as the rosy morning, lustful as the first born beam'. This failure of definition creates a scene in which the looker responds in the same way as the doer; it is impossible to distinguish between active and passive in this scene imagined by Oothoon.

But is this Oothoon's imagination or Blake's? And is Oothoon, as Marcus Wood believes, a 'white English female', a 'daughter of Albion' herself or is she a slave seen in visions by the daughters of Albion?[7] If, as Blake suggests in *Milton*, it is possible to 'become' what you 'behold', visions can muddle the categories of race, power, gender. The ambiguities that the poem sets up are like those of Fuseli's *Nightmare*, simultaneously about the dreamer and the dream. The sun imagery in Blake's passage serves to naturalise the act of looking, rendering as innocent the mechanism which in pornography produces a physical response in the viewer. The sun looks on, blushing with arousal as it views the outdoor 'wanton play' of the lovers. The image is a little like Donne's poem, 'The Sun Rising', but *only* a little. Donne's sun is an authority figure and a time keeper, waking the lovers to a world of necessity. He is an antagonist with fantasies of power which the lover must challenge: 'Thy beams, so reverend and strong/ Why shouldst thou think?/ I could eclipse and cloud them with a wink'. The indoor world of Donne's lovers is protected by curtains from the 'reverend' disapproval of the sun. Blake's lovers belong in a world made by the generative force of an ungendered sun. Oothoon seems to be sexualised by looking and to offer the same path to Theotormon. Finding pleasure in the sun, Oothoon looks at it. The strangeness of the process is evident in her ability to look directly at the sun without going blind. Perhaps like the Sophians of George Cumberland's 1798 utopia, *The Captive of the Castle of Sennaar*, she sees the sun as the source of 'Holy Energy', an image of divinity that is visible to all.

But Blake does not choose the route of turning the sun into the divine. In *The French Revolution* it is 'another's brain' or 'another's high flaming rich bosom' that is imagined as the sun:

> But go, merciless man! enter into the infinite labyrinth of another's brain
> Ere thou measure the circle that he shall run. Go, thou cold recluse, into the fires
> Of another's high flaming rich bosom, and return unconsum'd, and write
> laws.   (E294)

Returning 'unconsum'd' is impossible for Blake cannot imagine meeting without the transformation of one or another. This process is more extreme than the mechanisms of sympathy described by Adam Smith. Sympathy, which operates through the imagination, allows us to 'place ourselves in' the 'situation' of someone else, to 'conceive ourselves enduring all the same torments' and to 'enter as it were into his body'.[8] Smith's careful 'as it were' ensures that the process remains a virtual one, controlled by the consciously artificial process of simile. Both Blake and Fuseli, however, consistently treat the metaphorical as if it carried the same degree of reality as the 'real'. Both choose to illustrate and so to make real the similes used by Milton or by Shakespeare. Blake's 1795 colour print *Pity*, for instance, makes real a simile from *Macbeth*: 'And Pity, like a naked new-born babe,/ Striding the blast, or heav'n's cherubim hors'd/ Upon the sightless couriers of the air'. Instead of a safe comparison, an 'as it were', Blake suggests the process that Jonathan Lamb describes as 'horrid sympathy', 'an identification with something quite different from the self'.[9] Lamb takes this term from *Paradise Lost* book X when Satan sees his company of fallen angels turning into serpents: 'horror on them fell,/ And horrid sympathie; for what they saw,/ They felt themselves now changing'. Something similar is described in the Bard's Song of *Milton* in the phrase: 'he became what he beheld', which describes the response of Los to the creation of Urizen's body, a response that produces the female (E97). Blake's command to 'enter into the infinite labyrinth of another's brain' and 'into another's high flaming rich bosom' makes the meeting transformative.

According to Smith, feelings without an adequate explanation will not produce sympathy. The feelings produced in Oothoon by her imagined scene are therefore inappropriate in so far as the situation is not one that *should* produce the feelings that she invests it with. The test of appropriateness, of whether 'bringing the case home to ourselves' will produce the same feeling in us, reveals that we cannot share Oothoon's response. Smith depends on the domestic to determine normality and rule out extreme, unusual or excessively bodily experiences: when 'upon bringing the case home to himself, he finds that they do not coincide with what he feels, they necessarily appear to him unjust and improper'. For Smith both sex and gender are problematic: 'all strong expressions' of 'the passion by which Nature unites the two sexes' are 'upon every occasion indecent', indeed all the passions that originate from the body produce a failure of sympathy.[10] Yet Smith also insists on the difference of women since to 'talk to a woman as we would to a man is improper' and 'an intire insensibility to the fair sex, renders a man contemptible in some measure even to men'.[11] *Visions* exists at a tangent to this account: while the ability of a male author to produce the visions of women suggests the power of sympathy to cross divisions of gender, the poem fails to differentiate the feminine as a distinct form of experience. Blake does not observe the need to limit the degree of feeling or to ignore passions that originate from the body. In so far as Oothoon's suffering after the rape reflects Theotormon's distress rather than her own, and her pleasure in the imagined scene reflects his pleasure, the rules that mark out appropriateness are broken. Rather than becoming like him, she seems to become him.

Blake later defines the Bible as 'a Poem of probable impossibilities fabricated for pleasure as moderns say but I say by Inspiration' (E616).

The scene described by Oothoon exemplifies the work of poetry in imagining 'probable impossibilities', reversing likelihood in its scene of jealousy overcome and pain discharged.[12] In this poem, the appearance of feelings is all that we have since the narrative that explains the emotions is sketchy and inadequate. Whereas Smith insists that knowledge of the situation must control the appearance of passion, in *Visions* appearance is all and the visual is not contained by reason. Yet the visions of the 'Daughters of Albion' are conveyed to an audience represented with faces buried in their knees, or looking downwards. Only one woman looks up to the sky and her 'eyes are fix'd' on things located in vision or in fantasy (Figure 1).

VISUAL ENTHUSIASM AND NATIONAL CULTURE

In the 1795 *Song of Los* the 'Kings of Asia' announce edicts 'That the lust of the eyes may be quench'd' (E69). Whether 'lust' describes the older sense of pleasure or the newer sense of sexual appetite, tyranny is represented as needing to attack visual culture which, unlike verbal culture, is readily accessible to all classes. Looking is sexual and sexuality is visual. Written at the height of Pitt's reign of terror, the reference to the Kings of Asia may point to the tyrannical behaviour of despots nearer to home where forms of repression challenge the pleasure of looking.[13] Newly politicised in the mid-1790s, the 'free born joy' of looking had been at the centre of a debate about Britain's visual culture since the beginning of public exhibition culture in London in the early 1760s. Polite culture depended on regulating 'the lust of the eyes', setting up a model of public visual culture which announced its triumph over bodily urges.[14] Ronald Paulson argues that Hogarth's 1753 *Analysis of Beauty* offered a theory of art based on the erotic, and this, as John Barrell points out, placed it 'in direct confrontation with the theory proposed by Shaftesbury and founded on the suppression of desire'.[15]

Oothoon's 'happy' and 'lovely copulation' not only cross the boundaries set up by polite visual culture but revive issues that still preoccupied the 1790s. The third volume of John Ireland's *Hogarth Illustrated*, published in 1798 by John Boydell, the proprietor of the Shakespeare gallery, offered a lengthy commentary on a previously unpublished Hogarth print called *Enthusiasm Delineated*.[16] This was the 1760 version of a print that Hogarth revised and published in 1762 as *Credulity, Superstition and Fanaticism* and Blake, who valued Hogarth as an artist who engraved his own prints, attacked a rival engraver, Tom Cooke, for 'cutting down

Figure 1. *Visions of the Daughters of Albion*, copy A, plate 9, 1793. © The Trustees
of the British Museum.

Hogarth' with his own version of this print, published in 1798, the same
year as Ireland's volume (E505).[17] Ireland's second volume mentions Blake
as the engraver of Hogarth's painting of the *Beggar's Opera*, and the third
volume lists his engraving in an appendix.

Figure 2. William Hogarth, *Enthusiasm Delineated,* from John Ireland, *Hogarth Illustrated Vol III and last,* March 1798, John Boydell. © The British Library Board (131b7).

But I am interested here in Hogarth's *Enthusiasm Delineated* (Figure 2) not as a source for Blake's work but as evidence for the persistence of concerns about the association between looking and sexuality through the 1790s and particularly for the way in which it reveals the strong association between enthusiasm, sexuality and the visual. Sexuality, here, is produced by a regulatory discourse. Polite exhibition culture traced its origin in the display of paintings at the Foundling Hospital organised by Hogarth in the 1740s where looking at art was part of the public exercise of sympathy.[18]

Hogarth's own role can therefore be interpreted in two ways: either, as Paulson reads him, as a voice of the unruly, corporeal imagination outlawed by polite culture or, as Solkin presents him, as a formative voice in the creation of a polite culture through his satires.

Enthusiasm Delineated is the first print that Ireland discusses in the 1798 volume and he makes great claims for its significance: it reveals 'more mind' and is 'marked with deeper satire, than all [Hogarth's] other works'.[19] Ireland's lengthy commentary on the print and his account of the long-running debate about the growth of a public visual culture in Britain show how important the issues raised by Hogarth's print still were at the end of the eighteenth century. Hogarth's image shows a preacher (described by Ireland as 'a *Methodistical Papist*, or a *Popish Methodist*') whipping his congregation to a state of frenzy not just with words but with images, waving a series of puppets to catch their attention. The scene raises the familiar charge that Methodist meetings were erotically charged: Hogarth represents the enthusiastic congregation roused to madness by the preacher, reacting physically to his words, hugging each other or fondling small effigies. Like Oothoon, they break the rules of sentimental looking, becoming what they behold and acting out the words of the preacher as they fall to the ground or collapse into an embrace. The woman to the left, identified by Ireland as the famous bawd Mrs Douglas, 'who after a most licentious life, became a rigid *devoté*' of the Methodist Whitefield, falls to the floor grasping a doll-like effigy.[20] The images used by the preacher, represented as a series of puppets, are multiplied in the effigies that the viewers produce as they listen. In this image, the words of the preacher breed.

The emotional power of Hogarth's preacher derives from his use of the images of European art: 'This Proteus of the pulpit', as Ireland explains, 'poises a puppet in each hand.' The 'devil grasping a gridiron' on the left and the 'triple figure with the triangular emblem' on the right are the images 'by which Raphael, and some other painters, have profanely presumed to personify the Deity'.[21] God, Ireland assumes, cannot be represented. Blake disagrees: 'Think of a white cloud. as being holy you cannot love it', he wrote on his copy of Swedenborg's *Divine Love and Divine Wisdom*, 'but think of a holy man within the cloud love springs up in your thought' (E603). Ronald Paulson points out that the figures identified are those selected by Reynolds in the *Idler* no. 79 as the highest examples of 'the majesty of heroic Poetry'.[22] Hogarth thus criticises both European art, presenting Rome as 'a kind of puppet-show to the rest of Europe' and the tendency of popular visual imagery to embody spiritual realities.[23] European culture appeals to the worst elements of vulgar excess. Ireland reads *Enthusiasm Delineated* as an attack on the idolatrous conse- quences of enthusiastic religion: 'by the artists absurdly attempting to represent what are not properly objects of sight, that which they intended to be *sublime*, is rendered in the highest degree ridiculous'.[24] 'Absurdly attempting to represent what are not properly objects of sight' is exactly the charge that would be made against Blake's work in 1808 and 1809 by Robert Hunt in the *Examiner* when he asks 'how are we to find out that the figure in the shape of a body is a soul?' (BR260).

The problem was that enthusiasm was also seen as essential to the formation of a national visual culture. Not only does Hogarth admit that 'The arts are much indebted to Popery, and that religion owes much of its universality to the arts' but Ireland quotes Hogarth's admission that the absence of a developed culture of art in Britain is caused by 'our religion, which ... doth not require, nay absolutely forbids, images for worship, or pictures to excite enthusiasm'.[25] Whereas Protestantism is hostile to visual imagery, enthusiasm, like Catholic 'superstition', leads to an unstoppable generation of images. The concept of visual enthusiasm was particularly important to James Barry, Irish by birth, professor of painting at the Royal Academy and the man whom Blake called 'the really <Industrious> Virtuous & Independent Barry' (E576). Ireland quotes from James Barry's 1775 *An Inquiry into the Real and Imaginary Obstructions to the Acquisitions of the Arts in England* on the role of enthusiasm in visual culture: 'Where religion is affirmative, and extended', Barry writes, 'it gives a loose and enthusiasm to the fancy, which throws a spirit into the air and manners, and stamps a diversity, life, quickness, sensibility, and expressive signifi- cance over every thing they do.'[26] Barry blames the underdevelopment of visual arts in Britain on 'the accidental circumstance of the change of religion, which happened just at the time we should have set out in the arts'.[27] As an old man, Blake is described by Gilchrist, surprisingly, as speaking up for Catholicism: 'He had a sentimental liking for the Romish Church ... "He believed no subjects of monarchies were so happy as the Pope's".' Gilchrist reports Blake's sympathy for 'Milton, Harrington, and Marvel' but claims that it was Milton's republicanism not his Puritanism that Blake endorsed.[28]

If this is not just evidence of Blake's mischief making, it may represent the lasting influence of Barry's views on art. Barry's 1775 *Inquiry* was published when Blake was eighteen and seems to have been formative on Blake's own writing. Like Hogarth, Barry laments the flooding of Britain with art purchased in Italy by visually illiterate travellers on the Grand

Tour. Barry reminds his reader that Italians were selective in their response to the work of the classical period that they uncovered in the excavations beneath Rome: 'they only preserved what they thought worth it, the refuse they either threw with the rest of the rubbish back again into the cave, or suffered to be dispersed without care'.[29] Since 'the name of antique is with many passport sufficient, these cavas are opened once more' and 'this ill fated country of ours is to be crammed with nothing but rubbish from abroad'.[30] Blake's *Marriage of Heaven and Hell* presents a vision of the printing house in hell with 'a Dragon-Man, clearing away the rubbish from a caves mouth; within, a number of Dragons were hollowing the cave' (E40). Whereas the visual is to be valued, in both accounts it needs to be sorted and assimilated with care.

Ireland's commentary recognises that Hogarth's 1760 satire is as much concerned with the language of art as of religion. While the satire represents a scene in a chapel it also comments on the chaotic circumstances of the first public art exhibition held in the galleries of the Society of Arts in 1760. Like the preacher's congregation, the visitors to the 1760 exhibition of the Society of Arts did not pay and although the exhibition was a popular success it also quickly led to scenes of disorder, including broken windows which cost 13s 6d to repair.[31] In 1762 a one-shilling admission charge was introduced to filter the audience. Hogarth's image of 1760 must have suggested to early viewers the chaotic scenes that spoilt the first free exhibition, showing the dangers of uncontrolled sympathy produced by an overstimulation of the visual imagination.

This danger is particularly associated with the female spectator in *Enthusiasm Delineated*: the woman to the left falls to the ground clutching a small effigy, her pose like that of Bernini's St Teresa, or indeed the orgasmic women who populate Blake's illuminated poetry of the 1790s. The woman below the pulpit falls into a clinch with a young man while the thermometer to the right that takes the temperature of the Methodist's brain is calibrated from 'Revelation' down through 'Madness, EXTACY, Lust –Hot, Love – Heat, Luke Warm' right down via 'Low Spirits, Sorrow, AGONY, Settled Grief, Despair, Madness' to 'Prophecy'. As the author of a series of works in the 1790s which carry the subtitle 'A Prophecy', Blake would have appeared to be a target of Hogarth's satire. The Anglican discourse on enthusiasm (as evidenced in this print) invents a primal scene of sexual licence which suggests a sexual origin for spirituality and a common origin for Christian and pagan rites. These scenes reveal a fear that the ability to transcend the body in spirituality is doomed to failure since religious truth is only a masked memory of bodily pleasure. Swift's

Tale of a Tub presented religious enthusiasm as a vulgar form of 'Ancient Oracles' and offered 'an exact Description of the Changes made in the Face by Enthusiastic Preachers'.[32] In this fantasy of an upside-down world, the wind of inspiration enters the body through a funnel to the 'Posteriors', distorting the preacher's face through exit velocity. Swift explains that the winds of inspiration 'were frequently managed and directed by *Female* officers, whose Organs were understood to be better disposed for the Admission of those Oracular Gusts, as entering, and passing up through a Receptacle of greater Capacity'. In Swift's satire, women are linked to enthusiastic inspiration from 'the *Sibyls*' to the Quakers (described as 'certain refined Colleges of our *Modern Æolists*').[33] Swift's satire suggests that the uneducated fail to operate the metaphorical transmutation of the classics that makes such material safe for an educated reader. Women (like Oothoon) are particularly liable to produce the naïve bodily re-enactment that interprets inspiration as bodily ecstasy.

Ireland's commentary quotes repeatedly from George Lavington's 1749 *Enthusiasm of Methodists and Papists Compared*, a work composed in an unsuccessful attempt to prevent the passing of an Act which achieved legal recognition for the Moravians that year.[34] The focus on visual culture recognises that Moravians belonged within a European baroque culture and welcomed visual imagery in their worship.[35] According to Ireland, Hogarth's 1760 satire attacks Moravian visual culture along with the figurative traditions of Catholic art, expressing the iconophobia associated with Protestantism. For Blake, whose mother was, for a time, a member of a Moravian band, these targets would have resonated strongly and it seems likely that his reading of Hogarth would have represented the 'view from the street' that Barrell sees as going entirely unrecorded in the time.[36]

Lavington's trump card, saved for the lengthy last section of his three-part work, is the claim that Methodist meetings were merely a modern version of the Eleusinian mysteries.[37] In his own narrative of the 'egregious spectacles' or the 'blessed spectacles' the moralist becomes pornographer, revealing the justice of Lord Chesterfield's description of Lavington as 'the Baudy Bishop'.[38] Rejecting Warburton's account of the Eleusinian mysteries as a secret affirmation of an elite understanding of monotheism, Lavington claims that the greater mysteries culminated in looking at images of sexual organs and in ritual enactments of sex, drawing on abuses described in Warburton's footnotes to ask the question: 'were not the *natural Figures shewn?*'[39] The account of the approach to the greater mysteries is a masterpiece of vicarious voyeurism:

For these, they underwent *more tremendous Rites; Representations* were made to their *Eyes and Ears,* – of strange *Visions* and *Spectacles;* of *Voices, Howlings* of Men, Women, and Children; – Things which caused the most *dismal Agonies* of Body and Mind; Coldness, Sweats, Terrors, Consternation, Loss of Senses, or else the utmost Tortures, Despair and Madness.[40]

Burke's account of the role of the sublime in heathen religion seems to derive from Lavington; as Burke explains: 'Almost all the heathen temples were dark ... the Druids performed all their ceremonies in the bosom of the darkest woods, and in the shade of the oldest and most spreading oaks.'[41] Lavington creates the sexual sublime, drawing on terror, mystery and shame in a way that will recur in later disciplinary discourses and be parodied in Blake's 'A Little Boy Lost' in *Songs of Experience* and his accounts of druid religion. But Lavington also provides the model for a positive use of the sexual sublime by James Graham who, as Peter Otto suggests, drew on the structures of the sublime in the 1780s in his Temple of Health and Hymen.[42] Lavington's narrative turns vulnerability into power through knowledge of sexual mysteries, as the position of imagined spectator does also for Oothoon. Lavington, however, controls access to his text by his use of Latin: 'Are not the *Pudenda utriusa; Sexus, Conspectus Deorum & Dearum in Nuditate,* pretty Means of conveying such Doctrines?' (II, pp. 335–6). Sex is safe for the classically educated bishop but an outrage when assumed to form part of the power of Methodist or Moravian gatherings. Whereas Hogarth fears (or celebrates – depending on your reading) the imaginative power of the enthusiastic preacher, the annual Royal Academy show or Boydell's Shakespeare gallery offered semi-public spaces in which men and women could look at representations of naked bodies.

Oothoon offers to watch 'lovely copulation' in order to destroy the controlling power of a mental image: *Visions* is in this sense the antithesis of Lavington's account of the Eleusinian mysteries. If the torments of the eternal man described in *The Four Zoas* are those 'of love and jealousy' this is only because Blake's work is at ease with representations of bodily sexuality. The naked woman reclining on the cloud in *Visions of the Daughter of Albion* plate 3 is not framed and the sun reveals the pink-tinged blushing of her flesh. The 'free-born joy' of looking allows Oothoon to take on the right (often reserved for the male aristocratic connoisseur) of sexual fantasy, a right as fundamental perhaps as that of viewing the elite language of art objects. It is no accident that Blake, like Hogarth, focuses on the role of the female viewer and female sexuality, for it is the transformative power of looking and of sex that is linked with the kind of ecstatic looking which Blake describes. Visual culture is seen as inherently sexual in Blake's period, yet the frame offered by the commercial galleries selected the material on view or at least regulated the response of the viewer. While the sentimental culture modelled by Adam Smith attempts to regulate the enthusiastic viewing associated with the female viewer, keeping Oothoon out of the galleries, visual culture is seen by many as needing the bodily fantasies of Hogarth's satire. The strangeness of Blake's figure of Oothoon is closely allied to concerns that appear in the work of Blake's friend, Henry Fuseli.

CHAPTER 2

Fuseli and the 'female dream' of Europe

Fuseli's understanding of the dangers to art within bourgeois polite culture is contained most memorably in *The Nightmare* first exhibited in 1782, a work regularly parodied and issued in a series of engravings between 1781 and 1827 (the year of Blake's death). Although it would be rash to limit this iconic work to a single meaning, I want to explore here the implications of one particular reading. Markman Ellis draws attention to Burton's claim in *The Anatomy of Melancholy* that nightmares particularly afflict 'maids, nuns and widows' and cites a suggestive passage from John Bond's 1753 *An Essay on the Incubus, or Nightmare* which describes how an eighteen-year-old girl suffered from nightmares until she 'took a bedfellow of a different sex, and bore children'.[1] Similar assumptions of the health-giving powers of sex are evident in Erasmus Darwin's *Botanic Garden*, which tells of the miraculous recovery in Holland in 1636 of a girl struck down with the plague when her lover 'slept with her as his wife'.[2] Blake engraved a number of illustrations for *The Botanic Garden*. The utopian Sophians in Cumberland's *The Captive of the Castle of Sennaar* also believe in sexual healing. It seems likely, therefore, that Blake's circle would have read the pose of Fuseli's dreaming woman as an image of the power of sexual abstinence to produce both nightmares and heightened desire in just the way that Markman Ellis suggests.[3]

In 1794, the year after *Visions of the Daughters of Albion*, Blake's *Europe* describes another 'female dream': 'Eighteen hundred years: Man was a Dream!/ The night of Nature and their harps unstrung:/ She slept in middle of her nightly song,/ Eighteen hundred years, a female dream!' (E63). In *Europe* the 'female dream' contains desire within a Christian era through Enitharmon's plot that 'Woman, lovely Woman! may have dominion'. Andrew Lincoln suggests that Enitharmon 'figures the ascendance of "feminine" values in Christian ideology – maternal love, domesticity, chastity – values which privatize identity and desire'.[4] Milton's *Nativity Ode* tells how the birth of Christ banished the power of the Delphic oracles: 'Apollo from his shrine/ Can no more divine,/ With hollow shriek the steep of Delphos leaving.' Blake's revisioning of the *Nativity Ode* in *Europe* presents the Christian civil order with its legal codification of marriage as a return to the steep of Delphos. When the Shadowy Female begs Enitharmon to release her from the process of bearing 'all devouring kings' (E61) it is because Blake is challenging Burke's adoption of nature as part of a conservative order: it is not so much that Nature wants to stop producing offspring as that she wants to escape from the conservative and monarchical role into which Burkean rhetoric has forced her.

Both Blake and Fuseli, I suggest, continue the debate about Britain's visual culture that had preoccupied Hogarth and Barry. With Fuseli, however, this debate is coloured by his own sense of foreignness. Fuseli arrived in England in 1764, left on an ill-fated trip as a tutor to France, returned in 1766 and left again for Rome in 1770 to return to London finally in 1779. The complexity of Fuseli's representation of female sexuality has been put down to the blend of Zwinglian Puritanism, Rousseau's separation of art and morality and the companionship of a libertine circle of international artists in Rome.[5] Fuseli's fascination with sado-masochistic imagery, tyrannical women and with perverse sexuality has been contrasted with Blake's utopian domestic visions.[6] Fuseli has also been represented as politically conservative, comfortable with and dependent on aristocratic patrons and thus unlike the radical Blake of the 1790s.[7] But as the 'The only Man that eer I knew/ Who did not make me almost spew', it is perhaps worth reconsidering the opposition between a misogynist Fuseli and a liberatory Blake. Fuseli certainly shared Blake's belief in the power of visual enthusiasm, insisting on how 'favourably religious enthusiasm operated on Art'.[8]

Martin Myrone locates Blake, Fuseli and Gillray as the product of 'a kind of modernity that elevates specifically bourgeois values ... where art may become trash, enlightenment mutate into exploitation, the popular be exclusive'.[9] In the Tate Gallery's 2006 *Gothic Nightmares* exhibition, Blake's and Fuseli's work hung side by side, with the explicitly sexual drawings that Fuseli created in Rome occupying the same exhibition space as Blake's chaste neoclassicism. Fuseli's perspective on British culture is self-consciously that of an outsider: to Blake 'he was both Turk & Jew'; indeed Fuseli translated into German Mary Wortley Montagu's *Turkish Letters* in 1763. Nancy Pressly, however, argues that Fuseli's taste for spectacular excess derived from the growth of London's exhibition culture and its ability to address a more varied public: Fuseli brought to his experience in Rome, she argues, an association between sexuality and looking which we can see as a form of visual enthusiasm developed in the new London culture of spectacle.[10] Rome heightened Fuseli's taste for explicitly sexual imagery and extreme emotions within the libertine circles associated with John Tobias Sergel.

The civic humanist language within which much of the debate about public art took place at the end of the eighteenth century saw the creation of a public identity as dependent on shedding a sexual identity. John Barrell argues that civic humanism assumes an ability to read images in non-sexual terms, requiring the invention of 'narratives of a civic emancipation from sexuality'.[11] This identity allows apparently sexual narratives or works of art to be viewed in chaste terms as allegories, and some of the most convincing recent accounts have stressed the role of this discourse in Blake's treatment of femininity and of sexuality. Christopher Hobson identifies this discourse in Blake's early 'masculinist' work and David Fallon argues that 'the limits of republican discourse' explain the negative representations of the 'female' in Blake's early writing.[12] In particular, Fallon sees a resemblance between a sketch by Blake of a reclining female which is labelled 'Luxury' and a reclining figure above Enitharmon's head on plate 4 of *Europe*.[13] The question for this chapter, then, is whether Blake's reclining figures represent the dangers of excessive sexuality or the danger of sexual frustration.

Fuseli offered to Blake access to the complexities of European artistic culture which is explored in the 1794 *Europe*. Artistic culture, for Blake and Fuseli, is not merely part of the aesthetic but offers a route to understanding the political health of the culture that produces it. Fuseli's example offered to Blake not only an alternative model of feeling but an alternative method of countering the indolence of luxury. Fuseli's theory of art emerges in two works published soon after he arrived in England: the 1765 translation of Winckelmann that Blake owned during his apprenticeship to Basire and the *Remarks on the Writings and Conduct of J. J. Rousseau* that Fuseli published anonymously in 1767.[14] In the field of art theory, Winckelmann offers a parallel to Adam Smith's concern that bodies can disrupt the workings of sympathy.[15] In *Reflections on the Painting and Sculpture of the Greeks*, Winckelmann argues that the faces in the *Laocoon* group suggest the ability of the mind to transcend bodily experience, revealing a strength and even tranquillity that belies the suffering of the body: 'As the bottom of the sea lies peaceful beneath a foaming surface, a great soul lies sedate beneath the strife of passions in Greek figures.'[16]

The characteristic of 'the Greek works' for Winckelmann 'is a noble simplicity and sedate grandeur in Gesture and Expression'.[17]

It is the failure of the first female to remain within the limits set for art that horrifies the watching Eternals (civic humanist readers of Winckelmann or Smith it seems) in *The Book of Urizen*:

> Wonder, awe, fear, astonishment,
> Petrify the eternal myriads;
> At the first female form now separate
> They call'd her Pity, and fled   (E78)

Extreme emotions 'petrify' the Eternals, who respond by containing feelings within the regulatory structure of Smith's theory which announced that 'Pity and compassion are words appropriated to signify our fellow-feeling with the sorrow of others'.[18] It is the inability of the eternals to look at the intense feelings of others that produces sexual difference. In his unpublished 1789 *Aphorisms on Art*, Fuseli uses the word 'petrified' to describe the effect of extreme feeling on a spectator: 'The being seized by an enormous passion, be it joy or grief, hope or despair, loses the character of its own individual expression, and is absorbed by the power of the feature that attracts it.'[19] Passion here destroys individual identity, creating an 'allegory of sympathetic power' that parallels Blake's concept of states present as early as the contrary 'states' of Innocence and Experience but more fully developed in the late writing where 'States Change: but Individual Identities never change nor cease' (E132). Fuseli's rejection of Winckelmann is most clearly evident in the preface to his *Lectures* where he attacks the idea that pity enables a kind of control over feeling: 'in the group of the Laocoon, the frigid ecstasies of German criticism have discovered pity like a vapour swimming on the father's eyes; he is seen to suppress in the groan for his children the shriek for himself'.[20] Here pity does indeed divide the soul, leading the father to split his reaction for his children and for himself in order to control emotion and to keep it within bounds. Fuseli insists that feeling is as much a bodily experience as it is for Blake's Urizen when 'In harrowing fear rolling round;/ His nervous brain shot branches/ Round the branches of his heart' (E76). Winckelmann, according to Fuseli, 'reasoned himself into frigid reveries and Platonic dreams of beauty': 'To him Germany owes the shackles of her artists, and the narrow limits of their aims' (II, p. 14). Blake's 1806 letter to the editor of the *Monthly Magazine* in defence of Fuseli's painting of Count Ugolino returns to the question of the response of the viewer to suffering:

Mr. Fuseli's Count Ugolino is the father of sons of feeling and dignity, who would not sit looking in their parent's face in the moment of his agony, but would rather retire and die in secret, while they suffer him to indulge his passionate and innocent grief, his innocent and venerable madness, and insanity, and fury, and whatever paltry cold hearted critics cannot, because they dare not, look upon. (Undated letter published in *Monthly Magazine*, vol. 21 (1 July 1806), pp. 520–1, E768)

Here Blake recalls Fuseli's 1789 aphorism in which 'Ugolino is petrified by the fate that sweeps his sons'.[21] His sons are constrained by the intensity of their private familial feeling but it is the job of the critic and the viewer of public art to look at images which are too painful for the actors themselves. The artist represents the full range of passions: grief, madness, insanity and fury.

Fuseli's *Remarks on the Writings and Conduct of J. J. Rousseau*, anonymously published in 1767, address the role of sexuality in culture. This was a work described by a reviewer as 'sometimes libertine without one spark of wit to give it lustre'.[22] Both Fuseli and his friend John Armstrong circulated false rumours that the author was Sterne, a revealing (if stylistically unlikely) alibi since Sterne focuses on the difficult relationship between sensibility and sexuality, the fault line in Shaftesbury's account of a society built on altruism and empathy. Reviewing his own book for the 1767 *Critical Review*, Fuseli imagines that his 'character, in a summary way, will be sunk into that of a downright sceptic (perhaps atheist) and libertine' by hostile readers. Fuseli suggests that as private individuals band together to form the public an act of censorship occurs: 'the gentleman in private life should affront the public in a body, whom as individuals he would be far from offending'. Rejecting Hamlet's advice to the players, Fuseli claims that transgression is typical of 'true genius' which 'should *o'er step the modesty of nature*, and the decorum of habit'. He thus expects outrage from readers who fail to realise that 'sparkling wit, not contented with such flesh as the market affords in the public stews, should profanely wish to wanton itself with *the Word made flesh!*'.[23] Fuseli sexualises the figure of the genius as a sexual libertine. His frequent quotations from Shakespeare reveal his friendship with Garrick and his place within a culture which at this date permitted Hannah More to describe the headache she has got from 'raking out so late with that gay libertine Johnson'.[24] For contemporary readers of *Remarks on Rousseau*, libertinism was a feature of Fuseli's excessively metaphorical, allusive, undisciplined and playful style as much as of its content: in its use of unascribed voices, Fuseli's style is like Blake's in *An Island in the Moon,* embodying everything that Socrates objects to in *The Republic* and introducing a dangerous theatricality into writing.

Presenting himself as a cultural outsider, Fuseli claims that support for Rousseau 'must needs be displeasing to many sober-minded people, who conform to present modes, and readily subscribe, without farther inquiry, to adopted systems'.[25] Carol Hall points out that this was an unnecessary pose since the English public was sympathetic to Rousseau at this moment.[26] But Fuseli is correct in his pose in so far as he rejects Hume's account of the role of women in the creation of polite culture.[27] In *Remarks on Rousseau,* Fuseli addresses the question of the sexualisation of women that was central to what Emma Clery has named the 'feminization debate'.[28] John Aikin, after all, blamed the marriage of his sister, Anna Laetitia Barbauld, on the effects of reading *The Nouvelle Héloise.*[29]

Fuseli's polyphonic text imagines the consequences for the female reader in terms as lurid as any moralist but does not argue for censorship or prohibition:

To know that stays paint to the eagle eye of love, here their luxuriance of bosom and milky orbs of rapture, and there the slender waist and rising hips – that with the perfumes of their toilet contagion spreads – that aprons will invite Hamlet to build tabernacles between Beauty's legs – and petticoats appear to Romeo the gates of heaven –

– What will be the consequence of all this? –

They will open them – yea and dream at the same time, that virginity may drop a maidenhead, and matrimony pick it up; – that nature now and then lays a stumbling-block in Virtue's way to teach her to walk.[30]

Fuseli is clear that reading produces sexual excitement ('They will open them') legitimated by a dream which resolves conflict by enabling the coexistence of transgression and conformity. He imagines the dangers of Rousseau's *Héloise* for the female reader not only through echoes of *Epistle to a Lady* ('Most Women have no Characters at all') but also *Macbeth* ('I dare do all that may become a man;/ Who dares do more is none' (1.7): 'A man has a character, and dares to do no more than what becomes a man' (p. 45)). Like Pope and Shakespeare, Fuseli assumes that women are always already sexual and sees female desire as a force impossible to regulate or control:

Let temples, sacraments, parents, honour, nature, misery; let life, stript of all feminine endearments, vanity, delicacy, pride; let mangled conscience and hag-ridden disease; let hatred, jealousy, revenge – bar her gates, dispute her every inch of ground, fulminate her ear, assail her with torrents of tears, intangle her way with silken nets, or strew it all with daggers; – if a woman is bent on a purpose, swift as the thoughts of love, or lewdness, or fury, 'tis all one – she will throw herself headlong, and palpitate ecstasy on the bosom of perdition! – She will break your heart, or have her's broken. (pp. 45–6)

The energy of the prose, with its headlong phrases held back by the loosest of punctuation, suggests pleasure at a spectacle which runs counter to the construction of the respectable and desexualised woman. These energies have the power to resist the 'snug, less, narrow, pretty, insignificant' qualities of the private domestic world that he will later see as the foe to public culture. The woman 'bent on a purpose' is constructed through the same heightened language of *Sturm und Drang* through which Fuseli creates the voice of the 'genius'. The threading through of phrases from Shakespeare and from Pope suggests the close relationship of sexual passion and art.

Fuseli's multi-voiced work mocks the moral panic that dominated the British debate over reading and blamed the theatre and novels for female sexual desire. While the dream of the writer (or the reader of this overheated passage) is an erotic dream of the female body of 'luxuriance of bosom and milky orbs of rapture', the dream of the female reader is that sexual experience is trivial and can be contained in the social institution of marriage. Fuseli's language anticipates the overheated imaginings of Lewis's *The Monk* where the revelation of Matilda's breast is the undoing of Ambrosio: 'And, Oh! that was such a breast! The Moonbeams darting full upon it, enabled the Monk to observe its dazzling whiteness. His eye dwelt with insatiable avidity upon the beauteous Orb.'[31] The work of the female dream, in this passage, is to imagine the possibility of a frictionless assimilation of desire into culture. Fuseli specifically attributes the repression of sexuality in children to religion, describing how Catholicism uses the language of monstrosity to describe desire. He finds the same fear of the sexual imagination of children and of women in English attacks on the theatre or reading that claim ''tis all one – 'tis reading – 'tis the playhouse – 'tis sentiment – 'tis those damned romances that have turned her head – And will for ever, I am afraid – till fathers and mothers learn to be something more than the parents of their own passions –' (pp. 41–2). Fuseli seems to sympathise with women's desire for sexual self-determination, seeing as entirely logical their refusal of suitors chosen by their parents.

These years saw virulent attacks on female sexuality in works such as Bienville's *Nymphomania*, translated from French in the 1770s. Although Bienville's work received hostile reviews, its linking of the imagination with sexuality and its focus on female dreams make it a context for the

contemporary debate about female sexuality and for Fuseli's work. Bienville's section on the dangers of the imagination is illustrated by the story
of Julia, separated from a suitor by mercenary parents, who turns for
comfort to novels on the advice of her maid: 'These books were like a
burning-glass which collects the rays of the sun, in order to fix them on
one particular spot, which they must set on fire. The imagination of Julia
was this blazing spot, the flames of which, soon communicating with
her heart, broke out with a redoubled fury.' [32] Oothoon's ability to look at
the morning sun, fixing her eyes 'in happy copulation', repeats an account
of reading which translates fantasy into the burning rays of the sun.
Bienville wants to distinguish between a safe form of looking at 'nature'
and a more dangerous fancy associated with art and monstrosity
(a distinction that is often absent for Blake):

Hitherto, nature alone had spoken; but now, illusions, chimeras, and extrava-
gancies began to act their parts. The lascivious and voluptuous images which
she devoured with her eyes, at once excluded from her mind those sentiments of
honour, of piety, of modesty, and of reserve, which nature had, till then, respected,
and which she never could have overcome, without the aid of art. (p. 172)

Yet in its sudden shifts of register, Bienville's work is also open to Blake's
reading in *Visions of the Daughters of Albion* which sees masturbation as a
symptom of parental or societal repression. As Foucault argues, sexuality
is created by a regulatory discourse. Thus Bienville assumes that women
experience sexual pleasure more intensely than men: 'In women, there
are more organs than one, for the purpose of exciting venereal pleasures.
First, the *Clitoris* which, according to an universal opinion, is the
most exquisite seat of pleasure' (pp. 51–2). For Fuseli's dreamer in *The
Nightmare* as for Bienville's Julia, thwarted desire will produce a sleep
haunted by the monstrous forms of imagination. The linking of
masturbation and commerce is familiar in the period, as Barker-Benfield
describes: '"Autonomous hedonism" was the capacity freely to take
pleasure in one's own feelings, aroused by fantasy, in the privacy of
one's own imagination, enjoyed under the new conditions of literal
privacy – feelings, fantasy, and privacy all sponsored by the rise of
commercial capitalism.' [33] It is not the existence of female desire but its
privatisation that is seen by Fuseli as threatening to public culture: the
danger of the female dream is that it imagines a domestic resolution of
desire.

Jonah Siegel has argued that the discovery of the role of sexuality in
ancient culture in excavations at Herculaneum was potentially traumatic

for a culture which had accepted Smith's and Winckelmann's vision of an ancient world that could transcend sexuality.[34] But for Fuseli the sexuality of the ancient world would have made sense within a biological narrative of culture as moving from birth to maturity and senescence.[35] In cyclical models, the vigour of culture could be imagined in terms of adolescent sexual drives while refinement of culture leads to an emasculating softness. The problem, in this model, was not so much the role of male sexuality as the place of female desire, newly powerful within a commercial culture: did the female dream constitute luxury or the energy of visual enthusiasm? And how could it be regulated? Fuseli's travelling companion in his journey to Italy in 1770 was the physician John Armstrong, a friend of Wilkes and James Thomson and the author (among other works) of a 1733 poem, *The Oeconomy of Love*, that gives expression to a Lucretian view of the inescapability of the sexual drives.[36]

The Oeconomy of Love assumes that culture follows a biological model and opens with an invocation to Venus, for 'oft on Thee/ The Muses wait, oft gambol in thy Train,/ Tho' Virgins', which echoes but also adapts the famous opening of Lucretius' *De Rerum Natura*.[37] Lucretius described Venus as the force behind the natural world: 'At THY Approach, GREAT GODDESS . . . The Clouds disperse, the Winds most swiftly waste'. Luxury is sexual but not decadent in Creech's translation of this passage:

> For THEE does subtle Luxury prepare
> The choicest Stores of Earth, of Sea, and Air:
> To welcome THEE, she comes profusely drest
> With all the Spices of the wanton EAST:
> To pleasure THEE, ev'n lasy Luxury toils:[38]

For Armstrong, Venus is the engine of culture and of art: his account of the Italian journey he began with Fuseli describes his disappointment in finding the Florence Venus lacking 'that vain wanton conscious triumphant Beauty I expected, from the description of some Travellers'. This Venus: 'looks timorous, bashful and coy; almost distrest and unhappy. In her present humour you would think it must cost the gallant God of War himself, a great many stratagems and perceive in her that amorous Fire, that Meaning, those Expressions, which make even an ugly woman charming.'[39] The absence of female desire is a disappointment here, though in Rome Armstrong is delighted to discover a male god who would satisfy any woman: 'If I was a Woman, I should be more in with the APOLLO than as a Man I am with the VENUS. For I have seen many women whom I should prefer to the VENUS; but never such a beautiful

graceful sublime figure of a man as the Apollo is.'[40] Whereas most critics
have seen Fuseli's art as driven by a conflicted and fearful view of female
sexuality, Armstrong's jovial acceptance of female desire as a source of art
may be closer to Fuseli than it seems.

On his return to London in 1779 Fuseli was struck by the limits of
British culture; a caricature he included in a letter to James Northcote
shows Britain populated by artistic mice with the names of Ozias Humphrey, Romney and Benjamin West. Switzerland serves as a chamber pot
to the monumental figure of the artist who bestrides three countries,
France, Switzerland and England, while a winged penis (an image derived
from Payne Knight's researches) flies off to Italy.[41] Whereas Siegel reads
this image as a lament for the artist 'inescapably placed in the courtyard of
a museum whose objects he is constrained to copy', it is also a lament for
what Fuseli now sees as the constraints of Protestant visual culture. At the
end of his life, in his last academy lecture, Fuseli would complain of the
effects of privatisation on a culture of public art: 'The ambition, activity,
and spirit of public life is shrunk to the minute detail of domestic
arrangements – every thing that surrounds us tends to show us in private,
is become, snug, less, narrow, pretty, insignificant.'[42] In a 1793 review,
Fuseli criticised the claim that the 'greatest praise' of art is 'to furnish the
most innocent amusement for those nations to whom luxury is become as
necessary as existence'.[43] Luxury here demands an 'innocent amusement'
that is suitable for feminine sociability. Returning to London at the end of
the 1770s Fuseli may already have been aware of the pressure of movements to contain and regulate sexuality. His remedy for what he sees as
limitation within a feminine private sphere is often to emphasise sexuality
as a means of attacking the limits of the polite.

THE FEMALE DREAM

In his *Aphorisms on Art*, Fuseli announced the subject of the dream as
'[o]ne of the most unexplored regions of art … and what may be called
the personification of sentiment'.[44] Disseminated as prints for private
display, Fuseli's images frequently focus on female dreams whether
the subject is classical as in *Sleeping Woman with a Cupid* etched by
Fuseli in 1780–1 (W81) or *Allegory of a Dream of Love* engraved by Blake
around 1790 (W112). Fuseli chooses dreams from Shakespeare, as in *Queen
Katharine's Dream* from *Henry VII*, engraved both by Bartolozzi in 1788
(W77) and by Blake in 1804 (W213) or *Titania's Awakening*, reproduced
as a stipple engraving by Thomas Ryder in 1803 from one of Fuseli's

Midsummer Night's Dream paintings for the Boydell Shakespeare gallery (W119). Fuseli's Milton gallery provided *The Dream of Eve*, a stipple engraving of 1804 by Moses Haughton (W179). The reduction in scale in the engraved versions could be seen as an aspect of the feminisation or privatisation of culture. In 1793 James Barry worried that the engravings of his paintings for the Society for the Encouragement of Arts, Manufactures and Commerce would change the meaning of the images. Scale had to be limited so that 'the prints should come within such a compass as by being covered with glass to make a part of furniture'. In Barry's view, human figures simply did not work on a small scale:

> The size of glass and of the largest double elephant paper, not admitting those two longest prints to exceed three feet in length, their proportionate height, according to the pictures, could not be more than ten inches, which would reduce the figures to a contemptible size, inadequate to the expression of the subject, and afford but a poor idea of pictures forty-two feet in length each, and where every thing was of the natural heroic size.[45]

Blake's illuminated books, especially but not only the *Songs*, adopt a tiny format with writing so small as to challenge the power of the reader to distinguish letters and identify characters. The debaters in *An Island in the Moon* question whether an epic imagination can express its visions in a world of bourgeois consumerism. Jerome, immersed in competitive fantasies, dreams both of overtaking Double Elephant (perhaps the painter Richard Cosway, named after a size of paper) and of seeing the apocalypse:

> If I had only myself to care for I'd soon make Double Elephant look
>   foolish, & Filligree work I hope shall live to see–
>   The wreck of matter & the crush of worlds
>   as Younge says   (E456)

'Filigree work' suggests the scale and delicacy of miniature, of Austen's little pieces of ivory, yet within this feminised form the aim is still to represent 'The wreck of matter & the crush of worlds'.

For Blake, however, private collections can also offer an escape from the world of fashion: in 1803 he describes the private collection of his friend and patron Thomas Butts as providing a 'Green House' for his work: 'But whatever becomes of my labours I would rather that they should be preservd in your Green House (not as you mistakenly call it dung hill). than in the cold gallery of fashion. – The Sun may yet shine & then they will be brought into open air' (E724). The 'Green House' is presumably the glass behind which Butts places Blake's work and the 'cold gallery of fashion' may be Boydell's Shakespeare gallery. Boydell himself presented his commercial enterprise as a form of 'Public patronage':

for here the Painter's labours will be perpetually under the public eye, and compared with those of his contemporaries – while his other works, either locked up in the cabinets of the curious, or dispersed over the country, in the houses of the different possessors, can comparatively contribute but little to his present fortune or future fame.[46]

But Blake sees the galleries as a form of confinement which can only be avoided with the help of Butts's 'Green House'. The private offers an escape from the fashionable world until the public sphere can undergo the revolution that Fuseli demanded.

Fuseli's *The Nightmare* is an image both of a dreamer and of her dream that appears to be set in a contemporary bedchamber. Even though the table and the couch belong to the modern world, the incubus imports an older sexual culture into the modern commercial world.[47] Fuseli's Gothic imagination depends on the assumption that women are naturally both sexual and social; Knowles reports his remark on convents: 'How self-contradictory that "animal of beauty," as Dante calls woman, should exchange her claims to social admiration and pleasure, and the substantial charms of life, for the sterile embraces of a crucifix or some withered sister.' The convent is the product of 'Tyranny, deception, and most of all, that substitute for every other want, "the undistinguished space of woman's will".' [48] Although Blake's concept of the 'Female Will' has been read as a misogynist or Christian moral attack on active female sexuality, it seems more likely that it is an echo of Fuseli's understanding of 'Woman's will' as the female control of female sexuality.[49] Fuseli uses Gothic conventions as a means of making error explicit, revealing the power of female sexuality by means of images drawn from a culture which denies sexuality.

In 1793, three years after Fuseli was elected to the Royal Academy, his choice of subject matter was attacked by his fellow academician Robert Bromley as 'frivolous, whimsical, and unmeaning'.[50] While imagination is chaste, dreams are dangerously unregulated:

A man may carry the flights of imagination, even within the walks of the chastest art or science, till they become mere waking dreams, as wild as the conceits of a madman. The author of observations on Fresnoy *de arte graphica* very properly calls these persons 'Libertines of painting': as there are libertines of religion, who have no other law but the vehemence of their own inclinations.[51]

Bromley also claims that Michelangelo's imagination is 'capable of being licentious' (I, p. 40) and attacks what he detects as pagan or Catholic in art. He associates these qualities with the feminisation and popularisation of culture:

Books are written of a light and fantastic nature by those who cannot write otherwise, and yet will write something. And so it is with painting; the mind of the artist can but give such subjects as are consecutaneous to its turn. – *The Nightmare, Little Red Ridinghood, The Shepherd's Dream*, or any dream that is not combined with the important dispensations of Providence, and many other pieces of a visionary and fanciful nature.[52]

The public representation of fantasy marks a descent from the seriousness required of public art: 'the painter who should employ his time on such subjects, would certainly amuse the intelligent no more than the man who should make those subjects the topics of a serious discourse'.[53] Bromley assumes that art must serve a Christian moral agenda.

Given that this attack coincides with Blake's treatment of the 'female dream' in *Europe* it seems likely that Blake's poem is a mark of solidarity with Fuseli as well, perhaps, as a comment on his work. John Howard identifies *A Midsummer Night's Dream* as a parodic context for *Europe*, but it may be Fuseli's *Midsummer Night's Dream* paintings on show in these years in the Boydell Shakespeare gallery as much as the Shakespeare text that Blake invokes.[54] Theseus's definition of the imagination from *A Midsummer Night's Dream* was quoted in Boydell's 1789 preface to the Shakespeare gallery catalogue to set verbal above visual imagination, offering Shakespeare's definition as an unattainable goal for the artist: 'It must not then be expected, that the art of the Painter can ever equal the sublimity of our Poet. The strength of Michael Angelo, united to the grace of Raphael, would here have laboured in vain. – For what pencil can give to his airy beings "a local habitation and a name."'[55] Boydell, like Hunt in 1809, assumes that spirits are disembodied and that painters are hampered by the necessity to embody their visions. In his copy of Swedenborg's *Heaven and Hell* Blake, however, suggests that he is troubled by this definition of the imagination. An earlier reader had written on his copy: 'And as Imagination bodies forth y[e] forms of things unseen – turns them to shape & gives to airy Nothing a local habitation & a Name.' Blake replies: 'Thus Fools quote Shakespeare The Above is Theseus's opinion Not Shakespeares You might as well quote Satans blasphemies from Milton & give them as Miltons opinions' (E601). Blake's concern may be that Theseus locates the imagination, giving 'to airy Nothing a local habitation & a Name' that becomes part of a

Figure 3. Henry Fuseli, *Titania and Bottom c.* 1790. © Tate, London, 2010.

private and domestic world. Theseus is like Urizen, who will proclaim: 'Let each chuse one habitation:/ His ancient infinite mansion' (E72). The Burkean 'ancient infinite mansion' is a place in which identity is fixed by inherited estate. At the same time, the famous definition, incorrectly in Blake's view, suggests that an 'airy Nothing' is always superior to an imagined form.

Fuseli's 1790 *Titania and Bottom* nevertheless both embodies the imagination and represents a scene rich in ambiguities and suggestive of the unstable registers of the project of painting Shakespeare, forcing the viewer to consider whether power in Shakespeare's *Midsummer Night's Dream* is held by Theseus, Oberon or Titania. As Nicola Bown points out, Titania appears in Fuseli's painting (Figure 3) as a figure of power rather than the humiliated pawn of Oberon's scheme.[56] The painting could easily be illustrated by the lines from *Europe*: 'Enitharmon laugh'd in her sleep to see (O womans triumph)/ Every house a den, every man bound; the shadows are filld/ With spectres' (E64).

Fuseli's image recalls his analysis of the role of power in female desire: 'Female affection is ever in proportion to the impression of superiority in the object. Woman fondles, pities, despises and forgets what is below her; she values, bears and wrangles with her equal; she adores what is above her.'[57] In this painting, Titania 'fondles, pities, despises and forgets' Bottom. Titania is associated by William Hayley with Elizabeth I, an 'imperious Old Maid' in his 1785 *Essay on Old Maids* where he remarks that the comparison 'As a fair Vestal throned by the West' in *A Midsummer Night's Dream* is a 'sublime compliment' to the queen.[58] Fuseli's imperious Elizabeth in the 1797 illustration of *Queen Elizabeth and Essex* that Blake engraved for Charles Allen's *History of England* can thus be read as a figure of female power that recollects Wollstonecraft's analysis of the corrupting influence of power on women who 'as well as the rich of both sexes, have acquired all the follies and vices of civilization, and missed the useful fruit'.[59] Fuseli represents Elizabeth's anger at a failure by Essex to recognise her authority: 'Her anger, naturally prompt and violent, rose at the provocation; and she gave him a box on the ear.'[60] Enitharmon has been seen as a figure recalling the power of the supposed voluptuary Marie Antoinette; She may instead be seen as a figure of the chaste queen Elizabeth, who uses the control of sexuality to cement her autocratic rule and to maintain a hierarchical society through the regulation of sexuality.[61] As a figure of female power, as Erdman suggested, she also suggests Queen Charlotte's active role in government during the madness of the king.[62]

But just as Gothic shows the control of sexuality producing heightened and monstrous forms of sexuality, so the female dream of the resolution of conflict also, inadvertently, transmutes sensibility into passion. In 1798 Fuseli used a version of the Titania and Bottom design for an illustration of *The Cave of Spleen, with Umbriel Receiving from the Goddess the Bag and Vial* (W153) for Du Roveray's illustrated edition of *The Rape of the Lock*. The bag holds female passions: 'Sighs, sobs, and passions, and the war of tongues./ A vial next she fills with fainting fears,/ Soft sorrows, melting griefs, and flowing tears.'[63] These are passions that women must learn to control: yet for Fuseli, who argued against the control of the passions demanded by Smith and Winckelmann, these unruly feelings were also the stuff that art is made from. They are not so different from the turbulent passions to which Blake's Los is subject in *Jerusalem*:

> Los rag'd and stamp'd the earth in his might & terrible wrath!
> He stood and stampd the earth! then he threw down his hammer in rage &
> In fury: then he sat down and wept, terrified! Then arose
> And chaunted his song, labouring with the tongs and hammer   (*J*1:6:8–11, E149)

The sexualised pagan culture that Milton thought banished by the birth of Christ is still active in the female imagination and cannot be fully contained by commercial society.

For Fuseli, then, sexuality can reverse the problems of an age of luxury: 'In an age of luxury women have taste, decide and dictate; for in an age of luxury woman aspires to the functions of man, and man slides into the offices of woman. The epoch of eunuchs was ever the epoch of viragoes.'[64] Luxury, in this aphorism, is a state in which male castration gives rise to an anti-sexual female power. The reclining sketch of Luxury that David Fallon notes can therefore be read, like the dreamer in Fuseli's *Nightmare* whose pose she repeats, as a figure of sexual frustration. Titania's sexuality and that of the attendant fashionable coquettes is directed both to a provocation and to a denial of erotic pleasure. In *Titania and Bottom*, two female attendants either side of the central couple stand for the female control of sexuality, with arms crossed, eyes lowered and topped with exaggeratedly fashionable headgear. For Fuseli, the coquette epitomises the power of luxury to divert sexual drive and thus upset the economies of gender and sexuality.

The results are imaged in *Titania and Bottom* and in the *Cave of Spleen* through the device of miniaturisation or puppets used by Hogarth in *Enthusiasm Delineated*. Like Hogarth, Fuseli represents people cradling tiny images: in his hand, Bottom holds a miniature male figure, a displaced phallus standing in for the empty darkness between the legs of Bottom's massive form. With his hands upraised and his back to the viewer, the tiny figure recalls an image that Fuseli and Blake were working on around this time: the figure of the *Fertilization of Egypt* (Figure 4) for Darwin's *Botanic Garden* published in 1791. Anubis, the dog god of the Nile, becomes in *Titania and Bottom* one of the toys of a feminised culture, the dog head displaced on to the demeaning ass's head that marks Bottom's subjugation to female power or the power of the marketplace. Instead of a virile pagan culture which worships fertilisation, the culture which was being redis-covered by the researches of men like Darwin and Payne Knight, Fuseli sees his own time as one which replaces sex with things. Blake's claim to Butts in 1801 that 'Miniature is become a Goddess in my Eyes' (E715) is clearly problematic.[65] His claim in the advertisement for his 1809 exhibition to have rediscovered miniature in fresco, however, shows the ways in which Blake, like Fuseli, rediscovers public art by drawing on feminised forms: 'Fresco Painting is properly Miniature, or Enamel Painting; every thing in Fresco is as high finished as Miniature

Figure 4. *The Fertilization of Egypt* from Erasmus Darwin, *The Botanic Garden,* 1791.
© The Trustees of the British Museum.

or Enamel, although in Works larger than Life' (E527). The detail of
miniature is restored to 'Works larger than Life'.

The gods of the ancient world, banished by the Christian world,
reappear stripped of their sexual energy in the fairies of Hannah More's
Sensibility: an Ode. When More imagines sensibility as a 'pow'r/ Who
shedd'st thy gifts upon the natal hour,/ Like fairy favours', she creates a
world free from the disruptive force of sexuality. It is this redefinition of
the fairy world as safe that Blake and Fuseli reject in the 1790s. Masculinity is displaced in class terms on to the 'rustic' who stands for men outside
the world of luxury and the feminised polite.

The Fuseli/Blake image of the *Fertilization of Egypt* reverses Milton's
banishment of 'The brutish gods of *Nile . . . / Isis* and *Orus,* and the Dog
Anubis' in the *Nativity Ode.* In Bromley's criticism of Fuseli the Nile
becomes a figure for the dangerous category of genius that Fuseli claimed

for himself: 'Genius is to the human mind what the Nile is to Egypt, the prolific source of all that has ever embellished and enriched it in every way ... To manage it, art was called forth at first; and when managed, every art and elegance followed what was become so enriched.'[66] Bromley, like Winckelmann, sees Egyptian art as excessively sexualised and fertile, in need of regulation from 'art and elegance'; he therefore turns Fuseli's critique of culture against him, drawing on Winckelmann's contrast between Egypt as a place of political tyranny and Greece as a place of liberty.[67] In line with the assumptions of climate theory, Bromley distinguishes between 'genius' as the product of hot countries which are 'calculated to give an enthusiasm to the mind' and liable to tyrannic government and 'taste' which occurs in temperate climates and belongs with constitutional government (I, pp. 43–4). Fuseli gives the role of policing the heated male genius to the cooler temperament of the educated woman who understands Greek liberty and who allows an equal interchange between the sexes. Fuseli's Titania is a manifestation of the hothouse sexuality of a hierarchical world in which female power restricts access to pleasure in an economy of sado-masochism.

The *Fertilization of Egypt*, therefore, is an image of the sexual power of visual enthusiasm, a power which is limited by the rules of politeness of a commercial, feminised society but which Fuseli's work can invoke. Humphry Repton's 1789 catalogue to the Boydell Shakespeare gallery describes Fuseli as having 'indulged the wildness of his fancy, with his usual enthusiastic energy'.[68] This quality particularly worries Repton in the painting of *Lear and Cordelia* and he claims that 'there is an enthusiastic ardour in this astonishing Artist, which, while it delights, will sometimes "o'erstep the modest bounds of nature"'.[69] Fuseli had flaunted his willingness to overstep the 'modest bounds of nature' in the *Remarks on Rousseau*, associating himself explicitly with the visual energy of enthusiasm. But binding produces energy in Fuseli's painting much as in *Europe* Enitharmon entrances Orc with erotic play: 'And we will crown thy head with garlands of the ruddy vine;/ For now thou art bound;/ And I may see thee in the hour of bliss, my eldest born' (E62). Boydell's catalogue contextualises *Titania and Bottom* by quoting the passage from *A Midsummer Night's Dream* in which Titania lulls her captive to sleep:

> *Queen.* Come, sit thee down upon this flowery bed,
>   While I thy amiable cheeks do coy,
> And stick musk-roses in thy sleek smooth head,
>   And kiss thy fair large ears, my gentle joy.[70]

Figure 5. William Blake, *Oberon, Titania and Puck with Fairies Dancing, c.* 1786.
© Tate, London, 2010.

To some viewers, the strange rituals enacted by fashionably dressed
women and presided over by a female mistress of ceremonies might have
represented a tawdry masquerade version of the Eleusinian mysteries.

In Blake's 1786 version of the last scene of *A Midsummer Night's
Dream,* perhaps illustrating the lines 'Hand in hand, with fairy grace,/
Will we sing, and bless this place', it is notable that the fairies are
the same size as the king and queen, suggesting the absence of the
hierarchical relationships of the Fuseli painting (Figure 5). Not only
are class hierarchies absent: in the figures of Oberon and Titania,
feminine power is also conspicuously absent as the queen twines her
hands seductively round the upright body of her husband. While she
watches Puck and the dancing fairies, her body melts into that of her
husband. Puck, perhaps the mischievous fairy of the introduction to
Europe, faces the viewer.

By contrast, the 1794 *Europe* shows sexuality under the tyranny of
power as Fuseli's massive sleeping figure of the rustic Bottom is recreated
as Orc, a figure of revolutionary energy bound by another queen,

Enitharmon. The shift in sexual imagery carries with it a coded account of shifted political realities. But Blake may also associate the binding of revolutionary energy with the confinement of possibility associated with the commercial galleries. In 1796, Blake's friend George Cumberland criticises the claims of Boydell and others that the nation's visual culture has 'arrived at the pinnacle of perfection'. Cumberland sees this claim as a reflection of commercial self-interest:

It promotes their profits, and so far, if taken with large allowance, it does no harm; but it does hurt indeed both to art, to poetry, and the country's ideas, when such authors, as *Shakspeare*, are undertaken to be finally illustrated, by exhibitions of pictures, painted according to the orders, and the ideas, of men; who so far from being able to guide this triumphal chariot of the British Apollo, are scarcely worthy to hold the horses heads: pictures painted on the gallop of rivalship, the spur of necessity, and under the lash of power.[71]

Jonah Siegel sees Fuseli's use of nudity in his 1771 illustration to *Hamlet, The Danish King Poisoned While He Sleeps*, completed within the male libertine environment of Rome as 'extraordinary – especially if compared with Fuseli's own depictions of scenes from Shakespeare in Boydell's gallery and elsewhere'.[72] Yet if Fuseli's *Titania and Bottom* represents the limitation of possibility, it is also an image of pleasure. Fuseli's review of his own work for the *Analytical Review* stresses the pleasurable elements of the scene: 'The moment chosen by the painter, when the queen, with soft languor, caresses Bottom … gave him licence to create the fanciful, yet not grotesque group, which he has so judiciously contrasted, as not to disturb the pleasurable emotions the whole must ever convey to a mind alive to the wild, but enchanting graces of poetry.'[73] Imagining the queen caressing Bottom, Fuseli both draws attention to the sexuality of the scene and implies that they are confined within the gallery by the company of lesser works, including those by Reynolds. Rather than providing a contrast with the annual Royal Academy shows, Boydell's gallery becomes part of the fashion system. Although a depiction of 'soft langour', this scene nevertheless allows the painter 'licence': the sexualised scene of pleasure is the place in which the mind becomes 'alive'.

The 'female dream' limits meanings within a depoliticised sphere of fashion but can also provide an escape into another mode of looking, deriving a new form of sexual desire from the eroticised response to a scene of binding. The sexual gaze therefore potentially renews culture, allowing a short cut from the softness of luxury to the energy of virile culture. The feminised culture that Fuseli represents is one which diminishes masculinity but also reveals the sexual content of female dreams. Fuseli's small figures are alive although miniaturised, re-animated by the imagination of the artist or the viewer.

BLAKE AND VISUAL PORNOGRAPHY

Martin Priestman presents Blake as ambivalently caught between 'a libertarian or even libertine insistence on bodily and sexual fulfilment' and 'a distrust of material "Nature"' derived from Thomas Taylor's neoplatonic understanding of the mysteries.[74] The print known as *Allegory of a Dream of Love*, a joint project of Fuseli and Blake from about 1790, offers a test case for critics that stress either of the two alternatives that Priestman describes (Figure 6). To David Bindman, it is a work whose 'obviously erotic intention ... would cast an interesting sidelight upon Blake's practice as a commercial engraver and perhaps, in this case, publisher'.[75] This clearly pornographic image carries an inscription that seems, hypocritically, to announce the delusive nature of erotic dreams. As such this is pornography that pretends to be moral. This image has been

Figure 6. Henry Fuseli, eng. William Blake, *Allegory of a Dream of Love c.* 1790.
© The Trustees of the British Museum.

read as a statement of Blake's (and Fuseli's) neoplatonic disregard for the body, yet it can equally, and more coherently, be read as a critique of the cultural construction of sexuality.

The problems derive from the way that the elephant-headed figure points to a Latin inscription from *Aeneid* VI, 896, 'FALSA AD COELUM MITTUNT INSOMNIA MANES', which, in Dryden's translation, describes the 'deluding lies' that pass through the gate of 'polish'd iv'ry' in the 'silent house of Sleep'.[76] The passage itself was seen as problematic and much discussed in Blake's time. As Urania Molyviati-Toptsis points out, the line is puzzling since Aeneas returns from the underworld through the delusive gates of ivory having been granted a true vision of the future.[77] William Warburton solved this problem in *The Divine Legation* by reading *Aeneid* VI as a coded account of the Eleusinian mysteries, a move which will 'unriddle the enigma, and restore the poet to himself'. Warburton argues that Virgil uses Homer's story of the two gates to distinguish between 'the reality of another state' and 'the shadowy representations of it in the shews of the mysteries: so that, not the things objected to by Æneas, but the scenes of them only, were false; as they lay not in HELL, but in the TEMPLE OF CERES'. The '*falsa insomnia* do not signify *lying*, but, *shadowy dreams*'.[78] Both Blake and Fuseli would have been familiar with Erasmus Darwin's notes to *The Botanic Garden* since they were both working on illustrations around 1790. Darwin's lengthy note reads the iconography of the Portland vase as a representation of the Eleusinian mysteries and explains that the Egyptians represented psyche, the soul, as a butterfly and in later periods as a 'lovely female child with the beautiful wings of that insect'.[79] Unlike Warburton, Darwin suggests that the story of Cupid and Psyche is one of sexual fulfilment.[80]

Blake would probably also have known a very different account of the Eleusinian mysteries in Thomas Taylor's 1792 *Dissertation on the Eleusinian and Bacchic Mysteries*. Taylor's reading is esoteric, 'principally derived from manuscript writings, which are of course in the possession of but a few'.[81] For Taylor, the mysteries speak of the degradation of the body which contaminates and finally kills the soul: they 'signify that such a soul in the present life might be said to die, as far as it is possible for soul to die; and that on the dissolution of the present body while in a state of impurity, it would experience a death still more durable and profound'.[82] Whereas Bindman takes the image as clearly erotic, David Weinglass, in the spirit of Kathleen Raine's influential work, argues that the woman's erotic dream 'falls into the category of delusive visions ... the offspring of such visions (including the cupids) are driven out by the rising sun, represented here by the Egyptian god Harpocrates (in the form of a herm), who epitomizes truth'.[83]

The herm also recalls the priapic term in one of the sexually explicit drawings that Fuseli completed in Rome in the 1770s.[84] Fuseli's image is complicated by the decision, as Marina Warner points out, to represent the 'way of false dreams' in terms of 'a hyperbolic masturbatory scene, with a phallic elephant goblin poised on the floor'.[85] Blake has usually been seen as conforming to the masturbation phobia that characterised his period. But another reading is possible. In the 1793 *Visions of the Daughters of Albion* where 'The virgin/ That pines for man; shall awaken her womb to enormous joys/ In the secret shadows of her chamber' (E50), masturbation is a positive by product, one of the '*rewards* of continence' (my emphasis) of the negative regulatory discourse of 'religion'. Sexuality, or touch, is a means of escape from the body: one of the windows which light the 'caverned man' in (some copies) of *Europe* that allows him to 'pass out what time he please, but he will not;/ For stolen joys are sweet, & bread eaten in secret pleasant' (E60). The delusive nature of the dream may lie in the failure to 'pass out what time he please', in the choice to keep the dream secret and unfulfilled, just as Urizen hides his fantasies:

> His prolific delight obscurd more & more
> In dark secresy hiding in surging
> Sulphureous fluid his phantasies.   (E75)

Christopher Hobson reads these lines as a condemnation of masturbation, but the fear of masturbation may be Urizen's rather than Blake's.[86]

Secrecy rather than bodily sexuality may therefore be read as the theme of the *Allegory of a Dream of Love*: the scene is framed by curtains and the figure of the herm behind the couch has his finger to his lips in a gesture which reminds the viewer of the secrecy with which the sight must be guarded and recalls the two female attendants in *Titania and Bottom*. The figure of Ganesh hints at the syncretic mythographers' account of the sexual origin of religion. David Weir suggests that Fuseli may well have been Blake's source in the 1790s for knowledge of Hindu mythology since it was probably Fuseli that Joseph Johnson employed to review and to excerpt Sir William Jones's *Asiatick Researches* for the *Analytical Review* from 1789 onwards.[87] The first review is signed 'F.' and announces that he has 'been favoured with the use of a copy of the work by a friend, immediately on its arrival'.[88] Identifying the *Analytical Review* as the source for Blake's probable knowledge of Hindu mythology, Weir shows that Blake would have been able to access much of the material contained in rare and costly books and would have done so within the context of republican politics. From Jones (perhaps via Fuseli) Blake would have known that 'Ganesa' was the elephant-headed god who represented the fount of wisdom.

Both in its eroticism and in the openness of the curtained chamber the Blake/Fuseli image suggests the power of imagination to create the world envisaged in *America*, where the fires of Orc leave 'the females naked and glowing with the lusts of youth' (E57). Yet the print also represents the claustrophobic privacy associated by Blake and Fuseli with the feminising of culture in their time. In making this scene public through the medium of their print, Blake and Fuseli attack the requirement of secrecy imposed on sexuality by their culture.

WOLLSTONECRAFT AND THE POWER OF PASSION

The theme of the corrupting power of secrecy in sexual matters is also important to Mary Wollstonecraft. I want to suggest here and throughout this study some (perhaps surprising) continuities between Blake's reading of sexuality and that which Wollstonecraft shares with Fuseli. Marilyn Butler considered that in 'sexual matters the Jacobins thought and as a group behaved (whatever their opponents claimed) like forerunners of the Evangelicals'.[89] Cora Kaplan detected a class-based project of defining a bourgeois sexuality in Mary Wollstonecraft's horror at the brutishness of the body in the 1792 *Vindication of the Rights of Woman*.[90] Likewise, Helen Bruder argued in 1992 that 'amongst a group of writers who broadly shared Blake's political sympathies there is little if any support for his belief in the liberating potential of sexuality'.[91] Identifying this context as the Jacobin novelists and writers who gathered around Joseph Johnson's dinner table, Bruder portrayed these writers as defining both their radicalism and their sexuality in terms of a principled bourgeois opposition to a decadent and libertine aristocracy.

But Mary Hays, Mary Robinson and Mary Wollstonecraft reveal a more complex understanding of female sexuality than critics have so far fully acknowledged. What Wollstonecraft's 1792 *Vindication* attacks is not female desire but the figure of the 'coquette', a woman in the mode of Fuseli's *femmes fatales* who derives pleasure from control rather than desire, from flirtation rather than love. Jane Moore argues that 'Wollstonecraft does not prohibit women's sexual passion *per se*, but only

the sexual gaming that so often accompanied it in aristocratic circles'.[92]
For Wollstonecraft as for Fuseli, passion is proof of immortality when she
writes: 'They, therefore, who complain of the delusions of passion, do not
recollect that they are exclaiming against a strong proof of the immortality
of the soul.'[93] It is the inability of women to experience passion that she
criticises: 'it is not against strong, persevering passions; but romantic
wavering feelings that I wish to guard the female heart by exercising the
understanding: for these paradisiacal reveries are oftener the effect
of idleness than of a lively fancy'.[94] Harriet Guest is surprised that
Wollstonecraft is less critical of the 'wanton who exercises her taste to
render her passion more alluring' than of the fashionable, shopping
obsessed woman.[95] But Wollstonecraft, like Fuseli, sees sexual passion as
the antithesis of the luxury of the commercial world. She argues against
the attempt to keep women 'from the tree of knowledge' (p. 164), and
although she rejects the sexualisation of the concept of knowledge in
relation to women, her use of the word 'passion' makes clear her inclusion
of sexual knowledge. The 'regulation of the passions', she insists, 'is not,
always, wisdom' (p. 185). 'On the contrary ... one reason why men have
superior judgment, and more fortitude than women, is undoubtedly this,
that they give a freer scope to the grand passions, and by more frequently
going astray enlarge their minds' (p. 185). While rejecting the reduction of
women to bodies, her account of passion crosses the divide between body
and spirit.[96]

It is less clear, however, that Blake distinguishes between a positive
'passion' and negative fancy. In two copies of *Europe*, copy H (1795) and
K (1821), Blake added a plate which presents the poem as the product of
erotic fantasy, the work of a 'mocking fairy' with whom the narrator
strikes a bargain:

> He laughing answer'd: I will write a book on leaves of flowers,
> If you will feed me on love-thoughts, & give me now and then
> A cup of sparkling poetic fancies; so when I am tipsie,
> I'll sing to you to this soft lute; and shew you all alive
> The world, when every particle of dust breathes forth its joy.   (E60)

This added narrative frame seems to present the poem itself as a product
of the 'female dream'. The source of imagination is 'love thoughts' and
the muse needs to be 'tipsie', a model of inspiration akin to those of the
libertine artists of Rome, gathered under the sign of Sergel's Bacchus and
drawing on the Dionysiac origin of imagination. In *Milton* (dated 1804)
the 'Muses who inspire the Poets Song' are the 'Daughters of Beulah'

whose 'Realms/ Of terror & mild moony lustre, in soft sexual delusions/ Of varied beauty' allow 'The Eternal Great Humanity Divine' to plant 'his Paradise' (E96). But in each of these passages there are also doubts: Blake will only include the laughing fairy of *Europe* in two copies, and if the muse needs to be tipsie, the 'garlands of the ruddy vine' are also used by Enitharmon to bind Orc in *Europe*. Beulah, the moony, feminine space that Blake describes particularly in *Milton*, is associated with the definition of the imagination from *A Midsummer Night's Dream*:

> Some Sons of Los surround the Passions with porches of iron & silver
> Creating form & beauty around the dark regions of sorrow,
> Giving to airy nothing a name and a habitation
> Delightful! with bounds to the Infinite putting off the Indefinite   (E125)

The function of art in this passage is to contain and frame extremes of passion, creating beauty by means of a limitation of range. The Shake-spearian echo suggests a form of art which offers a place of safety since the emanations call for 'a habitation & a place/ In which we may be hidden under the shadow of wings', an escape from the 'great Wars of Eternity' (E129). To be 'hidden' in terms of the discourse of public art is of course negative.

In so far as Beulah can be read in terms of art, these lines echo the repeated laments of Blake's period at the limitation of the visual arts by the commercialised market which prevents the creation of the great forms of public art: the female dream is Beulah and thus models the anxieties of the period about the shaping cultural power of female desire, evident in the bourgeois model of the polite. It is revealing that Fuseli's biographer John Knowles wrote in 1831:

Perhaps to no man can the following lines be more aptly applied than to Fuseli:

> The poet's eye, in a fine frenzy rolling,
> Doth glance from heaven to earth, from earth to heaven;
> And, as imagination bodies forth
> The forms of things unknown, the painter's brush
> Turns them to shapes, and gives to airy nothing
> A local habitation, and a name.[97]

Blake perhaps doubts the efficacy of his own privatised art which through its choice of a limited print run and elaborate hand-colouring places itself within the context of bourgeois taste.

CHAPTER 3

A history of softness: William Hayley and The Triumphs of Temper

One of the most compelling images of a positive feminine sphere was provided by Hayley's 1781 poem *The Triumphs of Temper*, a work that presents women as defined by the quality of 'softness'. From early in the eighteenth century, the problematic status of femininity is represented through the word 'soft', used most memorably in Pope's claim (through the voice of Martha Blount) that women are 'Matter too Soft'. Hayley's work marks the move from the view that woman is a softer (and so weaker and more malleable) man to the view that woman is made of something quite different from man and something that is potentially better. Both views are accommodated by Hayley's poem which he presents as a revision of 'that most excellent and enchanting Poem' *The Rape of the Lock* for his own woman-centred culture.[1] Whereas Pope concentrated on 'Female Foibles', Hayley will 'aspire to delineate the more engaging features of Female Excellence' (p. ix) and where Pope saw women as 'Matter too Soft', Hayley will reinstate Milton's positive vision of Eve as a being created 'For softness' and 'sweet attractive grace' (iv.298).[2]

The eroticised language of Hayley's 1781 poem prepares the way for the fervour of Della Cruscan magazine poetry in the later 1780s and Erasmus Darwin's sexualised account of the natural world at the end of the decade. It may be the combination of femininity as a subject and eroticisation as a mode that explains the extreme hostility that Hayley attracted in the nineteenth century from Southey and Byron up to George Saintsbury's description in the 1914 *Cambridge History of English Literature* of Hayley's poetry as 'impossible'. It is Robert Merry's Della Cruscan poetry, however, that Saintsbury describes as 'the nadir of the art'.[3] In the 1781 edition of *The Triumphs of Temper* the word 'soft' occurs on 48 out of 166 pages, often more than once. If 1771 is the high point of weeping in *The Man of Feeling*, 1781 marks the high point of the word 'soft' used in Hayley's poem in consistently positive ways.

Hayley is not alone in using or overusing the word 'soft' in the 1780s: 'soft' is a word that Charlotte Smith uses repeatedly in the 1786 *Elegiac Sonnets* published with the encouragement of and dedication to her then neighbour William Hayley. But it is Hayley's account in *The Triumphs of Temper* of a heroine 'Possest by Sympathy's enchanting sway .../ Unconscious of the dawning day' (p. 5) that epitomises his culture's 'female dream' in its attempt to recapture a positive meaning for soft matter.

Wollstonecraft attacks the association of softness with femininity in her 1792 *Vindication*, rejecting the notion that 'all women are to be levelled, by meekness and docility, into one character of yielding softness and gentle compliance'.[4] But she too can be tipped into Hayleyan mode by the subject of 'human rapture':

A shadowy phantom glides before us, obscuring every other object; yet when the soft cloud is grasped, the form melts into common air, leaving a solitary void, or sweet perfume, stolen from the violet, that memory long holds dear. But, I have tripped unawares on fairy ground, feeling the balmy gale of spring stealing on me, though november frowns. (p. 201)

The frequency of the word 'soft' in Blake's illuminated works and in his manuscript poetry is striking: it is used to describe Thel's 'soft voice' (E3); Oothoon is the 'soft soul of America' (E45); Bromion claims her 'soft American plains' and she writhes 'her soft snowy limbs'. As used by Blake, the word is associated with femininity, with the natural world (in the 'Soft soul of flowers Leutha!' of *Europe* and 'my soft cloud of dew' in *Ahania*). In Blake's writing, however, softness carries also a series of negative meanings as in the 'flames of soft delusion' in *Europe* and 'soft sexual delusions' of *Milton* book 1. Hayley makes softness synonymous with sensibility and it is not surprising that Enitharmon's looms 'vibrate with soft affections, weaving the Web of Life' in *Milton* (E100). More sinisterly, it is Cathedron's looms that produce 'A Polypus of soft affections without Thought or Vision' (E120).

As Blake turns against the word soft and cognate forms, softness also becomes associated with Hayley. Blake's *Milton* opens with an address to 'Daughters of Beulah! Muses who inspire the Poets Song' which surprisingly recalls the opening of *The Triumphs of Temper*: 'Daughters of Beauty, who the song inspire,/ To your enchanting notes attune my lyre!' The word 'soft' is also associated with the figure of Satan in the Bard's song when 'with most endearing love' he 'soft intreated Los to give to him

Palamabrons station'. Whereas softness is often a quality of the natural
world seen as female, in Satan it is associated with manners:

> Satan labour'd all day. it was a thousand years
> In the evening returning terrified overlabourd & astonish'd
> Embrac'd soft with a brothers tears Palamabron

These are all manifestations of 'Satans soft dissimulation of friendship', a sign
of the feminisation of Satan and the blurring of roles that seems disturbing in
the Bard's Song when Satan takes over the harrow of Palamabron.

The bond between Blake and Hayley was forged through the language of
sentiment. In July 1800 Hayley sent Blake the gift of the copy of *The
Triumphs of Temper* that had belonged to his only son Thomas Alphonso,
who had died in May. The copy carried the inscription: 'For it belonged to
my departed son./ Thus from an Angel it descends to Thee'. Tom had been
apprenticed to John Flaxman and the overdetermined gift thus ties Blake into
Hayley's world as proxy son: when Blake moved to Felpham later the same
year his projects included painting a head of Hayley's dead son for his library
and engraving a new set of illustrations by Mary Ann Flaxman, the sculptor's
half-sister, to *The Triumphs of Temper*. *The Triumphs of Temper* was one of
the best selling poems of its time, a poem that has received little serious critical
discussion but which is important not only as an index of constructions of
femininity but also of female taste, a work that is both revealing of its time
and capable of carrying diverse meanings to its readers. Sales were astonishing, with over sixteen editions between 1781 and 1814, and Hayley regularly
revised and updated the text to keep it in tune with his audience.
G. E. Bentley suggests that Blake saw the illustrations to *The Triumphs of
Temper* as the kind of project that could secure his financial future. Blake
wrote: 'I am now Engraving Six little plates for a work of Mr H's for which
I am to have 10 Guineas each & the certain profits of that work are a fortune
such as would make me independent supposing I could substantiate such a
one of my own & I mean to try many.'[5] If he were to follow Hayley's
example, the female market would be crucial to Blake's future.

'Enthusiasm' is first used by Blake in an unequivocally positive sense in
the letter of consolation to Hayley written four days after the death of his
son in May: 'Forgive me for expressing to you my Enthusiasm', Blake
writes, 'which I wish all to partake of Since it is to me a Source of
Immortal Joy' (E705). Annotating Lavater's aphorism no. 630,[6] Blake
did not react to the word (E599), nor when annotating Swedenborg's
Divine Love and Divine Wisdom does Blake use 'enthusiasm' in a particularly positive sense (E606). But in 1800 'enthusiasm' is part of the bond

that links Blake to Hayley and Hayley to Blake. In August, writing to John Hawkins (who had tried to organise money for Blake to visit Rome in 1784) Hayley mentions a 'lady' who displays 'a mixture of modesty, affection, & Enthusiasm'. His letter moves immediately from the lady to Blake: 'I cannot write the word Enthusiasm without recollecting that worthy Enthusiast, the ingenious Blake, who appeared the happiest of human Beings on his prospect of inhabiting a marine Cottage in this pleasant village' (BR94).

Hayley places Blake within a sentimental category that understands enthusiasm as a bourgeois affective mode quite unlike the 'dangerous secular and religious enthusiasms swirling around the London of his time'.[7] He can thus write to Flaxman in July 1800 describing Blake as 'our good enthusiastic Friend' and in November 1801 to John Johnson of 'our good enthusiastic Blake'.[8] Hayley is here bestowing on Blake an identity he uses for himself when he describes *The Triumphs of Temper* as 'one of those pleasing and innocent delusions, in which a poetical Enthusiast may be safely indulged' since it lies within 'the limits of Composition, and the character of modern Times' (p. v). In his 1796 *Life of Milton* Hayley repeatedly identifies 'sublime religious enthusiasm' as the characteristic quality of the poet and he describes himself as 'the enthusiastic biographer' in a letter to Cowper.[9] In Blake's case, it seems that the label of enthusiasm (itself the product of a regulatory discourse) is the product of his penetration of bourgeois society and of his contact with those bourgeois friends who offer him this identity. He implicitly accepts this identity when a few months after arriving in Felpham, Blake signs off a letter to Hayley, 'believe me to be your affectionate, Enthusiastic, hope-fostered visionary, William Blake' (E715).

The word 'polite' similarly mutates in Blake's vocabulary. In 1798, 'polite' is strongly negative when Blake describes Bishop Watson's attack on Paine as the work of a 'modern polite gentleman' who would 'see Christs discourses Expung'd' (E612). But the two letters in which Blake is labelled as the enthusiast enclose letters in which 'polite' is used positively; writing to Thomas Butts, Blake comments that 'The Villagers of Felpham are not mere Rustics; they are polite & modest'. The word 'polite' here loses constraints of class and education. Blake's optimistic sense that a liberal culture can be inclusive seems to be related to the lull in the long war with France offered by the peace of Amiens. In October 1801, cheered by the prospect of peace, Blake writes to Flaxman that: 'The Reign of Literature & the Arts Commences. Blessed are those who are found studious of Literature & Humane & polite accomplishments. Such have their lamps burning & such shall shine as the stars' (E717–18). Peace enabled the Flaxmans along with other British artists to visit Paris to see Napoleon's new acquisitions in the Louvre.[10] In an 1800 letter to Cumberland, Blake imagines his cottage as a lighthouse: 'See My Cottage at Felpham in joy/ Beams over the sea a bright light over France'. Hayley's retirement in Sussex allows a glimpse of a European culture which will support true art.

In a letter of 1800, Thomas Butts tells Blake that staying at Felpham will not make him 'a better Painter or a better Poet', but 'that you will be a better Man'. Butts expects that Hayley's company will free Blake from 'certain opinions imbibed from reading, nourished by indulgence, and riveted by a confined Conversation'. Whereas Wollstonecraft can be sceptical about the value of 'the muddy current of conversation' as a means of forming and conveying ideas, Butts believes in sociability as a means of regulation.[11] In contrast, Wollstonecraft sees women's sociability as one reason for the formation of sentiments rather than passions: 'by living more with each other, and being seldom absolutely alone, they are more under the influence of sentiments than passions'.[12] Although Hayley liked to picture himself as the 'hermit', he was remembered by John Johnson for his 'eminently great conversational ability'.[13] Butts hopes that Hayley's company will replace 'dim incredulity, haggard suspicion, & bloated philosophy' in Blake with 'opinions which harmonize society'. Both Butts and John Johnson assume that Hayley belongs to the mainstream of social circulation.[14]

It was Blake's failure (or refusal) to please the gendered audience that Hayley's poem addressed that was blamed for the failure of the 1803 edition of *The Triumphs of Temper*. Hayley wrote to Flaxman, 'I am sorry to say that the Ladies (& it is a Ladys Book) find Fault with the Engravings' (BR157). The sixth edition of *The Triumphs of Temper* in 1788 contained seven illustrations by Thomas Stothard, engraved by Sharp and Heath in the fashionably soft style. The frontispiece reproduces Romney's painting of *Serena Reading* and the fifth illustration again shows Serena reading, this time as she walks.[15] The new engravings focus on the darker elements of the poem, representing the father figure, who resembles Hayley, in a guise which is strangely tyrannical. Maria Flaxman's illustration to canto IV, 'From this the nymph her useful lesson took' (l. 328), shows a scene of domestic conflict and Serena as a rebellious daughter who gathers confidence as she catches sight of Chesterfield's defence of the stage. Meanwhile Sir Gilbert angrily reads the scandal in the newspaper and the spinster Penelope looks on disapprovingly. Blake's linear engraving style rejects the stipple engraving method that he had mastered early in his career and that more easily rendered softness.

THE GORDON RIOTS AND THE GENESIS
OF 'THE TRIUMPHS OF TEMPER'

The power of *The Triumphs of Temper* in its time derives from its ability to channel fears and hopes about the redemptive role of bourgeois women. In his *Memoirs* Hayley juxtaposes writing the poem with witnessing the Gordon riots, describing how he encountered 'groups of the most fiend-like wretches, who were then exulting over the spoil which they took from the house of Lord Mansfield'. This passage is followed immediately by Hayley's return to Sussex and the writing of the poem: 'he began on his return to his retirement, an extensive performance of which he had for some time entertained an idea' (1, pp. 207–8). The Gordon riots were understood by many as a collective outbreak of madness and the poem describes the role of bourgeois women in maintaining the sanity of the nation. Writing in the third person, Hayley explains that 'His observation of the various effects of spleen on the female character, induced him to believe, that he might render an important service to social life, if his poetry could induce his young and fair readers to cultivate the gentle qualities of the heart, and maintain a constant flow of good humour' (1, p. 208). Hayley sees femininity as providing the connective tissue in the social world by maintaining the 'gentle qualities of the heart'. Blake's conception of femininity as connection appears in the role of the emanation and in the ability of the daughters of Albion to 'hear her woes, & eccho back her sighs' (E51).

Blake's writing of the 1790s portrays not only the feminised discourse of sympathy but also the figures of disruption and disorder that Hayley associates with the riots and that he excludes from his poem. In a long speech to Parliament on 20 June 1780, Burke attacked the petitions from various Protestant associations as evidence of 'bigotry and fanaticism' and singled out for criticism a petition against the rebuilding of a school destroyed by the riots: 'he read the names of several taken from thence with a mark – he threw others into ridicule, and he quoted, in a facetious manner, the names of several women – not being able to read and write themselves, these monsters were desirous of preventing others from receiving education'.[16] Presenting education as the route to religious toleration, Burke went on to describe his own education by a Protestant Dissenter. The project of avoiding riot and disturbance by educating women was taken up by Hannah More, one of Burke's friends and admirers from Bristol.

In More's 1788 poem on 'The Slave Trade' Burke's female monsters join with Milton's allegory of Satan, Sin and Death to produce the 'unlicens'd monster of the crowd,/ Whose roar terrific bursts in peals so loud,/ Deaf'ning the ear of Peace'. More identifies this monster in a footnote in her collected poems of 1801 with the Gordon riots and describes the genealogy of 'mad Liberty':

> Of rash Sedition born, and mad Misrule;
> Whose stubborn mouth, rejecting Reason's reign,
> No strength can govern, and no skill restrain,
> Whose magic cries the frantic vulgar draw
> To spurn at Order, and to outrage Law[17]

Elizabeth Kowaleski-Wallace comments that More represents the danger of free debate among the 'frantic vulgar' metonymically, as the 'stubborn mouth' which standing for 'revolutionary license' is 'magnified and animated, and it seems to have a life of its own. It is an orifice of corruption, with its foul odor and its "pestilent" breath, suggesting still other orifices of the body.'[18] Buried in this image is not only Milton's narrative of nightmare reproduction but Swift's '*Female* officers, whose Organs were understood to be better disposed for the Admission of those Oracular Gusts'. Literacy seems to Burke and More to offer protection against a form of madness associated with female sexuality. By contrast the 'sober Goddess' of Liberty is the 'pure daughter of the skies' – a formulation echoed in the description of Thel as the 'virgin of the skies' (E5) – who represents the power of women to redeem the nation by developing their minds.[19] More's female Liberty is derived from Cowper's account of the Gordon Riots where 'Liberty blush'd and hung her drooping head,/ Beheld their progress with the deepest dread'.[20] In More's poem, Cowper's allegorical figure of Liberty becomes part of bluestocking culture; her project through the 1790s and beyond is to disseminate these values through bourgeois culture.

Finding fault with Milton's allegory of Satan, Sin and Death, Johnson claimed that Milton reflected a culture not yet reshaped by female readers: 'The women had not then aspired to literature, nor was every house supplied with a closet of books.'[21] Hayley's aim is to achieve just this reshaping of culture. *The Triumphs of Temper* rejects the Tory claim to be the woman's party announced by Samuel Johnson's association of Milton's republicanism with a failure in 'domestick relations'. Hayley defended Milton's literary and personal treatment of women in his *Life of Milton* and in early editions of *The Triumphs of Temper* Hayley rejects Swift's view of femininity by punishing him in the Cave of Spleen. In an uncharacteristically vicious passage (which Hayley apologises for in a footnote and omits from later editions), Swift's 'spleenful brain' is daily ripped from his 'pierc'd skull' by the fiend Derision. Hayley was thrilled by Gibbon's report that his heroine Serena 'was very warmly befriended by two powerful sponsors, the Duchess of Devonshire, and my Lord North'.[22] These 'two powerful sponsors' position the poem in a political middle ground which appeals to the nation rather than a political party. Harriet Guest points out that Hayley's heroine Serena 'seems able to speak a language of patriotism which is more disinterested than that of her father because it is purified of party feeling, superior to the newsworthy business of high politics'.[23] Like Sin interposing between Satan and Death, Serena is a figure of conciliation, healing conflict and offering a Whig model of moderation. Her father, 'A faithful Whig, who, zealous for the state,/ In Freedom's service led the loud debate' turns 'every day, by Transmutation rare' into 'a Tory in his elbow chair'.[24] Serena has the power to soften the tyranny of her father 'when her young charms/ Wind round her hoary Sire's reluctant arms' (p. 102). Hayley insists in his 1782 *Essay on Epic Poetry* on the ability of women to write epic and so to contribute directly to public culture but his *Triumphs of Temper* also suggests the power of women to prevent conflict and heal the divisions of the nation.

Hannah More's 1782 *Sensibility: an Ode* praises 'sweet Serena's poet', recognising a kinship between the ability to triumph over temper described in his poem and the method of controlling pain derived via Elizabeth Carter from Epictetus.[25] More's subject is the meaning of suffering and addressing her poem to Mrs Boscawen, a recently bereaved mother, she argues that although sensibility heightens pain it also enables a circulation of feeling that makes happiness possible:

> For tho' in souls where energies abound,
> Pain thro' its numerous avenues can wound;
> Yet the same avenues are open still,
> To casual blessings as to casual ill. (pp. 276–7)

Unregulated feeling 'Breaks out in wild irregular desires,/ Disorder'd passions, and illicit fires' (p. 288), but Sensibility, channelled into 'avenues', is associated with the power of the educated mind to control the body and to render feeling within the bounds of morality. More is clear that Sensibility is available only to the educated and is something that the 'happy vulgar' (p. 278) cannot experience:

> They never know, in all their coarser bliss,
> The sacred rapture of a pain like this:
> Then take, ye happy vulgar, take your part
> Of sordid joy which never touch'd the heart.

The idea that poverty prevents the development of feeling and limits the power to experience both pain and pleasure recalls the view of the 'sage' in Cowper's 'Hope' that 'The poor, inur'd to drudgery and distress/ Act without aim, think little and feel less'.[26] While she sees hedonism as pagan, More believes that Hayley shares her view that education enables forms of mental experience denied to the 'vulgar'. While Hayley's poetry attempts to silence the conflicting feelings voiced by Thel's grave plot, in her insistence on the value of pain More rejects the freedom from suffering offered to Thel in the vales of Har.

'THE TRIUMPHS OF TEMPER' AND BLUESTOCKING CULTURE

The Triumphs of Temper gives form to the feminine dreams of the 1780s, a decade in which Roger Lonsdale long ago argued that 'women virtually took over, as writers and readers, the territories most readily conceded to them, of popular fiction and fashionable poetry'.[27] Removing the latent conflict within More's own writing, Hayley's poem for women reflected back to women readers an image of a culture that seemed to be their own work. A host of magazine verses in the 1780s and 1790s celebrate Hayley as the bard of bluestocking culture: Imoinda in 'Stanzas occasion'd by reading the Triumphs of Temper, a Poem by Mr. Hayley' in the *Town and Country Magazine*, vol. 14 (August 1782) offers her own prayer to Hayley's Sophrosyne (in perhaps inadvertently sexual terms):

> Thy friendly hand relief could bring,
> Refuse not the desir'd request;
> Then would I still with pleasure sing
> The kind restorer of my rest.
>
> Divine Sophrosyne! oh hear,
> Tho' at thy shrine so lately sung
> A bard, whose numbers full and clear,
> Flow in soft cadence from the tongue.[28]

The 'Bas-Bleu Intelligence' in the *Argus* of 10 March 1790 describes the sympathy of the bluestockings for Hayley after the failure of one of his plays: 'When the prints diurnal came,/ And display'd Great HAYLEY'S name,/ With criticisms dire surrounded,/ Which in rude sarcasm abounded'.[29] Hayley's *Triumphs of Temper* celebrates bluestocking sociability in its picture of a Heaven of Sensibility without paternal authority. Hayley's heavenly women 'Who deeply drink of intellectual joy' are ideal readers, discerning but open; the queen of this heavenly realm is 'Warpt by no envy, by no love misled,/ Equal she holds the living and the dead' (p. 136). The admiration was mutual, for just as women readers saw Hayley as celebrating bluestocking culture, so Hayley saw femininity as a means of accessing poetic power. Hayley views poetry as a 'declining Art': 'The ages ... are past, in which the song of the Poet was idolized for its *miraculous effects*' (p. v). The extraordinary success of the poem suggests that Hayley's plan was a smart move.

Adam Smith saw 'Society and conversation' as 'the best preservatives of that equal and happy temper, which is so necessary to self-satisfaction and enjoyment'.[30] In Hayley's poem it is up to women to maintain the 'equal and happy temper' that regulates society. Hayley's 'Temper' is not the external form of regulation offered by conduct books but a form of internal regulation which tunes the Æolian harp of the female mind, to 'regulate, unseen,/ The softer movements of this nice machine' (p. 10). Temper allows passion to be experienced safely since 'the rough swell of the insurgent tides/ By the mild impulse of the Moon subsides' (p. 44). Barred from attending a masquerade (the test that the heroine fails in Elizabeth Inchbald's *A Simple Story*), Hayley's Serena maintains her temper by writing an 'Ode to Sophrosyne' (p. 45), reproducing the technique of self-regulation used by Richardson's Clarissa when she recites Elizabeth Carter's 'Ode to Wisdom' and draws on Carter's stoic philosophy derived from Epictetus. The move in *Clarissa* from epistolary prose to verse is a sign of the mastery of the flux of feeling and the form of *The Triumphs of Temper* models its message. Hayley used this technique himself during the first year of Blake's stay at Felpham when he would write sonnets through the night in a form of therapy for the grief of his son's death.[31]

Hayley was at the centre of a culture of female literary productivity, a middle-brow culture that for a time defined the nation's idea of educated and feminine 'Liberty'. He attributed his love of reading to 'hearing poems read to him with taste and feeling by his mother' and was known for his encouragement of women writers, including Charlotte Smith (who lived at nearby Woolbeding in Sussex in the 1780s), Helen Maria Williams and Anna Seward.[32] The reissue of *The Triumphs of Temper* in

1795 in a series of seven works 'printed in an uniform size . . . and each adorned with Plates' for the mainstream publishers Cadell and Davies defines the taste of Hayley's world, including work by two of Hayley's neighbours: John Sargent's *The Mine* and Charlotte Smith's *Elegiac Sonnets*. The volumes are 5 or 6 shillings (the average price for new poetry in the period) and all are already successful, often the sixth, seventh or eighth editions.[33] By providing illustrations for the Armstrong by Stothard, including works by Charlotte Smith, and commissioning a critical essay to the Akenside by A. L. Barbauld, the project both invites women readers and announces their integration into mainstream culture. The collection belongs to a liberal network: Smith and Barbauld were among the 'lady defenders of the Revolution' toasted in 1792 at the British Club in Paris.[34] And 1795 was the year that Hayley published *The National Advocates*, a poem 'inscribed' to the lawyers Erskine and Gibbs 'in praise of their exertions in defence of Thomas Hardy, Horne Tooke and others'. This is a culture within which women's voices are perhaps more significant than ever before and within which earlier discourses of gender and sexuality are being challenged.

FEMININITY AND SOCIABILITY

This culture also gave Blake his first recognition as a writer as well as an artist. *Poetical Sketches*, Blake's first and only conventional publication in 1783, was the result of his participation in the social circle of the Rev. A. S. Mathew and Harriet Mathew. This was a milieu in which women not only actively contributed but probably set the tone. It was Harriet Mathew who persuaded her husband to join Flaxman in paying half the cost of printing Blake's poems and it was this volume that Flaxman sent to Hayley in April 1784.[35] Mrs Mathew was in contact with bluestocking circles, described in a memoir of Flaxman as 'one of the most highly-gifted and elegant women of that day . . . the intimate associate of Mrs. Montague, Mrs. Barbauld, Mrs. Chapone, Mrs. Brooke, &c.'[36] Although there has been some discussion of whether Blake's notebook satire *An Island in the Moon* represents the Mathew circle, until recently more critical attention has been given to identifying the male characters than the female. Whereas Ellis and Yeats took the scenes as an account of 'the literary evenings in Mr Mathews's drawing room' (masculinising the salon), S. Foster Damon's claim that Blake 'must be satirizing far more important people' displays the tendency of critics to minimise reference to circles dominated by the codes of bourgeois femininity in interpreting

Blake's writing.[37] Jon Mee suggests that *An Island* may date from later in the 1780s and reflect something of the more disputatious conversational style of Joseph Johnson's gatherings, partly on the grounds that 'women in the satire are represented neither as simply insisting on polite restraint nor as unusually disputatious' but as joining 'in the collisions on different sides of the question with everyone else'.[38] Godwin, after all, records his irritation at his first meeting with Wollstonecraft when she dominated the conversation and prevented him from drawing out Paine, who was 'no great talker'.[39]

The key role given by Hume and others to bourgeois women inevitably provoked satire in the 1780s and Blake's *Island in the Moon* clearly draws on current satiric conventions, developing out of his work in 1784 on four issues of the *Wit's Magazine*, then edited by Thomas Holcroft.[40] Robert Essick points out that the August 1784 issue of the *Wit's Magazine* contained an 'Expedition to the Moon' that takes on several of the same 'intellectual pretensions' as *An Island in the Moon*.[41] Blake's first task for the magazine was to reproduce Thomas Stothard's image of *The Temple of Mirth* for the frontispiece to the first issue in January.

The image Blake engraved (Figure 7) shows Mirth as a classical goddess, laurel wreath on her head and book in hand, holding forth to a mixed gathering of men and women who hold their sides and even, in the case of one man, fall to the floor laughing. The temple is decorated with busts of Swift, Sterne, Voltaire and other humorists. Though significantly more homogeneous in terms of class, the scene of an unruly crowd invites comparison with Hogarth's Methodist meeting in *Enthusiasm Delineated*. Words rather than images move this group and they listen to a woman rather than a male preacher. Rather than a woman falling to the floor, Stothard's image shows a man felled by uncontrollable laughter. In 1799, Blake told Dr Trusler that 'his Eye' was 'perverted by Caricature Prints, which ought not to abound as much as they do. fun I love but too much Fun is of all things the most loathsom' (E702). Blake's comment can be understood in terms of the contrast between the two versions he engraved of this print. His first version (Figure 7), closely following Stothard's design, epitomises 'a sweetness, softness and feminization of tone'.[42] This version adopts the style of Stothard's successful illustrations to *The Triumphs of Temper*. Blake's revised version (not illustrated) conforms to the more broadly caricatured style of his work for the next three issues of the *Wit's Magazine* after designs by the caricaturist Samuel Collings. The difference in style between the two versions is that which Hogarth described in his 1743 etching *Characters and Caricaturas*.[43]

Figure 7. William Blake, *The Temple of Mirth*, after Thomas Stothard, 1784.
© Tate, London, 2010 (first version).

The criticism of the caricature style in Blake's letter to Trusler suggests
that Blake is unhappy with a style that renders the body and its desires
grotesque, setting it in a carnivalesque world that is easy for the public
sphere to disown and to marginalise. Some critics have suggested that a
Bakhtinian mode of the grotesque describes Blake's acceptance of bodily
processes and the clearly grotesque imagery of some of the pencil annotations to the *Four Zoas* manuscript might also reveal Blake's view of the
body as perverse.[44] It might be the case that Blake refuses to offer a
hierarchy of bodily modes, incorporating the language of satire and the
grotesque into his epic vision. Yet it is also possible that the grotesque
sublime of the body most powerfully expressed in *The Book of Urizen* is
not only satiric but represents a Urizenic corruption of vision.[45] Tristanne
Connolly argues that the centrality of the *Book of Urizen* account of the
creation of the body is demonstrated by Blake's decision to reuse
the narrative with only small changes in *The Four Zoas* and in *Milton*.[46]
The Urizenic body, as Connolly observes, 'works against itself, is built to
frustrate itself from its beginnings'.[47] Yet the retelling has a specific

function: in the Bard's Song of *Milton*, the narrative is part of the reason that Milton must descend, it announces what Peter Otto calls Blake's 'critique of transcendence'. The narrative is imbued with Urizen's horror of the body, a product of reason's fear of embodiment. It reveals, in other words, the corrupted view of the body that still persists in contradistinction to the paradisiacal image of sexuality that Milton created in *Paradise Lost*. Blake's preference for 'Characters' over 'Caricaturas' not only conforms to Hayley's project to endorse female sensuality within cultural forms that are or can be respected but rejects the mode of the grotesque as a means of incorporating the body in culture. By giving women 'characters', Hayley and Blake can refute Pope's claim that 'Most women have no characters at all'.

The 'happy copulation' that Johnson associated with the collisions of wit appears in Blake's first version of *The Temple of Mirth*, which suggests a sense of delight in the mixed sociability it describes and adopts a different mode from that of Fuseli's contribution to the genre, an etched frontispiece after his own drawing, *The Mighty Mother Sails Through the Air* (Figure 8) to Theophilus Swift's *The Temple of Folly* published in 1787 by Joseph Johnson.[48] Fuseli shows a bare-breasted Folly complete with fool's cap topped with a crescent moon and standing not on the traditional globe but on a balloon. As we might expect, Fuseli sexualises the image, focusing it on the mighty mother's breasts. Sexuality here becomes simultaneously a means of satirically animating the desexualised sphere of Folly and a recognition of the power of a trivial world to coopt the sexual. It is not clear whether Folly encourages or sees through the crazy world described.

In *The Temple of Folly*, the poet is taken to a world in which anger and energy are tamed: 'The playful pard, and courteous tyger dwell:/ The civil mastiff welcomes at the gate,/ The lion fawns, and wolves forget their hate.'[49] This tame world echoes Sarah Scott's 1762 image of bluestocking sociability in *Millenium Hall* where Mrs Mancel comments: 'There is I confess something so amiable in gentleness, that I could be pleased with seeing a tyger caress its keeper.'[50]

More topically, and more significantly, the world of *The Temple of Folly* echoes Hayley's heaven of sensibility in its freedom from conflict. Like Blake's islanders, Theophilus Swift's world is entranced by Lunardi's balloon flights and by Lunardi's book which is humorously described as 'giving an account of his first voyage to the moon' (p. 75). Clearly radical in its identification of the followers of Folly as 'Priests of all nations, Brahmins, Imans, Friars,/ With all the trump'ry that blind zeal inspires'

Figure 8. Henry Fuseli, *The Mighty Mother Sails Through the Air* from *The Temple of Folly*,
1787. © The British Library Board (1346i46).

(III.247–8), Theophilus Swift attacks the depoliticisation of feminine
consensus culture. Fuseli may have met Theophilus Swift (a distant
relation of Dean Swift) at Joseph Johnson's house and in its wide-ranging
satire, which includes the failure of the travelled dilettanti to appreciate
British painters, the account of feminine folly reflects the hostility of the
Johnson circle not only to commercial femininity but to the political
conservatism of some bluestocking culture.[51]

The same concerns emerge when Wollstonecraft laments the insipidity
of the conversation of English women in her 1792 *Vindication*:

The conversation of French women, who are not so rigidly nailed to their chairs
to twist lappets, and knot ribands, is frequently superficial; but, I contend, that it
is not half so insipid as that of those English women whose time is spent in
making caps, bonnets, and the whole mischief of trimmings, not to mention,
shopping, bargain-hunting, &c. &c.[52]

The function of feminine chatter in Blake's notebook satire, however, is more difficult to define. Miss Gittipin does not belong to the feminine literary culture celebrated by Hayley's *Triumphs of Temper.* She wants to look rather than read:

Now here said Miss Gittipin I never saw such company in my life. you are always talking of your books I like to be where we talk. – you had better take a walk, that we may have some pleasure I am sure I never see any pleasure. theres Double Elephants Girls they have their own way, & theres Miss Filligree work she goes out in her coaches & her footman & her maids & Stormonts & Balloon hats & a pair of Gloves every day & the sorrows of Werter & Robinsons & the Queen of Frances Puss colour & my Cousin Gibble Gabble says that I am like nobody else I might as well be in a nunnery ... (E456–7)

Miss Gittipin's voice is closer to that of Smollett's garrulous servant, Win. Jenkins, in *Humphry Clinker*:

God he knows what havock I shall make among the mail sex, when I make my first appearance in this killing collar, with a full soot of gaze, as good as new, that I bought last Friday of madam Friponeau, the French mullaner – Dear girl, I have seen all the fine shews of Bath; the Prades, the Squires, and the Circlis, the Crashit, the Hottogon, and Bloody Building, and Harry King's row.[53]

Michael Phillips suggests that Catherine Blake 'may be reflected in that "Ignorant Jade" Mrs Nannicantipot' who 'speaks to Quid in the final fragment as though they were married'.[54] Although the topic of debate for Blake's islanders is 'the Ladies discourses' and battle lines are constructed in predictable ways with ladies set against the male philosophers and book lovers, the debate is as much about class, education and culture as about gender.

Unlike Wollstonecraft, Blake delights in the minute particulars of the inconsequential and disordered, ungrammatical and unedited 'Ladies discourses' and chooses to represent their speech (much as in his long lined poems narrative control is ceded to a series of often hard to distinguish voices who argue, speak and lament). It is out of the chatter and conflict of *An Island* that the *Songs* emerge. The women of *An Island* are more frivolous and more fashionable than either the bluestockings of Mrs Mathew's gatherings or the women of Joseph Johnson's circle. Their speech represents the uneducated women that Hannah More targeted. The very disorder of associative speech of Blake's Miss Gittipin is as disruptive as enthusiasm and as resistant to order as Blake's long-lined poetry. The witty exchanges of conversation are bracketed with the energy of the enthusiastic preacher when Mrs Sigtagatist recalls her childhood pleasure in emotionally unrestrained preaching:

there was I up in a Morning at four o clock when I was a Girl. I would run like the dickins till I was all in a heat. I would stand till I was ready to sink into the earth. ah Mr Huffcap would kick the bottom of the Pulpit out, with Passion, would tear off the sleeve of his Gown, & set his wig on fire & throw it at the people hed cry & stamp & kick & sweat and all for the good of their souls. (E452)

Like the bawd rolling on the floor in Hogarth's *Enthusiasm Delineated*, these women bring something of the disorderliness of the crowd into sociability.

The failure of the scheme to send Blake to Rome tilted his career towards the bourgeois London culture of the Mathews and towards the *Songs* whose form (at least) derives from a domestic genre of children's poetry. Martin Myrone suggests that some of the illustrations to *Songs of Innocence* echo contemporary embroidery designs, part of 'a now largely lost domestic visual world of decoration and design, of printed writing papers, ephemeral religious prints, decorative wares and furniture'.[55] Blake's illuminated books, after all, are material objects, produced both by his own research in the process of printing and Catherine's expertise in watercolour. Whereas Wollstonecraft regrets the attention that women give to sewing, William Hayley's willingness to value 'the many excellent pictures, which we have lately seen produced by the needle' as evidence of female creativity, recognises the material nature of art.[56]

In *An Island in the Moon* the discussion of epic and of science takes place in the same physical space as gossip about fashion and personality. The satire reveals concerns about whether the world of Folly allows the space for epic ambitions and for the renovation of public culture to incorporate the energy of enthusiasm. But it is clear that for Blake the feminine world of gossip and chatter, of disputatious associative talk, can give birth to poetry. Something like Theophilus Swift's 'courteous tyger' and 'playful pard' reappear in 'The Little Girl Lost' of *Songs of Experience*:

> Leopards, tygers play,
> Round her as she lay;
> While the lion old,
> Bow'd his mane of gold.   (E35)

The leopards and tigers here, however, belong potentially in a narrative of sexual awakening for Blake sees potential in a culture that the Johnson circle distrust.

'SOFT RAPTURES': SOFTNESS AND SEXUALITY

Although Hannah More endorsed *The Triumphs of Temper*, Hayley's poem is important precisely because it resists More's desexualised understanding of sensibility. When a friend suggested that his poem of thanks to More for her positive reference in *Sensibility* was too warm, Hayley insisted that 'she must be very prudish indeed; (which I am very far from supposing her to be,) if my verses offend her in that point of view'.[57] Hayley's poem to More belongs to the modes of Della Cruscan literary flirtation:

> How may he scorn all human harms!
> How blissful his condition!
> Who shall encircle in his arms
> So lovely a magician![58]

In so far as he encouraged women to write and to publish, Hayley also stands against More's desire to control women's writing. Hayley's magazine readers valued his work because it seemed to them to endorse the flood of female authors that appalled Hannah More in her 1799 *Strictures*: 'Who are those ever multiplying authors, that with unparalleled fecundity are overstocking the world with their quick-succeeding progeny? They are NOVEL-WRITERS; the easiness of whose productions is at once the cause of their own fruitfulness, and of the almost infinitely numerous race of imitators to whom they give birth.'[59] More here reveals her horror of writing that fails to dematerialise the process of production and carries the taint of sexuality. Excessive literary productivity becomes associated with sexual incontinence.

Hayley's feminised world tends towards a new indirection in its handling of sex: the 1795 series that led with *The Triumphs of Temper* contained a reprint of John Armstrong's 1744 *The Art of Preserving Health* rather than the still current 1733 poem *The Oeconomy of Love*, and the new introduction by John Aikin displays some anxiety about the treatment of sexuality, noting quizzically that Armstrong writes with 'great force' of 'the condition of one unnerved and exhausted by excess in amorous delights', a topic which is 'deviating from the express subject of the book; since love as a passion, and the appetite for sexual enjoyment, are distinct things'.[60] Whereas an 1811 edition is worried by Armstrong's politics, in the 1795 edition it is the treatment of sex that worries Aikin, perhaps because political conflict was increasingly played out in coded terms in relation to morals and to manners.[61]

Whereas Hannah More in 1782 describes sensibility as allowing the mind to triumph over the body, Hayley suggests that the cultivation of Temper will allow women to access a safe form of sensuality blocked by errant feeling. Hayley is concerned with the danger of Sensibility, which he sees as a state of quickly shifting 'Rapture and Agony' linked in 'Nature's loom'.[62] As well as a public meaning, Hayley's poem had a secret personal subtext for the uncontrollable alternation of 'Rapture and Agony' represented Hayley's diagnosis of (what he saw as) his wife's mental illness. In his *Memoirs* Hayley describes his wife's symptoms as a 'fluctuation of her spirits' which 'was rapid to an alarming degree'.[63] She was 'a most pitiable sufferer, whose nervous infirmities admitted only of such palliation, as may be gained by tender and liberal care "To manage well/ The restless mind".'[64] It was no coincidence, therefore, that the publication of *The Triumphs of Temper* coincided with the birth of Thomas Alphonso to the daughter of Hayley's old wet nurse. Owning a copy of *The Triumphs of Temper* both let Tom into the secret of his birth in coded form and offered an implied justification for his father's infidelity. By 1799, however, the story was the subject of widespread gossip. In January that year, Farington noted in his diary the details of Hayley's unhappy marriage which he had heard from Flaxman:

Mr. Hayley married the daughter of a clergyman, who was Dean of Chichester. Her mother had been subject to fits of insanity, which the daughter inherited. She had no children by Hayley and expressed that he should take the daugtr. of his Nurse (his foster sister) into his House *in Her place.* This Hayley did, and they all lived together cordially, and by this young woman Hayley had the boy above-mentioned.[65]

Saree Makdisi writes that in 'Blake's illuminated books, organs and body parts, even whole organisms, do not work the way they are supposed to'.[66] Hayley's writing for and about women addresses what he sees as the malfunctioning of the sexual system. In 1811 he wrote to Walter Scott describing 'a *Secret History* relating to the marvellous Organisation and Infelicities' of his wife.[67] Hayley explained to Scott that his wife was the unhappy product of an attempted sexual cure for her own mother's madness: Hayley's father-in-law had been advised that his wife's madness would be cured by giving birth and she had conceived while unconscious. The story is a peculiarly unhelpful example of the belief in the power of sexuality to cure illness prevalent in Hayley's circle, which also reveals the continuance of long-standing beliefs that character is formed in the moment and circumstances of conception. Hayley's *Temper* rests on an assumption that sexual experience is fundamental to mental equanimity and that sensibility requires a bodily sensuality that More saw as hostile to feeling and typical of the vulgar. It was entirely appropriate that Romney painted Emma Hart, the embodiment of sensuality, as Sensibility and incorporated a reference to Hayley's *Triumphs of Temper.*

Hayley embraces the way in which the language of softness is used in erotic writing as when John Armstrong's 1733 *The Oeconomy of Love* sings the praises of '*Love*, in thy soft Raptures when/ Timeliest the melting Pairs indulge'.[68] Armstrong was a close friend of James Thomson and his poem transmits the concerns of Restoration sexual culture through the safer topic of the natural world in a Lucretian tradition that runs from James Thomson's *Seasons* to Erasmus Darwin. It is no accident that Thomson overworks the word 'soft' in the eroticised 'Spring' for it is this discourse that Hayley invokes, smuggling eroticism into a didactic work through a language that emphasises touch. Blake's *Poetical Sketches*, which probably reflect the taste of Harriet Mathew and of Flaxman, recalls Thomson's language in 'To Spring': 'O deck her forth with thy fair fingers; pour/ Thy soft kisses on her bosom'.[69]

Hayley's poem offers a defence of female eroticised fantasy and welcomes the sexual charge of private reading, a subject of widespread concern to the period. Serena feels so strongly 'Sweet Evelina's fascinating power' that she reads past midnight:[70]

> But, as warm clouds in vernal aether roll,
> The soft ideas floated in her soul:
> Free from ambitious pride, and envious care,
> To love, and to be lov'd, was all her prayer:
> While these fond thoughts her gentle mind possess'd,
> Soft slumber settled on her snowy breast.   (p. 5)

Puberty, in Hayley's lascivious words 'those important years,/ When the full bosom swells with hopes and fears' (p. 2), creates a secret self 'When conscious Nature prompts the secret sigh,/ And sheds sweet languor o'er the melting eye' (p. 2). Hayley accepts without demur the parallel between erotic female fantasy and the work of the poet: 'The Poet dreams of everlasting Fame .../ The softer Virgin dreams of endless Love' (pp. 49–50). An 1809 watercolour by Blake suggests that he joins Hayley in these assumptions. (Figure 9) Blake's image literally interprets a simile from Shakespeare's *Henry IV, Part I* (IV. i. 108–9): 'As if an angel dropped down from the clouds'. In this image, the female reader is placed in a version of Hayley's heaven of Sensibility. Languidly reclining on a

Figure 9. William Blake, *As if an angel dropped down from the clouds*, 1809. © The Trustees
of the British Museum.

cloud, she plays with her exposed nipple and sees the text of her reading
become embodied in a handsome male angel, whose body is tilted
to allow a good view of his genitals. The prancing horse replaces the
sinister horse's head in Fuseli's *Nightmare* and the whole scene is lit by the
sun, rejecting the secret indoor, night-time location of much of Fuseli's
erotic imagery. In the early nineteenth century, evangelicals attacked the
reading of Shakespeare as dangerous, and Blake clearly rejects their
campaigns.[71]

The backlash appears as early as Cowper's poems of the early 1780s
which attack just the sexualised female dream that Hayley endorses:

> Ye novelists who marr what ye would mend,
> Sniv'lling and driv'ling folly without end,
> Whose corresponding misses fill the ream

With sentimental frippery and dream,
Caught in a delicate soft silken net
By some lewd Earl, or rake-hell Baronet;
Ye pimps, who under virtue's fair pretence,
Steal to the closet of young innocence,
And teach her unexperienc'd yet and green,
To scribble as you scribble at fifteen;
Who kindling a combustion of desire,
With some cold moral think to quench the fire,
Though all your engineering proves in vain,
The dribbling stream ne'er puts it out again;[72]

The attraction of *The Triumphs of Temper* to female readers of the Romantic period rests in its ability to provide an answer to the concerns of the period about the place of fantasy, sexuality and feeling. It is Cowper's disapproval, however, that dominates the later nineteenth century and reappears in a vicious review in *Blackwood's* of Hayley's *Memoirs* after his death in 1823 which describes him as a 'heartless, brainless versifier ... who certainly will henceforth rank at the very bottom of the scale of English drivellers'.[73]

THE TURN AGAINST SOFTNESS

For the 1803 edition on which Blake worked, Hayley replaced the word 'soft' wherever possible, reducing the pages on which the word appears from forty-eight to thirty-three. The 1781 'So shall this Zone, if justly I'm obey'd,/ Bring my soft spirit to thy certain aid' changes in 1803 to 'So shall this zone, if my command's obey'd,/ Bring my quick spirit to thy certain aid'. In canto II, 'soft spirit' (p. 24) changes to 'light spirit' (p. 24), 'Courtesy's soft lustre' (p. 30) to 'courtesy's mild lustre' (p. 31), and in canto III, the 'soft Maid' (p. 53) to the 'kind nymph' (p. 54). In canto V, one appearance of the 'soft Serena' (p. 117) changes to the 'fond Serena' (p. 115) and another (p. 118) to 'griev'd Serena' (p. 116).[74] Yet even these changes do not allow Hayley to rediscover his ability to access the female reader. Wollstonecraft rejects his prescription for the regulation of temper when she writes in 1792: 'As a sex, men have better tempers than women, because they are occupied by pursuits that interest the head as well as the heart; and the steadiness of the head gives a healthy temperature to the heart.' In More's 1808 novel *Coelebs* her mouthpiece Sir John attacks *A Sentimental Journey* (Sterne's 'corrupt, but too popular lesser work') which became the mischievous founder of the school of sentiment. A hundred writers communicated, a hundred thousand readers caught the infection. Sentimentality was the disease which then required to be expelled. The reign of Sterne is past. Sensibility is discarded, and with it the softness which it must be confessed belonged with it.[75]

Whereas softness was once associated with sympathy, More now sees it as belonging with luxury and indolence: 'Their flexible young hearts would have been wrought upon by the actual sight of miseries, the impression of which was feeble when it reached their ears at a distance, surrounded as they were with all the softnesses and accommodations of luxurious life.'[76] Blaming Blake for the failure of the edition, Hayley cannot see that the poem itself may no longer speak to the liberal audience he could once address so successfully.

The exaggerated marking of femininity in Hayley's use of the word 'soft' may be a symptom of the approaching shift from a one-sex model (in which woman is a lesser man) to a two-sex model in which woman is made of something quite different from man. Robert Southey has been identified (on somewhat dubious grounds according to the Opies) as the author of the now familiar nursery rhyme that provides the different ingredients of boys and girls:

> What are little boys made of made of?
> What are little boys made of?
> Snips & snails & puppy-dogs' tails
> And such are little boys made of.
> What are young women made of, made of?
> What are young women made of?
> Sugar & spice & all things nice,
> And such are young women made of.[77]

Certainly the end of the eighteenth century was particularly concerned with the question 'What are young women made of?' But by the end of the century, softness is more easily associated with the natural world than with women. As the links between softness and sexuality and between women and sexuality become less acceptable, it is transferred to childhood and to nature: it is the Derwent that 'compos'd' Wordsworth's 'thoughts/ To more than infant softness'.

Although the 1780s associated softness with eroticism and with the presence of women within a shared culture, the word is increasingly associated with an attempt to split culture along the dividing lines of gender, politics and class. Erdman links the attack on the workings of Pity in The Four Zoas ('If you would make the poor live with temper/ With pomp give every crust of bread') with an 1800 speech in which Pitt called on the nation to 'act with proper temper, firmness and sobriety'.[78] The passage in *Four Zoas* VIIa with its plan to 'Compell the poor to live upon a Crust of bread by soft mild arts' could equally be read as an attack on the conservative rhetoric of philanthropy and the work of Hannah More. The reference to 'soft mild arts' and to living 'with temper' shows here how Hayley's feminised rhetoric has been adopted by More's conservative project.

Hayley's apparently safe image of feminine eroticism appealed to conservative writers at the end of the century. Whereas T. J. Mathias attacked both Hayley and Darwin, Hayley received the dubious compliment of a defence from Polwhele in the 1798 *Unsex'd Females* on the grounds that *The Triumphs of Temper* blends 'the invention of Spenser' with 'the perspicuity and melody of Pope'.[79] Although Hayley's poem emphasises female sexuality, in Polwhele's terms it is not 'unsex'd' because Hayley describes a 'sexed' form of female sensuality, rejecting Wollstonecraft's claim that men and women are made of the same thing. For Polwhele, the very fact that Hayley uses Pope's Rosicrucian machinery of Gnomes, Sylphs, Nymphs and Salamanders makes him safe as this machinery is specifically offered as feminine.[80] Polwhele may realise that for both Pope and Hayley female sexuality necessarily serves male desire. For Polwhele, the crucial need is to preserve gender difference and what worries him is not the sexualisation of women but the adoption by women of what he sees as a male sexual identity. Thus Polwhele believes that Pope would share his horror at 'The Amazonian band – the female Quixotes of the new philosophy'. Although Hayley's *Triumphs of Temper* claims to reverse Pope's gendered hierarchy, Polwhele is probably correct in misreading Hayley as Pope.

Blake's hostility towards the soft culture represented by Hayley represents a rejection of the divided categories that are being set up at the end of the century. If softness is coded as feminine it also potentially excludes writing that appeals to women from addressing the public. Blake's work also rejects rules of politeness that impose an embargo on the memory of the energies of the Gordon riots. Whereas Hayley contains sexuality within a discourse of politeness, Blake draws on the iconographic tradition deriving from Milton's allegory and Swift's *Tale of a Tub* that More used to satiric effect in her image of 'Mad Liberty'. Rendered as part of visual culture in works by Hogarth, Fuseli and James Barry and illustrated by Blake in the early 1800s, Blake's most powerful version of the allegory of Satan, Sin and Death appears in the Preludium to *America* and the Preludium to *Europe*. Fuseli, Barry and Blake present the moment in Milton's allegory at which Sin attempts to prevent conflict between her father/partner Satan and her child/rapist Death.

In Blake's poetry of the 1790s, Sin's place is taken by the Shadowy Female who does not resist but welcomes Orc's sexual energy or even violence.[81] Even if Blake did not share the religious partisanship of the Protestant associations, these poems use a sexual narrative to recall events that appalled the sensibilities of the radical dissenters. As Saree Makdisi points out, the bourgeois radicals of Johnson's circle carefully dissociated themselves from the possibility of armed and active revolt.[82] But in the Preludiums to *America* and *Europe* Blake represents the ambiguous energies of revolution unleashed by the willing cooperation of the natural world or the nation.

In Blake's usage, the word 'soft' is not simply a code for femininity: to enter Beulah is to become *like* women or children, for in *Milton* book II 'Into this pleasant Shadow all the weak & weary/ *Like* Women & Children were taken away as on wings/ Of dovelike softness' (E130, emphasis added). The gender essentialism of Hayley's model disappears as Blake argues that 'Man in the Resurrection changes his Sexual Garments at will' (E212). Little over a year into Blake's stay in Felpham, the assumption of a shared language breaks down. Enthusiasm now signals to Blake all that separates him from Hayley's culture: 'My Enthusiasm is still what it was', Blake writes, 'only Enlarged and confirm'd.' The word 'enthusiasm' reclaims its combative sense and appears for the first time in the illuminated poetry in the preface to *Jerusalem*, dated 1804 in a plate that Blake subsequently defaced:

The Enthusiasm of the following Poem, the Author hopes [*no Reader will think presumptuousness or arroganc[e] when he is reminded that the Ancients acknowledge their love to their Deities, to the full as Enthusiastically as I have who Acknowledge mine for my Saviour and Lord, for they were wholly absorb'd in their Gods.*] (E145)[83]

At the same time, the Rosicrucian machinery that Hayley adapted from Pope and that Darwin took from Hayley reappears in a more sinister role in *Milton* book II where 'The Fairies, Nymphs, Gnomes & Genii of the Four Elements' are 'Unforgiving & unalterable': 'These are the Gods of the Kingdoms of the Earth: in contrarious/ And cruel opposition: Element against Element' (*M* II:31[34], 17–24, E131). In *Jerusalem* chapter 1 the four gates of Golgonooza are guarded by (sixty-four thousand each of) genii, gnomes, nymphs and fairies (*J* 1:13:26–9, E157). The discourse of sexuality indicated by this machinery is now seen as specifically bourgeois, part of the ideological construction that guards the gates of Golgonooza against dangerous meanings and (as we will see in the next chapter) produces art that fits smoothly into the ideology of a nation at war.

Bourgeois women were seen as facilitating a civilised and non-combative style of conversation, calming conflict and placing bounds on rude, crude or sexual talk. Sarah Scott's portrait of 'rational cheerfulness and polite freedom' in *Millenium Hall* is predicated on the ability of women to regulate sexuality in mixed society and offers the example of Lady Mary Jones whose 'vivacity seemed under the direction of modesty': 'In her greatest flow of spirits, she hazarded no improper expression, nor suffered others to do so without a manifest disgust.'[84] The result is a form of conversation which rejects the dazzle and debate of aristocratic gatherings where 'Every person was like a bent bow, ready to shoot forth an arrow; which had no sooner darted to the other side of the room, than it fell to the ground, and the next person picked it up, and made a new shot with it'.[85]

> Eternity is the place of the 'Arrows of Love' in the last plates of *Jerusalem*:
> And the Bow is a Male & Female & the Quiver of the Arrows of Love,
> Are the Children of this Bow: a Bow of Mercy & Loving-kindness: laying
> Open the hidden Heart in Wars of mutual Benevolence Wars of Love
> (*J* IV:97:12–14, E256)

The Bow is equally 'Male & Female' and the 'Wars of Love' recall Wollstonecraft's claim that Milton wrongly models eternity as a place of angels. Jane Moore points out that Wollstonecraft rejects Milton's model of eternity because of 'the conviction that the human condition, unlike the angelic, is one of struggle'.[86] Women and men have rational faculties precisely in order to pursue good, which necessarily requires coming into contact with temptation. Blake's view of Love is here more conflictual than the regulatory discourse of 'sexuality' produced by bourgeois politeness and epitomised in the success of Hayley's *Triumphs of Temper*.

CHAPTER 4

The Essay on Old Maids *and the learned lady*

Hayley's library was well stocked with works on sex aimed at a male readership: the sale of his library after his death contained not only books by More and Wilberforce but also a three-volume 1754 edition of the works of Crébillon in French (Paris, 1754), a 1784 copy of *Les Liaisons Dangereuses*, Diderot's *Bijoux Indiscrets* in French (1753) and English (1749) and many other texts of the libertine enlightenment. He owned Mandeville's *Virgin Unmask'd* of 1757 and works of comparative anthropology such as *Marriage Ceremonies*, 1760, as well as books on sex like *Charmes de l'Amour Conjugal*, 1784.[1] This interest in sex emerges in his three-volume prose work of 1785 *A Philosophical, Historical, and Moral Essay on Old Maids by a Friend to the Sisterhood*. With new editions in 1786 and 1793, *An Essay on Old Maids* was Hayley's most successful work after *The Triumphs of Temper*. The third edition of 1793 contained new illustrations by Thomas Stothard and coincided with a new engagement by Blake with the theme of sexuality in *America* (advertised in October 1793) and *Europe* of 1794.

The success of this work is as revealing as that of *The Triumphs of Temper*. Whereas *The Triumphs of Temper* contained its account of sexuality within the limits of a feminised discourse, under cover of anonymity Hayley's three-volume prose work of 1785 mounts an explicit and extensive attack on his culture's regulation of female sexuality. Whereas the first work for women flattered the self-image of bluestocking culture as disseminated through the magazines, the second acted as a safety valve for a libertine account of sexuality no longer acceptable within a feminised culture.

Hayley's 1785 work is about the cultural role of virginity, an issue which is central to Blake's 1789 *Book of Thel* as well as to *Milton* and *Jerusalem*. The lily Thel questions in the vales of Har is a 'little virgin of the peaceful valley' (E4); the cloud addresses her as the 'virgin of the skies' (E5); the 'matron Clay' speaks of her 'virgin feet' and the poem ends when

'The Virgin started from her seat, & with a shriek./ Fled back unhinderd till she came into the vales of Har'. Likewise, Ololon's status as the virgin is emphatically reiterated in the passage in *Milton* book II where she appears to Blake before his cottage:

> And as One Female, Ololon and all its mighty Hosts
> Appear'd: a Virgin of twelve years nor time nor space was
> To the perception of the Virgin Ololon but as the
> Flash of lightning but more quick the Virgin in my Garden
> Before my Cottage stood for the Satanic Space is delusion
> For when Los joind with me he took me in his firy whirlwind
> My Vegetated portion was hurried from Lambeths shades
> He set me down in Felphams Vale & prepard a beautiful
> Cottage for me that in three years I might write all these Visions
> To display Natures cruel holiness: the deceits of Natural Religion[.]
> Walking in my Cottage Garden, sudden I beheld
> The Virgin Ololon & address'd her as a Daughter of Beulah[:]
> Virgin of Providence fear not to enter into my Cottage
>
> (*M* II:36[40]:16–28, E137)

In so far as Blake sees a girl walking in his 'Cottage Garden' and welcomes her into his cottage, this scene both recalls and revises events that marred Blake's last summer in Felpham. On 12 August (as Blake described it to Butts) a soldier 'was invited' into his garden without his knowledge by a gardener who was working there: 'I desired him as politely as was possible to go out of the Garden, he made me an impertinent answer[.] I insisted on his leaving the Garden[;] he refused' (BR 158). Afterwards, the soldier (named Scofield or Scholfield) claimed that Blake had damned the King and that his wife had offered to fight for Bonaparte. A charge of sedition was brought against Blake and heard at Chichester in January 1804. This episode – evidence either of Blake's pro-French sympathies or his aptitude for conflict – is recalled in *Jerusalem* where a character called 'Skofield', one of the 'Spectre sons of Adam', appears several times. The soldier's presence in his garden perhaps seemed to Blake one of the 'invasions of privacy' that characterised, according to John Barrell, the highly politicised atmosphere of the time.[2] In the very different scene of Ololon's entry into Blake's garden in *Milton*, a poem that shares a symbolic date with Blake's trial for sedition, the invasion of privacy is transformed.

Despite the frequency of the word 'virgin' in Blake's work, Christopher Hobson finds Blake's 'attitudes to virginity ... hard to gauge'.[3] Andrew Lincoln reads the figure of Ololon as an attempt to restore to Protestant culture the compassionate role of the Virgin in Catholic culture in an explicit reference to Hannah More's reforming work.[4] Lincoln not only detects a reconsideration by Blake in the post-1800 poetry of qualities coded as feminine and thus devalued within both Protestantism and civic humanism but also suspects that Blake's political position shifts towards an idiosyncratic endorsement of some elements of Barruel's counter-revolutionary reading of culture. Lincoln sees Blake turning against Hayley's enlightenment culture (and the task of painting Voltaire in Hayley's library) and finding a new sympathy for some elements of the evangelical project. Within the context of the period's debate about sexuality, however, Blake's re-imagining of the category of the virgin reveals the consistency with which he maintains into a new century the critical reading of gender and sexuality born in the revolutionary 1790s.

Hayley alludes teasingly to a series of precursor texts with the admission that the title 'might entrap some indelicate reader'.[5] Whether Hayley is referring to Wilkes's 1755 *Essay on Woman* or to Mandeville's 1709 *The Virgin Unmask'd* (also published as *The mysteries of virginity: or, A full discovery of the difference between young maids and old ones*) which Hayley owned in a 1757 edition, his protestation about attracting the wrong kind of male reader ('for readers of that class must be undoubtedly masculine') is an attempt to retain the imagined female reader of his text.[6] Hayley's anxiety emerges from a sense that reading is inevitably policed by gendered rules. What links Hayley's *Essay* with both Wilkes and Mandeville is his assumption of the naturalness of female sexuality even though codes of politeness render impossible the kind of graphic description offered to her niece by Mandeville's 'Elderly Maiden Lady': 'Sometimes when you thought you was not observ'd, how passionately would you throw yourself backward, and clapping your Legs alternatively over one another, squeeze your Thighs together with all the Strength you had, and in a Quarter of an Hour repeat the same to all the Chairs in the Room?'[7] Instead, Hayley offers a medicalised understanding of female sexuality within the codes of sensibility:

A frame of glowing sensibility requires a proper field for the exercise and expansion of all its general affections; and when this is denied to it, such obstruction will sometimes occasion the very worst of evils, a sort of stagnation both in heart and soul, a disorder for which language can afford no name, and which, being a compound of mental and bodily distemper, is more dreadful to support, and perhaps more difficult to cure, than any distinct maladies either of mind or body. (I, p. 10)

In this passage, Hayley both stresses the interconnection of body and spirit ('a sort of stagnation both in heart and soul', 'a compound of mental and bodily distemper', 'distinct maladies either of mind or body') and suggests that the sexual disorder he describes lies outside the structures of language. Within Hayley's world, 'language can afford no name' for a whole area of human experience. Hayley's nameless disorder is perhaps the condition of Blake's 'nameless female' of the Preludium to *America* (E51) and the 'nameless shadowy female' of the Preludium to *Europe* (E60). Blake's Milton descends for the sake of his lost emanation 'To go into the deep her to redeem & himself perish?' making the journey that Thel feared, achieving the circulation that (in another form) Hayley saw as necessary for the healthy functioning of bodies and of society.

For Hayley, sexuality is fundamental to the human need for 'tenderness' and 'sensation'. The words that Hayley uses of the old maid are 'obstruction', 'stagnation', 'disorder' and the *Essay* aims to 'promote the circulation of good-will and good-humour in bodies where they are frequently supposed to stagnate' (I, p. xix). Flow is here associated with health, just as the inverse, standing water, is dangerous in the Proverb of Hell 'Expect poison from the standing water' (E37), or in the words of the harper in the 'Memorable Fancy' whose 'theme was, The man who never alters his opinion is like standing water, & breeds reptiles of the mind' (E42). Appropriately it is Urizen who creates 'A wide world of solid obstruction' (E72) and it is his blocked world that produces a 'destructive torrent' of sexual energy: 'cataracts of fire blood & gall/ In whirlwinds of sulphurous smoke:/ And enormous forms of energy' (E72).[8] Like a chimney sweep himself, Hayley in his *Essay* must clear blockages and 'sweep away those black and bitter particles, which form a lodgment on the brain ... to give that degree of cleanliness and comfort to the pericranium of his reader, which the brush of the Chimney-sweeper secures to the house of his employer' (I, p. xiv). The sexual connotations of the chimney sweeper are here probably intended.

Similar assumptions about the necessity of circulation and the danger of blockage are common to radical discourse in Blake's period: Mary Hays's Emma Courtney describes the destructive power of blocked sexuality in images of water: 'I regret these natural sensations and affections, their forcible suppression injures the mind – it converts the mild current of gentle, and genial sympathies, into a destructive torrent.' In another passage, monasteries are imagined not only as blocking circulation but as creating a negative circulation of polluted sexuality; according to Emma Courtney 'monastic institutions and principles' produce 'as from a polluted source, streams, that ... spread through society a mingled contagion of dissoluteness and hypocrisy'.[9]

Anna Clark comments that 'those who feared sexual desire as polluting and disorderly, and those who celebrated it as liberating and transcendent, often assumed that sexual desire itself is a powerful, natural force, like rushing water, which must be contained lest it overflow and wreak havoc'.[10] But for the pro-sex discourse of Blake's time, the power of sex becomes destructive when flow is blocked.

Blake imagines the contamination of human experience in *Milton*, where the Ulro contains

> a vast Polypus
> Of living fibres down into the Sea of Time & Space growing
> A self-devouring monstrous human Death Twenty-seven fold
> Within it sit Five Females & the nameless Shadowy Mother
> Spinning it from their bowels with songs of amorous delight
> And melting cadences that lure the Sleepers of Beulah down
> The River Storge (which is Arnon) into the Dead Sea:
>
> (*M* 11:34[38]:24–30, E134)

The Polypus blocks the flow of the 'Sea of Time & Space' with its 'fibres'. A source of fascination to the period, the Polypus was considered to be neither vegetable nor animal and was thought to reproduce asexually by breaking off parts of itself; Sarah Scott's *Millenium Hall* describes how 'That insect alone, of all creation, does not continue maimed by amputation, but multiplies by it'.[11] Darwin's *Zoonomia* describes the polypus, found in 'stagnant waters' in July, whose young branch out from the adult like the branches of a tree, and 'require no mother to supply them with a nidus'.[12] In *Milton*, 'The 'Five Females & the nameless Shadowy Mother' who spin the polypus 'from their bowels' use 'songs of amorous delight' to lure 'the sleepers of Beulah' into a non-sexual place, a 'Dead Sea'. This 'self-devouring monstrous human Death' is a version of what Hayley calls 'the very worst of evils' for the amorous songs are merely a trick to create a stagnant world, offering, like the coquette, an asexual version of the erotic.

'THELYPHTHORA' AND THE SEXUALITY DEBATE

Perhaps the most significant precursor to Hayley's 1785 *Essay* in his library was Martin Madan's 1780 *Thelyphthora*.[13] Martin Madan, Cowper's cousin, was the chaplain at the Lock Hospital for prostitutes infected with venereal disease and a celebrated preacher when in the 1780 *Thelyphthora* he effectively ended his career with the suggestion that polygamy was the answer to prostitution. As Felicity Nussbaum shows,

Madan's solution was not as extraordinary as it now seems but a serious reconsideration of a lingering alternative direction for the institution of marriage, regularly invoked as a (rejected) alternative in Richardson's novels.[14] It has long been suggested that Blake's choice of the name Thel is a reference to Madan's work although the nature of Blake's response to Madan is disputed.[15] Like Wollstonecraft's *Vindication of the Rights of Woman* a decade later, *Thelyphthora* was notorious and its arguments familiar even to those who had not read it; indeed, Cowper probably wrote his *Anti-Thelyphthora* on the basis of a discussion with John Newton without having read his cousin's work.[16] But Hayley's nervous revisiting in the *Essay on Old Maids* of the issues that Madan raises makes his knowledge of the work indisputable. Like *The Triumphs of Temper*, *Thelyphthora* is an attempt to heal the ills of the nation caused by the trauma of the American war; but Madan's proposal threatened the very basis of the nation's self-image, attacking its sense of difference from the East and the view that it uniquely enshrined the protection and cultivation of women's happiness. A host of quickly written pamphlets attacked Madan and produced a wide-ranging debate on sexuality.

In one pamphlet Richard Hill imagined the consequences of legalising polygamy on domestic happiness: 'nothing could be expected at home but quarrels, jealousies, and brawlings among the rest of the females, and at best, dissatisfied looks from a nauseated husband'. The idealised private space that underpins the public sphere in eighteenth-century Britain turns in his pamphlet into a place of nightmare: 'every habitation where peace at present dwells, is liable to be turned into a temple of discord, if not into an human slaughterhouse, by wives cutting their own, each others, or their husband's throats, or hanging or drowning themselves in fits of frantic jealousy'.[17] Cowper's 'If John marries Mary, and Mary alone' imagined a similar outcome: 'Should John wed a score, oh! The claws and the scratches!/ It can't be a match:- 'tis a bundle of matches.'[18] Blake's 'William Bond' from the Pickering manuscript which dates from the Felpham period recognisably echoes the voices of this debate. Set beside the poems that the polygamy debate provoked from Cowper, however, Blake's method is different: instead of one voice, we hear the voices of a narrator, of William and of Mary Green. This time, surprisingly, the wife accepts rejection:

> O William if thou dost another Love
> Does another Love better than poor Mary
> Go & take that other to be thy Wife
> And Mary Green shall her Servant be　(E497)

But her answer also recalls the eighteenth-century proto-feminist attack on marriage, the recognition that 'Wife and servant are the same/ But only differ in the name', as Lady Mary Chudleigh put it in 1703. Whereas most contributions represent the would-be polygamous husband as a carefree libertine, William Bond is full of fears: 'I wonder whether the Girls are mad/ And I wonder whether they mean to kill'. Richard Hill dedicates his work 'To all the good Wives in the Kingdom', but the position of Blake's poem, which shifts viewpoints and meanings mid-poem, is harder to define. In 'William Bond', a narrator offers the concluding moral extrapolation of the story: 'Seek Love in the Pity of others Woe'. But the reduction of love to pity is countered by the ejection of the angels by the fairies, as Mary wakes to find herself on her bed beside 'her William dear'. The narrator of 'William Bond' uses neither the word 'husband' nor 'wife', referring only to 'Sister Jane'. What the poem debates is the nature of the 'Bond' in William's name, a negative version of Cowper's 'Marriage Bond Divine'.

Those who did read *Thelyphthora* would have encountered a much more sophisticated and serious work than the pamphlet war suggested. Madan's work at the Lock Hospital offered first-hand evidence of the failure of the schemes of earlier philanthropists to control the endemic prostitution of the eighteenth century.[19] His solution in *Thelyphthora* is radical, logical and based on a utopian understanding of sexuality. With a typically Protestant disregard for ceremony Madan argues that because there was no marriage ceremony in Eden, the union of Adam with Eve took place through intercourse; in God's eyes sexual intercourse is marriage. Madan's argument is informed by a thorough-going idealisation of sexuality offered in a spirit of sympathy for women; since every act of intercourse effectively married the sexual partners, men must be considered legally married to and financially responsible for any and every woman that they seduced. A careful reading of the Bible convinced Madan that polygamy was frequently acceptable in Old Testament societies and could therefore not be proscribed in modern times. Madan is consistently hostile to the 1753 Hardwicke Marriage Act, which claimed to improve the lot of women and which became central to eighteenth-century Britain's case to be a nation which offered a unique form of protection to its female citizens.

Madan's learned work claims to represent a true Protestant understanding of sexuality which derives from Milton and removes corruptions introduced by Catholicism. In an image echoed by Mary Hays, Popish celibacy is seen as dangerous because it attempts to dam the natural force of sexuality: 'When we endeavour to stop the course of a river by laying a dam across the stream, the effect must be, that it will either make its way, bearing down all before it, or it will make a passage over its banks, and overflow and destroy the country' (I, p. 178). It is this charge that is acted out in the gothic novel, with its image of the convent as the place of deformed sexual relations.[20] According to Madan, the Reformation acceptance of a married priesthood is a sign of a healthy sexual culture which defines not only sexual but gender identities by discouraging sodomy; he quotes 'the excellent authors of the History of Popery' in their claim that 'a certain unnatural vice in England' was unheard of until 'priests were forbidden marriage'.[21] Britain's Protestant identity is seen as rooted in a normative heterosexual identity which values sexuality and enables domestic happiness.[22] Although recent accounts have associated a belief in the spirituality of sexual love with such marginal religious groups as the Swedenborgians and Moravians, this assumption is also present in members of the established church.

Madan offered a sweeping historical narrative of the growth of hostility towards sexuality within Christian culture, ascribing the New Testament prohibition of polygamy to a fear of sexuality in the early Christians and analysing the early Christian cult of virginity. Madan points the reader who 'has a mind to see how far folly and enthusiasm can carry people on these subjects' to 'Tertullian's epistles to Eustachius – to Gerontius – and against Helvetius; Tertullian on Chastity; Chrysostom on Virginity; Cyprian on the discipline of Virgins; and Oecumenius on I Cor. vii. – then he will begin to find out how MARRIAGE ITSELF was vilified' (I, pp. 176–7). Unlike most biblical commentators, Madan tried to make the New Testament conform to the Old, in the process using the Bible to authorise alternative forms of sexual regulation. Serious responses therefore focused on the issue of misreading the Bible. Kinnaird reasserts the superior authority of the New Testament over the Old:

> If words can convey any precise idea, it evidently appears from these passages in the New Testament, that some of the leading principles of the Mosaic law were abrogated by Christ himself; and that in their stead a new system was set up, of an infinitely more refined and spiritual nature.[23]

But Madan is clearly aware of following in the footsteps of Milton, for whom a reform of the laws of marriage similarly derived from an intense investment in the spirituality of marital sex: Milton's first divorce tract, *The Doctrine and Discipline of Divorce*, faced the same problem of privileging an apparently pro-divorce statement in Deuteronomy 24:1–2 over

Christ's words reported in Matthew 19:3–9. James Turner argues that Milton's sexual idealism is most evident in the divorce tracts which propose that if 'the love of husband and wife does not re-enact, "at least in some proportion", the original creation of Eve-Eros in the Garden, the marriage should be immediately dissolved'.[24]

It was the orthodoxy of Madan's background that made his work so inflammatory. Although a friend of the Countess of Huntingdon, Madan remained within the Anglican church and emerged from the class that was committed to the advancement of women's education and learning. He was the son of the writer Judith Madan, immortalised by John Duncombe in 1754 as Cornelia in *The Feminiad,* a work closely associated with Samuel Richardson's circle. Duncombe presents British femininity as the contrary of Eastern tyranny; Britain is what it is – a utopia for women – because 'The freeborn sons of Britain's polish'd isle' drove the Siren of sexual attraction

> to that dreary plain,
> In loathsome pomp, where eastern tyrants reign,
> Where each fair neck the yoke of slav'ry galls,
> Clos'd in a proud seraglio's gloomy walls,
> And taught, that level'd with the brutal kind,
> Nor sense, nor souls to women are assign'd.[25]

Duncombe tells how Britain's rejection of a Restoration culture which sexualised women produced a society whose highest achievement was the work of female writers. Only by controlling sexuality did Britain distinguish itself from the Orient. The production of what Cora Kaplan describes as 'a class sexuality for a radical, reformed bourgeoisie' is fundamental to this account in which women are figured as innocent victims of male lust.[26] Madan understands women as lacking sexual desire and represents them as victims of male lust, 'as lawful prey to the lust, treachery, cruelty, and mean artifices of licentious and profligate men, who can seduce and then abandon them at their will'.[27] Britain, in Madan's work, is the country that should protect women and his disagreement with his cousin William Cowper is about the means of offering that protection. In Cowper's *Anti-Thelyphthora* Sir Marmadan mounts a chivalric defence of the 'trembling sex' (l.97), prefiguring by a decade Burke's account of the French Revolution as an attack on women. If Madan were to have his way, Cowper argues, Britons would turn into 'mahometans' (ll.107–8).[28] In Madan's account, however, Muslim cultures offer more protection for women as well as greater protection of fertility and population increase: 'With regard to the depredations which are made on married women, how may the Mahomedans shame us!' (II, p. 90).

A number of writers with connections to Blake and Hayley read Madan's proposal carefully and in some cases sympathetically, using Africa as a utopian alternative to British forms of sexual regulation.[29] This utopian imagination is nowhere more clearly represented than in the *The Captive of the Castle of Sennaar*, which describes the utopian African civilisation of Sophis. Blake's image of apocalypse as sexual rapture at the end of the 'ASIA' section of the *Song of Los* reverses the terms of the attacks on Madan, suggesting a positive meaning both for sexuality and for the Oriental. The contrast between British and Muslim sexual cultures is a constant theme in the period, as Felicity Nussbaum points out.[30] But it is also clear that in Blake's immediate circles, the 'polygamous Other' offered an alternative that was seen as superior to some aspects of a hypocritical and crisis-laden British complacency.

The role of marriage in defining Britishness remained crucial from Godwin's critique in the *Essay Concerning Political Justice* to Barruel's claim in 1798 that an anti-social conspiracy which weakened the bonds of marriage was one of the direct causes of the French Revolution. In the 1792 *Vindication*, Wollstonecraft rejects Madan's argument that polygamy is necessary because female births naturally outnumber males, citing the same authority, Johann Reingold Forster's 1788 *Observations*, that Madan uses.[31] But she accepts Madan's proposal that men should bear financial responsibility for the consequences of seduction: 'The necessity of polygamy ... does not appear; yet when a man seduces a woman, it should, I think be termed a left-handed marriage, and the man should be legally obliged to maintain the woman and her children.'[32] Hannah More in her 1799 *Strictures on the Modern System of Female Education* claims that protecting the bond of marriage would save the nation in time of war. Hayley's *Life of Milton* is therefore entering a significant debate when it defends Milton's questioning of the rules of marriage in the Divorce Tracts as an expression of a continuing search for a utopian sexuality in the wake of the failure of the English revolution.[33] Hayley's own unhappy marriage informs his defence of Milton's view of marriage which he presents as taking the reader into 'the heart and mind of Milton', proving 'how keenly he felt the anguish of connubial infelicity' (p. 84). In his *Life of Milton* he also sees political meanings in Milton's attempt to 'establish a more enlarged system of domestic liberty, at a time when connubial discord was so common, in consequence of civil dissension'.[34] Locke had argued that society originated in the bond between man and wife, this was the 'first society' from which derived 'that between parents and children', and later master and servant. These bonds 'each of these, or all together, came short of political society'. As the hope of changing 'political society' faltered in the 1790s, energy shifted to imagining ways of recreating what Locke saw as the 'first society'.[35]

In *Milton* an echo of Madan's argument appears when 'the Divine Voice was heard in the Songs of Beulah':

> She shall relent in fear of death: She shall begin to give
> Her maidens to her husband: delighting in his delight
> And then & then alone begins the happy Female joy
> As it is done in Beulah, & thou O Virgin Babylon Mother of Whoredoms
> Shalt bring Jerusalem in thine arms in the night watches; and
> No longer turning her a wandering Harlot in the streets
> Shalt give her into the arms of God your Lord & Husband.
> Such are the Songs of Beulah in the Lamentations of Ololon
>
> (*M* 11:33[36]:17–24, E133)

Just as Madan proposed polygamy as the answer to prostitution, so here the Divine Voice suggests that giving 'Her maidens to her husband' will end prostitution.[36] The role of prostitution in commercial London is encapsulated in Blake's typically opaque word cluster: 'Virgin Babylon Mother of Whoredoms'. These words offer in compacted form an analysis of the dark but inextricable underside of the bourgeois construction of the asexual woman, inverting the meaning of the apocalyptic Whore of Babylon. In place of the Whore of Babylon as an indictment of sexual excess, Blake introduces the Virgin Babylon who represents the anti-sexual power of the marketplace and the deflection of sexuality via Moral Virtue to feed the machine of war.

Blake's opaque word cluster seems to require the gloss he provided in an 1809 image for Butts usually known as the Whore of Babylon.[37] The virgin/harlot is a complex figure whose crossed legs reveal her simultaneous arousal and rejection of sexual desires, recalling Blake's notebook comment:

> When a Man has Married a Wife
> he finds out whether
> Her knees & elbows are only
> glued together.

The fumes of her cup produce dancing figures of gnomes and fairies, the graces that Pope, Hayley and Darwin use to convey the sexuality of the natural world and they feed the seven-headed monster which represents the 'Seven deadly Sins of the soul' created by Urizen. This is the monster that eats the figures of drunken soldiers, crazed by the opium of rejected sexual love. The horns bear crowns showing that the monster represents the crowned heads of Europe fighting revolutionary France. The image can also be read as an inversion of Fuseli's *Nightmare*: instead of a male incubus resting on the stomach of the sleeping woman, a female Whore of Babylon crouches incubus-like on the back of the seven-headed monster. The sexuality of the nightmare is now channelled into war, for the beast's prominent veins show that he lives on blood.

Perhaps Thomas Butts, the 'Friend of Religion and Order' who was Blake's most significant and loyal patron from 1799 onwards, failed to see that Blake's image replaces the Whore of Babylon with the figure who appears in *Milton* as 'Moral Virtue the cruel Virgin Babylon' (E99), 'Mystery the Virgin Harlot Mother of War' (E117) and the 'Virgin Babylon Mother of Whoredoms' (E133). The word 'whore' does not appear in *Milton* and the usual title of the 1809 image for Butts misleadingly returns Blake's image to a familiar context. But perhaps these meanings were also opaque to Butts since his earnings derived from his work as Chief Clerk at the Commissary General of Musters, the government department that ensured the equipment of serving soldiers and recorded enlistments and deaths. In 1788 Butts signed a summons for Justices according to an act punishing mutiny and desertion.[38] It was in 1809 that Blake painted a miniature of Mrs Butts, which Robert Essick describes as a portrait of 'a dominating and fleshy woman, perhaps just ageing into corpulence'.[39] Essick likens the portrait to Blake's image of the Wife of Bath in the Canterbury Pilgrims. But this image is also surprisingly like the Virgin/Whore of Babylon that Blake painted for her husband (Figure 10).

Essick suggests that Blake's poem 'The Phoenix/ to Mrs Butts', dating from about 1794, marks an 'early shift away from the celebration of female sexual liberty', in that it 'gently chides the poem's addressee (figured as a "Fairy gay") to cease her pursuit of the Phoenix and return to the loving care of her children'.[40] This reading, however, misses the typically Blakean twist in the final couplet which endorses the energies of the fairy: 'But if thou seem'st a Fairy thing/ Then it flies on glancing Wing'. As so often, the meaning of Blake's text is complicated by containing conflicting voices.

The speech of the Divine Voice in *Milton* reads as an endorsement not just of Madan's proposal for legalised polygamy but of the pamphlet war's

Figure 10. William Blake, *The Whore of Babylon*, 1809. Pen and black ink
and watercolour. © The Trustees of the British Museum.

view of Madan as a spokesman for male libertinism. As in *Thelyphthora*,
the presence of the 'wandering Harlot' on the streets (here identified as
Jerusalem) is the consequence of the social regulation of sexuality in
marriage. This passage has been seen by Mary Lynn Johnson as 'one of
Blake's failings or blind spots'.[41] But it can also be read as one of the voices
of a multi-voiced text. The meaning and authority of this passage depend
on the force of the phrase 'heard in the Songs of Beulah', repeated after
the speech of the Divine Voice in the enclosing line: 'Such are the Songs
of Beulah in the lamentations of Ololon'.[42] The doctrinaire statements of
the 'Divine Voice' take for granted the terms of a world of unequal power,
of 'maidens' and 'husbands'. From a perspective in which the category of
the 'female' is inherently flawed, the offer of 'Female joy' suggests a kind
of masochistic 'joy' that differs from human joy, that necessarily produces

'lamentations'. Blake's poem picks up the voices of the debate, hearing one element of Madan's text through the voices of his contemporaries.

BIBLICAL SEX AND THE BOOK OF ENOCH

Hayley's *Essay* ignores the issue of polygamy but develops Madan's attack on the early Christian and later Catholic cult of virginity. In his third volume Hayley offers an extended and detailed analysis of the cultural role of virginity in literature including readings of Chaucer, Spenser, Shakespeare and Milton. The parallels between the second volume and Blake's account of the eighteen hundred years of the 'female dream' in *Europe* (E63) are particularly striking. Hayley claims that the Christian era is one of an 'infinite Increase of Old Maids' (II, p. 135) and pins the blame on St Paul: 'when we consider the extensive veneration which was justly paid to this apostle, we may fairly conclude, that the multitude of primitive Old Maids was infinitely increased by his First Epistle to the Corinthians' (II, p. 141).

Hayley's theme appears most clearly (and enjoyably) in the search for an 'antediluvian Old Maid' that opens the second volume and is accompanied in the 1793 edition by two illustrations, one of which is engraved by Blake's erstwhile partner James Parker. The tone is humorous and the material both exotic and erotic as Hayley offers the story of the attempted seduction of one of the virgins belonging to a religious order set up by Eve 'who were to continue virgins, and to preserve unextinguished the fire, which had fallen from heaven on the sacrifice of Abel' (II, p. 6). This section is a loosely embroidered version of the story in Genesis 6 of the 'fable of an amorous connection between the apostate angels and the daughters of men' (II, p. 6) that fascinated Hayley's period because it locates in the Old Testament a parallel to pagan accounts of the birth of heroes through the connection of gods and women. This story was used by the author of 2 Peter to suggest that the fall was caused by female sexuality and James Turner suggests that St Paul's insistence that women should be veiled 'because of the angels' recalls the desire of the angels for the daughters of men in Genesis 6.[43] For William Alexander's *The History of Women* (used and cited by both Madan and Hayley and a foundational text of the new class sexuality) the notion that the 'Sons of God' in Genesis 6 are angels is 'absurd and ridiculous'.[44] The story is merely a regrettable episode of human carnality: the family of Seth were 'so captivated with the beauty of the women, who appeared naked, that they yielded to their charms, and defiled themselves with them' (I, p. 31). Hayley points out that Milton used the story in *Paradise Regained.*

In Hayley's version, the angels of the Genesis account become a group of libertines who swear 'to assemble together on the ninth night of every year, and to recount, in order, the feats of their impurity' (II, pp. 16–17). Hayley is most probably using the 1715 translation of the surviving Greek fragments of the book of Enoch which describe the 'gallantry' of the angels with the 'daughters of men', but his account of the libertine pursuit of the resistant Kunaza is also in effect a comic retelling of *Clarissa*, his own century's defining narrative.[45] The libertine angels expect female compliance; as Pharmarus tells the prince of the company, 'thou hast met with no female, that could resist thy perfection' (II, p. 19). In this 'antediluvian romance', as in Blake's 'Proverb of Hell', 'Eternity is in love with the productions of time'. Like Thel, however, Kunaza is 'determined to give her virginity to the grave'.

In Hayley's version, the loss of Eden is also the loss of female sexual pleasure, a loss that Thomas Laqueur dates to the era in which Hayley is writing. The angel Pharmarus offers a vision of 'the first nuptial couch' of Adam and Eve, of the tree under which Eve reclined and which promises the lost knowledge of sexual pleasure: 'he ordained that every daughter of woman, who reclines beneath its shade, shall experience unutterable joy, beyond the common joy of her sex', a 'blessing ... long forgotten by the heedless offspring of man'. Hayley may be thinking here of James Graham's Celestial Bed that had been opened to the public at the Temple of Hymen in London in 1781. William Mason, the dedicatee of Hayley's 1782 *Essay on Epic Poetry*, had published his own anonymous satire *The Celestial Beds; or, a Review of the Votaries of the Temple of Health, Adelphi, and the Temple of Hymen* in 1781.[46] Mason's satire reserves its horror for the 'horrid creed' offered by Madan: 'But who are these Circassian dames?/ Damsels who use unnumber'd names?/ Wives, if Thelyphthora says true,/ To Christian, Pagan, Turk, and Jew' (p. 32). But rather than following Graham's emphasis on health and conception, Hayley specifically focuses on female sexual pleasure as knowledge lost to the present. Pharmarus warns Kunaza 'not to live and die in a foolish ignorance of delights, which thy frame has been fashioned to enjoy' (II, p. 31). Kunaza's continuing resistance, fortified by the offstage sound of a woman in labour, drives Pharmarus to rape and the angel Gabriel to imprison him in caverns under the earth (II, p. 36). Orc's struggle from underground captivity in the Preludium to *America* seems to continue this story.[47] In this version, the problems of Hayley's position on the cusp between two different sexual cultures emerge. Unlike Richardson he writes from a pro-sex position which (covertly) enjoys and indulges the figure of the male libertine. But like Richardson, Hayley is wedded to the idea of a gendered sexuality within which women resist sex. The result is that most unappealing of constructs: a comic account of rape. Violence appears as the inevitable result of the gendered account of sexuality to which Hayley subscribes and which he helps to construct.

At the same time, the Oriental story is used as a means to escape the limitations of national sexual culture. Accepting his century's construction of British womanhood, Hayley must necessarily locate his story in another land which is indeed an 'Other' land. Arguing for a positive view of Islam in Blake's work, Angus Whitehead mentions that Hayley owned Sales's translation of the Koran.[48] Hayley emphasises that the tale originates in the East, brought to him by a traveller friend 'who had promised to collect for me, in his travels over Europe and Asia, every scrap of antiquity that could afford me any light in my maiden researches' (II, pp. 12–13). In fact, as he probably knew, the book of Enoch story was preserved in a manuscript by the Ethiopian church which had been brought back to England by James Bruce, the Scottish traveller, in 1773 and deposited (although not yet translated) in the Bodleian Library. In his *Memoirs* Hayley claims to derive the story of the antediluvian maid from Joseph Warton and it may be that Joseph Warton was passing on his brother Thomas Warton's knowledge of the arrival of the manuscript in the Bodleian Library.[49] Hayley's work is best seen in the context of the use of orientalist fantasy within the libertine enlightenment, in works such as Crébillon's *The Sopha* and Diderot's *The Indiscreet Jewels* (both of which Hayley owned). Although Schuchard presents Hayley as offering an account of 'the ancient Jewish traditions of sacramental sexuality' it is clear that he instead follows his hero Voltaire in offering a libertine enlightenment attack on the religious use of sexuality.[50]

Hayley contributed an anonymous 'Ode to James Bruce' to a magazine in 1786 that Bruce included (without knowing the author) when he finally published his *Travels to Discover the Source of the Nile* in a lavish five-volume folio edition in 1790 that Hayley bought for his library.[51] The Nile, in Hayley's 'Ode', functions as body to Britain's intellect:

> Remember, as my fruitful tide
> Throws verdant life on lands below;
> So, round the world, 'tis Britain's pride
> New streams of mental light to throw![52]

Hayley's 'fruitful tide' uses the trope that Darwin and his illustrators Blake and Fuseli repeat in their image of *The Fertilization of Egypt* published in 1791. If Africa is the corporeal partner of mental Britain, these writers might be seen as constructing a view that underpins an emergent colonial order. But for Blake in the 1790s, African civilisations stand for the integration of body and soul. In the 1795 *The Song of Los*, '*heart-formed Africa*' is the location of the bard's song and the words of the poet are set to the music of '*four harps at the tables of Eternity*' which seem to recall the striking full-page illustrations of African harpists in the 1790 folio edition of Bruce's *Travels*. In Cumberland's 1798 *Captive of the Castle of Sennaar* the utopian civilisation of Sophis is a society in which the mental and the physical are in balance and women are fully incorporated as citizens.

James Bruce considers the role of women in Islamic culture sympathetically and at length. His account of the book of Enoch follows directly on a lengthy discussion of the functioning of polygamy in which he praises *Thelyphthora* and rejects the idea that Madan offers a libertine's charter.[53] Bruce argues that in permitting divorce 'without any cause assigned' and 'as many concubines as he can maintain' Islamic law already provides for male sexual desires (1. pp. 286–7). Like Wollstonecraft, Bruce assumes that motherhood makes women into citizens and he claims that by permitting polygamy and increasing the chances of a woman bearing children, Mahomet 'secured civil rights to each woman' (1, p. 283).

THEL AND THE COY VIRGIN

With its echo of *Thelyphthora* and portrait of another coy virgin, Blake's *Book of Thel* clearly enters the debate to which Hayley contributes. Yet Thel's actions in the poem are among the most contentious passages in Blake's poetry. Depending on the context that the critic provides, it is possible to read the poem in opposite ways. Wollstonecraft's writing offers a typically complex parallel. Despite its rejection of a sexuality defined by male libertinism, Wollstonecraft's 1792 *Vindication* insists on the necessity for women to eat of the tree of knowledge. By contrast, Thel flees from the sight of the 'secrets of the land unknown' back to a place where 'gentle may I lay me down, and gentle rest my head./ And gentle sleep the sleep of death', a land like Theophilus Swift's where 'The playful pard, and courteous tyger dwell'. As we saw in chapter three, Wollstonecraft's suspicion of Milton's account of the perfection of angelic love stems from a belief in the inevitability of conflict in human existence.[54] Thel's flight at the end of the poem is to a place without conflict rather than a place without sexuality for the vales of Har are filled with the 'life of this our spring', a place of 'milky garments', 'wine' and 'perfume'. This is a sexualised place imagined in terms of a Darwinian natural world where the loss of self leads to 'tenfold life, to love to peace and raptures holy'.

We saw in chapter two how Fuseli in his 1776 *Remarks on Rousseau* imagined female dreams as a means of denying conflict. In the voices that Thel hears in the vales of Har, conflict does not exist: there is no conflict of interest between the lamb and the lily of the valley, even though one eats the other: 'Thy breath doth nourish the innocent lamb, he smells thy milky garments,/ He crops thy flowers, while thou sittest smiling in his face'. Like the lamb in Pope's *Essay on Man* who 'Pleased to the last … crops the flowery food,/ And licks the hand just raised to shed his blood', the voices of the vales of Har lack a sense of continuous individual identity. Benefit to the other is benefit to the self and this absence of self is mirrored in the sequence of similes which fail to define Thel's identity:

> Ah! Thel is like a watry bow, and like a parting cloud.
> Like a reflection in a glass, like shadows in the water.
> Like dreams of infants, like a smile upon an infant's face,
> Like the dove's voice, like transient day, like music in the air   (E3)

This multiple fracturing of identity is akin to the disruption of identity in Oothoon's speech – like Oothoon, Thel alternates between first and third person. But for Thel, this shifting identity is associated with her status as the 'weeping virgin', the 'virgin of the skies'. Virginity here seems to allow the self to escape fixed form and to make possible the evasion of conflict, a skill on which Ololon will draw in *Milton*.

It is imagination that gives Oothoon her identity: she is described as 'a virgin fill'd with virgin fancies' as she offers to catch girls for Theotormon. It is not clear, then, that the choice of worlds for Thel is between celibacy and sexuality but between different modes of understanding identity and conflict. The underworld Thel flees recalls the Cave of Spleen described in both *The Rape of the Lock* and *The Triumphs of Temper*. In these two poems, the Cave of Spleen contains the feelings buried or disallowed by the sentimental world. In 'the land unknown' that Thel visits, Blake, like Wollstonecraft, represents the conflicts and feelings unacceptable to the polite world, incorporating the notches on the scale of the thermometer of feeling present in Hogarth's anti-enthusiasm satires, feelings of despair and suicide, of 'the poison of a smile', of an eyelid stored with 'a thousand fighting men'. These feelings are themselves conflicted since the voice of

the grave plot laments both the openness of the senses to intensity and the
limitation of the senses to sexual pleasure. The implication of this voice is
that sexual conflict cannot be contained within the the vales of Har. At the
end of the poem, Thel flees to a female dream like that of *The Triumphs of
Temper* which makes sexual desire safe but demands as the price the taking
on of a female identity. Blake's poem reveals the constraints of the Lock-
ean framework assumed by Pope and inherited by Hayley.

Following Helen Bruder's splendidly confrontational 1997 reading, the
earlier tendency to see the poem as critical of Thel's flight at the end of the
poem has been replaced by a critical orthodoxy that Thel rightly rejects a
world which requires conformity to predetermined female roles.[55] Previous
readings had either (following Kathleen Raine) seen Thel's refusal to descend
as a positive rejection of embodiment and of the contamination of the soul by
what Thomas Taylor saw as the degraded body or, following commentators
who saw Blake as a prophet of 'free love', as a regrettable rejection of
sexuality. Bruder's reading borrows from both earlier versions in so far as it
takes the world that Thel rejects as that of heterosexual sexuality and
motherhood but views her rejection positively. Bruder differs from Raine
in so far as her reading is not hostile to the body or bodily pleasures.

In a sophisticated historicisation of Bruder's reading of the poem,
David Worrall has recently presented Blake's *Book of Thel* as a 'specific
refusal of Swedenborg's doctrine of conjugal love, a subject topical to
contemporary Swedenborgians who were proposing to establish an
African colony based on its principles'.[56] Worrall reads the 'Vales of
Har' as an image of 'the region of Swedenborgian sexual union and
conjugal polity – and from which Thel flees' (p. 26). Yet the vales of
Har are the place *to* which she flees at the end of the poem: 'The Virgin
started from her seat, & with a shriek./ Fled back unhindered till she came
into the Vales of Har' (E6). Thel is described as 'mistress of the vales of
Har' (E4) and the 'beauty of the vales of Har' and is thus associated with
the place that in *Tiriel* was associated with aged tyranny, where Har and
Heva are 'like two children' (E277). The vales of Har are a place where
sexuality is controlled within the female dream that Hayley services and
Blake may see this world as one in which sexuality is regulated within a
coercive marital structure. The voice from the grave plot speaks of the
openness of the senses of taste, hearing and sight but sexual desire is
treated in a different way from the other senses:

> Why a Tongue impress'd with honey from every wind?
> Why an Ear, a whirlpool fierce to draw creations in?

Why a Nostril wide inhaling terror trembling & affright.
Why a tender curb upon the youthful burning boy!
Why a little curtain of flesh on the bed of our desire?   (E6)

It is the limitations on desire that send Thel back to a dream in which conflict is defused.

Blake represents the New Testament in the 1795 *Song of Los* as the product of a culture hostile to sexuality, casting both Adam and Noah as resistant to Urizenic laws and Jesus as the tragic recipient of 'A Gospel from wretched Theotormon' (E67). In order to ensure the increase of population, another creed is dispensed to Mahomet:

> The human race began to wither, for the healthy built
> Secluded places, fearing the joys of Love
> And the disease'd only propagated:
> So Antamon call'd up Leutha from her valleys of delight:
> And to Mahomet a loose Bible gave.   (E67)

Just as Blake is able to use the words 'lust' and 'copulation' positively in this period, so the word 'loose' with its suggestion of illicit sexuality becomes associated with an escape from a constricting set of laws. Madan assumes that the population of Britain is declining and offers polygamy as a means to raise the birth rate by removing 'those multitudes who live and die in celibacy' (II, pp. 275–6). *The Song of Los* similarly describes how 'The human race began to wither' and values sexuality as a means to restore population. Whereas Edward Larrissy takes the reference to the Koran as 'a loose Bible' as evidence of Blake's negative orientalism and argues that Leutha 'represents the sinful character of sex under the law', she can also be seen positively: her 'valleys of delight' are the places of the 'joys of Love', joys that Christian traditions forget.[57] Larrissy is surely wrong to argue that the Koran is rejected because it 'countenances polygamy' and to detect in this passage an image of the sinfulness of female sexuality.

The female Grave in Blake's 1795 *Song of Los* speaks with a voice that recognisably echoes that of Thel's grave plot. It is a voice of unregulated sexuality which is contained within the writing of Hayley and Darwin:

> The Grave shrieks with delight, & shakes
> Her hollow womb, & clasps the solid stem:
> Her bosom swells with wild desire:
> And milk & blood & glandous wine
> In rivers rush & shout & dance,
> On mountain, dale and plain.   (E69–70)

The verbs here are all active: 'shrieks', 'shakes', 'clasps', 'swells', 'rush & shout & dance' and produce what Bruder describes as a picture of the 'wildly orgasmic female grave'.[58] This voice resists the taming of femininity in Hayley's culture.

Blake's female Grave, like the voice from the grave plot that Thel hears, derives from images that have been seen as characteristic of 'the misogynist imagination' such as the 'womb-like darkness of chaos' that Pope associates with the goddess Dulness in *The Dunciad.*[59] In John Armstrong's *Oeconomy of Love*, Milton's hell provides an image for the female genitals when the new husband tricked by a fake virginity discovers: 'Hell's ever open Gates:/ An unessential Void; where neither Love/ Nor Pleasure dwells, where warm Creation dies/ Starv'd in th'abortive Gulph' (18). The grave, in Marvell's Ode, is 'a fine and private place/ But none I think do there embrace'. But in Blake's image, the grave is simultaneously sexual and maternal. If sexual rapture is positive then the active contribution of the female earth is an image of transformation and of revolutionary change.

BLAKE, HAYLEY AND MISOGYNY

'Prudence is a rich ugly old maid courted by Incapacity', states one of the 'Proverbs of Hell' (E35). Emma Clery argues that 'Old Maids and whores are the quintessential female types in a climate of misogyny'.[60] Hostility towards 'Mahometan' culture is also axiomatic within bluestocking discourse, as when a young Elizabeth Robinson (later Elizabeth Montagu) commented that 'there is a Mahometan error crept even into the Christian church that Women have no Souls'.[61] These indicators should, therefore, securely locate the work of Hayley and of Blake as a misogynist backlash to the new prominence of women. But Clery's categories are designed to identify the conditions of the debate earlier in the eighteenth century. Although Dror Wahrman takes *An Essay on Old Maids* as symptomatic of the work of gender distinction of the end of the eighteenth century, Hayley's subject is not just gender but sexuality and class.[62]

Hayley sees the 'old maid' as deprived of 'the delights, of that state, to which *all human beings* are invited by the voice of nature and reason' (emphasis added); rather than expressing the new understanding of gender he here attacks the new formation of 'woman' as different in kind rather than in degree. Hayley also attacks the class stratification fundamental to the new idea of the bourgeois woman that he had celebrated in his 1781 poem. Madan distinguishes between the figure of the sentimental prostitute as the victim of seduction who represents 'the weakness and credulity of helpless women' and that of the street prostitute seen in 'the wards of a public hospital, to which the harpies are consigned by the force of a disease, which, after having communicated to numbers of men, threatens their own destruction'.[63] Blake's 'London' yokes together the figure of the domestic woman with that of the street prostitute outside, breaking down the walls that protect the safety of the domestic interior.

Hayley draws on familiar misogynist tropes in his account of the practical joke played by 'a friend' on the old maids of the neighbourhood when he repeatedly knocked on his own front door at midnight in order to bring them out to snoop. Here the old maid turns into a figure of moral surveillance, mobilising an image that reappears in the work of Hayley's friend Charlotte Smith in the 1790s. As Harriet Guest observes, Austen's Henry Tilney will present spies as 'necessary to the constitution of modern British society as a kind of benevolent neighbourhood-watch scheme, policed not by any government or its agents but by a network of neighbours whose surveillance is reassuring and protective' when she writes *Northanger Abbey* at the end of the 1790s.[64] Guest notes that in Charlotte Smith's novels of the early 1790s, 'spies are by no means always political agents, tolls of government or the law; they are also servants, gossips and scandal mongers'.[65] Smith adopts Hayley's motif and develops his sense of a society constrained by a regulatory moral discourse.

Yet Hayley's narrative also subverts its own misogyny, challenging the physiological assumption on which the joke is based. The prankster maintains 'that the curiosity of an Old Maid is so fiery a passion, that she, who is thoroughly inflamed by it, may expose her shrivelled body, without danger of cold, to the most unwholesome of nightly vapours' (1, p. 26). The rheumatic fever which strikes down the most elderly and infirm woman not only rebukes the misogyny of the trick but proves that the old maid is physiologically of the same kind as a fertile woman. Hayley assumes that women of all ages, as well as men, share sexual desires; the curiosity of the old maid is the result of an 'insatiate thirst for information' by which 'her soul seems to be continually flying, in a giddy circuit, to her eyes, ears, and tongue; she appears inflamed with a sort of frantic desire to see all that can be seen, to hear all that can be heard, and to ask more questions than any lips can utter' (1, p. 20). Hayley quotes *Hamlet*, 'Such curiosity is a kind of ravenous monster, which hangs upon its prey,/ As if encrease of appetite did grow/ By what it fed on' (1, p. 21). Whereas Hamlet sees female monstrosity as the result of 'appetite', for Hayley it is the result of sexual repression.

Perhaps the most telling evidence of Hayley's rejection of gender difference is his use of lines from Gray's *Ode to Spring* (a poem that, as Jerome
McGann points out, Blake also reworked in 'The Fly' of *Songs of Experience*) to describe the old maid as 'A solitary fly', 'Without a hive of hoarded
sweets' (I, p. 9).[66] Gray is 'a justly-admired poet, who might himself be
called (I mean not to derogate from his genius or his virtues by the
expression) an Old Maid in breeches' (I, p. 9). Yet Hayley also recognises
that the *Ode to Spring* contains what he calls a 'more forcible, poetic
language'. Although the image of the male 'old maid' could of course be
a covert reference to Gray's supposed homosexuality, Hayley's use of this
image (and Blake's turning of the image against Hayley himself) refer, as
I have argued elsewhere, not to homosexuality but to desexualisation.[67]
This image also points to Gray's dualistic splitting of body and soul which
Blake questions in 'The Fly' which asks 'If thought is life/ And strength &
breath' (E24). The body is part of thought and the fly is human, as Blake
suggests in his 1798 illustration to Gray's *Ode to Spring* for Mrs Flaxman
where 'two pink-winged flies hover over' the figure of Gray 'pointing
derisive fingers' while others 'on the tree are nursing a baby'.[68]

At the same time Hayley is clearly worried that his *Essay* will be seen as
misogynist: the first two editions carry a dedication to Elizabeth Carter and
Hayley's tone is that of the modern man of feeling, devoted to challenging
'that coarse and contemptuous raillery, with which the ancient maiden is
perpetually insulted'.[69] Hayley abides, superficially, by Harriet Byron's
warning in *Sir Charles Grandison* (1753–4) that spinsters must no longer
be seen as figures of fun: 'those women who have joined with the men in
their insolent ridicule of Old Maids, ought never to be forgiven'.[70] Nevertheless more than half the first volume is devoted to 'the Particular Failings
of Old Maids' which include 'curiosity, credulity, affectation, envy and ill-
nature'. Part of the trouble, of course, is Hayley's sex, which debars him
from criticising particular constructions of femininity: what appears as
misogyny in a male authored text can be used by female writers such as
Wollstonecraft to define a negative construction of femininity.[71] There is a
potential double standard in the willingness to infer positive motivation in
female writers who use the tropes of misogyny to critique a particular
construction of femininity but to deny this reading to male writers. Sarah
Scott's account in the 1762 *Millenium Hall* of Mrs Susanna Morgan who
had 'lived immaculate to the age of fifty-five' surpasses Hayley in its venom:

Tormented inwardly with her own ill-nature, she was incapable of any satisfaction but what arose from teazing others; nothing could dispel the frown on her

brow, except the satisfaction she felt when she had the good fortune to give pain to any of her dependants; a horrid grin then distorted her features, and her before lifeless eyes glistened with malice and rancorous joy.[72]

The hostile stereotype of the 'old maid' provides Scott with a negative frame for her positive account of female community, enabling her to deflect potential criticism of her portrait of female celibacy. The schools the women endow 'seldom celebrated fewer than two marriages in a year, sometimes more'.[73] The narrative histories of Scott's novel provide a series of alibis for the adoption of a celibate life and deny the ambition to free the majority of women from the duty of motherhood.

Nevertheless Hayley's discomfort in attacking bluestocking culture is evident in his shifting tone, sometimes the voice of a sentimental celebration of femininity, sometimes libertine and satiric. He is pre-eminently a writer of his time in his lack of confidence in the universality of his voice, which is apologetically male as well as anxiously anonymous, insecure in his simultaneous sympathy for women and dislike of an ascetic strand in eighteenth-century feminism. The bulk of the bluestocking writers were published during the Romantic period and seemed in the wake of the Revolution debate to offer a less threatening version of feminism than that of Wollstonecraft and Hays.[74] Hayley's essay most probably responds to the appearance of the last edition of *Millenium Hall* in 1778 and the story of the search for the antediluvian maid clearly repeats the technique of Swift's attack on Astell. Revealingly, Hayley cites Swift's *Tatler* attack in the story of

a certain society of modern ladies, under the guidance of a seraphic president, intitled Madonella; a lady whose adventures are related with infinite humour in the first volume of the Tatler, and who, having devoted herself and her associates to a life of virgin purity and retirement, was rapidly and ingeniously induced to take an active part in the necessary increase of the world. (II, p. 80)

The issues that Hayley raised in 1785 continued to be pertinent to his culture and his *Essay* continued to sell.

Clery points to the way in which Mandeville in *The Virgin Unmask'd* and Defoe in *Roxana* represent 'feminist arguments within a text that otherwise insists upon the debased nature of women'.[75] Hayley's *Essay on Old Maids*, by contrast, joins its attack on the repression of female sexuality with a continuing defence of women's literary power. Although the dedication to Carter was removed from the third edition of 1793 Hayley added an appendix containing the lost works of a tenth-century Saxon nun Hroswitha or Rosvida which were published in 1501.[76] This act of reparation for the offence caused to Carter and Seward indirectly comments on the work of women writers of his own time, for Hayley claims that if Hroswitha had been alive in 'our age and country, she would have proved a second Hannah More' (III, p. 208). It is significant, then, that the subject of Hroswitha's sacred dramas is sensual love. Hannah More differs from Astell in her devotion to Milton and it is over the reading of Milton and the perceived threat to the Protestant understanding of sexuality that Hayley and Blake choose to ground their opposition to the evangelical movement.[77]

The absence of women from eternity has been central to the feminist case against Blake. For many commentators it has seemed obvious that sexuality, motherhood and infancy are located in Beulah as the place of femininity defined in essentialist biological terms. The difference of Beulah and Eternity is perhaps better understood in terms of differing understandings of the word 'sexuality' or of differing sexual cultures. It is clearly inappropriate to assume that there is a single entity called 'sex' or 'sexuality'. In its account of the Daughters of Beulah, 'Muses who inspire the Poets Song' (E96), *Milton* follows Hayley in addressing the image of the muse. Elizabeth Carter (to whom Hayley dedicated *An Essay on Old Maids*) is one of *The Nine Living Muses of Great Britain* in the engraving Joseph Johnson commissioned for the *Ladies New and Polite Pocket Memorandum-Book* for 1778 from Richard Samuel's painting exhibited at the Royal Academy the following year.[78] Blake, however, produces muses whose 'Realms' of 'mild moony lustre' are also places 'Of Terror' (E96).

The 'soft sexual delusions' are those of a polite culture that offers access to a world of intellectual debate under specific terms. This place of 'mild moony lustre' may recall the idealised scene of polite intellectual debate described by Hayley in Sir Hilary Highman's scheme to institute regular debates each full moon at his inherited estate on his return from Greece with a Greek wife:

> He particularly admired that cast of conversation which used to form the most delightful part of an ancient attic entertainment, and he often wished to substitute something of this nature in the room of those dull or disgusting topics of discourse, which produce such a heavy effect in the rural visits of our English gentry.[79]

This Beulah-like gathering is a model of enlightened intellectual debate, open to both sexes. Whereas Blake draws for inspiration on the daughters of Beulah, Milton, 'who walkd about in Eternity/ One hundred years', wrote, as Johnson pointed out, before culture was reshaped by the presence of women and is thus separated from his sixfold emanation. Eternity seems hierarchical and oppressive: Milton 'obey'd, he murmur'd not'.

Just as Fuseli could find inspiration in the soft sexual reveries of the female dream, so the Bard's narrative of the events of Beulah wakes Milton, who 'rose up from the heavens of Albion ardorous!' (E108). If the 'sexual' is the place where the rules of politeness constrain communication, it is also a place where this constraint produces an erotic dream. Thus after a definition of the difference between the 'human' and the 'sexual', Blake naturally writes: 'If you account it Wisdom when you are angry to be silent, and/ Not to shew it: I do not account that Wisdom but Folly' (E98). Beulah is the place where sexual pleasure is regulated and controlled, for 'They perverted Swedenborgs Visions in Beulah & in Ulro' (*M* 1:22[24]:46, E117). This is the place where the sexual Jerusalem is condemned 'as a Harlot' and in her place is raised 'Mystery the Virgin Harlot Mother of War'. 'Babylon the Great' is the place not of sexual excess but of the kind of failed sexual regulation described by Martin Madan, the world in which the projects of the philanthropic reformers cannot stem the tide of prostitution and of venereal disease, in which Madan's scheme itself reinstates the divided understanding that it seeks to replace.

Blake's *Milton* is therefore centrally about the cultural meaning of virginity, and this word takes on a complex range of meanings. It is significant that Ololon's meeting with Milton provokes the appearance of 'Rahab Babylon'. As G. A. Rosso demonstrates, Blake's figure of Rahab is a recoding and reinterpretation of a figure 'revered to this day in both Jewish and Christian traditions'.[80] Blake's Rahab is negative not because she is sexual but because she uses her sexuality to enable the destruction of the people of Jericho by Israel. Just as he reverses the figure of the Whore of Babylon to produce the Virgin Babylon, so Blake again reverses the apparent meaning of a figure, turning a national heroine into a negative figure of chauvinist nationalism. She is 'A Female hidden in a Male, Religion hidden in War/ Namd Moral Virtue' (E142–3). Virtue here is associated with the protection of national boundaries as well as with sexual morality. Rahab is associated with empire and with purity, with the use of the discourse of moral virtue to justify political aggression. What Blake identifies is a culture which defines Liberty in opposition to the 'mad Liberty' of the crowd, that defines sensibility in terms of mind not body and that outlaws the desires of the body.

But whereas Hayley's writing is part of the bourgeois debate which produces sexuality as a field of discourse, Blake rethinks the meaning of virginity. The character called the 'virgin Ololon' splits as the 'virgin' separates 'away from Ololon'. Virginity here takes on meanings far wider than the sexual terms which concern Hayley. Catherine McClenahan points out that Albion is described as an 'Aged Virgin Form' in *Jerusalem* 39 'despite his "masculine" identity, because "he" mechanically and jealously guards "his" pre-eminence as a nation and empire against all change and successfully fends off all attempts at revolution or even reform by the ruling class at home'.[81] The confrontation with Ololon at the end of *Milton* is imaged as a remaking of identities in the womb, a place of chaos and of creation when the 'virgin Ololon' asks: 'Is this the Void Outside of Existence, which if enterd into/ Becomes a Womb?' Much as the female grave in *The Song of Los* was a place of sexual rapture, so here the womb is a place of radical transformation, a place that is equally a void and a grave. Even though Hayley's analysis in the *Essay on Old Maids* appears to mesh closely with Blake's figure of the virgin, Hayley's work belongs within a discourse which cuts sexuality off from the society that produces it. To read the meeting of Milton and Ololon in terms of Hayley's discourse of sexuality would be to produce a poem which culminates in the moment in which 'a Virgin of twelve years' loses the identity of 'the virgin'. We are relieved to know that Ololon is a collective identity who only adopts a 'female form' as a disguise, for 'They could not step into Vegetable Worlds without becoming/ The enemies of Humanity except in a Female Form' (E136–7). If Ololon's age is significant, she is cast as a pre-sexual female, who can exploit the softness of femininity to infiltrate the hostile vegetable world without being caught in the mesh of a divided or 'sexual' identity. Rejecting the identity of the 'virgin' Ololon casts off one of the sexual garments, categories which define identity in terms of sexual experience since 'Man in the Resurrection changes his Sexual Garments at will/ Every Harlot was once a Virgin: every Criminal an Infant Love!' (E212). The feminine is revealed as a powerfully subversive identity which can destroy the categories of Hayley's world.

MALTHUS AND THE REHABILITATION OF THE 'OLD MAID'

The figure of the 'old maid', as Karen O'Brien shows, becomes newly important in Malthus's 1803 second edition of the *Essay on the Principle of Population*. The woman who does not reproduce is now seen as conferring a social benefit, helping to solve the problem of nature's excess fertility.

Rejecting the possibility of contraception, delayed marriage and a period of elective celibacy become, for Malthus, the best hope of population control. Moreover he feels that sexual delay works to the advantage of women: the 'passion is stronger, and its general effects in producing gentleness, kindness, and suavity of manners [are] much more powerful, where obstacles are thrown in the way of a very early and universal gratification'.[82] Malthus here proposes a view of sexuality, of women, of society and of poverty that is diametrically opposed to that of Blake's circle and in significant features to that of Blake himself. The Sophians of Cumberland's 1798 novel, due for publication in the same year as Malthus's first edition, ask in amazement whether 'at the first genuine impulse of tender desire' Europeans can 'check the current of creation, and ... delay its exigent service at the command of those who are past feeling the divine impetus'.[83] This misguided intervention is the work of 'men, who dare to interpose their feeble wills to postpone the great unerring and explicit laws of propagation' (p. 67). O'Brien shows that Malthus's case for delayed marriage and the cultural rehabilitation of the old maid was supported by 'women writers throughout the century', including Maria Edgeworth and Hannah More, who saw a link between political economy and the cause of female education.[84] In this alliance, women writers accept that sexual regulation is a remedy for economic ills. But the processes by which we 'make somebody poor', as Blake suggests in 'The Human Abstract' of *Songs of Experience*, are also open to economic and political remedy.

CHAPTER 5

Cowper's fear: nature, population, apocalypse

According to Marshall Brown writing in 1991, Cowper was 'a bachelor in an age of poetic sterility'. Brown uses the term metaphorically to refer to Cowper's need to control meaning: Cowper was 'the reverse of a disseminator...content to sit at home and peruse the papers, he would not participate in the active dissemination of news, unless it were the one kind of news that always remains pure and unfragmented, the Good News of the Gospels'.[1] Though she might not have liked his tone or his preference for multivalent meanings, Hannah More would have recognised Brown's Cowper. More prefaced her 1799 *Strictures on the Modern System of Female Education* with an epigraph from *The Task*:

> Domestic Happiness, thou only bliss
> Of Paradise that has surviv'd the Fall!
> Thou art not known where PLEASURE is ador'd,
> That reeling Goddess with the zoneless waist.
> Forsaking thee, what shipwreck have we made
> Of honour, dignity, and fair renown![2]

This passage is a confection of lines 41–2, 51–2 and 58–9 from book III. The selective reading produces a Cowper who fits More's message and identifies a negative meaning of 'PLEASURE' that Blake would abhor. *Milton* offers strength to the Londoners 'at the Asylum/ Given to Hercules, who labour in Tirzahs Looms for bread/ Who set Pleasure against Duty' (E122). In More's epigraph, the 'reeling Goddess with the zoneless waist' recalls the kinds of vulgar femininity that Hayley offered to contain in *The Triumphs of Temper*. The short-lived coinage 'zoneless' (emerging in 1748 and dying out after 1822) derives from the equally short-lived adjective 'zoned' meaning 'Wearing a zone or girdle. Hence, virgin, chaste'. The impermanence of these words suggests the chronological specificity of this language. Emma Hamilton, probably no fan of Hannah More, thanked Hayley for his ability to define a neat (behavioural) waist: 'if it had not been for the good example Serena taught me, my girdle would have burst'.[3] In his years at Felpham, Blake must have become newly aware of how Cowper was being posthumously used in the shaping of a culture of bourgeois femininity.[4]

I have argued so far for a revisionary reading of Fuseli, Wollstonecraft, Madan and Hayley that finds in their work versions of a pro-sex discourse that Blake negotiates and debates. Both while Cowper was alive and posthumously via Hayley, however, Blake encounters a writer whose work fears sexuality. My argument that Blake remains faithful to the radical pro-sex discourse of the 1790s in his later work (despite negative references to the 'sexual', to the 'corporeal' and to the 'female will') is therefore challenged by Blake's allegiance to Cowper in the much quoted annotation to Spurzheim's *Observations on Insanity*:

Cowper came to me & said. O that I were insane always I will never rest. Can you not make me truly insane. I will never rest till I am so. O that in the bosom of God I was hid. You retain health & yet are as mad as any of us all–over us all–mad as a refuge from unbelief–from Bacon Newton & Locke. (E663)

The phrase that lodges in most critical writing is 'mad as a refuge from unbelief' and the conclusion usually drawn is that Blake reveals his newly orthodox Christian belief. Critics see Blake as abandoning his earlier sympathy for enlightenment speculation and radical anti-clericalism as he moves, in the early nineteenth century, closer to the counter-revolution, echoing Barruel's conspiracy theories and mimicking the turn in Coleridge's writing against the classical. Even Martin Priestman, who presents Blake as influenced by nascent atheist currents in the 1790s, assumes that this is no longer the case after 1800 when there is 'a return to something like recognizable Christianity in Blake's work'.[5]

The supposed shift in Blake's religious sympathies is often associated with growing misogyny as if, in both religious and sexual terms, Blake simply loses his radical vision. Focusing on sexuality, however, Christopher Hobson sees Blake's post-1803 work as transcending the limitations of early poetry which 'idealized male aggression', producing in the late epics a newly tolerant view of sexuality.[6] The annotation to Spurzheim is important because it reveals the consistency of Blake's religious sympathies: the passage Blake annotates, as both Morton Paley and Jon Mee point out, is a discussion of the supposed link between Methodist enthusiasm and madness, a link vividly illustrated in Hogarth's 1760 satire, *Enthusiasm Delineated*.[7] Blake's marginal comment willingly takes on the identity of mad enthusiast described by Spurzheim, and in doing so suggests something of how Blake reads Cowper. 'Thou readst black where I read white' (E524), writes Blake in the *Everlasting Gospel*: whether he is reading the Bible or Milton, Blake repeatedly constructs meanings which invert those of other readers. This difference is nowhere more evident than in his reading of Cowper, where Blake reads the 'mad' Cowper that Hayley saw but that his *Life* attempted to conceal. The mad Cowper is a writer driven by a powerfully sexual imagination.

HAYLEY, COWPER AND THE 'BLUSH UNSEEN'

Hayley saw sexuality as a problem for Cowper and a component in his mental vulnerability. A passage at the end of the *Life* describes the separation from his early love Theodora as one cause of his first breakdown:

Nature had given him a warm constitution, and had he been prosperous in early love, it is probable that he might have enjoyed a more uniform and happy tenor of health. But a disappointment of the heart, arising from the cruelty of fortune, threw a cloud on his juvenile spirit. Thwarted in love, the native fire of his temperament turned impetuously into the kindred channel of devotion. The smothered flames of desire uniting with the vapours of constitutional melan-choly, and the fervency of religious zeal, produced altogether that irregularity of corporeal sensation, and of mental health, which gave such extraordinary vicissi-tudes of splendour and of darkness to his mortal career ... (II, p. 222)

In this passage religion merely diverts 'the native fire of his temperament'. As usual, Hayley identifies free-flowing circulation as necessary to good health and sees writing as a means of regaining mental balance. Cowper's writing is itself a form of 'flow' derived from feeling since *The Task* is a 'Poem of such infinite variety, that it seems ... to have flowed, without effort, from inspired philanthropy'.[8] As a poem flowing from 'philan-thropy' Hayley represents *The Task* correctly as the poem that inspires More's attempt to contain social unrest through charity and through pity. Blockage of another kind, according to Hayley, explains the return of Cowper's depression in 1798 when 'a scorbutic habit, which, when his perspiration was obstructed, occasioned an unsearchable obstruction in the finer parts of his frame' (II, p. 211). On land, scurvy was seen as most common in the winter months and the recommended cure was open air, fruit and greens.[9] Cowper's interests in walking and horticulture were therefore suitable activities for the diagnosis of constitutional scurvy. But Hayley's passage also echoes his account of the pathology of the old maid which argued that 'A frame of glowing sensibility requires a proper field for the exercise and expansion of all its general affections; and when this is denied to it, such obstruction will sometimes occasion the very worst of evils, a sort of stagnation both in heart and soul'.[10] Hayley clearly sees Cowper in the same terms he used for Gray in the *Essay on Old Maids* as 'an old maid in breeches'. He quotes a letter in which Cowper imagines the pleasures of quiet domesticity with the Unwins in terms of Gray's image of the rose 'born to blush unseen'.[11] Neither for Cowper nor for Thel is the 'blush unseen' an image of lost potential.

Blake's mad Cowper in his annotation to Spurzheim voices distress caused as much by sexuality as by religion, particularly since Blake is himself alert to the interrelation of two areas which contemporary culture was seeking to separate. Hayley may have shared with Blake his view that Cowper's insanity was expressed in terms of religious enthusiasm but was caused by an obstruction or blockage of the flame of his warm temperament. This blockage produces the construct of 'sexuality' that paradoxically allows access to Golgonooza: 'For Golgonooza cannot be seen till having passd the Polypus/ It is viewed on all sides round by a Four-fold Vision/ Or till you become Mortal & Vegetable in Sexuality' (E135).

When *The Task* was published in 1785 readers assumed that the domesticity to which the poet alluded was marriage and it is this meaning that is assumed by Hannah More's 1799 epigraph.[12] But Hayley's 1803 *Life* revealed that his portrait of 'Domestic happiness' was based on his non-sexual relationship with Mrs Unwin. Hayley quotes Cowper: 'Man's love of woman's not so pure,/ Nor when sincerest, so secure' (I, pp. 223–4) and presents the relationship as 'a connexion so extraordinary', 'an attachment perhaps unparalleled'. The relationship appears as a utopian redefinition of possibility which 'tho' not sanctioned by the common forms of life, was supported with perfect innocence, and endeared to them both, by their having struggled together, thro' a series of sorrow' (I, p. 30). Hayley's *Life of Cowper* suggests the possibility of recreating society through sociable rather than sexual bonds.

Hayley's Cowper is thus feminised rather than sexual: '[t]owards women in particular', Hayley reported, 'his behaviour and conversation were delicate and fascinating in the highest degree' (II, p. 222). Women provide a form of benign policing, as in Gray's poem 'A Long Story' in which two young women visit – or invade – the writing poet in the retirement of his cottage, leaving a spell that summons him to a trial before an assembly of women, the 'Lady Janes and Joans', presided over by a peeress. Blake illustrated this minor poem at length in the unique volume he produced in 1798 for the library of Ann Flaxman (Figure 11).

Figure 11. William Blake, *The Poems of Thomas Gray*, design 22, *A Long Story*, 1797–1798. Watercolour with pen and black ink and graphite. © Yale Center for British Art, Paul Mellon Collection.

Blake's illustration shows the male poet within a domestic interior whose privacy is penetrated by women. Helen Bruder sees this image as Blake's playful acknowledgement to his friend Ann Flaxman that the male imagination 'must submit to womanly judgement'. Certainly in Cowper's own work, the judgement of women (or 'ladies') determines true worth: the 'worst effect' of smoking 'is banishing for hours/ The sex whose presence civilizes ours' (1, p. 225). Yet the hierarchical distribution of space can be read more negatively as an image of the way in which rank and gender police the work of the poet.[13] From Wollstonecraft's point of view, female aristocratic power is a malformation of human identity. Blake's image contains the ambiguities of Beulah or even the more negative phrase the 'female will', in the ruffs, bonnets and wimples that the seated old maids sport in the 1800 years of the 'female dream'. Although Gray's poet speaks in his own defence, 'The ghastly prudes with haggard face/ Already had condemn'd the sinner'. Blake's watercolour illustration uses a technique akin to extra-illustration or Grangerisation in which a printed text is cut and pasted within a unique watercolour frame: a form associated with women encloses a male text.[14]

Heaven in the *Life of Cowper* is policed by the rules of politeness: 'If the most eminent departed authors could revisit the human scene, after residing in a purer sphere, and revise their own productions', Hayley writes, 'they would probably annihilate all the virulent invectives, which the intemperance of human passions has so abundantly produced.'[15] Hayley's heaven echoes Cowper, whose poem 'Conversation' describes his hatred of aggressive arguers: 'They fix attention, heedless of your pain,/ With oaths like rivets forced into the brain'.[16] This is the (Beularised) world in which Blake's Milton, the most 'eminent departed' author, is 'Unhappy tho in heav'n' (E96). It is the job of the Bard to make sure that heaven can still hear the inchoate sounds of work, of living and dying to which Milton is forced to listen in the song of the Bard:

> Loud sounds the Hammer of Los, loud turn the Wheels of Enitharmon
> Her Looms vibrate with soft affections, weaving the Web of Life
> Out from the ashes of the Dead; Los lifts his iron Ladles
> With molten ore: he heaves the iron cliffs in his rattling chains
> From Hyde Park to the Alms-houses of Mile-end & old Bow
> (*M* 1:7:27–31, E100)

The conflict of the Bard's song involves ill-controlled feeling ('he wept!', 'she trembled!'), rage which 'flam'd high & furious' and, in place of the vapours that Hayley imagined as dampening Cowper's fire, 'Thick fires contending with the rain, thunder'd above rolling/ Terrible over their heads' (E102). Rather than returning from heaven to 'annihilate all the virulent invectives, which the intemperance of human passions has so abundantly produced',

> Ololon descended to Felphams Vale
> In clouds of blood, in streams of gore, with dreadful thundering
> Into the Fires of Intellect that rejoic'd in Felphams Vale   (E143)

Blake's *Milton* challenges the cult of Cowper for which Hayley's *Life* provides the template, rejecting a model of sexless marriage and a form of sociability constrained by feminine politeness. Blake's Milton leaves heaven to search for his emanation, yet his emanation is, like most lost objects, in the usual place but hidden: he imagines that he is in heaven without his emanation ('What do I here before the Judgment? without my

Emanation?' E108). Yet Ololon descends at the beginning of *Milton*
book II in search of Milton. What Milton has failed to realise is that
heaven contains Ololon; it is not the sexless place described by Hayley.

Cowper's sexual and gendered identity has been a fruitful area for
academic discussion.[17] Andrew Elfenbein argues that 'Cowper's perceived
mixture of masculine and feminine qualities' scandalously suggested the
possibility of homosexuality and linked this gender identity to the 'character of genius'.[18] Elfenbein suggests that Francis Jeffrey's reference to
Cowper's 'feminine gentleness and delicacy of nature' in a review of
Hayley's *Life* implies a recognition of the homosexual identity of a
lifelong bachelor.[19] By contrast Christopher Hobson detects in Cowper's
association of sodomy with privilege in *Tirocinium* the presence of a
homophobic discourse of republican virtue that has also been detected
in Blake's writing and offered as an explanation for elements of anti-
feminism in his work.[20] The discourse of effeminacy returns in Blake's
notebook attack on Hayley: 'Thus Hayley on his Toilette seeing the Sope/
Cries Homer is very much improvd by Pope' (E505) and perhaps in the
image of the hermaphrodite in *Milton*: 'A mournful form double; herm-
aphroditic: male & female/ In one wonderful body' (E108).[21] While
Blake's image of Hayley 'on his Toilette' could indeed be read as latent
homophobia, it could also reflect his sense of Hayley as contributing to an
idealisation of a desexed culture. The charge of narcissism, characteristic
of the image of the coquette, belongs to a discourse which attacks the
hoarding and manipulation of sexuality as a form of economic power, as
in the figure of the old maid in the Proverbs of Hell.

Fuseli and Blake, I have argued, fear that luxury desexualises culture,
blocking or diverting sexual energy. Cowper not only imagines luxury in
sexualised terms but reveals an intensely sexual view of nature concealed
beneath the surface of the green land that brings peace. Like *The
Triumphs of Temper*, *The Task* is an inheritor of *The Rape of the Lock*,
written to order and taking as its nominal subject a material part of the
domestic world. But whereas Hayley accepts the subject of femininity as
a means of taming enthusiasm and accessing poetry, Cowper attempts to
escape a world sliding into luxury and decadence. Lady Austen's choice
of subject carried a hint of scandal since *The Sofa* was the title of a work
of the libertine enlightenment, a 1742 novel by Crébillon *fils* that appears
in the second scene of Hogarth's *Marriage à la Mode* on the sofa of the
aristocratic lady's dressing room as a signal of her scandalous tastes. In
this oriental fantasy a young courtier, Amanzei, tells how his soul was
condemned to inhabit a series of sofas in punishment for 'his inordinate

desires'. The 'immortal Brahma' chooses a sofa for the transmigration
of his soul as a more humiliating vehicle even than a reptile (the
punishment accorded, of course, to Satan). With this experience he can
report 'that there are few chaste women on the Sopha' (p. 27). Amanzei
is condemned to migrate from sofa to sofa until a man and woman,
truly in love, use him to consummate their passion. Despite its inscription from Homer, Fuseli and Blake's image *Allegory of a Dream of Love*
(discussed in chapter 2) could well function as an illustration to Crébillon's
novel. The word 'soft' appears twenty-one times in the 1781 English
translation in phrases such as 'soft preludes of enjoyment' (I, p. 50),
'soft desires' (I, p. 182), 'the soft impulse insensibly increased upon her'
(II, p. 225).[22] 'Soft' is here thoroughly eroticised and liberation from
imprisonment in the material (sofa/body) comes through passion. Hayley
owned Crébillon's *The Sopha; a Moral Tale* both in French and in an
English translation.[23] Ozias Humphrey's 1803 remark to Farington that
'Hayley was the *workbasket poet* of that day, – His verses were upon every
Girl's Sopha' suggests not only the anodyne nature of his poetry for
women but also its insistent eroticism.[24] Hayley's sympathy for a culture
of aristocratic libertinage is suggested in his (anonymous) *Two Dialogues*
of 1787, a debate between Lord Chesterfield and the moralist Dr Johnson
which Chesterfield wins.[25] Chesterfield is also praised in *The Triumphs of
Temper* for his 'liberal' attempt to 'defend the violated stage'.[26] Hayley's
Life of Cowper therefore suppresses the conflicts of his liberalism to
produce a hypocritical politeness, a 'mournful form double; hermaphro-
ditic: male & female/ In one wonderful body' (E108), revealing the
inability of liberalism to confront conflict except through burying
unacceptable selves.

Whereas Hayley uncovered a positive meaning for softness in *The
Triumphs of Temper*, Cowper's negative use – a direct descendant of
Pope's 'matter too soft' and the ancestor of Lady Bertram's sofa in
Mansfield Park – generates a form of anti-sensualism that characterises
elements of British nineteenth-century culture and that Blake describes in
Jerusalem, where the construction of 'Babylon the City of Vala, the
Goddess Virgin-Mother' depends on the destruction of Jerusalem 'our
Harlot-Sister', 'To be for a Shame & a Curse, and to be our Slaves for
ever/ So cry Hand & Hyle the eldest of the fathers of Albions' (E163).
Here the liberal hypocrisy which Blake detects (in a small but symptomatic form) in Hayley's construction of the evangelical Cowper produces
the monstrous image of Hyle, a name for a cultural process rather than the
individual who would continue to assist Blake's flagging career.

Blake's negative image of Hayley as Hyle (the Greek word for matter)
in *Jerusalem* consigns him to imprisonment in the sofa; yet Blake's
own writing belongs to a tradition quite different from that of Cowper's
anti-materialism. Whereas Cowper assumes that luxury marks a final
descent into decadence, Blake, as we saw in chapter 2, assumes that
sensual pleasure and ornament are part of healthy cultures. One of the
tasks of the daughters of Beulah at the end of *Milton* book 1 is to prepare
'couches soft'. As the sons of Los create time, 'Moments & Minutes &
Hours/ And Days & Months & Years & Ages & Periods', they also offer
places of rest:

> And every Moment has a Couch of gold for soft repose,
> (A Moment equals a pulsation of the artery),
> And between every two Moments stands a Daughter of Beulah
> To feed the Sleepers on their Couches with maternal care.
>
> (*M* 1:28[30]:44–9, E126)

The first state of 'Humanity in its Repose' is 'a most pleasant Sleep/
On Couches soft, with mild music, tended by Flowers of Beulah'
(*M* 11:34[38]:9–10, E134). Blake echoes the communal living of the
Sophians in *Captive of the Castle of Sennaar* who enjoy afternoon rests
on couches in a large hall: 'He then led me into the hall, where we trod
softly, most of the company being composed in tranquil sleep; and
having placed me on a couch … he retired to his own; when, calmed
by that peaceful joy which reconciliation ever inspires, and lulled by the
soft murmurs of the gliding brook, I soon dropped into a sweet and
profound repose.'[27] Cumberland's account of the cultivation of sensual
pleasure in an African utopia escapes the rhetoric of luxury that frightens
both Cowper and Rousseau in *Émile*. Rousseau can accept that childhood
is a time when 'the soft and pliant fibres … readily yield to impression',
but growth into manhood demands that this softness is left behind: Émile
must not be indulged 'in soft and uninterrupted slumbers' (I, p. 231).[28]
Particularly to be feared is: 'A soft bed, in which we lie buried in feathers
or eider-down' which 'dissolves, as it were, the whole body' (I, p. 232),
for within a dualist model, matter threatens to dissolve the self. While
softness is associated with eroticism it remains positive in Blake's work:
it is in the Notebook verses associated with the failure of the 1809
exhibition that the softness of 'Feather pillows' and 'Bartolloze' begin to
signify a culture that rejects the energy of sexuality, polices public art
and fosters war. The couches of Beulah can always turn into Albion's
death 'couch' (E104).

Cowper's narrative of the rise of luxury is derived from John Brown's 1758 *An Estimate of the Manners and Principles of the Times*. Cowper had acknowledged Brown in 'Table Talk' as a prophet unheeded in his time and warned

> that effeminacy, folly, lust,
> Enervate and enfeeble, and needs must,
> And that a nation shamefully debas'd,
> Will be despis'd and trampl'd on at last

Nevertheless there is a significant difference between this warning and that of Brown against 'vain, luxurious, and selfish Effeminacy'.[29] Brown describes how crude pleasures, including lust and obscenity, are displaced in commercial society by the pleasures of acquisition, food, clothing and gaming. The process of amassing wealth leads not only to emulation or vanity but also refinement. Even obscenity tends to be replaced by *double entendre*: 'As Excess of Delicacy hath destroyed our *Force of Taste*, it hath at least had one laudable Effect: For along with this, it hath carried off our *Grossness of Obscenity*.'[30] Like Fuseli later on, Brown is worried that the distinction of the sexes is lost in a culture of luxury which turns a crude form of male sexuality into a measured form of fashionable politeness, both masking and endorsing sexuality within culture. The presence of women sexualises sociability even as it ensures politeness:

In ancient Days, *bare* and *impudent Obscenity*, like a common Woman of the Town, was confined to *Brothels*: Whereas the *Double-Entendre*, like a modern fine Lady, is now admitted into the *best Company*; while her *transparent Covering* of Words, like a *thin* fashionable *Gawze* delicately thrown across, *discloses*, while it seems to *veil*, her *Nakedness* of Thought.[31]

Cowper's love of domesticity potentially places him within the pathology of blended genders that Brown delineates – as Hayley's and Jeffrey's accounts of Cowper as a feminised man confirm.

Brown identifies the kind of debility from which Cowper himself suffered as a sign of the times: 'OUR effeminate and unmanly Life, working along with our Island-climate, hath notoriously produced an Increase of *low Spirits* and *nervous Disorders*, whose natural and unalterable Character is that of *Fear*' (p. 48). Cowper's fear and his celebration of the domestic affections make him ripe for Brown's diagnosis of effeminacy since Brown laments the way in which commerce and wealth produce a focus on the domestic rather than on 'the *Love* of our *Country*' and of 'the Principle of *public Spirit*': 'DOMESTIC Affections', he writes, 'are not yet generally extinguished: There are kind Fathers, kind Mothers,

affectionate Children, Sisters, Brothers' (p. 36). In Hayley's account in the
Life, Cowper retires to and celebrates the feminine and the domestic:
'Reserved as he was, to an extraordinary and painful degree, his heart and
mind were yet admirably fashioned by nature for all the refined intercourse, and confidential delights both of friendship and of love.'[32]
Cowper, however, shifts the emphasis of Brown's account of 'effeminacy'
because it runs the danger of including his own disorder of nervous fear.
He gives it a more specifically sexual interpretation in order to exclude his
own pathology from the account and to allow the idealisation of the
domestic. In Cowper's version of the discourse, luxury is sexual and
located in the city.

As a school friend of Charles Churchill and fellow member in the 1750s
of the Nonsense Club, Cowper is only one remove from the libertine
circles of the Medmenham monks. Cowper's return to writing in the early
1780s is clearly related to his distress at the publication of *Thelyphthora*,
for Madan was not only Cowper's cousin but the friend and clergyman
who had counselled him in his first mental breakdown. Cowper's account
of 'Domestic Happiness' rests on a fascination with violent sexuality in
nature as an image of apocalypse and with the city as the location of
monstrous fecundity and promiscuity. It is as a poet of sexuality that
Cowper is important to Blake's conception of Vala which can be read as
an analysis of the consequences of the discourse on luxury that constructs
Cowper's idealisation of nature. In *Jerusalem*, 'Vala produc'd the Bodies.
Jerusalem gave the Souls' (E163) but the split between body and soul is
mended when Albion 'found Jerusalem upon the River of his City soft
repos'd/ In the arms of Vala, assimilating in one with Vala' (E164).
Cowper uses Nature to distance appetite: the 'rural walk' in *The Task*
book 1 is a means of ensuring that he can live 'Guiltless of pampered
appetite obscene'.

THE SEXUALITY OF NATURE

Whereas Darwin sees the natural world as manifesting the binomial
sexual categories of Linnaeus, Cowper's view of nature reveals his desire
to retire to a place without sexuality. Although the 1989 edition of the
OED quotes Cowper writing about Erasmus Darwin's poem *The Loves
of the Plants* as the first example of the modern use of the word
'sexuality' to mean 'the quality of being sexual or possessing sex',
Cowper's view of nature is more conflicted than that of Darwin and
his view of sexuality more anarchic and disruptive.[33] For Cowper, the

location of sexuality in the natural world seems to offer some defence against the fears that human sexuality brings, enabling him to maintain a view of bourgeois femininity as asexual. In the violence of the natural world, Cowper images his fear of the unregulated sexuality of the London crowd.

'Where man is not nature is barren', claims one of the 'Proverbs of Hell' (E38). Blake's proverb reveals his understanding of the sexuality of the natural world. But Blake's account of natural sexuality is often associated with violence. In the figures of Vala, Rahab and the shadowy female, Blake's writing offers plentiful scope for the identification of misogyny, imagining the forcible rending of the veil, the uncovering of a secret place which carries both sexual and earthly meanings. Whereas Cowper fears the opening of the earthly grave at the moment of apocalypse at which he may be thrown into eternal damnation, Blake imagines the Last Judgment in equally sexual terms as the ecstatic female grave of the *Song of Los*. At this level, then, the relationship between the sexual imaginary of Blake and Cowper is simple: what Cowper fears Blake welcomes. More puzzling, however, is the way in which Blake enters the debate over the meaning of natural violence. Perhaps one of Blake's most perplexing annotations is his contribution to what becomes a threeway debate between Bishop Watson, Tom Paine and his own 1798 comments on his copy of Bishop Watson's *An Apology for the Bible*. Blake writes, 'The Earthquakes at Lisbon &c were the Natural result of Sin.'[34] The comment is the more surprising because Blake portrays the claim that 'Womans love is Sin!' (E62) as the work of the female will in *Europe*. Albion is at his lowest ebb when in *Jerusalem* chapter 1 he calls to Vala 'O that thou wert pure!/ That the deep wound of Sin might be clos'd up with the Needle' (E166). In seeing the Lisbon earthquakes as 'the Natural result of Sin', Blake seems to part company with the enlightenment attack on the idea of the vengeful God which was made explicit in the theological debate provoked by the Lisbon earthquakes of 1755 in Voltaire's *Candide*. Although Blake does not link the Lisbon earthquake with female sexuality, the connection is implicit in the patterns which emerge in his own writing where 'Nature' is associated with Vala and Vala is associated with 'the deep wound of Sin'.

Book II of *The Task* derives from Sir William Hamilton's account of the Sicilian and Calabrian earthquakes in 1783, published in the *General Evening Post* which Cowper read avidly.[35] The paper reported Hamilton's thesis presented to the Royal Society that the earthquakes were the result of volcanoes on the sea bed. Hamilton argued that the horrid boiling of the sea during an earthquake was caused by 'exhalations or eruptions from cracks at the bottom of the sea' and had a volcanic origin. Hamilton described how:

the motion of the earth had been various, and, according to the Italian denomination, *vorticoso, orizontale,* and *oscilatorio,* either whirling like a vortex horizontal, or by pulsations, or beating from the bottom upwards; that this variety of motions had increased the apprehensions of the unfortunate inhabitants of those parts, who expected every moment that the earth would open under their feet, and swallow them up; that the rains had been continual and violent, often accompanied with lightning and irregular and furious gusts of winds; that from all these causes the face of the earth of that part of Calabria was entirely altered ... that many openings and cracks had been made in those parts; that some hills had been lowered and others quite levelled; that in the plains deep chasms had been made ...[36]

Cowper is certain that the earthquakes are God's punishment for man's sin: 'Such evil sin hath wrought'. He explains the fact that the earthquakes were not in Britain but in the relatively less sinful Sicily by the belief that 'God may choose His mark,/ May punish, if He please, the less, to warn/ The more malignant.' The earthquakes are just one of many signs that 'the close of all' is at hand. Cowper adopts the viewpoint of the earth, personifying her in imagery derived from the Song of Songs as a woman longing for God:

> How does the earth receive him? – With what signs
> Of gratulation and delight, her king?
> Pours she not all her choicest fruits abroad,
> Her sweetest flow'rs, her aromatic gums,
> Disclosing paradise where'er he treads?
> She quakes at his approach.   (II, pp. 49–50)

The land devastated by the earthquakes is not the 'old/ And crazy earth' that Cowper invokes at the beginning of the book but a land described by Hamilton as 'the most beautiful and fertile country I ever beheld: a perfect garden of olive trees, mulberry trees, fruit trees and vines'. God's punishment of this fertile land in Cowper's imagination takes a sexual form:

> Her hollow womb
> Conceiving thunders, through a thousand deeps
> And fiery caverns roar beneath his foot.
> The hills move lightly and the mountains smoke,
> For he has touch'd them. From th'extremest point
> Of elevation down into th'abyss,
> His wrath is busy and his frown is felt.   (II, p. 50)

Cowper's image of God touching the land uses the same trope of the sexual earth or of woman as nature that reappears in Blake's famous question, 'And did these feet in ancient time/ Walk upon England's mountains green?' (E95). England, in Blake's lyric, awaits the touch of the lord with the same eagerness as Sicily in Cowper's *The Task*. Blake borrows – or shares – Cowper's image of the earth as a woman but reverses the valence. Neither Blake nor Cowper belongs within the modern understanding of sexuality, instead reusing the Bible's association of seismic change with sexual experience.

The Lisbon quake, with its epicentre offshore in the Atlantic ocean, is echoed in *America*, where the turbulence that Albion's angel believes is his work is really the result of Orc's undersea volcanic eruption:

> And as a sea o'erwhelms a land in the day of an earthquake;
> Fury! rage! madness! in a wind swept through America
> And the red flames of Orc that folded roaring fierce around
> The angry shores, and the fierce rushing of th'inhabitants together: (E56)

When 'Rintrah roars & shakes his fires in the burdend air' in *The Marriage of Heaven and Hell*, he inadvertently echoes Hamilton's account of 'rains ... continual and violent, often accompanied with lightning and irregular and furious gusts of winds'. Thunder and lightning, rain and winds, pulsations and vortex are everywhere in Blake's writing where the Last Judgment occurs 'whenever any Individual Rejects Error & Embraces Truth' (E562). Cowper sees the Sicilian earthquakes as God's warning of punishments in store for Britain and understands the loss of America as actual punishment for Britain's folly: 'Our arch of empire' is now 'A mutilated structure, soon to fall'. Blake celebrates the moment that 'Empire is no more!' in 'A Song of Liberty' and uses Cowper's picture of a punishing god from *The Task* to describe the work of Albion's Angel who sends an earthquake in *America*. Rather than the work of God as in Cowper, or of natural forces as in Hamilton, the tsunami and the fires are here the work of man.

What most distinguishes Blake's use of the earthquake is the loss of fear. Hamilton can find humour in the scenes he describes, particularly in his enlightenment glee at discovering that the schoolboys of Reggio relish their new found freedom and the nuns 'constantly walking about, under the tuition of their confessor ... seemed gay, and to enjoy the liberty the earthquake had afforded them'. In his hastily written journal, Hamilton reveals, 'the remark stands thus; "*Earthquakes particularly pleasing to nuns and schoolboys.*"' Earthquake has similar effects in *America* where 'The

Figure 12. William Blake, *The Marriage of Heaven and Hell*, copy H, plate 1.
© Fitzwilliam Museum.

doors of marriage are open, and the Priests in rustling scales/ Rush into reptile coverts, hiding from the fires of Orc' (E57). Hamilton comments several times on the ability of animals to anticipate a quake: 'I was assured here (where they have had such a long experience of earthquakes) that all animals and birds are in a greater or lesser degree much more sensible of an approaching shock of an earthquake than any human being.' Blake similarly describes a world in a state of heightened awareness. Sounding not at all like the victim of a sexual assault, Oothoon in *Visions* reflects on the multiple senses of the animal world:

> With what sense is it that the chicken shuns the ravenous hawk?
> With what sense does the tame pigeon measure out the expanse?   (E47)

The frontispiece to *The Marriage of Heaven and Hell* (Figure 12) shows figures embracing in a volcanic space below ground. The teeming multitude of little figures rise up from the flames of fiery embrace to repopulate a wintry world above. Here the surface of the natural world acts as a veil over the buried energies of a hell or a heaven below ground.

This scene could be read in terms of the fertility of a volcanic region but Blake's couples, as Christopher Hobson argues, seem in many copies of the work either to fail to specify gender or to include pairs of women embracing.[37] The prolific energy they produce is not that of Darwin's vegetable sexuality but of an ungendered eroticism.

In Blake's version, the revolutionary moment of the early 1790s is imaged by the opening of a volcanic abyss which recalls Hamilton's account of 'several deep cracks in this neighbourhood, not one above a foot in breadth; but which, I was credibly assured, had opened wide during the earthquake, and swallowed up an ox, and near an hundred goats'. Blake's non-mimetic cross-section through the earth reproduces the pictorial conventions of popular religious imagery such as the often reprinted anonymous image of *The Tree of Life* (Figure 13) printed by Bowles and Carver at 69 St Paul's Church Yard.[38] The world outside the heavenly city in the Bowles and Carver image occupies the same pictorial space as hell in Blake's frontispiece and is perhaps a source of Cowper's account of the corrupt city. This popular print shows '*this present* Evil World *with the Industry of* Gospel Ministers *in endeavouring to pluck* Sinners *from the Wrath to come*'. Heavy gates on the right, like the gates of hell that Sin guards in Hogarth's painting of *Satan, Sin and Death*, offer a view of the flames of the 'Bottomless Pit'. This scene contains a fashionably dressed crowd, some of whom listen to, and some of whom ignore, the preachers Wesley and Whitefield. To the left are scenes of 'Chambering & Wantonness' perhaps based on Hogarth's *The Harlot's Progress*. Before the gates of hell is 'Babylon Mother of Harlots' in a form which strongly resembles Blake's later images of the Virgin Babylon. Blake's satiric version reminds the viewer of the revelation of Matthew 22.30 that 'in the resurrection they neither marry, nor are given in marriage, but are as the angels of God in heaven'. Heaven/hell is here full of embracing angels free of the constraints of marriage: an apparently anti-sensual passage turns into a statement of revolutionary eroticism. The 'Broad Way' which in the Bowles and Carver print leads down to the 'Bottomless Pitt', in Blake's frontispiece leads out of hell up to a wintry heaven and the path out of hell is easier for Blake's couples than for Satan in *Paradise Lost* because they do not have to talk their way past the portress of hell's gates. In Blake's image, fashionably dressed women

Figure 13. Anon, *The Tree of Life*. Published by Bowles and Carver, undated.
© The Trustees of the British Museum.

Figure 14. William Blake, *The Marriage of Heaven and Hell,* copy H, plate 3.
© Fitzwilliam Museum.

belong in the wintry scene above ground; the polite, fashionable world that thinks it is heaven needs the energies of the bodies below ground.

This pattern of imagery is typical of its historical moment, a time when a follower of Richard Brothers wrote that 'We live in a period distinguished by the most extraordinary events, one pregnant with the fate of Empires and Thrones – wonderful changes have already taken place, and still the portentous clouds thicken, and spread around the political horizon.'[39] The groan of the 'Eternal Female' in labour that opens 'A Song of Liberty' is a sign of revolutionary change and she is represented as a woman giving birth at the bottom of plate 3 of *The Marriage*, in a position that surprisingly recalls the images of orgasmic women in Blake's poems of this period. Neither passive nor weak, her ecstatic body mirrors the unfolding baby as it reaches strongly out and up (Figure 14). Although this figure is the only unambiguous visual representation of birth in

Blake's visual text, the illuminated books teem with tiny figures that suggest the multiplication of life forms, even the homunculi thought to inhabit the sperm. These little figures (and the insects and birds which sprinkle the text) might be functional devices to prevent foul biting when the etching acid works too strongly on an extended area but it is Blake's choice to turn them into living forms. It is clear that the volcanic eruption imagined by Blake marks not the end of the material world but the renewal of its fertility. In this sense Blake's imagination is closer to Hamilton's account than to Cowper.

But Blake also uses the image of earthquake in a way which is more disturbing and more violent. Descending to the earth in *Milton* book 1, Milton witnesses the conflict of Orc and the shadowy female who conceals Jerusalem and Babylon: 'in vain' Orc 'Stretch'd out his hands of fire, & wooed: they triumph in his pain'. This conflict again produces the image of an earthquake:

> Thus darkend the Shadowy Female tenfold & Orc tenfold
> Glowd on his rocky Couch against the darkness: loud thunders
> Told of the enormous conflict[.] Earthquake beneath: around;
> Rent the enormous Females, limb from limb & joint from joint
> And moved the fast foundations of the Earth to wake the Dead
>   (*M* 1:18[20]:46–50, E112)

As in *The Task*, earthquake is imaged as the tearing apart of a female form: Orc rends the Shadowy Female who aims to prevent change by weaving 'this Satan for a Covering' (E111–12). Whereas the earth is punished in *The Task* for her sexual desire, here it is the resistance of the 'enormous Females' that provokes violence. Blake here seems to work through the compacted logic of his claim in response to Watson that 'The Earthquakes at Lisbon &c were the Natural result of Sin'. If this statement is un-ravelled via Blake's use of the term 'sin', it becomes clear that Blake sees earthquake as the natural (or logical) consequence of the imposition of (the category of) sin. The characters of Blake's epic poetry act out the logical consequences of the assumptions that they encode: if St Paul prescribed the veil for women 'because of the angels' (1 Cor. 11:10), in reference to the love of the angels for the daughters of men described in Genesis 6 (the story that is retold in the book of Enoch) then the veil that Vala represents is an attempt to make safe the power of female sexuality. It is the unleashing of this sexual power that Blake associates with the imagery of apocalypse and Last Judgment. Acting out the compacted assumptions of Blake's shorthand statement that the earthquakes are the natural result of (the category of) sin, Blake's poetry follows his own definition of prophecy in the annotations to Watson: 'Thus/ If you go on So/ the result is So'.[40]

If *Milton* deals with the ways in which Milton's work has been revised in the years since the death of the poet, the violence of this scene may represent Blake's interpretation of sexual ideology in the last years of the eighteenth century which emerges so clearly in Hayley's writing.[41] The *Essay on Old Maids* assumes the necessity of rape in its retelling of the story of the book of Enoch. At the same time, Blake's encounter with Cowper at Felpham would have emphasised Cowper's role in the construction of an evangelical culture of regulated sexuality. While there, Blake produced two paintings intended for the sides of the fireplace in the rectory of John Johnson, Cowper's cousin and Hayley's friend, representing *Winter* and *Evening* designed to illustrate passages from *The Task* book IV, lines 120–9 and 243–60.[42] In this scheme, the fire is framed and controlled by images of cold and dark. Blake's image of winter for John Johnson portrays an old man wrapped in white shroud-like death clothes (Figure 15). These are the 'sexual garments'. Whereas Blake portrays winter in the *Poetical Sketches* and the wintry Urizen as figures of oppression, Cowper welcomes winter: 'I love thee, all unlovely as thou seemest,/ And dreaded as thou art.' Although it draws on Thomson's *The Seasons*, *The Task* is weighted disproportionately towards images of winter with successive books on 'The Winter Evening', 'The Winter Morning's Walk' and 'The Winter Walk at Noon' and thus avoids the sexualised imagery of Thomson's 'Spring' and 'Summer'.

In book III of *The Task*, the volcanic fires of the previous book are made safe by domesticity when Cowper muses by the fire watching 'the sooty films that play upon the bars'. In a notebook verse, Blake takes the fireside as a symbol of the political limitations of domesticity, the failure to make change that he also detects in Sensiblity's cult of pity:

> Who will exchange his own fire side
> For the stone of anothers door
> Who will exchange his wheaten loaf
> For the links of a dungeon floor   (E500)

By contrast, the fire that consumes the frontispiece to *The Marriage* becomes an image of apocalypse and the 'strangers', the fragments of burnt wood that Cowper and later Coleridge will watch, rise up to rekindle the enthusiasm of the world above.

Figure 15. William Blake, *Winter*. © Tate, London, 2010.

In the *Book of Urizen*, 'Eternity shudder'd when they saw,/ Man begetting his likeness,/ On his own divided image' (E79). Cowper's disgust at the city as a place of 'sloth and lust,/ And wantonness and gluttonous excess' produces a comparable revulsion. It is a place where the worst become what they behold: 'In cities, foul example on most minds/ Begets its likeness' (II, p. 36), a version of what Jonathan Lamb describes as 'horrid sympathy'. Cowper imagines the city in terms drawn from Milton's allegory of Satan, Sin and Death as a place where 'Rank abundance breeds/. . . sloth and lust,/ And wantonness and gluttonous excess.' The city, then, is hell, situated under the earth, a source of horrid energy. Rather than sharing his period's fear of the city as a place that destroys fertility through disease, Cowper seems to predict the fear of overpopulation that will become explicit in Malthus. Cowper compares the swarming births of 'Profusion' to the plagues with which Moses struck Egypt, 'a race obscene,/ Spawned in the muddy beds of Nile, came forth/ Polluting Egypt', seeing the fertile mud of the Nile not as the origin of life but of 'a race obscene', a source for him of intense disgust. By contrast Blake's *The Book of Ahania* links physical fertility with the fertility of the imagination. S. Foster Damon takes Ahania, Urizen's emanation, as a figure of Pleasure, the figure who reappears as an unruly and oversexed woman in Cowper and More.[43]

Urizen sees his rejected feminine part as 'Sin'. Horrified at his own 'Lust' his sexuality becomes 'Unseen, unbodied, unknown,/ The mother of Pestilence' and the repression of sexuality produces the nightmare world of the 'corrupted continent'. David Worrall suggests that Urizen's imagination recalls the image of the flooding of the Nile, represented in 1791 in Blake's engraving of Fuseli's illustration *The Fertilization of Egypt* for Darwin's poem *The Botanic Garden*.[44] Urizen's blocked imagination produces a flood of monstrously fertile forms:

> For his dire Contemplations
> Rush'd down like floods from his mountains
> In torrents of mud settling thick
> With Eggs of unnatural production
> Forthwith hatching;   (E85)[45]

Cowper's early response to Madan in 'Love Abused' draws on the same trope of the mud of the Nile. He imagines lust contaminating the pure waters of the British Eden: 'And earth, a second Eden shows,/ Where'er the healing water flows'. But Madan threatens to unleash a flood:

> if from the dykes and drains
> Of sensual nature's fev'rish veins,

> Lust, like a lawless headstrong flood,
> Impregnated with ooze and mud,
> Descending fast on ev'ry side
> Once mingles with the sacred tide[46]

The flood breaks out from the 'dykes and drains' which should both contain and release pressure. Cowper's language is like that which Mandeville used to describe the social function of prostitution as 'those Drains and Sluices we had to let out Lewdness ... those Ramparts and Ditches within which the Virtue of our Wives and Daughters lay so conveniently intrench'd'.[47]

It is the terrifying recognition that the British Eden requires the operation of 'dykes and drains' that makes Cowper's response to Madan so powerful. These images return in Cowper's account of the monsters bred in the mud of the Nile by lust in *The Task* book II. The 'plague' that destroys society is found by Cowper in 'the skirts/ of the robed pædogogue' whose words pollute the land. The task of the poet is to follow the example of Moses in opposing falsehood:

> So when the Jewish Leader stretched his arm
> And waved his rod divine, a race obscene
> Spawn'd in the muddy beds of Nile, came forth
> Polluting Ægypt.[48]

Blake's *Book of Ahania* tells a different story. It is Urizen's refusal to recognise his own lustful thoughts as good that produces the language of Sin and Pestilence. Blake's annotation to Watson therefore potentially takes on a new meaning: if 'Sin' is the cause of earthquake, then that consciousness of sin is the production of Urizen. Ahania's narrative claims the right to challenge the authority of Urizen's account, creating multiple versions, competing truths. Cowper insists that 'truth' derives solely from the Bible, 'the fountain head', 'the sempiternal source/ Of light divine'. But Blake's rejection of the sole authority of the Hebrew scriptures in *All Religions are One* allows the fertile imagination of the writer to create as many stories as Ahania can babies:

> 10: When I found babes of bliss on my beds.
> And bosoms of milk in my chambers
> Fill'd with eternal seed
> O! eternal births sung round Ahania
> In interchange sweet of their joys.

11: Swell'd with ripeness & fat with fatness
Bursting on winds my odors,
My ripe figs and rich pomegranates
In infant joy at thy feet
O Urizen, sported and sang;   (E89)

These lines critique just the division between a female celebration of child-birth and a male fixation on apocalypse that Mellor sees in Romantic writers.

Mellor describes a 'feminine mode of thought' in the Romantic period which rejects the disruption of apocalypse but celebrates in the courtship novel the generational rhythms of reproduction and childbirth.[49] Yet women's writing in the period is for the most part singularly quiet on the subject of the bodily pleasures of sexuality, birth and reproduction. The courtship novel ends before sex takes place. Blake's celebration of bodily maternal pleasure recaptures a language of eroticism which is threatened in the period. Felicity Nussbaum explains the interest in polygamy in the period in part as a response to the new emphasis on breastfeeding among middle-class women which, she suggests, was seen as causing male sexual deprivation.[50] Hayley, indeed, records his father's refusal to allow his mother to breastfeed him on the grounds that 'she must inevitably injure the delicacy of her frame', a decision that, in tune with his time, he considers as a threat to his survival.[51] For Hayley, the erotic and the maternal are necessarily opposed. Urizen's rejection of Ahania similarly splits reproduction from pleasure. But in Ahania's 'babes of bliss' and 'bosoms of milk' sexual pleasure includes birth and suckling as an 'inter-change sweet of their joys'.[52] Whereas the Urizen narratives describe a rational fear of the body, Ahania's song is a celebration of maternity.

Cowper's opposition between the healthy country and the corrupt city is disturbed by the realisation that cities are 'nurs'ries of the arts/ In which they flourish most'.[53] In London philosophy finds 'her eagle eye/ With which she gazes on yon burning disk/ Undazzled, and detects and counts his spots.' 'All healthful, are th'employs of rural life', writes Cowper in book III (p. 123). With its account of the city as both diseased and fertile, Cowper repeats the pattern of Hogarth's satires on enthusiasm, linking the generation of visual imagery to the uncontrolled and sexualised response of the crowd. Even more troubling is that riot and the arts belong together: 'London is, by taste and wealth proclaimed/ The fairest capital in all the world,/ By riot and incontinence the worst' (p. 37). Cowper must therefore seek out forms of art, conversation, the news-papers, or thinking, which deny their own artificiality. *The Task* invents an image of art produced by asexual domesticity in contact with nature. Cowper dreams of a 'low-roof'd lodge' he calls 'the *peasant's* nest':

> And hidden as it is, and far remote
> From such unpleasing sounds as haunt the ear
> In village or in town, the bay of curs
> Incessant, clinking hammers, grinding wheels,
> And infants clam'rous whether pleas'd or pain'd,   (II, p. 13)

The pleasure of rural life lies in its escape not just from the 'mad multitude' but also from the 'unpleasing sounds' of work and children.

Hayley's *Life of Cowper* ends with Blake's design of Cowper's weather house and peasant's nest which are accompanied by lines from *The Task* book I:

> Peace to the Artist whose ingenious thought
> Devised the Weather-house, that useful toy!
> Fearless of humid air and gathering rains
> Forth steps the Man, an emblem of myself,
> More delicate his tim'rous mate retires.   (II, p. 12)

Blake's picture shows a world divided by gender: the woman stays indoors while the man ventures out. In front of the peasant's nest are Cowper's three hares, an experiment, according to Hayley, in 'educating a little group of tame Hares' (I, p. 89). Vince Newey sees Cowper's pet hares as an exercise in regulation that showed how the multitude could be controlled through education and labour and anticipated Hannah More's later social projects.[54] If Blake provided an image of two hares for Mrs Butts to work in needlepoint, as Essick suggests, the image may have suggested the regulatory function of the 'female will' to him.[55] In *The Task*, Spring is a careless mother who 'brings her infants forth with many smiles,/ But once delivered, kills them with a frown'. The bourgeois woman can create a safer embroidered version: 'A wreath that cannot fade, of flowers that blow/ With most success when all besides decay.' Bourgeois women redeem the careless habits of Nature, who epitomises the behaviour of the plebeian woman. This image becomes part of Albion's misguided search for virtue in *Jerusalem* book I:

> Vala! O that thou wert pure!
> That the deep wound of Sin might be clos'd up with the Needle,
> And with the Loom: to cover Gwendolen & Ragan with costly Robes
> Of Natural Virtue, for their Spiritual forms without a Veil
> Wither in Luvahs Sepulcher.   (*J* 1:21:12–16, E166)

Cowper imagines Nature as a philanthropic benefactor: 'Beneath the open sky she spreads the feast;/ 'Tis free to all – 'tis ev'ry day renew'd'. The fault of the poor is their own: 'Who scorns it, starves deservedly at home'.

Yet if Cowper seeks in nature an escape from the grotesque sexuality he associates with the city, this escape is never secure for the natural world he finds is always potentially sexual: the surface of the earth can split open at any point to reveal a gulf which is at the same time the womb and the grave. In this sense, Cowper's imagination is fundamentally like Blake's and unlike Darwin's. It is Cowper's sexual imagination that drives Blake's reconfiguration of Darwinian nature in *Milton*. The lamentations of Beulah over Ololon cannot see the sexual power of nature, a power which opens into eternity:

> Thou percievest the Flowers put forth their precious Odours!
> And none can tell how from so small a center comes such sweets
> Forgetting that within that Center Eternity expands
> Its ever during doors, that Og & Anak fiercely guard[.]   (E131)

When Blake uses the language and imagery of apocalypse, of a last harvest and vintage, of new heaven and earth, he does so with meanings which are shifted as drastically as he shifts such words as 'harlot' and 'virgin', or such figures as Rahab and the Whore of Babylon. Book 1 of *Milton* ends with an account of the harvest and the vintage but 'the Sons of Los' and 'the Labourers of the Vintage' turn out not to describe the end of the world but 'the Constellations in the deep & wondrous Night' that

> rise in order and continue their immortal courses
> Upon the mountains & in vales with harp & heavenly song
> With flute & clarion; with cups & measures filld with foaming wine.

If the stars 'continue their immortal courses' this is not an ending but the birth of a new order. The natural world becomes 'the Vision of beatitude,/ And the calm Ocean joys beneath & smooths his awful waves!' Blake's revision of Cowper removes the opposition between art and nature for the beauty of the natural world at the end of *Milton* book 1 is the work of the sons of Los: it is constructed, not natural, as surely as sentiment also is a construction: 'The Sky is an immortal tent built by the Sons of Los' (E127). Cowper's pleasure in *The Task* derives from watching the work of the labourer: 'Wide flies the chaff,/ The rustling straw sends up a frequent mist/ Of atoms sparkling in the noon-day beam.' Blake instead imagines the artist as a labourer.

THE PLEASURE OF THE PEEP-SHOW: COWPER
AND VISUAL CULTURE

The mind of the old maid, according to Hayley, produces a limited and vulgarised form of visual culture:

Her head may be compared to one of those raree-shew-boxes, which are filled with splendid and successive pictures of one magnificent object: at the first peep you may discern the temple of Hymen; the structure presently vanishes, but disappears only to make room for a more captivating view, either of the temple itself, or of some delightful avenue, which is terminated by the same noble edifice.[56]

The raree-shew-box is an image for culture as gaudy, meaningless spectacle, a standard trope in the period for spectacle rendered safe by miniaturisation and framing, a reduced version of Lavington's Eleusinian mysteries rather than the carnivalesque of Hogarth's enthusiasm satires. In *Tristram Shandy*, Toby's innocent looking is compared by Widow Wadman to the raree-shew: 'Honest soul! thou didst look into it with as much innocency of heart, as ever child look'd into a raree-shew box.'[57] This raree-shew is not just innocent but sexually damaged. In *The Sorrows of Young Werter*, love which is deprived of sexual fulfilment turns life into a peep show: 'It is the optic machine of the Savoyards without light. As soon as the little lamp appears, the figures shine on the whitened wall.'[58] Yet in the 1789 translation by Daniel Malthus, Werter defends the optical illusion for 'if love only shews us shadows which pass away, yet still we are happy, when, like children, we are transported with the splendid phantoms'. Here the technology of the peep-show facilitates erotic dreaming and Daniel Malthus's translation endorses the power of sexuality in a way that his son Thomas will not in his *Essay on Population*. The innocence of Cowper's peep-show view of the world is therefore questionable. The framing of the scene controls the danger and renders the 'great Babel' portrayed by Bowles and Carver as a safe form of entertainment:

> 'Tis pleasant through the loopholes of retreat
> To peep at such a world; to see the stir
> Of the great Babel and not feel the crowd;
> To hear the roar she sends through all her gates
> At a safe distance, where the dying sound
> Falls a soft murmur on the uninjured ear.[59]

Here the noise of the crowd is tamed and softened. When Blake's Milton calls on Ololon to free culture from the constraints of feminised politeness, 'To cast aside from Poetry, all that is not Inspiration/ That it no longer shall dare to mock with the aspersion of Madness/ Cast on the Inspired, by the tame high finisher of paltry Blots,/ Indefinite, or paltry Rhymes; or paltry Harmonies' (E142), he not only attacks sentimental culture but distinguishes between two versions of Cowper's poetry.

The culture war that Blake describes is acted out in illustrated editions of Cowper in the early nineteenth century. In 1806 Fuseli provided the illustrations for a new edition of Cowper's two-volume *Poems* printed for Joseph Johnson.[60] According to Farington, Fuseli considered 'Cowper the best of all the Poets of his period; above Hayley &c. & even Darwin. He had imagery and his stile was more perfect and pure'.[61] Reviewing Cowper's *Iliad* for the *Analytical Review*, Fuseli set Homer's epic vision in contrast to a fashionable and effeminate world: 'When we consider the magnificent end of epic poetry, – to write for all times and all races – to treat of what will always exist and always be understood, the puny laws of local decorum and fluctuating fashions ... cannot come into consideration.'[62] His review praises Cowper for restoring the otherness of Homer's voice and resisting the temptation to resolve difference: 'He neither "attempts to soften or refine away" the energy of passages relative to the theology of primitive ages, or fraught with allegoric images of the phenomena of nature, though they might provoke the smile of the effeminate, and of the sophists of his day.'[63] The 'effeminate' here is the reader locked into the values of his own age who laughs at primitive cultures. Fuseli singles out the scene of the 'toilet of Juno' in *Iliad* xiv as if in comparison with Pope's account of Belinda at her dressing table to suggest that Pope's Homer is contaminated by the feminisation of the age which Pope *affects* to satirise in the *Rape of the Lock*. Cowper (according to Fuseli) avoids this danger for although 'We are admitted to the toilet of Juno' there is 'no idle *étalage* of ornaments ready laid out, of boxes, capsules, and cosmetic'.[64] Precisely because the scene described by Fuseli lacks the jumble of a consumer culture it carries a strong erotic charge: 'the zone embraces her breast, perfumes rise in clouds round her body, her vest is animated with charms'. Fuseli thus defines a mode of sexuality which is distinct from that of the commercial world portrayed by Pope on Belinda's dressing table.

The two versions of the frontispiece 'The Poet's Vision' show both how Fuseli sexualises Cowper in 1806 and how his vision is revised for

Figure 16. Henry Fuseli, *The Poet's Vision* (unused design), 1807. © The Trustees
of the British Museum.

publication (Figures 16 and 17). In both versions, Cowper, reclining on
a sofa, receives inspiration from a muse. In the unused design, the
muse appears in a break in the clouds holding her lyre up and out of
Cowper's reach, her Grecian dress slipping to reveal her breasts. In the
sky behind, a horse which recalls Fuseli's *Nightmare* rears its head. The
poet reaches up to touch the muse or to grasp her lyre, slipping off his
couch and letting his books fall to the floor. Poetry, it is implied,
allows Cowper to access an erotic charge denied by his waking
thoughts. This undeniably erotic image was replaced for publication
by a soberer version in which the poet sleeps, lyre in his hands. He is
now safely asleep and the motherly muse remains fully clothed. Her
wings suggest the angelic and hint that her inspiration is spiritual
while only a mischievous watching child acts as chaperone for the

Figure 17. Henry Fuseli, *The Poet's Vision*, engr. Abraham Raimbach, pub. J. Johnson, London, 1 March 1807. © The Trustees of the British Museum.

encounter. Despite this revision Fuseli's Cowper illustrations offer a very different image from those of Richard Westall for an edition of 1810 published by John Sharp. Fuseli represents indoor scenes from Cowper, creating a kind of hothouse sexuality that emphasises the gendered, night time scene of contemporary pornography. Westall's illustrations instead show outdoor scenes and focus on nature rather than the private world of the imagination. Westall was the artist whom Boydell employed to illustrate *Milton* after the failure of the Milton edition that Johnson planned in the 1790s, edited by Cowper and illustrated by Fuseli. Westall's Cowper illustrations portray the poet that Hannah More revered in highly sentimental images of landscape that are extra-ordinarily detailed and cover the full page.[65] The cottager in 'Truth' is a docile figure who has clearly attended one of More's schools.

CHAPTER 6

Blake reads Richardson: anthologies, annotation and cultures of reading

In 1804 Blake claimed to be won over to Richardson, writing to Hayley: 'Richardson has won my heart I will again read Clarissa &c they must be admirable I was too hasty in my perusal of them to percieve all their beauty' (E754). James Chandler suspects 'one of those moments of tactical compromise with Hayley's polite culture that he later regretted' and sees Blake's hostile reference to *Clarissa* in his annotations to Boyd, written before the period at Felpham, as more revealing.[1] But Blake's remark may not be disingenuous if his model of feeling owes more to Fuseli than to Adam Smith. Fuseli saw *Clarissa* as the supreme work of feeling: in old age he insisted to his biographer Knowles that 'if Richardson is old, Homer is obsolete. Clarissa, to me, is pathetic – is exquisite; I never read it without crying like a child.'[2] *Milton* opens with a question about feeling. The Muses are commanded to 'Say first! what mov'd Milton' and again 'What cause at length mov'd Milton to this unexampled deed[?]' (E96). David Fallon suggests that this question recalls the moment in *Paradise Lost* book XI when Adam watches a vision of Cain's murder of Abel and Michael ('he also moved') echoes his emotion.[3] Milton's search for Ololon and Ololon's encounter with Milton allow the release of intense emotions that reshape identity.

Blake's response to *Clarissa* may be as complex as his response to *Paradise Lost* and as capable of identifying the multiple meanings of a text in his contemporary culture. The sentimental *Clarissa* that Chandler describes in which conflict is 'quite literally resolved into [a] specific set of sentiments' (p. 109) extracted and listed at the end of the book was not the only version that Blake might have encountered. A reader of the 1759 fourth edition added a comment on the critical debate that the novel produced, noting that Dr Johnson believed Richardson had taught 'at once Esteem & Detestation' towards Lovelace but that Dr Beattie feared 'some Readers will be more inclined to admire the gay profligate than to fear his Punishment'.[4] The meaning of *Clarissa*, like that of

Blake's poetry, is complicated by the presence of voices that cannot be securely controlled. Mary Wortley Montagu thought Richardson's novels likely to do 'more general mischief than the Works of Lord Rochester'.[5] Pointing to the repeated comparisons between Lovelace and Satan, Tom Keymer sees the attraction of Lovelace to many contemporary readers as 'a precise parallel' with 'Blake's famous remark that Milton "was a true Poet and of the Devil's Party without knowing it"'.[6] If Satan in the Bard's song of *Milton* is a Hayley-like modern polite liberal, does this mean that Blake covertly reads *Clarissa* from the point of view of Lovelace? The meaning of *Clarissa* depends on identifying a culture of reading, something that has proved difficult for modern readers of Blake's own texts. Although *Clarissa* has seemed to recent critics to confirm the cultural shift established by the rise of women as writers and as readers, how Blake and even how Hayley reads Richardson is less easy to determine.[7]

Hayley's 1768 edition of *Clarissa* was the revised version with added letters and footnotes which try to control the reader's response, blackening Lovelace and glorifying Clarissa further. That Blake sees *Clarissa* as a moral text is suggested by his 1800 annotations to Boyd which place Richardson below Homer on the grounds that 'the grandest poetry is Immoral the Grandest characters Wicked' (E634). Blake's positive comments in 1804, however, accompany a copy of Barbauld's newly published edition of Richardson's correspondence that Blake, now back in London, had collected for Hayley.[8] Claudia Johnson describes this edition as an attempt 'to assert the increasingly controversial authority of middle-class dissenters to speak on behalf of the nation'.[9] Richardson had seemed at the vanguard of progress in his ability to recognise and celebrate female virtue in Duncombe's 1754 *The Feminiad*. But after 1800 the role of 'the sex's friend' was being claimed by more conservative voices. Richardson was now seen by many as not only old fashioned but marred by the crudity of an impolite age. Jocelyn Harris describes how '[c]ultivated people read his correspondence with mingled distaste and merriment, not attending to the serious discussions of aesthetics and seeing only the plump little bourgeois printer immersed in the pettiness of daily life'.[10] Barbauld included a letter from Colley Cibber which described reading *Sir Charles Grandison*:

The delicious meal I made of Miss Byron on Sunday last has given me an appetite for another slice of her, off from the spit, before she is served up to the public table. If about five o'clock to-morrow afternoon will not be inconvenient, Mrs. Brown and I will come and piddle upon a bit more of her.[11]

Reviewing Barbauld's edition Francis Jeffrey picked on this letter as an example of the impoliteness of the age to which Richardson belonged.

Rather than apologise for his impoliteness, Barbauld's introduction celebrates Richardson's humble origins and emphasises the power of reading to make literature available to those without a classical education. Her Richardson is an original genius imagined in terms of Edward Young's 1759 *Conjectures on Original Composition*. She describes how the young Richardson found his inspiration in humble materials: 'Some observation struck the young sense; some verse, repeated in his hearing, dropt its sweetness on the unfolding ear; some nursery story, told with impressive tones and gestures, has laid hold on the kindling imagination, and thus have been formed, in solitude and obscurity, the genius of a Burns or a Shakespeare' (I, pp. xxxv–xxxvi). John Barrell has shown how conservative writers of the period constructed a fantasy of rural retirement which 'was itself thoroughly embedded in a political notion of how the poor should behave'.[12] Barbauld's account of Pamela's parents draws on the images used by Cowper and Hannah More and recaptures the figure of the cottage from conservative discourse: 'It is not the simplicity of Arcadian shepherds: It is such as people in low life, with the delicacy of a virtuous mind, might fall into without any other advantages than a bible education. It is the simplicity of an English cottage' (I, p. vxii).

This image is one that clearly appeals to Blake, who wrote in September 1800 to Flaxman of his Felpham cottage: 'It is a perfect Model for Cottages & I think for Palaces of Magnificence only Enlarging not altering its proportions & adding ornaments & not principals' (E710). For Blake, the cottage provides the model for the palace in a republican nation.[13] Barbauld insists that reading is 'still ... the cheapest of all amusements', available even to the manual labourer: 'the severest labour has its intervals, in which the youth, who is stung with the thirst of knowledge, will steal to the page that gratifies his curiosity, and afterwards brood over the thoughts which have been there kindled, while he is plying the awl, planing the board, or hanging over the loom' (p. xxxiv). Barbauld's manual worker enjoys the right to solitary brooding that Blake begins to question in his time at Felpham when he apologises that 'my Abstract folly hurries me often away while I am at work, carrying me over Mountains & Valleys which are not Real in a Land of Abstraction where Spectres of the Dead wander' (E716). The right to private reflection is potentially political in this period: in 1801 Thelwall describes the growth of his 'political enthusiasm' and explains that 'this enthusiasm had been fostered, rather than crushed, by the broodings of solitude'.[14] Richardson printed his novels on presses in his own shop and his control of his own process of production offers a model for Blake's own experiments in evading the rules of the fashionable market. Blake's pleasure in the Barbauld edition may therefore implicitly rebuke Hayley for what Blake sees as an attempt to edit him out of a culture which Hayley is ready to open to bourgeois women writers. Whereas Hayley encouraged women to write epic poetry in his 1782 *Essay on Epic Poetry*, he does not offer the same invitation to Blake.

Hayley, by contrast, must have been interested to read an edition of Richardson's letters published the same year as his own, largely epistolary, *Life of Cowper*, which quoted Pope's account of letters as 'Emanations of the Heart' and offered Cowper's letters as a contribution to England's claim to rival the literary culture of France.[15] Letters offer a kind of domestic intimacy, according to Hayley, 'gracefully displaying, without disguise and reserve, a most amiable character, and exciting by that display, a tender and lively affection in the reader' (p. v). Blake echoes this view in an 1801 letter to Butts that claims that the *Life of Cowper* 'will contain Letters of Cowper to his friends Perhaps or rather Certainly the very best letters that ever were published' (E716). Blake's surviving letters are quite different from the impolite, blunt, persona of the notebook. A culture that values letters as 'Emanations of the Heart' is also one that identifies the self within the limits framed by sociability.

'CLARISSA' AND THE MEANING OF RAPE

Margaret Doody sees Richardson's references to the rape of Lucretia, the event which led to the founding of the Roman republic, as a coded reference to the larger historical import of the story: 'To tell a rape story is a political act. A strong rape story is a story about the necessity for revolution' (pp. 108–9). In Doody's view, this revolution is not a 'further movement in the Whig or Tory direction' but 'the movement for the liberation of woman'.[16] This new understanding of the place of women is evident in Henry Boyd's introduction to his 1785 *Translation of the Inferno of Dante Alighieri*, which cites Hayley's call for a widening of epic in the notes to his 1782 *Essay on Epic Poetry*.[17] Hayley appeals to both Ariosto and Dante to authorise the celebration of femininity in *The Triumphs of Temper*, which carries an epigraph from Dante and announces an ambition to join the 'sportive wildness' of Ariosto with the 'more serious sublime painting of Dante'. Like Hayley, Boyd judges writing against the tests of feeling and delicacy: Dante is a 'venerable old Bard' (p. 27) who wrote 'before indelicacy became offensive' for 'rude and early Poets describe every thing, they follow nature to all her recesses' (p. 23).

The treatment of women is key to Boyd's discussion of the morality of the epic hero and takes as its test case the story of Dido and Aeneas:

Æneas indeed is a more amiable personage than Achilles; he seems meant for a perfect character. But compare his conduct with respect to Dido with the self-denial of Dryden's *Cleomenes* . . . Æneas, by the connivance of the Gods, leads the hospitable Queen of Carthage into guilt, and, by the command of the Gods, *piously* leaves her to ruin and despair.[18]

Although Blake continues to use moral categories, he appears to reject the test of morality: 'Every body naturally hates a perfect character because they are all greater Villains than the imperfect as Eneas is here shewn a worse man than Achilles in leaving Dido' (E633).

Yet Blake's assertion on his copy of Boyd's Dante that 'the grandest poetry is Immoral the Grandest characters Wicked' (E634) raises the possibility that, whatever he may assert to Hayley, he is a satanic reader of *Clarissa* who exploits the openness of the epistolary text to extract a libertine defence of free love. Lovelace also invokes the story of Dido and Aeneas but does so to justify his rape of Clarissa to Belford:

'Dost thou not think, that I am as much entitled to forgiveness on Miss Harlowe's account, as Virgil's hero was on Queen Dido's? For what an ungrateful varlet was that vagabond to the *hospitable* princess, who had *willingly* conferred upon him the last favour? . . .Yet this fellow is, at every word the *pius* Aeneas with the immortal bard who celebrates him.'[19]

If Lovelace's '*willingly*' is a blatant attempt to manipulate the reader (or himself or Belford), a misrepresentation highlighted by italicisation in the 1768 edition, he also, like Blake in the annotations to Boyd, sets the morality of the epic defined by the destiny of the nation against the morality of the novel which describes, as the subtitle to *Clarissa* puts it, '*The most Important Concerns of Private Life*'.

In one extended fantasy, Lovelace explores what society might be like if sexual partnerships could be dissolved at will by either party, a scheme he presents as 'infinitely more preferable' to 'the polygamy of the old Patriarchs; who had wives and concubines without number!' (v, p. 274). The scheme is presented as a return to natural freedom: 'could a man do as the Birds do, change every Valentine's day [A natural appointment! for Birds have not the sense, forsooth, to fetter themselves, as we wiseacre men take great and solemn pains to do]' (v, p. 270). Lovelace sounds momentarily like Oothoon when she celebrates 'Love! Love! Love! happy

happy Love! free as the mountain wind!' (E60), the voice of the couplet: 'He who binds to himself a joy/ Does the winged life destroy' (E470). The similarity seems to uncover Blake's utopianism as the voice of the self-interested libertine, endorsing the judgement of critics such as Anne Mellor and Robert Essick.[20] But there is a difference. Although Oothoon contributes to the same debate as Lovelace, she denies the coercive force of Lovelace's analogy with the natural world: 'wilt thou take the ape/ For thy councellor? or the dog, for a schoolmaster to thy children?' (E48). In resisting animal models – common to didactic works in the period – Oothoon refuses the reverse didacticism of Lovelace's libertine moralism, a moralism echoed in some late twentieth-century Blake criticism.[21] At the same time, whereas Lovelace is an inherently flawed advocate, Oothoon's utopian moment lacks the framing provided by character and narrative.

The ideas that Lovelace explores (however self-interestedly) bear comparison with Madan's attempt to enforce financial responsibility for male libertinism. Lovelace appeals to a tradition of civic humanist thought which looked back to Sparta as a state which produced active and masculine citizens and soldiers, proposing a means-tested tax payable to the state on each change of partner and state provision for any children subject to parental conflict who will be: 'considered as the Children of the Public, and provided for like the Children of the antient Spartans; who were (as ours would in this case be) a nation of heroes' (v, p. 271). His plan has something in common with Cumberland's utopian city of Sophis where children are raised by the community, attending a peripatetic school which tours the island learning (in Rousseauian mode) through practical example.[22] Lovelace claims that his plan would benefit women: 'I remember I proved, to a demonstration, that such a Change would be a means of annihilating, absolutely annihilating, four or five very atrocious and capital sins. – Rapes, vulgarly so called; Adultery, and Fornication; nor would Polygamy be panted after' (v, p. 271). The reader spots the irony but also hears an echo of the eighteenth century's long-standing debate about the regulation of sexuality. The words sound utopian: Lovelace believes that easily dissolved relationships would 'prevent Murders and Duelling', would do away with 'Jealousy (the cause of shocking violences)' and would increase female fertility. Warming to his theme, he imagines amicable partings between the lovers: 'Each, perhaps a new mate in eye, and rejoicing secretly in the manumission, could afford to be complaisantly sorrowful in appearance' (v, pp. 271–2). It is clear that the novel does not endorse Lovelace: the passage comes in a letter to Belford written shortly before the rape. Yet the fantasy provides a glimpse of an alternative destination for British culture in the eighteenth century. In letters such as this, *Clarissa* is part of the century's debate about the regulation of sexuality continued in the work of Madan, Cumberland, Hayley and Blake.

Richardson catches Lovelace within the nets of his narrative, which ultimately makes the task of detecting Lovelace's deception an easy one. While James Chandler identifies Blake's attack on the culture of sentiment as lying in the absence of connective links in the syntax of the lyric poetry, the assumption that a linear narrative, often quite a simple one, underpins Blake's poems is common in the most sophisticated readings. When Nicholas Williams, for instance, claims that the 'plot of' *Visions of the Daughters of Albion* 'is simply told' he constructs a sequential narrative which frames the strangeness of Blake's poem within a sentimental form, turning *Visions* into a version of *Clarissa*: 'She rushes to consummate her love with Theotormon, but is raped by the thunder god Bromion before she can reach him.'[23] Such narrativisation tends to introduce links that are missing for, as Martin Priestman points out, 'though "Bromion rent her with his thunders" certainly sounds like rape, Oothoon never makes an issue of her unwillingness'.[24] Equally problematic is Marcus Wood's attempt to make sense of the same poem in terms of narrative: 'The poem opens with the relationship of Oothoon and Theotormon. Oothoon, in a state of delight following their initial ecstatic, though apparently sexually unconsummated union, makes an impetuous crossing to America. She is immediately raped by Bromion.'[25] Here Wood introduces the curious motif of the 'impetuous crossing to America' (surely hard to arrange in the late eighteenth century unless like Oothoon you can walk on water) in order to make clear the assumption that Oothoon is an Englishwoman, one of the daughters of Albion.

Not only are the voices that make up *Visions* hard to ascribe to character roles and sometimes hard to tell apart but the narrative voice is also compromised, referring to Oothoon and Bromion as 'the adulterate pair' (E46), a description that might make sense to Theotormon but which sounds strange as an account of rape by a thunder god. Similarly odd is the simile that explains Oothoon's recovery: 'Theotormon severely smiles. her soul reflects the smile;/ As the clear spring mudded with feet of beasts grows pure & smiles'. Oothoon's dependence on approval from her lover is here endorsed within a beautiful image from the natural world. Rather than reflect on past experience, Oothoon's voice lacks a sense of self in its ability to reflect the feelings of others and in its openness to external experience. It is this openness that she tries to share with

Theotormon: 'I cry arise O Theotormon for the village dog/ Barks at the breaking day. the nightingale has done lamenting' (E47).

What is troubling about *Visions* viewed as a rape narrative is the implication that Oothoon achieves a form of liberation. When she speaks of her escape from a closed world ('They told me that the night & day were all that I could see;/ They told me that I had five senses to inclose me up' (E47)), it is hard to understand the time sequence: do these lines refer to her despair after the rape or to some earlier period before the poem begins? Even stranger is the ability of Bromion to sense the infinite nature of the world. It is his voice that reminds us:

> Thou knowest that the ancient trees seen by thine eyes have fruit;
> But knowest thou that trees and fruits flourish upon the earth
> To gratify senses unknown? trees beasts and birds unknown:
> Unknown, not unpercievd, spread in the infinite microscope,
> In places yet unvisited by the voyager. (E48)

Oothoon's words surprisingly suggest the unimportance of the event she has experienced. The 'happy copulation' and the 'lovely copulation' of which she speaks at the end of the poem evade the meanings produced by the narrative with which the poem opens.

The 'night' Oothoon escapes can therefore be read as the world structured according to a sentimental narrative of progress within which the crime of rape takes on a particular function.[26] Narratives of the period are fascinated with the subject of rape in particular because it stands for the world before the process of feminisation. With the rise of politeness, women were no longer thought to be living under the tyranny of men, and the civilising process was thought to be the guarantor of women's safety.[27] Martin Myrone identifies the painting on the wall behind the female readers of *The Monk* in Gillray's 1802 satire *Tales of Wonder* as a 'painting of a maiden seized (and thus saved from, or threatened with, rape) by a medieval warrior whose elongated limbs and dynamically stylized pose are unmistakeably evocative of Fuseli and his ilk'.[28] This caricature identifies the taste for rape narratives as part of bourgeois feminine culture. Hayley's *Essay on Old Maids* reminds his readers that 'the Roman empire was founded on a rape, and no less than six hundred and eighty-three Sabine virgins were forcibly converted into wives'.[29] The presence of rape in 'Oithona' proves to Hugh Blair both the antiquity of the poem (since it is a crime of the past) and the superiority of the civilisation of ancient Scotland since the response of the tribe recognises the affront to women: 'Women are carried away by force; and the whole

tribe, as in the Homeric times, rise to avenge the wrong.'³⁰ The treatment
of rape in this society reveals the level of refinement: 'The heroes show
refinement of sentiment indeed on several occasions, but none of
manners' (p. 18). In discovering rape as part of the modern world in
Visions of the Daughters of Albion, Blake dismantles the assumptions of the
enlightenment narrative: neither in Albion, nor America, nor the slave
plantations of Surinam has the civilising process done its job. The culture
that allows rape is not an 'other' place.

But Blake also attacks the threat of rape as a means of regulating
sexuality. Christopher Hobson is right to point out that the 'most
common sexual betrayal in the cautionary literature of the period, the
rape or seduction and abandonment of an unsuspecting girl, is made the
central situation of *Visions of the Daughters of Albion*, is alluded to in
America ... [E54], and is present as underlying threat in several of the
Songs, notably "The Little Girl Lost".³¹ But Blake attacks the regulatory
use of this threat. In 'The Little Girl Lost' it is the mother's fear that
disturbs Lyca's sleep ('How can Lyca sleep,/ If her mother weep') and the
child is as yet free from the fear central to the period's cautionary
literature: 'The kingly lion stood/ And the virgin view'd'. Alain Badiou
claims that the ethical system in place since the eighteenth century 'defines
man as a victim'; rather than an active subject, 'man is the being who is
capable of recognizing himself as a victim'.³² It is this culture of necessary
and universal victimhood that Blake attacks, creating the figure of
Oothoon to stand in contrast to the victim of sensibility, whether
Cowper's Crazy Kate or Richardson's Clarissa.

Whereas Oothoon rejects the identity of the victim of rape, the Preludium to *America* challenges the reader's ability to apply the label of rape.
The assumption that this scene is a representation of rape is virtually
universal within readings of the poem. The problem for most readers lies
in the lack of explicit condemnation of the episode: Christopher Hobson
argues that in the Preludium to *America* 'Blake presents the rape unprob-
lematically' and Helen Bruder sees the narrator as complicit in the scene
of rape.³³ Yet the assumption that the scene represents rape is itself flawed,
particularly since the response of the shadowy female's body is pleasure:
'It joy'd'.³⁴ The alternative that this scene simply describes a sexual
encounter is seldom considered, possibly because the Female's response
is physiological before it is affective: 'It joy'd' comes before 'She ...
smiled'. Sex is impersonal, and body parts are not part of a whole until
after the event: 'The hairy shoulders ... the wrists of fire ... the terrific
loins ... the struggling womb'. The passage epitomises the reversal of

cause and effect by means of which, in Chandler's account, Blake destroys the syntax of sentiment.[35] Importing a view of femininity as affective rather than sexual, the possibility that this is a narrative of mutual sexual desire seems too shocking for modern readers. The scene is read as rape because it is seen as part of a faulty narrative sequence in which seduction is the missing element.[36] It is more problematic to insist that this is an account of rape, for then the narrator, like Lovelace, assumes that rape will produce a compliant sexual partner.

Such a hypothesis is unnecessary both because we can have no access to the shadowy female's consciousness and because the event is not located in narrative sequence. If the treatment of sexuality in *Visions* and of physical attraction in the Preludium to *America* insists, as Hayley does in *An Essay on Old Maids*, on the reality of bodily pleasure in the face of a culture that in writing for women tends to obscure this possibility, it might make more sense to compare the Preludium to *America* with Hayley's reimagining of the book of Enoch in the *Essay on Old Maids*. Yet in contrast with Hayley, what is striking is that Blake avoids the trope of seducer (or rake) as educator in so far as sexual knowledge is not imagined as the preserve of the male. The women of *Visions* and the Preludium to *America* are always already aware of pleasure: Oothoon has 'plucked Leutha's flower', the womb in the Preludium is 'panting'. Unlike Hayley, who fetishises the virginity of Kunaza and sympathises with the libertine search for a virgin, Blake describes the sexual encounter of two virgins while at the same time challenging this category by describing the shadowy female as the 'virgin' *after* Orc's embrace: virginity can henceforth be found 'in a harlot, and in coarse-clad honesty/ The undefil'd tho' ravish'd in her cradle night and morn' (E54). Whereas Hayley offers a tale of seduction which culminates in forcible sex, both *Visions of the Daughters of Albion* and the Preludium to *Europe* begin with a sexual encounter. Sex is not the end of the story, as it is for Hayley and for Richardson in *Clarissa*, but the event which precipitates or allows the possibility of change. Whereas Clarissa loses her fluency after the rape and Hayley breaks off the narrative, the sexual experience of the Female is imagined as giving her a voice. Although she is 'dumb till that dread day when Orc assayed his fierce embrace', the Female becomes eloquent until the last line of the Preludium to *Europe*: 'I see it smile & I roll inward & my voice is past' (E61). If 'joy'd' refers to both pleasure and conception in the Preludium to *America*, the poem reveals an older view in which conception is dependent on orgasm. In so far as neither Richardson nor Hayley can write with any directness about female sexuality they belong to the new order.

The shift which *Clarissa* marks is to a new world in which female sexual pleasure becomes a functionless accident. E. J. Clery points out that by leaving open the question of Clarissa's pregnancy, Richardson leaves in doubt the 'last, faint hint of her carnal nature'.[37] Following Laqueur, Clery argues that it would not be possible to justify Richardson's assertion of the spiritual opposition of the sexes on anatomical grounds until early in the nineteenth century.[38] As early as Ian Watt's *Rise of the Novel*, the treatment of rape in *Clarissa* has been seen as epitomising what the novel can do: since rape by definition depends on the consciousness of the victim, the extraordinary lengths to which Richardson goes to allow the reader access to Clarissa's interiority are essential to prove that the act of sex was indeed rape and thus to clear Clarissa of the charge of sexual attraction. Ian Watt argued that the length of *Clarissa* is connected to the complexity of the sexual code within which Clarissa must operate: 'unawareness of sexual feeling on the heroine's part, which by others may be interpreted as gross lack of self-knowledge, if not actual dishonesty, becomes an important part of the dramatic development, deepening and amplifying the overt meaning of the story'.[39]

It is the lack of any such psychological interiority conceived of as separate from the body that makes it impossible to claim that the sexual act which begins the Preludium to *America* is rape. Blake's language of feeling is learnt from Fuseli's balletic bodies and Lavater's physiognomies that act feeling, refusing to separate body from soul or consciousness from physical experience. If Watt is right, the production of writing which records psychological interiority is a necessary prerequisite for the crime of rape to exist. But the failure of this cultural change to ensure female autonomy is suggested in a remark of Hayley in a letter to John Johnson: 'I thought you had known enough of feminine spirit, to know, that with the dear soft sex *silence generally means consent.*'[40] What Hayley learns is not to listen to 'the dear soft sex' but to observe the proprieties of the new order. Blair's comment might still be relevant: 'The heroes show refinement of sentiment indeed on several occasions, but none of manners.'

'CLARISSA' AS AN ANTHOLOGY

When Blake writes to Hayley, he has, he admits, only had time to skim Barbauld's edition:

I omitted to get Richardson till last Friday having calld thrice unsuccessfully <&> before publication have only had time to skim it but cannot restrain

myself from speaking of Mr Klopstocks Letters Vol 3–which to my feelings
are the purest image of Conjugal affection honesty & Innocence I ever saw on
paper. (E754)

Blake's reading technique is one which is typical of the user of anthologies, privileging the part over the whole and giving a new sense to Blake's
oft-quoted statement that 'To Generalize is to be an Idiot To Particularize
is the Alone Distinction of Merit' (E641). But if Blake read on, he would
have found in Barbauld a critic who explicitly rejects the readings of
conservative moralists, taking issue with the claim of Fordyce that the
heroine is exceptional, 'a rare pattern of chastity', as 'an idea very degrad-
ing to her sex'.[41] Richardson's triumph, she argues, is not the idealisation
of virginity but the continuation of purity after rape:

It was reserved for Richardson to . . . throw a splendour round the *violated virgin*,
more radiant than she possessed in her first bloom. He has made the flower,
which grew,

———— Sweet to sense and lovely to the eye,

throw out a richer fragrance *after* "the cruel spoiler has *cropped the fair rose, and
rifled its sweetness.*" (p. xcvi)

Blake might have remembered Oothoon's words: 'Sweetest the fruit that
the worm feeds on. & the soul prey'd on by woe' (E47). For Barbauld,
moral meanings are fixed by narrative sequence: *Gil Blas*, she warns, is
'a work of infinite entertainment, though of dubious morality' and
'rather a series of separate adventures than a chain of events concurring,
in one plan, to the production of the catastrophe' (I, pp. xvi–xvii). It is
when we get to the 'catastrophe' – in *Clarissa* the rape – that we know
who to trust.

Whereas Barbauld challenges conservative moralists, she rests the morality of her own reading in the connectedness of narrative and, in doing
so, shares the concerns of conservative contemporaries. The significance of
the rediscovery of the book of Enoch lay as much in its contribution to
breaking up the unitary authority of the Bible as to the story that it told.
For Cowper and More, the most important task was to teach methods of
reading that respected the authority of the whole over that of the part.
Cowper presents the cottager as a check to the rot of Voltaire's enlightened scepticism, a woman who 'for her humble sphere by nature fit,/ Has
little understanding, and no wit'. Poor but content, she presents an
exemplary understanding of the Bible for she 'Just knows, and knows

no more, her bible true,/ A truth the brilliant Frenchman never knew'.[42] Cowper's cottager is the model for Hannah More's 'Shepherd of Salisbury Plain' in the *Cheap Repository* series who is meant to show that the Bible produces unambiguous meanings but also reveals that a supposedly simple method of reading needs to be taught. In the mid-1790s, when Blake was engaged on the production of his Bible of Hell, the baffling books of *Urizen* and *Ahania* and *Los*, More's *Cheap Repository Tracts* attempt to convey to the newly literate poor a technique for reading the Bible safely. In doing so, as Kevin Gilmartin points out, More admits that the Bible requires the supplement of her own works: 'though "large" and "old", and "reverently" passed from generation to generation, the Bible is neither sufficient nor complete, and cottage literacy and discipline are instead vividly framed by More's own publishing enterprise'.[43] The shepherd explains his method:

I always avoid, as I am an ignorant man, picking out any one single difficult text to distress my mind about, or to go and build opinions upon, because I know that puzzles and injures poor unlearned Christians. But I endeavour to collect what is the *general* spirit or meaning of scripture on any particular subject, by putting a few texts together, which though I find them dispersed up and down, yet all seem to look the same way, to prove the same truth, or hold out the same comfort.[44]

More's commitment to the Bible as the single authorising text can be seen in the formation of the British and Foreign Bible Society in 1804 (the date which Blake set to the title pages of his *Milton* and *Jerusalem*), which is committed to 'the circulation of the Scriptures, and of the Scriptures only, *without note or comment*'.[45] But even for More, the fantasy of the wholly safe text was difficult to sustain. For ecumenical reasons the Bible Society agreed in the 1820s to include the Apocrypha in every Bible and this decision she only accepted grudgingly, to pacify 'the Papists': 'if the Papists will not take a Bible without it, is there any comparison between having a Bible with it, and having *no Bible at all*?'[46] Hannah More fears that uncontrolled meanings can be produced by fragmenting texts. Her worry is 'scepticism' which 'must break up the old flimsy system into little mischievous aphorisms, ready for practical purposes: it must divide the rope of sand into little portable parcels, which the shallowest wit can comprehend, and the shortest memory carry away' (VI, pp. 102–3). Breaking up texts is crucial to Blake. In *America*, Orc announces:

That stony law I stamp to dust: and scatter religion abroad
To the four winds as a torn book, & none shall gather the leaves;

But they shall rot on desart sands, & consume in bottomless deeps;
To make the desarts blossom, & the deeps shrink to their fountains,
And to renew the fiery joy, and burst the stony roof.   (E54)

The Bible is a loosely arranged collection of poetic tales like the Geez manuscript that Bruce brought back from Abyssinia, confirming the 'Fragment Hypothesis' of radical biblical scholars like Alexander Geddes who presented the Bible as poetry rather than as law.[47]

The moralisation of the narrative unity of the novel by women readers responds to the threat to reading practices from the use of anthologies to access literary culture. Although Barbauld imagined Richardson as studying 'the treasures of Shakespeare and of Milton, of Addison and of Locke', his literary references are for the most part drawn from Bysshe's *Art of Poetry*, a volume owned and used by both Blake and George Cumberland.[48] First published in 1702, with regular revisions up to the ninth edition in 1762, Bysshe's *Art of Poetry* offers a thematic collection of 'Allusions, Similes, Descriptions and Characters, of PERSONS and THINGS, that are in the best English POETS'. In 1736 Hogarth shows a copy of the *Art* on the desk of the Grub Street writer in the *Distrest Poet*.[49] William Gifford in 1791 blames Bysshe for the rise of a democratic literary culture: 'Happy the soil where bards like mushrooms rise,/ And ask no culture but what Bysche supplies!'[50]

Like the voices of *Visions*, Bysshe's text gives equal value to each excerpt. The first extract under FORTITUDE is Satan from *Paradise Lost* I:

> My Mind cannot be chang'd by Place or Time:
> The Mind is its own Place, and in itself
> Can make a Heav'n of Hell, a Hell of Heav'n. *Milt.*[51]

But no speaker is named and the result of the thematic organisation is to free the passages from control by author or context. Fragments of poetry become equally expressions of the Poetic Genius: each entry sets up an argument or definition, but does so without creating a narrative. Nevertheless, Bysshe's anthology is not value free, displaying a preference for Dryden and Restoration poets which cumulatively represents a specific culture. Bysshe provides Lovelace with a seducer's manual when he determines 'to act the part of Dryden's Lion' and quotes:

> *What tho' his mighty soul his grief contains?*
> *He meditates revenge who least complains:*
> *And like a lion slumb'ring in his way,*
> *Of sleep dissembling, while he waits his prey*   (1,237–8)

Lovelace has to be judged by his actions but Bysshe's categorisation also
offers a guide to how to read. If Lovelace seems to display nobility of soul
we only have to check Bysshe to find that the Dryden passage from
Absalom and Achitophel is filed under REVENGE. Clarissa, by contrast,
quotes from Elizabeth Carter's 'Ode to Wisdom', even if Richardson
provided her with the work of a female poet at first unknowingly. She
also uses Bysshe, most strikingly in 'paper x', the last of the fragmentary
scribblings which reflect the incoherence of her distress after the rape.
Bromion can momentarily access Oothoon's openness to experience, but
Richardson shows Clarissa creating new meanings from the same book as
her rapist.

In paper x the extracts are not identified by author but scattered across
the page, the typography setting some passages at right angles in a way
which destroys sequence (almost in the way Blake does in his inscriptions
on the Laocoön engraving). Three of the passages come from Bysshe's
DESPAIR, two from DEATH, one from ASTONISHMENT. But the final passage, taken like Lovelace's lion quotation from Dryden, *Absalom and
Achitophel,* is from LIFE:

> For Life can never be sincerely blest.
> Heav'n punishes the *Bad,* and proves the *Best.*

Clarissa's scribbled fragments seem to reveal the disintegration of the
identity that Richardson's novel celebrates: if a message of hope is buried
in her quotations, this meaning must be extracted by the reader, not
culled from a list of moral sentiments. Yet through her madness, Clarissa
clings to a sense of individual identity in a way that Oothoon does not:

> I cannot tell what – And thought, and grief, and confusion came crouding so
> thick upon me; *one* would be first, *another* would be first, *all* would be first; so I
> can write nothing at all. – at all – Only that, whatever they have done to me,
> I cannot tell; but I am no longer what I was in any one thing. – In any one thing
> did I say? Yes, but I am; for I am still, and I ever will be, *Your true –* (v, p. 303)

Individuality, defined here through the connection with Anna offered by
the letter, offers a hope of returning sanity, while the event is blotted out.
Elizabeth Bronfen sees the rape as causing 'the complete destruction of
any sense of self-esteem, of any self-supporting narcissistic sense of wholeness and value, so that ... her letters, following the event of rape, are
fragments articulating, in various modes, her sense of being "nothing"'.[52]
But Clarissa's insistence that 'I am; for I am still, and I ever will be, Your
true' here asserts an identity confirmed by affective connection, by what
Blake would call 'emanation'. Whereas Bronfen sees this breakdown as

the result of a loss of a sense of virtue, Barbauld and Wollstonecraft read *Clarissa* as asserting the continuation of her virtue. For Blake the crucial question seems to be that the female speaker should be able to give voice to her own experience. It is this problem that Oothoon confronts in language of extraordinary lyrical power. Clarissa's insistence that 'whatever they have done to me, I cannot tell' is echoed in Blake's notebook verse 'On the virginity of the Virgin Mary & Johanna Southcott': 'Whateer is done to her she cannot know/ And if youll ask her she will swear it so' (E501). The Virgin Mary 'cannot know' and Clarissa 'cannot tell' for neither as women have access to a language that includes sexual experience.

Leopold Damrosch sees 'The Sick Rose' as an ironic account of Clarissa's paper VII which calls on a familiar set of images to give form to her own sense of physical pollution:

Thou pernicious Caterpillar, that preyest upon the fair leaf of Virgin Fame, and poisonest those leaves which thou canst not devour! ... Thou eating Cankerworm that preyest upon the opening Bud, and turnest the damask Rose into livid yellowness! (v, p. 306)[53]

Read in tandem with paper VII, Blake's 'Sick Rose' shares the assumption contested by Barbauld, Wollstonecraft and Blake in *Visions* that rape destroys the purity of the victim. Whereas Clarissa's fragment speaks to the 'pernicious caterpillar', Blake's speaker addresses the rose and finds her sick. The parallel merely adds to the complexities of Blake's poem, raising the question of whether the anthropomorphising of botany offered by Darwin can naturalise conservative ideology, attempting to constrain human meanings within the rules of the 'natural'. This may explain why the Rosicrucian machinery used in *Milton* book II is 'Unforgiving & unalterable' (E131). The rejection of botanic analogy, after all, is a theme of Wollstonecraft's 1792 *Vindication* where she attacks Barbauld's use of flower imagery as part of 'a supposed sexual character'.[54] Contextual readings, however, can set up new meanings simply by changing the context. When Wollstonecraft refers to 'the worm in the bud' in the 1792 *Vindication* her allusion is to a passage from *Twelfth Night*: 'She never told her love/ But let concealment, like a worm i'the bud/ Feed on her damask cheek.'[55] If this is the worm in 'The Sick Rose', then it is the secrecy of the 'dark secret love' that makes her sick; the sickness is not caused by the male lover but by the rules of the social that enforce secrecy on female desire.[56]

Fragmenting the text, as More realises, allows the multiplication of readings and opens up the text to debate: the arguments of Lovelace can be considered irrespective of his actions; moments of pleasure can exist in *Visions of the Daughters of Albion* irrespective of the narrative succession of events that links the present to the past and the future. Whereas Richardson presents his work as a collection of familiar letters, Blake flaunts the fragmentary nature of his text, whether the mock anthology of *The Marriage of Heaven and Hell* or the reshuffled fragments that build into epics without continuity. Blake raids his own past work: lines from *The Book of Urizen* appear in the Bard's Song of *Milton*, although we would not expect that Urizen's hostility towards the body would become part of the voice of the Bard.

The critical valuation of fragmentary forms is now as standard in Blake criticism as More's or Barbauld's insistence on narrative completion was to their own historical moment. What is still questioned is the extent to which fragmentary reading and writing can be used to identify a specific cultural and political identity for Blake's work. Luisa Calè shows how the catalogue to Fuseli's Milton gallery 'disarticulates *Paradise Lost* at key junctures and excerpts climactic moments ... Expurgations and interruptions are marked by blanks between entries, and blanks and dashes within entries.'[57] At the same time Calè shows how Fuseli's gallery offers 'a montage of moving pictures', creating a narrative succession from visual images which in themselves tend to fragment temporal succession.[58] The tendency to celebrate disarticulation rather than (or as well as) wholeness is particularly evident in the annotations that an anonymous contemporary, possibly George Cumberland, wrote in ink against *Europe* copy D, now in the British Museum. The large majority of these annotations are drawn from Bysshe.

Most readers have thought that the annotations mutilate the text, defacing Blake's illuminations with uncomprehending attempts to find parallels which reveal merely the desperation of contemporaries.[59] But if the annotations are by Cumberland, they are the work of a friend and sympathiser: the fact that they are not even written on his own copy suggests that the comments were permitted by the owner of the book. H. J. Jackson argues that a 'very common use of marginalia during the period' was 'the circulation of manuscript notes as a way of disseminating personal opinions'.[60] They are not vandalism but suggest something of the expectations of the reading culture to which they belong. The annotations to *Europe* copy D read the images rather than the words, working to overcome one of the most familiar and difficult aspects of Blake's illuminated books, the frequent lack of correspondence between verbal and visual text. The annotator seems to value *Europe* for its images rather than its words and supplies parallel passages so as to produce a work which can be understood in isolation from Blake's own mythology, or his stories of characters with peculiar names. Cumberland's annotations function in a similar way to the two *Small Books of Designs*. Whereas for copy A Blake reprinted images from his illuminated books but masked out his text in order to produce instead something comparable to a visual anthology, a book of powerfully emotive images, in copy B Blake retitles his pictures with pregnant phrases which can be understood outside any narrative. Instead of characters and stories, the images represent powerful feelings and voices.

In *Europe* copy D, the annotations read images literally and piecemeal: plate 5 is titled by the annotator *A Comet*, using one of Bysshe's sections. Four quotations using the simile of a comet follow: from Rowe, *The Fair Penitent*, *Paradise Lost* II, Pope's translation of the *Iliad*, and Shakespeare *Henry* VI Part I. The organising principle of the annotations here is the simile, not the subject to which it refers following Blake's and Fuseli's practice as illustrators to choose to represent both the tenor and the vehicle of an image.[61] *Europe* does not include the word 'comet' which is used of Orc in *America*: the decision to turn to the word 'comet' in Bysshe therefore suggests knowledge of *America* as well as *Europe*.

Cumberland's marginal glosses can be seen as handing authority to the reader whose construction of meaning resists textual authority.[62] But if the annotation is seen as replacing Blake's challenging words with passages contained and explained by a title, they might be seen as rendering Blake's text safe. Cumberland may have been right when in March 1803 he refers in a letter to the Editor of the *Monthly Magazine* to 'A mind full of images, (such as the fruitful one of our own Blake)'.[63] But this form of fruitfulness may also be inherently lacking in power, allowing existing meanings to colonise the new text. David Erdman, however, takes the glosses as evidence that Blake 'inducted some people into the political meanings of even his more obscure symbols'.[64] Erdman assumes that there is a single correct reading of Blake's work and that this coded meaning was the shared possession of Blake's circle. Blake's illustration to the opening plate of the *Prophecy* (Figure 18), identified as *Pestilence and War*, shows, as Erdman points out, 'a female comet shaking evils from her hair, importing "change to times and states" and "Pestilence and War," according to George Cumberland's gloss'[65].

Cumberland's gloss, however, makes a suggestion exactly opposite to both the words of the plate and the likely Miltonic allusion. Whereas Milton's 'Prince of light' brings peace, Cumberland's gloss makes it clear that this child brings war.

Figure 18. William Blake, *Europe a Prophecy*, copy D, plate 5. © The Trustees of the British Museum.

If Blake's audience was limited to a handful of friends, who may have struggled to decode the meanings of his densely allusive and boldly revisionary work, then the illuminated books can be seen as representing a shrinking of possibility like that which Fuseli was lamenting at much the same period. But Cumberland's glosses represent a reader-centred process which takes material and imposes its own meanings on it. Cumberland uses Anne Radcliffe in a way which is more like Joanna Southcott's prophetic reading of Radcliffe than the reading methods of the educated. Cumberland announces the possibility of using all kinds of literature, even writers like Dryden and Pope whom Blake elsewhere associates with polite culture: 'Dryden in Rhyme cries Milton only plannd/ Every Fool shook his bells throughout the land' (E505). The marginal glosses impose a comprehensible narrative, turning the multi-layered mythology of Blake's

poem into a sequence which recognisably provides a radical's view of
Europe in 1793–4, a world in which the Assassin lurks to murder the
Pilgrim (in a poem from Radcliffe's *Mysteries of Udolpho*), 'Storms,
Tempests etc' announce (as in 'The Argument' to *The Marriage of Heaven
and Hell*) the coming turbulence brought by the *Comet* which titles plate
5 which leads to *War* (plate 7), *Mildews blighting ears of Corn* which
produces *Famine* (plate 9) and *Plague*.[66]

The titles of other plates remind the reader of the Gordon riots of the
previous decade since *Papal Superstition* leads to *Imprisonment* which is
overcome by *Fire*. Whereas the image of the final plate shows Los
carrying a dead woman and a fleeing child through encompassing flames,
Blake's text describes only 'The sun glow'd fiery red'. Once again, it is the
annotations that provide a clear link with the images, supplying (via
Bysshe) a passage from Blackmore's *Prince Arthur*: 'The impetuous
flames with lawless powr advance,/ On ruddy wings the bright destruction flies,/ follow'd with ruin and distressful cries,/ The flaky Plague
spreads swiftly with the wind/ And gastly desolation howls behind.'[67]
Whereas Blake's text seems to allude to the war with France ('in the
vineyard of red France appear'd the light of his fury'), Cumberland's
annotations recall the terrible memory of London burning in the Gordon
riots. Drawing on the rag bag of Bysshe's anthology, Cumberland creates
a coherent reading of *America*, unbothered by the triangulation of meaning between image and now two rival texts. Cumberland's annotations,
like the anthology from which (most) are drawn, happily raid Milton,
Homer, Virgil, Dryden, Shakespeare, Blackmore, Garth, Mason and
Beaumont and Fletcher to provide a narrative of the fears and hopes of
the 1790s.

Whereas anthologies strip poetic similes of context, freeing them for
reuse within a new frame of reference, they also preserve access to lost
cultural possibilities, splitting open the surface of a work to reveal meanings that are buried. Bysshe may be used by Richardson (and Lovelace),
Cumberland and Blake because his fondness for a Restoration sexual
culture offers a counterweight to new codes of sexuality. Blake's notebook
allows another glimpse of his reading practices on a Sunday at home in
August 1807: 'My Wife was told by a Spirit to look for her fortune by
opening by chance a book which she had in her hand it was Bysshes Art of
Poetry. She opend the following' (E696). The extract is from Aphra
Behn's 'On a Juniper-Tree, cut down to make Busks', a poem that typifies
the association between softness and desire: 'I saw 'em kindle with Desire/
While with soft sighs they blew the fire'.[68] Like the ending of *Visions*, this

poem describes a scene of voyeurism: the lovemaking of the couple is watched by a tree which is cut down at the end of the poem to make the stiffening parts of a corset. Behn, however, introduces an element missing from Blake's scene: a consumer culture which frames sexuality within the language of fashion, here in the form of a garment that lifts and offers the breasts to view. Although the poem emerges from an aristocratic culture of libertinage, the work of a royalist, in the anthology which Catherine held in her hand the lines belong less to an author than to a topic: the passage is the first extract under the heading 'Enjoyment'.[69] Read in this context, the entries (thirteen passages of Dryden and Dryden translations, Otway, Cowley, Rochester, Milton, Lee) present a Lucretian account of sexuality which is part of the natural world but also links body and soul, invoking a sexual ideology which would happily accommodate the works of Fuseli's friend, John Armstrong.

Blake uses Bysshe in a different way from Richardson. He is not above quoting from Bysshe to provide a title in *For Children* (1793) from Dryden's version of *The Knight's Tale*.[70] But for the most part he does not embed Bysshe's extracts but creates anew following Young's model of original composition: 'He that imitates the divine *Iliad*, does not imitate *Homer*, but he who takes the same method, which *Homer* took, for arriving at a capacity of accomplishing a work so great.'[71] It does not seem coincidental that Catherine's volume opens at 'Enjoyment', a long section made up of explicit erotic description. Barbauld recalls the old joke that books tend to open at or near favourite passages, unwittingly revealing the erotic preoccupations of the female reader: *'The Ladies' Library*, described in the Spectator, contains *"the Grand Cyrus*, with a pin stuck in one of the leaves, and *Clelia*, which opened of itself in the place that describes two lovers in a bower" '(p. 72).

If use made the volume fall open at 'ENJOYMENT', a fortuitous alphabetical juxtaposition means that it also opens at a section on 'ENTHUSIASM. See *Sybil*' (Figure 19).[73] Dryden's translations provide the greatest number of extracts in this long entry, a choice which might surprise us for, as Shaun Irlam points out, Dryden himself fears the power of enthusiasm, drawing 'a direct correlation between the figural interpretation (detortion) of scripture by religious Enthusiasts – Swift's "converting imaginations" – and a threat to the polity.'[74] Dryden fears the loss of authorial control: 'The Book thus put in every vulgar hand,/ Which each presumed he best could understand'.[75] In constructing an anthology heavily weighted towards Dryden but organised in terms of metaphor and figure, Bysshe subverts the intention of Dryden's work, which

Figure 19. Edward Bysshe, *The Art of English Poetry*, 2 vols., 1762, vol. I, pp. 194–5.
© The British Library Board (11603cc18).

according to the preface to *Religio Laici* is suspicious of the force of figuration: 'The Florid, Elevated and Figurative way is for the Passions; for Love and Hatred, Fear and Anger, are begotten in the Soul by shewing their Objects out of their true proportion.'[76]

More surprisingly, given Blake's opposition of the classical Daughters of Memory to the biblical Daughters of Inspiration in the preface to *Milton* (E95), the section on 'Enthusiasm' creates a classical genealogy, locating the concept in Virgil's account of the Cumaean Sibyl in *Aeneid* VI. This is the passage in which Virgil separates true from false inspiration, associating false inspiration with the prophetic frenzy of the Sibyl and with the religions of Asia Minor and further east. As Steven Connor explains,

Virgil engineers Aeneas's exposure to the frighteningly incontinent and dis-ordered voice of prophecy in order precisely to suggest the necessity for its control and formalization. The female seer is allowed privileged access to the divine voice in order that she will embody the lesson of the need for temperance.[77]

The first passage that Bysshe quotes is from Dryden's translation of the prophetic frenzy of the Sibyl in *Aeneid* VI:

> He comes: Behold the God! Thus while she said
> Her Colour chang'd, her Face was not the same,
> And hollow Groans from her deep Spirit came:
> Her Hair stood up; convulsive Rage possess'd
> Her trembling Limbs, and heav'd her lab'ring Breast:

This is the passage that provides Fuseli with the inscription 'FALSA AD COELUM MITTUNT INSOMNIA MANES' for the *Allegory of a Dream of Love* that was discussed in chapter 2. I argued there that the dream of love was not necessarily seen by Blake as delusory and the location of this passage by Bysshe within the category of 'Enthusiasm' complicates the attempt to distinguish between classical and biblical contexts even further. Swift and Lavington use Virgil's negative account of the Sibyl's frenzy to associate Catholic and Protestant sects with paganism and thus associate enthusiasm with a female bodily rapture. 'Enthusiasm' in the passages in Bysshe is possession by a god which leaves the female subject powerless and terrified. The Sibyl (in an image that Mary Shelley will use in her preface to *The Last Man* to suggest the female origin of prophecy) writes the words of the oracle on 'flitting leaves, the sport of ev'ry wind', like Orc in the Prophecy of *America*, who scatters 'religion abroad/ To the four winds as a torn book, & none shall gather the leaves' (E54).[78] Virgil's Sibyl, 'Struggling in vain, impatient of her Load,/ And lab'ring underneath the pond'rus God', also sounds like the unnamed female of the Preludium to *America* and to *Europe*. Enthusiasm here is an ecstatic state of inspiration over which the self has no control, a frenzied rapture. In the extract from Dryden's *Oedipus*, enthusiasm is imagined as birth: ''Tis great, prodigious! 'tis a dreadful Birth', a metaphor which reappears in the Preludium to *Europe* where the shadowy female labours to give birth to ideas: 'I wrap my turban of thick clouds around my lab'ring head;/ And fold the sheety waters as a mantle round my limbs' (E61).

Bysshe uncovers the prehistory of the negative genealogy which Milton uses in the allegory of Satan, Sin and Death in *Paradise Lost*, which reappears in satiric accounts of enthusiastic religion in the eighteenth century, and which Blake uses again in the Preludium to *America* and to *Europe.* The instruction to Catherine to open Bysshe's *Art of Poetry* is itself an example of possession by a spirit. So also is the voice of the Bard in *Milton*: 'The Bard replied. I am Inspired! I know it is Truth! for I sing/ According to the inspiration of the Poetic Genius' (E107–8). The Bard's confidence, which has worried readers, comes from speaking another's words. The Bard here knows that 'it is Truth'. In one version of *America*, the words of the Bard seem to horrify him: '*The stern Bard ceas'd, asham'd of his own song*' (E52). In Bysshe the experience is one of loss of control and the language sounds like rape:

> The more she strove to shake him from her Breast,
> With more and far superior Force he press'd;
> Commands his Entrance, and without Controul
> Usurps her Organs and inspires her Soul.

Yet this disordered state is more productive of change than the female dream ushered in by Enitharmon. It is this poetic genealogy that reappears throughout Blake's work, not only in accounts of the possession of female figures but also in the union of Blake and Milton, Milton and Los, or Los and Oothoon.

Because the language within which Blake imagines the transport of the shadowy female is that of the classical attack on female prophecy, we might assume that he sets it in opposition to the religious enthusiasm of the Bard, but this opposition depends on an antipathy between the classical and the Hebraic which does not operate in the early poetry. To achieve this separation, Blake would need to side with Swift and Lavington in their attempts to cast the religious enthusiasm of the Quakers, Methodists and Moravians as inherently pagan through an association with the ecstatic body of the female prophet. The female prophetic mode of the Preludiums describes an order in which offspring are free of parental control: as the shadowy female laments,

> I bring forth from my teeming bosom myriads of flames.
> And thou dost stamp them with a signet, then they roam abroad
> And leave me void as death: (E61)

The game the Blakes play, in which Bysshe is opened at random to discover the reader's fortune or a prophetic message, is a reading practice specifically associated with 'enthusiasm'. Adam Clark's 1800 *Letter to a Methodist Preacher, on his Entrance into the Work of the Ministry* warns against 'that disgraceful custom (properly enough termed) Bibliomancy: i.e. divination by the Bible ... I need scarcely observe', Clark explains, 'that this consists in what is called dipping into the Bible, taking passages of scripture at hazard, and drawing indications concerning the present and future state of the soul.'[79] Lavington had singled out the practice of using the Bible to draw lots as typical of Methodists: 'they have another way of knowing the Divine will, which is by casting *Lots*; and particularly by *opening the Bible*, where the *first passage* that offers itself to the *Eye* is to be their *Rule*.'[80] Lavington's aim is to discredit the Methodists and Moravians as following 'papist' and 'pagan' practices:

The *Heathens* had various ways of doing it: – as by jumbling together *loose Letters*, or *Words*, in an *Urn*, and making what Sense they could of such as were taken out by chance; – by dipping into some *Book* of high esteem, as *Homer*, or *Virgil*, and then applying to their purpose the first passage that offered itself, &c. (I, p. 70)

Although particularly important to Moravians, 'Bibliomancy' was a sign more generally of an impolite culture like that still flourishing in Joanna Southcott's writings into the nineteenth century: one in which books have magical properties. As Jacqueline Pearson points out, drawing lots by means of the *sortes Virgilianae* is a feature of women's reading in the period.[81] Books in *The Task* can be dangerous, semi-magical objects, 'talismans and spells/ By which the magic art of shrewder wits/ Holds an unthinking multitude enthrall'd' (II, p. 236).

Blake's (playful) use of such practices shows that he can find in classical and female literary culture a means of accessing inspiration. Female literary activity is both proof of the highly developed nature of society and of the ability of women to access a disintegrated self. But *Clarissa* challenges the assumption that the loss of coherent identity is to be celebrated, making the failure to achieve the identity offered by polite culture equivalent to siding with the rapist Lovelace. In her 1792 *Vindication*, Mary Wollstonecraft argues the need for 'a strong individual character'. Standing armies, she thinks, are technologies for acting out the fantasy of a few: 'because subordination and rigour are the very sinews of military discipline; and despotism is necessary to give vigour to enterprises that one will directs'.[82] Without a coherent self people become 'like the waves of the sea', mere tools for acting out the fantasies of their leaders as soldiers act out the kind of chivalric fantasy that both Cowper and Burke imagine:

A spirit inspired by romantic notions of honour, a kind of morality founded on the fashion of the age, can only be felt by a few officers, whilst the main body must be moved by command, like the waves of the sea; for the strong wind of authority pushes the crowd of subalterns forward, they scarcely know or care why, with headlong fury. (p. 97)

The construction of 'a strong individual character' is the effect of *Clarissa* and of Wollstonecraft's bourgeois feminism, a kind of individuality that structures identity against the disorganisation of Blake's lamenting females, from Oothoon, to Ahania, to Enion. That is why there are no females in Blake's eternity, for strength is necessary to intellectual war. At the same time, the ability of Blake's characters to split and metamorphose into emanations and spectres, to speak with other voices and divide into a multitude is itself a means of accessing other experiences. Wollstonecraft assumes that 'the strong wind of authority pushes the crowd of subalterns forward, they scarcely know or care why'. But Blake seems to assume that every person within the crowd is unique, differentiated by his own viewpoint which will 'know or care why': 'No man can think write or speak from his heart, but he must intend truth. Thus all sects of Philosophy are from the Poetic Genius adapted to the weaknesses of every individual' (E1). The dispersed identity of the female which echoes and laments is also, in the form of Jerusalem, the voice of the nation.

   This chapter offers an account of a fragmented reading which in many ways parallels Jon Mee's use of the term 'bricolage' to describe Blake's method. But I have also suggested that this process of cutting and pasting, reusing and fragmenting belongs with a feminised culture which encourages such processes as Grangerisation and extra-illustration. Andrew Lincoln has criticised Mee's account of bricolage as insufficiently specific to account for Blake's work because 'such combination is a feature of many different kinds of writing'.[83] Lincoln offers the example of Pope's combination of 'elements derived from classical epic with descriptions of modern "Dulness" in The Dunciad' to argue that the 'subversion of hegemonic authority from such transformative "recombining" of discourses ... is a common feature of many kinds of writing' (p. 233). Lincoln's claim is that the recombination of 'elements from across discourse boundaries such that the antecedent discourses are fundamentally altered in the resultant structures' is simply a definition of literature.

   What makes Mee's model distinctive, however, is that it associates Blake's form of transformative 'recombining' with an openness typical of the self-educated, or that Iain McCalman sees as typical of a particular culture of 'seekers'. It is not just that the result is different, as Lincoln is aware in his comment that Pope's use 'may intend to defend rather than undermine hegemonic values', but that the recombination works in a different way (p. 233). Saree Makdisi is preemptively aware of Lincoln's query in his 2003 account when he admits that 'In principle ... there is actually nothing unusual about this aspect of Blake's work. Whenever a text of whatever kind is cycled through – read in – different contexts, its meaning changes; that, after all, is what reading is all about.'[84] Whereas for Mee, the recombination of the bricoleur seems to allow an unself-conscious raiding of discourses, for Makdisi, what is special about Blake's work is that it forces on the reader a greater degree of self-awareness:

> Far more than most literary and artistic work, Blake's reminds us of the extent to which all texts are open and virtual; and hence, far more than most, it frees us from the determinism of those texts that pretend to be closed and definite – texts which are, for example, constitutive of 'state trickery'. (p. 169)

This chapter aims to reconsider and to differentiate between forms of this culture of fragmentation and recombination, including bourgeois reading practices particularly associated with women in the period. Of course overturning of fixed meaning threatens to depoliticise art, containing it within a safe sphere like that of Beulah. Indeed, the ability to freely change the meanings of discourses so beloved of critics reappears, as Frances Ferguson points out, in criticism of *Clarissa*:

> Lovelace has appeared in the role of the artist who is committed to a proliferation of meanings, and, in the terms of William Warner's deconstructive account of him, he has continually dispersed and recreated himself to acknowledge the absurdity of the connection between any particular form and any particular significance.[85]

Blake seems to realise both the danger of misreading and the danger of the constitution of the bourgeois sphere of art as play.

Keri Davies shows that some of the first purchasers of Blake's illuminated poems were keen book collectors who may have valued the work as aesthetic object rather than prophetic warning.[86] In tracing Blake's decision to adopt a labour-intensive method of book production, Michael Phillips has also suggested that Blake responds in 1793 to surveillance by neighbouring counter-revolutionaries in Lambeth by moving away from methods of reproduction which would appear to the authorities to belong with cheap and thus dangerous political handbills towards a safer, because more expensive and aesthetic (indeed also more obscure), form of prophetic illuminated poetry. By going up-market, Blake evades the imminent danger of imprisonment.[87] The culture of the unique artist's book certainly appealed to Hayley, even though he does not seem to have purchased any of Blake's illuminated books. His *Memoirs* tell of his passion for splendid books; while still at Eton he had six volumes 'transcribed in his own hand, and bound by the celebrated bookbinder, Roger Payne' (I, p. 28). The library for which Blake painted the heads of the poets was one of his chief pleasures. Producing the unique set of Gray's poems for Ann Flaxman in 1798, just before moving to Felpham, Blake worked within a form associated with feminine culture, cutting a printed text of Gray's poems and surrounding them with his own water-colour illustrations. Blake works at the limit of his bourgeois culture, always at risk of being recaptured by the sleepy world of Beulah.

CHAPTER 7

A 'blank in Nature': Blake and cultures of mourning

In February 1798, George Cumberland wrote to Horne Tooke with a worry about the representation of Mercury's sandals in the frontispiece to *The Diversions of Purley*. In the image that Sharp had engraved, Cumberland thought that 'it was impossible to say whether [Mercury] was taking off or putting on his Sandals and winged appendages'. He suggested that Horne Tooke should replace the image in the second edition with a new version in which it would be clear 'that he was pulling them off'.[1] Cumberland recommended 'that neglected man of genius, and true son of Freedom Mr Blake, as your engraver' for the job.[2] Why did it matter, and why did Cumberland think that Horne Tooke would go so far as to replace the image with one engraved by Blake?

A second puzzle: in the Bard's song of *Milton*, Los announces a day of mourning by a perplexing action: 'Los took off his left sandal placing it on his head,/ Signal of solemn mourning' (E101).[3] This 'mournful day', Los claims, 'Must be a blank in Nature' (E102). Although the meaning of a 'blank in Nature', as of the curious business of the sandal, is opaque to Blake's readers, the repetition of the words 'mournful' and 'mourn'd' make emphatic a theme that will continue into book II where Ololon descends 'With solemn mourning into Beulahs moony shades & hills/ Weeping for Milton'. It may be that Los's action inverts the characteristic gesture of the epic hero: in Cowper's *Odyssey*, a translation that Blake used at Felpham when he studied Greek with Hayley, the action of tying on a sandal is the formulaic prerequisite for the hero's journey, as when Telemachus sets off in book II: 'Athwart his back his faulchion keen he slung,/ His sandals bound to his unsullied feet,/ And, godlike, issued from his chamber-door'.[4] Two copies of *Milton*, after all, announce that 'Shakspeare & Milton were both curbd by the general malady & infection from the silly Greek & Latin slaves of the Sword' (E95). It is tempting also to see a link with Mercury's action of taking off his sandals which Cumberland saw as critical to the understanding of *The Diversions of*

Purley, a work in which Horne Tooke insisted on the materiality of language, denying the conservative claim that language describes acts of mind.[5] Blake's readers are often faced with a choice of whether to read apparent echoes and allusions as confirmation or parody. This chapter will suggest that the 'blank in Nature' that Los announces both parodies the neoclassical conventions of the visual language of mourning and invokes Horne Tooke's radical materialism. Blake's visions of heaven in illustrations for Blair's *Grave* in 1805, in the frontispiece for Malkin's 1806 *A Father's Memoirs of his Child* and in a series of versions of the Last Judgment on which he worked from 1805 to 1810 not only reject the sentimental conventions of pity but also insist on the bodily nature of the spiritual. It is with the consequences of these moves for the relationship of public to private in Blair's *The Grave*, and with the role of women in the *Vision of the Last Judgment*, that this chapter is concerned.

Although Los has a strange idea of 'solemn mourning', Blake's visual representations of death spoke powerfully to his own time. In these projects, Blake can be seen to address a specific audience, adapting his work to their particular requirements. Engraved by Schiavonetti, Blake's illustrations to *The Grave* were to become his best-known work in the nineteenth century: *Death's Door* in particular, according to Joseph Viscomi, 'was to Blake then what *Ancient of Days* is now'.[6] If, once again, we take Hayley's taste as an index of a dominant bourgeois culture, Blake's ability to speak his language of mourning is revealing. Hayley certainly possessed the copy of *Poetical Sketches* given to him by John Flaxman in 1784 as well as copies of the *Life of Cowper* and *Ballads* for which he commissioned engraving work, but *The Grave* seems to be the only work by Blake that remained in Hayley's library at his own death.[7] Just four days after the death of Hayley's son Blake shared his own sense of the absence and the presence of the dead: 'I am very sorry for your immense loss, which is a repetition of what all feel in this valley of misery & happiness mixed ... I know that our deceased friends are more really with us than when they were apparent to our mortal part' (E705). Blake offers 'a brothers Sympathy' for a grief which is at the same time particular and general. Yet he also signs his letter 'Your humble Servant' as if the sentimental culture of mourning which pretends to join sufferers in a family of the bereaved simultaneously reinstates class difference.

In Blake's time a shared language of epigraphs, memorials and grave-yard literature contributed to the recognition that private loss is 'a repetition of what all feel'. Philippe Ariès saw this as a time when the afterlife could be imagined as a continuation of a domestic bourgeois world, indeed the Swedenborgian belief that heaven contains families, children, schools and homes typified the bourgeois reshaping of heaven. [8] Even the death of royalty could be seen as a loss within the family; Hannah More's 1805 *Hints towards Forming the Character of a Young Princess* had set out a scheme of education that aimed to turn the monarchy into an exemplary bourgeois family and the public mourning at the early death of Princess Charlotte showed the success of her project.[9] In 1805, More announced the death of the idea of the public that had been crucial to civic humanism, contrasting republican Rome and modern Britain: 'In the former, the *public* was everything; the rights, the comforts, the very existence of *individuals*, were as nothing. With *us*, happily, the case is different, nay, even exactly the reverse' (I, p. 108). It took Shelley's 1817 *Address to the People on The Death of the Princess Charlotte* to make clear the political implications of the transposition of a bourgeois culture of sentiment to the public sphere.

The illustrated edition of Blair's *Grave* potentially contains Blake's vision within a culture that could present the death of a princess as a 'repetition of what all feel' as it evacuates the public sphere of conflict. Whereas Hogarth used *Enthusiasm Delineated* in 1760 to voice a concern about the disorderly viewers of the first public art exhibitions, critics in the early nineteenth century seem concerned instead about the function of art within the home. The illustrated *Grave* offers an image of the Last Judgment in a book available to all within the home while Blake's 1809 exhibition was held on the first floor of the house in which he was born and grew up.

THE 'WORLD' AND THE 'FAMILY FIRE-SIDE'

Malkin's *A Father's Memoirs of his Child* belongs with Hayley's *Memoirs of Thomas Alphonso Hayley, the young sculptor* (published as part of Hayley's own memoirs in 1823) and, to some extent, Godwin's 1798 *Memoirs of the Author of the Vindication of the Rights of Woman*[10] in so far as it belongs to a distinctively new genre of the domestic memoir, making public a grief that is rooted in a close personal bond. Malkin's text includes the letters written by his son, who died at the age of six, together with the narrative of the child's illness and death written by his wife Charlotte. Malkin was clearly anxious about the publication both in so far as it trespasses on private grief and in that it suggests that the public could be interested in the life of a young child. His 1795 *Essays on Subjects Connected with Civilization* announces confidently that 'With regard to any apology for the temerity of authorship, it is a commonplace compliment to the public, which may well be spared'.[11] *A Father's Memoirs*, however, reveals considerable, surely non-conventional, anxiety. The prefatory letter to Thomas Johnes (to whom Malkin gave a copy of Blake's *Songs of Innocence*) describes conversations in which 'it was impossible for me not to dwell on an event, which had drawn a deep furrow over the level of my happiness'.[12] Malkin explains that he was first persuaded to 'transmit a short sketch of this little life' to the *Monthly Magazine* (p. iii). The longer book he presents as a response to readers who 'required the sanction of some avowed authority' for his account of his exceptional child (p. iv). Still, however, Malkin hesitated, 'considering, how differently the world estimates the effusions which give pleasure by the family fire-side' (p. iv).

Although published by Longman, Malkin's book remains a semi-private undertaking, and although a thousand copies were printed most were never sold.[13] Its role is to afford some 'relief to the feelings' of the 'survivor' as well as being 'a tribute to' the merit of the 'departed' (p. iii). Malkin's model is that described by Esther Schor as 'the social diffusion of grief through sympathy'.[14] He therefore aims to follow Adam Smith's rule that the sufferer who longs to see his grief mirrored in his spectators, to see 'the emotions of their hearts, in every respect, beat time to his own', must work 'by lowering his passion to that pitch, in which the spectators are capable of going along with him'.[15] It is this necessary moderation of passion that produces the 'pity' which, according to Los in the Bard's song of *Milton*, 'divides the soul/ And man, unmans'. 'Man', in Blake's view, is a being capable of intense feeling. It is Urizen's creation of 'Laws of peace, of love, of unity:/ Of pity' (E72) that Blake regrets, not the human capacity for feeling. The Eternals in *The Book of Urizen* flee at the sight of the first female ('They call'd her Pity, and fled' (E78)) because reason denies feeling and creates sexual difference to control its power.

Charlotte Malkin's narrative survives in a private notebook intended as a record of her children's infancy which she began, perhaps as a new year's resolution, on 1 January 1801. It is this account that Benjamin Heath Malkin incorporates in his *Memoirs* with slight editorial changes. The notebook opens with a statement of intent; it is, she writes:

A Book, in which I wish to preserve the memory of any particular circumstances that relate to my children; such as any questions asked, or observations made by them which are in my estimation worth remembering: concerning that it will be both useful and pleasant to me to look back in future years (should they be granted me) to a little register of their early habits; to see in their own words their manner of expressing the ideas that arise in their infant minds; and to review their progress in virtue and knowledge, with more certainty and satisfaction, than I could do from memory alone unassisted by some such records.[16]

It is a selective record of the speech of the child chosen according to the tests of utility and pleasure which nevertheless aims to preserve unchanged the children's own voices. Charlotte managed only two further entries that year, on 3 February and 20 April. By the time she picked up her book again in September 1802, Thomas was dead. Writing only a few weeks after his death she entered instead a detailed account of his illness, death, post mortem and burial. Charlotte claims not to regret her failure 'to write down the various things said and done by my dearest Thomas'. The child's letters and writings now provide her 'greatest treasure'. In her belief that letters record and preserve the individuality of her lost son, Charlotte imbues them with the presence of voice: they allow that 'converse daily & hourly' which Blake believed he could achieve with his long-dead brother.

Memory, however, is always potentially a source of torment – a word particularly associated by Blake with the 'dark visions of torment' recorded in *The Book of Urizen* (E70). In *Jerusalem* Vala describes a world of suffering in which the poor and dispossessed 'view their former life: they number moments over and over;/ stringing them on their remembrance as on a thread of sorrow' (E164). Although suffering is caused by the injustice of man-made poverty, Vala's image recalls Locke's account of the dangers of association which he exemplifies in the pain of a bereaved mother: 'The Death of a Child, that was the daily Delight of his Mother's Eyes, and Joy of her Soul, rends her all the Torment imaginable; use the Consolations of Reason in this Case, and you were as good preach Ease to one on the Rack, and hope to allay, by rational Discourses, the Pain of his Joints tearing asunder.'[17] Bereavement reveals both the limits of rationality and the dangers of association for 'some, in whom the Union between these Ideas is never dissolved, spend their Lives in Mourning, and carry an incurable Sorrow to their Graves'. Adam Smith also illustrates the dangers of excessive sympathy through the example of maternal feeling. He describes how a mother transfers to her view of her sick child 'her own terrors for the unknown consciousness of its disorder'.[18] This process explains the human fear of death which transposes the fears of the living to a dead body that does not feel. Mourning can become excessive when 'we endeavour, for our own misery, artificially to keep alive our melancholy remembrance of their misfortune'.

Blake's period was fascinated by memory: according to Nicholas Dames, the great discovery of the eighteenth century was 'a powerful, detailed, dispersed faculty of "pure" or "desultory" memory'.[19] By contrast, Dames takes Elizabeth Bennet's injunction in *Pride and Prejudice* to 'Think only of the past as its remembrance gives you pleasure' as epitomising the beginning of a new idea of memory.[20] I suspect that Dames's new model is in fact a continuation of the sentimental culture of mourning described by Adam Smith which aims to contain and moderate pain. Charlotte Malkin's statement of intent in her new notebook is certainly in line with Elizabeth Bennet's advice: both women are concerned to control memory and to evade its dangers. For Wollstonecraft, a crucial benefit of education for women is the ability to construct abstract ideas through generalisation, a mental power that provides an enhanced ability to control feeling.[21] Transformed into a book of mourning, however, Charlotte Malkin's journal threatens instead to perpetuate pain. Conscious of the dangers of memory, therefore, Benjamin Heath Malkin edits his wife's private record to produce a public narrative.

Malkin also tries to edit out a third category of mourning, the dissolution of the self in the flight of enthusiasm. He welcomes the lapse of time since the death of his son which allows him to execute 'his censorial functions' (p. xiii), a censorship which protects against the opposite dangers of melancholy or enthusiasm: 'Under the influence of a calamity not yet overpast, the mind must either have lost its spring, or have been wound up to the opposite extreme of wild and hyperbolical enthusiasm.'[22] Writing only weeks after the death, Charlotte Malkin finds release in the flight of feeling – moments of religious rapture marked by one, two or three exclamation marks, ending her narrative with the words:

May we be found patient and resigned under so heavy a dispensation; and may we be prepared, by the exercise of every Christian virtue on earth, to meet our heart's best hope & joy in that blest abode, where we shall never more know the anguish of separation from him, but rejoice with him eternally in the presence of our God and Saviour!!——.

The published account chooses a different conclusion:

His star has faded from among the glories of this world: yet we believe that he still must occupy his sphere of usefulness in the system of creation, and pay homage to that Being who brought him out of nothing, but who will not reduce the lowest of his accountable creatures to that from which they came. (p. 162)

Charlotte's language of rapture is here replaced by a partially classicised apotheosis incorporated within a moderate language of Christian devotion.

What Benjamin Heath Malkin excises from his wife's account is the language of feminised enthusiasm: a language of rapture and of vision, of certainty and of angels. The danger of enthusiasm to women is a theme of Ann Batten Cristall's 1795 *Poetical Sketches*, the work of a friend of Wollstonecraft to which the Malkins (both 'B. Malkin, Esq. Hackney' and 'Mrs Malkin, ditto') subscribed in 1795, the year their son Thomas was born. Cristall explores both female feeling and sexuality in poems such as 'The Triumph of Superstition' and 'The Enthusiast' with characters that rival Oothoon's impetuous feeling and Bromion's tyrannical sexuality. In 'The Enthusiast', Arla's enthusiasm is expressed in loosely metrical poetry, expressive of 'force' and 'energy': 'Her soul was meek, her energy was strong,/ And force divine fir'd each seraphic song.'[23] Not only does enthusiasm set loose her passions ('The dormant passions of her nature woke') but it provokes visions: 'Angels she saw descending from on high,/ Unfolding all the wonders of the sky,/ And caught a glimpse of the DIVINITY' (p. 159).[24] Although Charlotte Malkin's father was the master of Cowbridge grammar school and her writing is fluent and highly literate, scarcely marred by deletions or misspellings, her private narrative is touched by the language of enthusiasm. Her husband edits this out, but their choice of Blake to work on the frontispiece allows the visionary language of enthusiasm to be discreetly invoked. The long excursion which introduces Blake in the preface, a digression to which a number of contemporary reviewers took exception, includes a discussion of Blake's enthusiasm which, according to Malkin, explains Blake's relative failure: 'Enthusiastic and high flown notions on the subject of religion have hitherto, as they usually do, prevented his general reception, as a son of taste and of the muses.'[25] Blake also confirms Malkin's belief that exceptional individuals (like his own dead son) are unlikely to experience life happily. As a figure representing what his son might have become, Blake stands not only for the genius but for the voice of the child and his poetry embodies the qualities that Malkin cuts from his wife's account. Displaced on to the visual, located in an artist, Malkin can still access and appreciate this language, attacking those who 'criticise the representations of corporeal beauty, and the allegoric emblems of mental perfections' (p. xxiii).

For Charlotte Malkin, heaven is a place of what her husband calls 'corporeal beauty'. It is 'that blest abode, where we shall never more know the anguish of separation from him, but rejoice with him eternally in the presence of our God and Saviour'. The first 'him' is not God but her son Thomas. The scene she describes is represented by Blake as *The Meeting of a Family in Heaven* in *The Grave*: in this image the family includes parents and children of diverse ages. God is nowhere to be seen and the spiritual forms of the dead carry their family positions with them into eternity.

This image, which would have carried no surprises to Swedenborgians, flouts Adam Smith's warning of the danger of transposing the feelings of the living to the dead. There is marrying in this bourgeois heaven. By contrast Albion has to remind Vala in *Jerusalem* that 'In Eternity they neither marry nor are given in marriage' (E176). The same biblical text (Matthew 22:30) is echoed in the last line of Wollstonecraft's *Mary* with the heroine sure that 'she was hastening to that world where there is neither marrying, nor giving in marriage'.[26] The heaven imagined by Blake's illustrations to *The Grave* and by the Malkins (who were deeply involved in this project) is one in which personal identity survives. Hayley's *Life of Cowper*, by contrast, reveals Cowper's doubts about the continuation of individual identity after death, quoting a letter from Cowper to his aunt in which he doubts 'whether we shall know each other' for 'the ties of kindred, and of all temporal interests, will be entirely discarded from amongst that happy society, and possibly even the remembrance of them done away'.[27] In Blake's illustration for *The Grave* a reunited husband places his hand tenderly on his wife's bottom: not only will families be reunited but bodily pleasures will form part of the heavenly state (Figure 20). It is surely conceivable that the heaven to which Wollstonecraft's *Mary* hastens contains bodily pleasure even though it lacks marriage.[28]

Malkin's voice is typical of the rational discourse of the Johnson circles: Godwin records his presence at dinner with Horne Tooke in 1796 and 1797 and on 17 May 1800 he attended the dinner for academicians at Fuseli's Milton Gallery along with Fuseli, Flaxman, Hoare, Johnson, Smith and many others.[29] His republican sympathies are evident in his 1795 *Essays on Subjects Connected with Civilisation*, which was attacked by Mathias in 1797 (BR223 fn). In this work, Malkin not only defends Paine implicitly but Wollstonecraft's 1792 *Vindication* explicitly, praising her for 'setting those prejudices in a strong point of view, which have prevailed to the exclusion of half our species from the common rights of humanity, and the unfettered exercise of reason'.[30] Malkin 'subscribes 'most cordially to the truth of her philosophy' and refers 'the reader for proof to the perusal of her arguments' (p. 260). Nevertheless he draws back from Wollstonecraft's 'wild wish ... to see the distinction of sex confounded in society, unless where love animates the behaviour'.[31] Malkin expects his reader to be shocked by Wollstonecraft's claim to have 'conversed, as man with man, with medical men, on anatomical subjects; and compared the proportions of the human body with artists' and is 'clearly of opinion, that the distinction of sexual character should be strongly marked'.[32]

The meeting of a Family in Heaven

Figure 20. William Blake, *The Meeting of a Family in Heaven* from Robert Blair, *The Grave*, 1808. © The British Library Board (c142e11).

Malkin's feminism is more cautious than Wollstonecraft's or Blake's and although he admits women to rationality and men to feeling he is careful to exclude the realm of the body and sexuality from his dream of a more equal world.

Fuseli's 1805 prospectus to *The Grave* presented Blake as an artist able to imagine the spiritual truths of death and eternal life within images drawn from the 'familiar and domestic'. The 'Author of the Moral Series before us', Fuseli writes 'has endeavoured to wake Sensibility by touching our Sympathies with nearer, less ambiguous, and less ludicrous Imagery, than what Mythology, Gothic Superstition, or Symbols as far-fetched as inadequate could supply' (BR211). Blake is now 'Author' rather than artist, working within the world of the 'Moral', of 'Sensibility' and of 'Sympathies'. As several critics have noted, it was the claim that Blake could 'connect the visible and the invisible World' that reviewers seized upon.[33] Robert Hunt in the liberal journal the *Examiner* insisted that 'the utter impossibility of representing the Spirit to the eye is proved by the ill effect it has on the stage' and selected an example from *The Tempest*: 'When the spirit Ariel, who should be viewless, and always fleeting as the air, appears, it is by means of legs which run no faster than her shoulders' (BR259).

Despite the male pronouns in Shakespeare's text, Ariel was played by female actors from the Restoration until the early twentieth century, in accord with the feminisation and sexualisation of the fairy world by Pope and others.[34] Rejecting the project of visualising Shakespeare (which had been crucial to Fuseli's career), Hunt tries also to insist on the contrast between the immateriality of polite femininity and the animality of Sycorax. The rejection of the pictorial representation of spirits as bodies is therefore a gendered issue.

Discussing the criticism, Robert Essick points out that Blake's practice of 'representing spirits with real bodies' (E541) conforms with 'most Western art from classical antiquity to the early nineteenth century' in which 'physical representation was given to gods, spirits of the dead, angels and other spiritual beings'.[35] But this convention was not always transparent and had previously been challenged within Christian iconography. Michelangelo's *Last Judgment* was itself a statement of the corporeality of heaven: Marcia Hall shows that 'what Michelangelo has represented is not simply judgment, but the Second Coming of Christ when everyone will be issued a new spiritual body to replace the worn-out physical body of earthly life'.[36] The problem for the reviewers of *The Grave* was specifically what they saw as the sexualisation of the spiritual and in their criticism sexuality acquires a new definition. James Montgomery, who liked the volume on its first appearance, wrote in 1854 that 'several of the plates were hardly of such a nature as to render the book proper to lie on a parlour table for general inspection' (BR277). At the same time, the relative success of Blake's illustrations to *The Grave* suggests that it may have been the perceived eroticism of the treatment that formed its attraction to a culture concerned to police sexuality.

In so far as *The Reunion of the Soul and the Body at the Last Day* (Figure 21) represents the body and the soul as equally embodied the image rejects the distinctively nineteenth-century assumption that women are more spiritual and less sexual than men. Robert Hunt was

Figure 21. William Blake, *The Reunion of the Soul and the Body* from Robert Blair,
The Grave, 1808. © The British Library Board (c142e11).

particularly concerned about how the female soul was to get inside the
male body. Hunt assumed that re-entry was to occur via the mouth:

The mouth of the lower figure is certainly a little open, but if this aperture is to
admit the body, I beg pardon, the soul above, it is somewhat too small, as it is no
longer than the mouth of the upper body, or soul!! To be sure, that figure is soul, and
can therefore enter without any difficulty or squeezing into ever so small a cranny,
just as MILTON describes his spirits contracting or enlarging at will. (BR260)

Blake answers this objection in *Jerusalem* where the Saviour reminds
Albion that in Eden 'We live as One Man; for contracting our infinite
senses/ We behold multitude; or expanding: we behold as one,/ As
One Man all the Universal Family' (E180). Like Albion, Hunt's mind
flips between the logic of time and eternity: 'the body, I beg pardon,
the soul'.

Appropriately for a culture which rests on an act of creation through the Word, Hunt imagines the soul as breath. But in *The Book of Urizen* Los creates the body through a combination of effortful physical work and the work of looking as he 'Kept watch for Eternals' (E73). As an image which can be read as a representation (though an odd one) of earthly lovers locked together in rapturous reunion, the *Reunion of the Soul and the Body* comes closer to the conventions of polite erotica than most of Blake's work, showing a clothed soul but a partially naked male body whose slipping garments reveal muscular, rounded buttocks, an image perhaps appealing to the female viewer. The overlapping faces, locked together by a beam of vision that runs from eye to eye, repeat a pose that is used to represent physical eroticism by a series of artists that Blake would have known, from the lovers below the pulpit in *Enthusiasm Delineated* to James Barry's 1800 *Jupiter and Juno on Mount Ida* (Figure 22).

In Blake's version, the visual language shared by polite pornography, by satires of religious enthusiasm and by classical art is used to envision the resurrection of the body. Instead of rising up to heaven, however, the resurrected body is joined on earth by the descent of the soul to form a renewed earthly life. Defying gravity, the falling soul will not squash the male body but join with it. The earth splits as the gravestones that recall Urizen's laws fall to the ground. Whereas the eye of the male figure (the body) is seen foreshortened in perspective, the eye of the female figure (the soul) is rendered schematically or as if part of a face turned towards us. We see the process of transformation by which two faces in profile change into a single face turned directly to the viewer. The two mouths join to produce a single mouth as in an optical trick. The image presents to us the morphing of two into one as the female enters the male through eyes, nose and mouth. In Blake's illustrations to Gray's 'A Long Story' the masculine domestic space of the poet was penetrated by young female visitors and in this image from Blair's *The Grave* we see female penetration of a male body. Whereas Blake's writing in the 1790s, in *Visions*, and in the Preludium to *America*, seems to describe male penetration of a female body, his late work is concerned instead with visual and verbal images of the female penetration of male space.

'TRULY GRAND AND REALLY POLITE'

It was the miniature painter Ozias Humphry, who in June 1806 had helped Blake get permission to dedicate his *Grave* designs to the queen, who also facilitated the commission of the Petworth *Vision of the Last*

Figure 22. James Barry, from A Series of Etchings by James Barry, Esq. from his Original and Justly Celebrated Paintings, in the Great Room of the Society of Arts, *Jupiter and Juno on Mount Ida, c.* 1804–5. © Tate, London, 2010.

Judgment.[37] For a writer and artist whose work centres on the moment of apocalypse and who viewed Michelangelo as the greatest of all artists, the ambition to represent the Last Judgment comes as no surprise. Nor is it surprising that Humphry should have set up a commission for Blake's work from Lord Egremont, a major patron of the arts who commissioned important work from Flaxman. Blake had almost certainly been introduced to Egremont at Petworth by Hayley when he was a near neighbour at Felpham. As a member of the Committee of National Monuments (known as the 'Committee of Taste'), Lord Egremont was involved in the decision to commission Flaxman to produce a monument to Nelson in St Paul's cathedral in 1807.[38] Yet Blake, it seems, conceived of the 1808 Petworth *Vision of the Last Judgment* quite specifically as a work for a female patron, the Countess of Egremont: in drafts of a letter to Humphry in January and February 1808 Blake writes that the work was 'completed by your recommendation [under a fortunate star] for The Countess of Egremont [by a happy accident]' (E552).[39]

Most commentators assume that the Petworth *Vision of the Last Judgment* was commissioned by Lord Egremont and addresses a male audience. This assumption may be encouraged by the 'misogyny and asceticism' of a subject which Steven Goldsmith understandably reads as showing the 'apocalyptic consummation of Babylon' which 'marks the end of all evils attached to material existence, from the imperfections of fallen language to the equally dangerous temptations of the female body'.[40] In the lengthy description of the *Last Judgment* drafted in 1810, Blake explains that his picture shows the harlot '[bound] seized by Two Beings each with three heads they Represent Vegetative Existence. <as> it is written in Revelations they strip her naked & burn her with fire' (E558). Such a topic might seem particularly inappropriate to Blake's female patron.[41] The Countess of Egremont, born Elizabeth Ilive, had been Lord Egremont's mistress since about 1784 when she was fifteen and, though the relationship was not exclusive, she was soon established, as 'Mrs Wyndham', the mistress (in that other sense) of Petworth. Her background is unknown (a family history suggests unhelpfully that her father was either 'on the staff at Westminster School' or 'a Devonshire farmer, or a Surrey rector'). In 1801, however, when Blake was staying in nearby Felpham, Egremont married his mistress of seventeen years by whom he already had seven children. The countess was a woman of wide-ranging interests who had won a silver medal from the Society for the Encouragement of Arts, Manufactures, and Commerce for designing a new form of lever for lifting heavy weights.[42] In December 1798, Joseph Farington describes 'Mrs. Wyndham, who lives with Lord Egremont' calling to see his pictures: 'She professed to have a great delight in painting and devotes much of her time to it.'[43] He reported that 'she seldom comes to town, not oftener than once a year, but thinks she shall come in the Spring to see the Orleans collection which I mentioned to her. – She appears to be abt. 36 years old.' Two days later, Farington writes that 'Hayley is in great favor with his Lordship' and describes how 'they went for a change to Hayleys house' when 'one of his children by Mrs Wyndham died' which 'affected them much'.[44] At just the date at which Blake's illustrations for Flaxman of Gray's 'A Long Story' provide a positive image of the generosity of an aristocratic lady, Mrs Wyndham was running up two receipted bills (dated 1798–9 and 1800–1) with Flaxman for 'plaister statues' and 'for models'.[45] Artists were welcome to visit Petworth and Farington is struck by Hayley's report that 'when there was no company they dined with Lord Egremont & Mrs Wyndham only'. This he considers 'as handsome a reception as they could reasonably expect'. Mrs Wyndham, or from 1801, the Countess of Egremont, seems to have acted as a link with visiting artists.[46]

By 1803, however, the countess was separated from her husband of two years and had moved out of Petworth. Farington's diary for 1804 mentions that she 'lives separate from Him in a House in Orchard St' and in 1807 Egremont bought her a house in Fulham.[47] Although in 1807 Farington reports having heard from Daniell, on whom she had just called, that 'Lord & Lady Egremont are to live together again' it seems likely that she enjoyed a considerable degree of autonomy as a viewer and purchaser of art. She clearly continued to visit artists' studios in London and if Blake's studio was on her list in 1807 she would already have been able to see the 1806 version of *The Last Judgment*, now in Pollok House Glasgow. It seems likely that both the purchase of the Petworth *Last Judgment* and the version of *Satan Calling up his Legions* described in the *Descriptive Catalogue* as dedicated to 'a Lady' reflect the taste of the countess rather than her husband, whose manner Farington (no democrat himself) describes as 'not likely to please at first' since '[t]here is a great deal of the Peer about Him, the effect of a habit of superiority'.[48]

Whereas Blake would have associated Lord Egremont with the classical imagery of commemorative sculpture, *The Vision of the Last Judgment* offers a 'blank in Nature' that disrupts the colonisation of the afterlife by bourgeois mores. Blake's notebook dedication suggests a certain intensity:

> What mighty Soul in Beautys form
> Shall dauntlessView the Infernal Storm
> Egremonts Countess can controll
> The flames of Hell that round me roll
> If she refuse I still go on
> Till the Heavens & Earth are gone   (E480–1, deletions omitted)

In this poem the countess is a positive figure of female power; or, as Farington puts it in 1807, she 'looks very well. She is abt. 40 years old'. The Petworth *Vision of the Last Judgment* is conceived for a very different audience from the bourgeois reviewers (whether liberal or anti-Jacobin) who objected to the bodily nature of Blake's imagination in the illustrations to *The Grave*: one that offered a flagrant rejection of the mores of bourgeois society.[49]

It is relatively straightforward, I think, to trace the influence of Fuseli's view of the role of the passions in Blake's conception of the Last Judgment. In his 1801 Academy lecture on 'Invention', Fuseli criticises

Michelangelo's limited account of the passions: 'Michael Angelo has wound up the destiny of man, simply considered as the subject of religion, faithful or rebellious; and in one generic manner has distributed happiness and misery, the general feature of the passions is given, and no more.' Fuseli contrasts this with a speculative account of how Raphael might have handled the subject:

he would have combined all possible emotions with the utmost variety of probable or real character: a father meeting his son, a mother torn from her daughter, lovers flying into each other's arms, friends for ever separated, children accusing their parents, enemies reconciled; tyrants dragged before the tribunal by their subjects, conquerors hiding themselves from their victims of carnage; innocence declared, hypocrisy unmasked, atheism confounded, detected fraud, triumphant resignation; the most prominent features of connubial, fraternal, kindred connexion.[50]

Even though Fuseli describes this as an account of 'all possible emotions', his list focuses on the reconciliation of conflict, on 'a father meeting his son', 'enemies reconciled'. Fuseli saw Raphael as a dramatic rather than epic painter and as such is the painter of sympathy and of private affection: Fuseli's later lectures suggest that Raphael is more fitting than Michelangelo to the privatised character of modern society.[51] This is not what Blake provides in *Jerusalem*, where Los hears 'in deadly fear in London … raging round his Anvil/ Of death' the sounds of deformed sympathies and private hatreds: 'The Soldiers fife; the Harlots shriek; the Virgins dismal groan/ The Parents fear: the Brothers jealousy: the Sisters curse' (E159).

Raphael was particularly admired by both Flaxman and Lord Egremont, and Ozias Humphry's commission from Blake for the *Last Judgment* followed immediately on his success in selling Egremont a painting by Raphael. Since Fuseli had presented Blake as the artist of the domestic and the familiar, Humphry may have offered him as capable of attempting a view of the Last Judgment that would contain 'all domestic, politic, religious relations; whatever is not local in virtue and in vice'. Blake replaces what Fuseli describes as the 'ostentatious anatomy' of Michelangelo's figures with more fluid and androgynous forms.[52] Where Michelangelo was innovative in his inclusion of a group of women, Blake goes further in including families, children and couples embracing.[53] Blake's 1810 description of the subject specifically addresses a female reader: 'The Ladies will be pleasd to see that I have represented the Furies by Three Men & not by three Women It is not because I think the Ancients wrong but they will be pleasd to remember that mine is

Vision & not Fable The Spectator may suppose them Clergymen in the Pulpit Scourging Sin instead of Forgiving it' (E557). One female visitor to Petworth estimated that the earl had forty-three children and the meeting up in heaven of all those complex relationships could have been a complicated business: the 'Ladies' that Blake addresses here are free from the constraints of 'Moral Virtue'. In 1810 Blake insists that Heaven is a place of passions:

Men are admitted into Heaven not because they have <curbed &> governd their Passions or have No Passions but because they have Cultivated their Understandings. The Treasures of Heaven are not Negations of Passion but Realities of Intellect from which All the Passions Emanate <Uncurbed> in their Eternal Glory The Fool shall not enter into Heaven let him be ever so Holy. Holiness is not The Price of Enterance into Heaven Those who are cast out Are All Those who having no Passions of their own because No Intellect. Have spent their lives in Curbing & Governing other Peoples by the Various arts of Poverty & Cruelty of all kinds Wo Wo Wo to you Hypocrites Even Murder the Courts of Justice <more merciful than the Church> are compelld to allow is not done in Passion but in Cool Blooded Design & Intention. (E564)

Steven Goldsmith therefore seems to me to be absolutely right when he argues that, on the whole, 'the Last Judgment picture suggests not asceticism but freedom from sexual restraint'.[54]

Where I differ from Goldsmith is in what might appear to be a detail: his sense of the relationship of the Petworth *Last Judgment* to the 1809 *Whore of Babylon*. Goldsmith is surely right to claim that in 'each of these pictures, "energy" is clearly sexual' but wrong to see this as 'fundamentally paradoxical'.[55] Goldsmith points out that 'the "fiery gulph" that defines the primary axis in the Last Judgment series is distinctly, almost pornographically, vaginal' and that in each version of the Last Judgment, 'but most clearly pronounced in the Petworth figure, the arrangement of the trumpeting angels suggests the labia'.[56] To Goldsmith, this curious hidden image confirms what Damrosch sees as 'an unresolved tension between apocalyptic truth and inadequate modes of representation'.[57] 'When Blake urges his (male) audience to engage with his picture with prophetic imagination', Goldsmith writes, 'he invokes a sexual act distinctly at odds with his apocalyptic hopes' (p. 151). What difference does it make if Blake imagined a female audience and if the 'sexual act' is not at odds with his apocalyptic hopes?

The association established by the satiric discourse on enthusiasm between the female genitals and the prophetic voice is capable, in Blake's work, of a positive meaning, one which simultaneously affirms the

Figure 23. William Blake, *The Spiritual Form of Nelson Guiding Leviathan*.
© Tate, London, 2010.

necessity of representation and rejects the assumption that Blake's work strives towards transcendence. Blake's constant drive towards parody and the inversion of received meanings appears in the first two paintings of his 1809 exhibition, *The Spiritual Form of Pitt* and *The Spiritual Form of Nelson Guiding Leviathan* (Figure 23) which both invoke Michelangelo's *Last Judgment* in their compositions.

In these two works, Blake critiques the selection of Flaxman to produce a monument to Nelson by reworking the *Last Judgment* as parody. In Blake's painting, Nelson is now accompanied by his monstrous sidekick Pitt, 'that Angel who, pleased to perform the Almighty's orders, rides on the whirlwind, directing the storms of war' (E530). There is also a distant and disturbing memory of Fuseli's 1790 *Titania and Bottom* in so far as a commanding central figure is surrounded by a whirling vortex of tiny figures which reveals Fuseli's painting as a parody of the Last Judgment in which Titania takes the role of the saviour. Just as Fuseli's 1790 painting represented a disordered economy of both gender and sexuality, so Blake's 1809 paintings analyse the way in which a corrupt culture of sexuality feeds a culture of war. These pictures belong with the 1809 *Whore of Babylon* (or Virgin Whore) as negative images of regulated sexuality.

By contrast, in *The Reunion of the Soul and the Body* and the *Vision of the Last Judgment* rapture creates a 'blank in Nature', opening the surface of the earth to allow the resurrection of the body. Since 'sexuality' (as Blake uses the word) is the antithesis of rapture, these images do not rest on ambiguity. Damrosch writes that '[i]n some mysterious way the sexual act must be the entrance to an apocalypse in which fallen sexuality will be burned up and replaced by something else'.[58] But in Blake's writing it is the 'Harlot' who is 'Mystery'. The discovery of 'mystery', 'paradox' and 'unresolved tension' allows Blake's critics to maintain a fundamentally dualist reading of his words and images, a reading that belongs to Beulah, the place 'where Contrarieties are equally True'. The mystery dissolves if what we call the 'sexual act' is potentially the opposite of Blake's 'sexuality'. The representation of the harlot in the series of pictures of the Last Judgment is key to Blake's meaning. She appears first of all in the lower right corner of the *Day of Judgment* for *The Grave*, moves to the rocky centre in the 1806 version and in the Petworth *Last Judgment* sits on the roof of the grave. Her position is now that of the risen soul, the youthful spiritual body in *Death's Door* who looks up to heaven while the aged body of the old man enters the grave below.[59] The figure of the harlot in the *Last Judgment* is the antithesis of the Virgin Whore: she is naked and no longer wears the skirt whose waist ruffle reminds the viewer of Elizabeth I's virginal adoration of Raleigh and of his military oppression of the Irish. Her abandoned pose, like the embrace of the resurrected couples, itself allows the moment of apocalypse.

CHAPTER 8

Wollstonecraft and the adulterous woman

The conventions of aristocratic sexual freedom clearly offered to the Countess of Petworth the possibility of evading moral censure. The rules of bourgeois sexuality, however, became increasingly clear at the end of the eighteenth century when for conservative writers Mary Wollstonecraft and adultery became inseparably linked in 1798. The immediate cause was the furore caused by Godwin's *Memoirs of the Author of Vindication of the Rights of Woman* published by Joseph Johnson in January 1798 with a second, amended version appearing in summer 1798.[1] Concern over the prevalence of prostitution or the rate of adultery had been a constant theme in the eighteenth century, but this new sex panic took a distinctly different form from the flurry of concern produced by Madan's *Thelyphthora* in the aftermath of the Gordon riots and the American war.[2] This time the concern was not so much with the consequences of male sexuality, evidenced in the polygamy debate and the continuing concern about prostitution. Instead, the end of century sex panic focuses specifically on the question of female sexuality, seeming to bear out Laqueur's thesis that at just this time women are newly categorised as sexually passive.[3] The shift that several Blake critics have detected from a concern in the poetry of the 1790s with the consequences of aggressive male sexuality to a concern in the writing and art after 1800 with the negative consequences of 'Moral Virtue' in the vindictive punishment of homosexuality extends to a defence of female sexuality that critiques the terms of the new definition of gender.

To some extent, this new sex panic is a response to the fear of French invasion which peaks around 1798. Barruel's *History of Jacobinism* translated in 1797 offered three ready-made conspiracies as the work of French philosophy: 'the Anti-Christian conspiracy, the second the Anti-monarchical conspiracy, the third the Anti-Social conspiracy'.[4] The Anti-Social conspiracy was seen by Barruel as an attempt to destroy the structure of marriage and conservative English readers detected Godwin as a prime agent of this conspiracy. Did not Godwin reveal that the conversation when he first met Wollstonecraft had been about Voltaire? The spectacle of Wollstonecraft's life provided by Godwin in his *Memoirs of the Author of the Vindication of the Rights of Woman* in 1798 after her death the same year was the trigger that the counter-revolution needed. Gail Bederman argues that Malthus's 1798 *Essay on Population* 'was originally written to satirize both Mary Wollstonecraft, the most notorious unwed mother of her day, and William Godwin, whose memoirs of his late wife included detailed and approving accounts of her love affairs'.[5] Bederman suggests that Malthus had no need to spell out the further object of his attack. In choosing the subject of sexual incontinence, his satire on Godwin's sudden deviation from the role of celibate philosopher and Wollstonecraft's life and loves would easily be detectable by his early readers. A preoccupation with Godwin's view of sex was common among anti-Jacobin writers at just the period when Malthus was writing his essay.

At the turn of the century, public debate also focused on the issue of adultery. Not only was there an increase in cases for 'criminal conversation' in the last decades of the eighteenth century, but Lord Auckland's 1800 bill to criminalise adultery was debated at length in Parliament.[6] Although Auckland's bill was not passed into law, the aim of imprisoning or fining any man found guilty of sex with another man's wife reflected the assumption of female sexual passivity. Katherine Binhammer shows that the lawyer Thomas Erskine, 'whose success at winning high settlements for plaintiffs in crim. Con. actions was legendary, rose to prominence because of his ability to exploit the structural presupposition of female sexual passivity'. Erskine, the defence lawyer in the treason trials (and the subject of one of Hayley's poems), set the bourgeois culture of the family against the threat of aristocratic libertinism.[7] Since male defendants necessarily argued for active female compliance, what was on trial in 'criminal conversation' cases according to Binhammer was 'not the individual guilt or innocence of the men involved but the sexuality of the new domestic woman'.[8]

This issue was central to Hannah More's 1799 *Strictures on the Modern System of Female Education*, which opens with a resounding call for moral reform as the only hope of withstanding the nation's enemies in time of war. More sees marriage as central to resisting what Barruel calls the 'anti-Social conspiracy' and predictably attacks '*The female Werter*' (using the phrase Godwin had chosen in his Memoir of Wollstonecraft) to warn of the social dangers of female desire. More singles out Wollstonecraft as the first female author to offer 'a direct vindication of adultery' and to assert 'that adultery is justifiable, and that the restrictions placed on it by the laws of England constitute one of the *Wrongs of Women*'.[9] More's attack draws on resounding lines from book III of *The Task*:

> The adult'ress! What a theme for angry verse,
> What provocation to the indignant heart
> That feels for injured love! But I disdain
> The nauseous task to paint her as she is,
> Cruel, abandoned, glorying in her shame.

Ironically Wollstonecraft had borrowed Cowper's phrase when she described street prostitutes who 'trample on virgin bashfulness' and 'glorying in their shame, become more audaciously lewd than men' in the 1792 *Vindication*.[10] Attacking Wollstonecraft as an adulteress, More turns this language against her: the adulteress, by implication, imports the sexual morality of the street into the bourgeois home. More thus adopts the satiric strategy developed by Malthus.

Since knowledge of the debate was so widespread, and hostile commentary so ubiquitous, it is hardly necessary to argue for Blake's knowledge of the Wollstonecraft scandal.[11] When Blake portrays 'Mary' in *Jerusalem* as an adulterous wife, attacked by a distraught Joseph, the collocation of the name 'Mary' and 'Adulteress' inevitably recalls the attacks on Wollstonecraft. It is usually assumed that Blake's contact with Mary Wollstonecraft was limited to the early 1790s when Joseph Johnson was giving him engraving work and Blake illustrated her *Original Stories from Real Life* published in 1791. But Blake's contact with Malkin in the years up to 1806 suggests his continuing contact with circles which would have felt a pressing interest in the outcry that followed Wollstonecraft's death and Godwin's biography. Malkin's defence of Wollstonecraft in 1795 and his subscription to Ann Batten Cristall's *Poems* the same year shows that he moved in circles sympathetic to Wollstonecraft. Blake's unqualified praise of Cumberland's 1798 *Captive*, the year of the Wollstonecraft scandal and Malthus's *Essay*, makes the argument that around this time he develops a virulent hostility towards active female sexuality particularly improbable. Andrew Lincoln's identification of Ololon with Hannah More and Blake's turn towards Christianity with the evangelical response to Barruel seems to me an example of the dangers Blake runs through his consistent technique of parodic inversion of terminology.[12] As I have argued throughout, the 'Female Will' is instead a term for repressive morality in Blake's work, satirically reversed in meaning.

The identification of Mary as 'a Harlot & an Adulteress' is a repeated theme of Blake's late writing. *Jerusalem* presents Joseph's attack on his unfaithful wife:

> Joseph spoke in anger & fury. Should I
> Marry a Harlot & an Adulteress? Mary answerd, Art thou more pure
> Than thy Maker who forgiveth Sins & calls again Her that is Lost
> Tho She hates. he calls her again in love.   (*J* iii:61:5–8, E211)

Blake is radical in his claim that Mary conceived Jesus through an adulterous physical union and the notebook draft of the Everlasting Gospel is even more explicit, presenting Mary as an adulteress:

> Was Jesus Chaste or did he
> Give any Lessons of Chastity
> The morning blushd fiery red
> Mary was found in Adulterous bed   (E521)

Whereas recent critics have identified in Blake a horror at the body, the Everlasting Gospel identifies the body as divine: 'Thou Angel of the Presence Divine/ That didst create this Body of Mine' (E521).

Wollstonecraft's friends seemed to have opted, for the most part, for silence, leaving the attack on Wollstonecraft to the anti-Jacobins. When Malthus dated his preface June 1798, Blake's friend George Cumberland had already completed his utopian novel, *The Captive of the Castle of Sennaar* which I have cited throughout as offering a close parallel to Blake's own vision. G. E. Bentley, Jr, assumes that Cumberland wrote his tale in 1797 and it cannot therefore have been written as a direct response to the *Memoirs* which Godwin was revising in November 1797 and published on 29 January 1798 (according to Godwin's diary entry).[13] Cumberland asked Horne Tooke 'to look' the manuscript 'over before it went to Press' on 22 January 1798. Nevertheless early readers drew an immediate connection with the Wollstonecraft scandal, and Cumberland's place in the same circles as Godwin suggests that he may reflect something of their debate over sexuality in this period. Cumberland sent the printed (but unpublished) book to Thomas Taylor, who immediately made the link with Wollstonecraft, responding on 16 October 1798:

I think it more entertaining than instructive, more ingenious than moral. I will not, indeed, I cannot suppose that you would undertake to defend lasciviousness publickly; & yet it appears that it is as much patronized by the conduct of your Sophians as by the works of Mrs Woolstonecraft. You will doubtless excuse the freedom of this opinion, when you consider that as I am a professed Platonist, love is with me true only in proportion as it is pure; or in other words in proportion as it rises above the gratification of our brutal part.'[14]

Taylor's view of sex is quite different from Cumberland's and quite unlike Blake's.

CUMBERLAND, FLAXMAN AND THE INNOCENCE OF LOOKING

Cumberland's utopia is notable not only for its advocacy of 'lasciviousness' but for its picture of a society in which women are full citizens and part of public culture. Their active contribution ensures that the erotic culture of Sophis is quite different from that of the 'corrupted continent' of Europe. Cumberland suggests that women are unlikely to forget the material nature of visual culture and that this memory of the body is healthy for the public sphere.

Cumberland's account of women as viewers of art is coloured by the time he spent in Rome after 1784, the year of Flaxman's unsuccessful attempt to fund Blake's trip to Rome, when Cumberland came into an inheritance that allowed him to give up his work as a clerk in the Royal Exchange Insurance Office. Unlike Fuseli, who mixed in cosmopolitan libertine circles in Rome, John Flaxman and his wife Ann arrived in Rome the same year as Cumberland and left in 1794. Cumberland, who had already visited Florence and Rome in 1785, eloped to Rome in 1787 with the wife of his London landlord, Mrs Elizabeth Cooper. They stayed until 1790 and may never have married.[15] Cumberland therefore had good personal reasons to object to the vicious attacks on Wollstonecraft unleashed by Godwin's *Memoirs*. His view of women also bears close comparison with that of Wollstonecraft's own writing.

Fuseli's *Aphorisms on Art* give women an important role in resisting the slide of culture into effeminacy: 'The female, able to invigorate her taste without degenerating into a pedant, sloven or virago, may give her hand to the man of elegance, who scorns to sacrifice his sense to the presiding phantoms of an effeminate age.'[16] The heroine of Mary Wollstonecraft's 1788 novel *Mary*, visiting Lisbon, marks out her difference from fashionable ladies by her desire to 'view the ruins that still remained of the earthquake', a sublime sight that implicitly raises key issues about natural evil discussed in the debate between Rousseau and Voltaire.[17] The fictional Mary's taste in paintings is equally revealing: 'she was particularly fond of seeing historical paintings', a topic that 'as the ladies could not handle ... well, they soon adverted to portraits'.[18] Cumberland's 1796

Thoughts on Outline gives another glimpse of the debate about how women look at art. Like the older John Armstrong, Cumberland is explicit that a sexual response is a natural element of our reaction to great art and believes that the Greek 'Minervas, Venuses, and Jupiters' were 'taken from living examples'.[19] Looking at a beautiful woman, Cumberland thinks, is a superior pleasure to looking at sculpture: 'there is but one thing that can have more intrinsic value than a very fine piece of sculpture, which is, a beautiful young woman, with an accomplished mind, and generous heart; for she combines in all her actions the graces and beauties of a pure statue'.[20] In *Thoughts on Outline*, a volume for which Blake provided the engravings, Cumberland insists on the right of women to view naked statues: 'let our travelled ladies, who have walked without harm with gentlemen through every Museum in Europe, and beheld all that Grecian Art, even when it was playful, could shew, teach their countrywomen, that true modesty disdains not to examine, with a steady eye, the masculine parts of the antique statues'.[21] Helen Bruder comments that Ann Flaxman's unpublished *Journey to Rome* dwells 'on the pleasure derived from the contemplation of male bodies'.[22]

Cumberland suggests that women might be particularly able to view nakedness innocently through their exposure to the nakedness of children: the 'masculine parts of the antique statues', he writes, 'are as chastely represented as those of children by the hand of nature, which innocence may, and does daily, behold unblushing'.[23] Cumberland here echoes Wollstonecraft's insistence in the 1792 *Vindication* on her own right to view the body: 'I have conversed, as man with man, with medical men, on anatomical subjects; and compared the proportions of the human body with artists'.[24] The chastity of art is a product both of the inherent virtue of the viewer and of the form of representation. For Cumberland, looking is transformative, making the viewer into what he sees: his preface quotes from Petvin's *Letters concerning Mind*: 'If there be a BEAUTY IN VIRTUE, certainly the mind must have a feeling of it, whilst it has it under view ... It must be felt and understood *together*, we must *be in some measure what we behold*.'[25] The formulation is significantly different from Blake's repeated phrase 'he became what he beheld' (E97), used in the nightmarish account of the creation of Urizen's body but only in its retelling in *Milton*, because, for Cumberland and Petvin as for Wollstonecraft, what we see is conditioned by what we are. Cumberland quotes Petvin: '"a man must be tolerably good before he can have any tolerable notion of goodness"'.[26] Writing to Dr Trusler, Blake makes the same assumption when he writes that 'Every body does not see alike' (E702).

What Jonathan Lamb describes as 'horrid sympathy', the nightmarish power of looking to turn the viewer into what they behold, is clearly invoked by Blake as an account of the fear of the visual that dominates conservative discourse.[27] Within this theory, the vulnerable or naïve viewer cannot withstand the sight of intense or frightening imagery without naïvely acting out what is seen. This is the fear that governs Hogarth's satire of the enthusiastic crowd and produces the view that only (pre)regulated emotions can be represented.

Like Cumberland, Wollstonecraft insists on the ability of women to achieve the kind of disinterested, abstract and so innocent viewpoint that was assumed to be available to educated men, a claim that outrages the conservative Polwhele in *The Unsex'd Females* of 1798:

Miss Wollstonecraft does not blush to say, in an introduction to a book designed for the use of young ladies, that, 'in order to lay the axe to the root of corruption, it would be proper to familiarize the sexes to an unreserved discussion of those topics, which are generally avoided in conversation from a principle of false delicacy; and that it would be right to speak of the organs of generation as freely as we mention our eyes or our hands'.[28]

In the view of Wollstonecraft and others in her circle, modesty can coexist with sexual knowledge.[29]

Looking at art is especially important in *The Captive of the Castle of Sennaar*, which opens with the figure of the innocent captive common to radical fiction of the period. Cumberland's imprisoned philosopher artist perhaps recalls Count Cagliostro, whom Cumberland had visited in Rome.[30] Cumberland's captive decorates his cell with *trompe l'oeil* paintings that create the impression of a room filled with elegant statuary and furniture.[31] Apparently hanging on the wall is 'the portrait of a female of a divine countenance and figure, reposing on a sopha, and embracing a child as lovely as a cupid, while another lay sleeping at her feet'. The painting is one of several references to the story of Cupid and Psyche which is also frequently invoked in his *Thoughts on Outline* with its pictures of 'Venus councels Cupid', 'The conjugal union of Cupid' and 'Cupid and Psyche'. In the 1798 work, the entrance to the land of Sophis is marked by a figure of 'a winged Cupid' and acceptance as a citizen of Sophis is dependent on female desire. It is only when it is established that Lycas is 'in possession of the affections of a female citizen' that he is granted residence and the death of his wife Mica and his children by her forces him to leave the utopian society.[32]

The painting in the philosopher's cell is thus an image of loss, a work by which art can fill the 'blank of nature'. It is also a statement of the positive role of ornament. Annotating his copy of Reynolds's 1798 *Works* Blake argues against the claim that: 'The regular progress of cultivated life is from necessaries to accommodation, from accommodations to ornaments.' Reynolds takes the cyclical model of culture to mean that ornament characterises the decadence of culture and is a negative product of feminine commercialism. Blake rejects this model, asserting that 'Necessaries Accomodations & Ornaments are the whole of Life' (E637) (He wrote first: 'are Lifes wants'). It is Satan's hirelings who destroy 'Cultivated Life' and 'Ornament'. Pleasure, luxury, ornament are all necessities and can be imagined through erotic reverie.

Whereas Reynolds sees the right kind of public art as a defence against decadence, in the hands of Hannah More in 1799 the arts themselves in a late stage of a civilisation may come to be pernicious:

In a state of barbarism, the arts are among the best reformers; and they go on to be improved themselves, and improving those who cultivate them, till, having reached a certain point, those very arts which were the instruments of civilization and refinement, become instruments of corruption and decay; enervating and depraving in the second instance as certainly as they refined in the first.[33]

More describes a private use of painting as a form of moral self-regulation in her 1808 novel *Coelebs* in the tale of the extravagant aristocrat Lady Melbury whose failure to pay for the artificial flowers which adorn her at parties leads to the death of a flower girl. Lady Melbury uses art as a memento of her sin:

'With a little aid from fancy, which I thought made it allowable to bring separate circumstances into one piece, I composed a picture. It consisted of a detached figure in the background of poor Stokes, seen through the grate of his prison on a bed of straw: and a groupe, composed of his wife in the act of expiring, Fanny bending over a wreath of roses, withered with the tears she was shedding, and myself in the horrors in which you saw me,
Spectatress of the mischief I had made.
Wherever I go, this picture shall always be my companion. It hangs in my closet, my dear friends,' added she, with a look of infinite sweetness: 'whenever I am tempted to contract a debt, or to give into any act of vanity or dissipation which may lead to debt, if, after having looked on this picture I can pursue the project, renounce me, cast me off for ever!'[34]

This painting is a moralised version of Sterne's imagined captive in *A Sentimental Journey*. It is also an anticipation of Dorian Gray's portrait, belonging in a 'closet' in so far as it represents the conscience of its owner.

Retiring to her domestic privacy, the middle-class woman who protects
the conscience of the nation contemplates her guilt, like a female Satan,
'Spectatress of the mischief I had made'.[35]

Cumberland's 1796 *Thoughts on Outline*, dedicated to Charles James
Fox, argues for a free press and for the promotion of the arts:

What better use, indeed, can we make of that freedom of the press, which is yet
left us, than to seek the good of the country, whose constitution confers it? What
better use of life, and liberty of thought, than to give our ideas free scope, when
sincerely desirous of promoting a straight direction in the tender plant of those
arts, which may hereafter adorn and raise the character of the nation to which we
belong?[36]

The decision not to publish Cumberland's *Captive* was guided by Erskine's response to a pre-publication reading which 'deemed it dangerous,
under Mr Pitts' maladministration, to publish it'.[37] Erskine was worried
by a passage in which Lycas generalises about repressive societies: 'either
single tyrants framing arbitrary laws, and, by hereditary force, over-awing
the multitude; or ten or a dozen men, under pretext of guardianship,
dividing, among themselves, the property of millions' (p. 78). Cumberland
sees commercial culture as controlled by political tyranny. But his
bereaved prisoner artist is still committed to active intervention: his words
are 'life and light'. He watches from his small barred window and his
voice warns boats of a sunken rock when the Nile floods: 'scarce a week
passes in which I do not save many lives: I am now at the station of
humanity, 'tis that which keeps me so close at this little window' (p. 10).
This scene is surely remembered in Blake's image, already quoted, of his
Felpham cottage as a lighthouse in 1800: 'See My Cottage at Felpham in
joy/ Beams over the sea a bright light over France'.

Cumberland's scene, like More's, revises the passage from
A Sentimental Journey in which Yorick imagines a prisoner in the Bastille
in such detail that he weeps – only to realise the fallacy and foolishness of
tears for a product of his imagination that he has himself imprisoned.
Whereas Sterne's image shows the inefficacy of sentiment, the captive here
actively helps those outside his cell, acting as an image of Charles James
Fox, who is one 'whose *honesty* alone, if he should again accept the helm,
is capable, under Providence, of re-conducting into harbour the misman-
aged vessel of the British state' (pp. iii–iv). Fox, like the philosopher artist,
is the pilot of the ship of state, capable of bringing it into harbour.
Solitary sexual fantasy is compatible, in Cumberland's novel, with active
and benevolent activity.

THE 1809 EXHIBITION

Recent critics have raised the possibility that after 1800 Blake shifts significantly towards sympathy for some elements of the evangelical movement, indeed that his work shares the missionary project of the early nineteenth century; in addressing the Jews in *Jerusalem*, it has been argued, Blake joins the contemporary project.[38] But the exhibition takes on some highly visible evangelical and missionary campaigns in particular the disciplinary use of the adulterous woman. An eager visitor to public art exhibitions, Blake is likely to have seen Rembrandt's *Christ and the Woman Taken in Adultery* when it was on view in London in 1807, first at Christie's then at the home of its new owner, John Julius Angerstein. The painting, as Philippa Simpson describes, attracted 'rapturous critical response': 'For the hordes of artists and cognoscenti who swarmed around this celebrated Rembrandt, even the most hyperbolic praise failed to do the work full justice. The president of the Royal Academy, Benjamin West said that "All who approached it pulled off their hats" in reverence'.[39] Blake's decision to include *The Penance of Jane Shore* as the final painting (NUMBER XVI) in his exhibition is represented in the catalogue purely in terms of technique and artistic consistency, to 'prove to any discerning eye, that the productions of our youth and of our maturer age are equal in all essential points' (E550). But this small painting also acts as a statement of ideological consistency, a coded reference to Blake's continuing defence of active female sexuality. Despite its commercial setting and its function as a selling exhibition, Blake's 1809 exhibition functions as an alternative national gallery, a comment on the kinds of paintings that the nation chose to mark its public identity. Whereas Rembrandt shows the adulteress as a tiny figure, kneeling before a standing Christ and dwarfed within a huge space by a dimly represented but intimidating throne, Blake's early painting shows the erect and dignified figure of Jane Shore, the mistress of the dead king Edward IV led in disgrace in St Paul's church.

Bentley suggests that Blake's first image of Jane Shore may have been one of the 'two designs from the History of England' that Malkin describes Blake as working on 'after drawings which he had made in the holiday hours of his apprenticeship' at the end of his time with Basire.[40] Blake's likely source was Rapin de Thoyras's *History of England* dating from the 1730s which presents Shore as an idealised figure, 'surprisingly beautiful, and withal of a Generosity very uncommon in Persons of her Character'.[41] But the story of Jane Shore, the bourgeois wife who became the king's mistress, would also have been familiar to Londoners from

Nicholas Rowe's 1714 *The Tragedy of Jane Shore*, one of the most popular and frequently performed plays in the period, a vehicle for Sarah Siddons and a key play in Mary Robinson's career. Rowe's play casts Jane Shore as an idealised figure who willingly takes on her status as outcast: 'Let me be branded for the public scorn,/ Turn'd forth, and driven to wander like a vagabond,/ Be friendless and forsaken, seek my bread/ Upon the barren, wild, and desolate waste' (IV, p. I).[42] If the version exhibited in 1809, as Bentley suggests, was completed in 1793 it is the product of the same year as the *Visions of the Daughters of Albion*. Like Oothoon, Shore is opened by suffering to a consciousness of others, losing a sense of her own separate self and of the separateness of sexuality from other categories. In Rowe's play, Shore likens herself to 'the hireling' who 'With labour drudges out the painful day,/ And often looks with long expecting eyes/ To see the shadows rise and be dismiss'd' (v.i, p. 68). Female suffering is part of the continuum of human experience which includes that of the 'the hireling'. The performances of Rowe's *Tragedy of Jane Shore* in the 1790s resist attempts to return women to the domestic sphere, representing the abject mistress as a figure on the public stage.

The visitor to Blake's exhibition presumably had the option of taking the painting as an image of the repentant whore but the association of Jane Shore with the actress and writer Mary Robinson confirms the combative nature of Blake's painting. Herself a royal mistress (one of the Prince Regent's many conquests), Robinson was also a friend of William Godwin. Under the pseudonym of Ann Frances Randall, Mary Robinson was the author of the 1799 *Letter to the Women of England*, which carries an epigraph from Rowe's *The Fair Penitent* and quotes a phrase from a key speech in *The Tragedy of Jane Shore* that attacks the double standard: 'Mark by what partial Justice we are judg'd;/ Such is the Fate unhappy Women find,/ And such the Curse intail'd upon our kind' (I.ii).[43] Mary Robinson had taken the role of Alicia when *The Tragedy of Jane Shore* was performed at Covent Garden on 27 January 1783.[44]

Including Jane Shore in his exhibition, Blake places the 'harlot' alongside his own ambiguous images of national heroes (Figure 24). Whilst the nation was engaged in turning St Paul's cathedral into a mausoleum of the great, Jane Shore is seen doing public penance in the same place. Dressed in a blue robe like Mary, the harlot stands alongside Pitt whose shift recalls his identity as the virgin in contemporary caricatures which mocked his apparent lack of interest in sex.[45] Whereas the focus on sexual morality coincided with a concern over the protection of the nation's integrity against foreign invasion,

Figure 24. William Blake, *The Penance of Jane Shore in St Paul's Church*, 1793.
© Tate, London, 2010.

Blake's Jane Shore offers an alternative figure of the nation and in doing so rejects the new model of bourgeois woman that in More's work defines national identity. While Malkin defended Wollstonecraft in 1795, so Blake here rejects the evangelical scapegoating of the adulterous woman.

'WAHĒINE! WAHĒINE! THAT IS, WOMAN! OR, WE ARE WOMEN'

In the 1809 exhibition, Blake reasserts this belief through comedy. *The Goats* chooses a ludicrous moment in a missionary work, and in doing so focuses directly on the question of the role of the body in culture. The setting is Otaheite, modern Tahiti, the location for one of the most powerful recent reimaginings of Paradise, a sexual utopia as it had seemed on its discovery by Cook and Bougainville, even if that paradise was swiftly ruined by venereal disease.[46] Blake was clearly struck by the description of women swimming round the missionaries' boat: 'Though

Figure 25. James Barry, *The Thames, or the Triumph of Navigation*, etching, published 1792 (1 May 1791). © National Portrait Gallery, London.

it was now dark two females swam off, in hopes, no doubt, of a favourable reception; but finding they could not be admitted, they kept swimming about the ship for near half an hour, calling out, in a pitiful tone, Wahēine! Wahēine! That is, Woman! Or, We are women!'[47] In these women Blake finds a means to reject the domestic ideology of his time. The scene of women swimming perhaps recalled to Blake a painting by James Barry, who seems to have been much in his mind in these years. Barry's painting of *Commerce, or the Triumph of the Thames* for the Society of Arts, Manufactures and Commerce in the Adelphi (Figure 25) was part of the most ambitious project of historical painting to be realised in the period and as such an important image for Blake of the kind of painting that would be possible in a society that recognised the value of public art. Barry's Adelphi painting would have been easily identifiable to educated viewers as a reworking of a celebrated sculpture of *The Nile* in the Vatican Museum, a statue showing the river god surrounded by small putti and other mythical creatures which was ceded to France under the 1797 Treaty of Tolentino and reached Paris in 1803.[48] Not only was the statue particularly praised by Vasari but it was frequently reproduced in prints and in small models. Thomas Banks incorporated a small relief copy on the pedestal of his 1804–5 monument in St Paul's cathedral to George Blagdon Westcott killed in the Battle of the Nile in 1798.[49] In recreating this scene, Blake once again addresses the nation's cult of the hero.

In Barry's painting prostitutes take the place of the *putti* who accompany the Nile, swimming along with a selection of male dignitaries and making visible the painful truth of the economic centrality of prostitution to England as a commercial nation. Among the 'Nereids carrying several articles of our manufactures and commerce of Manchester, Birmingham', Barry explains in his catalogue, are some who are not behaving themselves: 'if some of those Nereids appear more sportive than industrious, and others still more wanton than sportive, the Picture has the more variety and I am sorry to add the greater resemblance to the truth'.[50] Barry's wanton nereids reveal that the lack of 'trades and employments' for women is 'a source of infinite and most extensive mischief' and thus identify prostitution as an economic rather than a moral problem. The women swimming in the Thames show the problematic role of women no longer, or not only, valued as sources of population and excluded from the economic life of the nation except perhaps through prostitution.

Blake's (lost) comic episode represents the resurgence of animal sexuality in the face of attempts at regulation by missionaries, likening Tahiti to the Thames. It also announces the naked body as the subject of art. The passage that Blake illustrates describes a 'savage' girl who 'was rather stout, but possessing such symmetry of features, as did all her companions, that as models for the statuary and painter their equals can seldom be found'. The missionaries are intent on clothing the girls but 'they could not all succeed so well as the first in getting clothed; nor did our mischievous goats even suffer them to keep their green leaves, but as they turned to avoid them they were attacked on each side alternately, and completely stripped naked'.[51] Perhaps Blake was prophetic in this painting, for, as Vic Gatrell describes, in 1814 'a Thames Police Act was passed in order to deprive common people of their rights to bathe in the Thames in daylight, on pain of a fine'. This attempt at controlling the Thames did not go unchallenged when a Thames Bathing Bill the following year attempted to undo 'a most injurious encroachment on the comfort of the lower classes'. It was Wilberforce and his friends who resisted this move, claiming that it would make it impossible for decent people to approach the Thames 'from the number of persons undressing themselves, and exposing their naked bodies to view'.[52]

Barry died in 1806 but was remembered with a two-volume edition of his *Works* published by Cadell and Davies in 1809. Blake's 1809 exhibition and the accompanying *Descriptive Catalogue* go out of their way to assert his continuing allegiance to the kind of visual culture associated by Hogarth, Ireland and Barry with enthusiasm. Barry's 1783 catalogue describes stumbling upon a full-length portrait of George I in Northumberland House and being struck by how badly the painter has handled the body. Imagining himself in the company of a writer, perhaps Pope, 'and at his elbow a native of Otaheite, or rather a cultivated Athenian', he considers how he would defend the abysmal handling of the body to a spectator from another culture: 'what answer could he give to the questions that might be asked? Was it because this Mr Jervoise had studied no more of the human figure than the mere face, that he has managed all the rest of this picture in so incorrect, slovenly, and strange a way: what is this intended for, a leg; and this, and this, what is it?'[53] The figure of the Tahitian spectator is a familiar one in the period because of the huge impact of the visit of the Tahitian chieftain Omai in 1774, but whereas Cowper imagines Omai in *The Task* regretting the loss of Britain on his return to the shores of Tahiti, Blake reads the work of the missionaries as comic and doomed to failure. The savage girls delight in their nakedness, and imagining them (if he can fight off the demons of Correggio) allows Blake to create art.

This issue is most important in the vast centrepiece of the exhibition, the lost painting of *The Ancient Britons*, whose strangely red colouring is explained by Blake as the result of habitual nakedness: 'The flush of health in flesh, exposed to the open air, nourished by the spirits of forests and floods, in that ancient happy period, which history has recorded, cannot be like the sickly daubs of Titian or Rubens' (E545). Blake here echoes George Cumberland's account of the painting of the naked body in *The Captive*: 'have you never observed, that all prominent parts of muscles blush, like the cheeks, when exposed to fine air? The fleshy parts of muscles are red, porous, and consequently are the warm points of the body'.[54] Blake also draws on Barry's belief 'that the ancient Britons were as naked as other savages; and that the practice of boxing alone, in our countries, furnishes more frequent exhibitions of the naked and of the best kind, than any that are now to be met with in Italy'.[55] The meaning of the *Spiritual Form of Pitt* and *The Spiritual Form of Nelson* lies as much in the use of a naked but feminised body for Nelson and a clothed form for Pitt as in any other element of the complex iconography.[56]

Blake's distress at the failure of the exhibition appears in the much-revised verses called 'Blakes apology for his Catalogue' in his notebook.[57] In the notebook verses, Hayley, Flaxman, Cromek, Stothard, Schiavonetti and Reynolds have all sold out to a feminised culture:

> If I eer Grow to Mans Estate
> O Give to me a Womans fate
> May I govern all both great & small
> Have the last word & take the wall   (E502)

If this verse, like so many of the others in the notebook, is about visual culture, then 'take the wall' might suggest that female tastes control the hanging decisions at the exhibitions such as the Royal Academy. Blake imagines himself as outside the 'sexual' system: he is not part of 'Mans estate', though if he were to enter this system he (like Ololon) would choose a female identity. Although this verse could reveal a simple form of misogyny, female control can also be read as shorthand for a culture of 'Moral Virtue' increasingly dominated by conservative evangelical concerns. The verses do not attack individual women: Nancy Flaxman is excerpted from the grumbling about her husband as are Mrs Butts and the Countess of Egremont. The real antagonist in this series of verses is softness, whether detected in the work of Rubens, in chiaro scuro which obscures line, or in the need to cater to a taste which at the same time obscures and fetishises sexual desire. The 'Imitation of Pope A Compliment to the Ladies' suggests that this culture which appears to be woman-centred masks a dislike of women beneath a façade of elaborate compliment. Women really stand in this culture on a scale of importance below heroes, men, animals, furniture and 'table stool and chair':

> Wondrous the Gods more wondrous are the Men
> More Wondrous Wondrous still the Cock & Hen
> More wondrous still the Table Stool & Chair
> But Ah More wondrous still the Charming Fair   (E506)

The quality of softness is seen as the price of admission to a compromised public sphere:

> Having given great offence by writing in Prose
> Ill write in Verse as Soft as Bartolloze

The first draft put 'feather pillows' for the later 'Bartolloze' (E865), suggesting the world of the sofa conjured at the beginning of Cowper's

Task. Blake is responding to the taste for stipple engraving which could achieve peculiarly soft effects, suitable especially it was thought for feminine subjects, a style at which Bartolozzi excelled. But here, the soft style of stipple engraving is generalised to include verse.

The rhyming couplets retain Blake's impolite London accent, insisting that 'crime in' rhymes with 'Rhyming':

> Some blush at what others can see no crime in
> But nobody sees any harm in Rhyming

Although rhyme is a technique that blurs difference, in Blake's use here it affirms difference. Blake's verse asserts that sexual cultures differ, for some blush 'at what others can see no crime in'. Support for Pope's rhymed Homer places Hayley now in opposition to attempts by Cowper, assisted by Fuseli, to produce an English *Iliad* that captures the new poetic freedom:

> Thus Hayley on his Toilette seeing the Sope
> Cries Homer is very much improvd by Pope   (E505)

In his notebook verse, Blake chooses for himself the role of contrary to the culture of softness:

> While I looking up to my Umbrella
> Resolvd to be a very contrary fellow

Instead of looking up to heaven, all he can see is his umbrella, which rhymed, non-standardly, with 'fellow' and again gives us Blake's impolite London accent.[58] Rhyme, ironically, protects Blake from assimilation to the polite. Hayley was remembered as a keen umbrella user but Blake's umbrella here constructs his own protective mundane shell. Blake's hostility, focused on the comical figure of a transvestite Hayley, identifies the way in which a feminised culture has shifted in the years he has been away from London from one which endorses bodily pleasures to one in which femininity stands for the duty of moral reform to solidify the status quo.

Whereas sexuality, like enthusiasm and mourning, appeared to offer an entry for Blake into a polite world, Blake's later work distinguishes between sexual cultures, rejecting not just the enlightenment libertinism which Hayley himself disavows but the evangelical model of culture. Not only does Blake refuse to offer a utopian account of the role of sexuality in civilisation like his friend George Cumberland but he becomes increasingly sceptical of the ways in which a sexualised discourse protects the status quo. Darwin's Lucretian eroticisation of the natural world seems to block the entrances to Golgonooza.

By contrast, Hannah More's power as a cultural critic lies in part in her ability to draw on eroticism for her own ends, channelling the sexual energies of enthusiasm to the purposes of social order. Hogarth admitted the necessity for religion to draw on enthusiasm when in 1762 he issued a new version of his 1736 print *The Sleeping Congregation* to point the contrast between the enthusiastic and the Anglican congregation. The Anglican preacher in *The Sleeping Congregation* peers shortsightedly at a written text and presides over a church largely free of images. What images there are come from the royal crest and God is represented merely by a diagram of a triangle, a symbol which is echoed in the hats hooked up on the walls and pew boxes and even (inverted) in the witch-like hats of some of the old women. The young woman at the front, her breasts framed by the busks of her corset, is ignored by the congregation – an object of desire only to the viewer of this far from abstract print (and the clerk or curate whose furtive look points the way for the viewer). It is this image that Cowper recalls in a discussion of ineffective preaching in *The Task*:

> Sweet sleep enjoys the Curate in his desk,
> The tedious Rector drawling o'er his head,
> And sweet the Clerk below[59]

The role of enthusiasm became controversial once again in 1800 when Hannah More was accused of employing Methodists in her Sunday schools in Blagdon. More appeared as a dangerous radical to conservatives like Richard Polwhele who once again appealed to Lavington. Polwhele's 1800 *Anecdotes of Methodism* reminded the reader that Lavington 'always spoke of the Methodists, as a fraternity compounded of hypocrites and enthusiasts'.[60]

Polwhele is sure that Methodism equals sexual 'uncleanness' since 'it is really not to be wondered, that persons of all ages and descriptions, assembled in the middle of the night, should be tempted "to work all uncleanness"'.[61] Polwhele continued his campaign when in 1820 he issued a new edition of Lavington's work with a 312-page introduction attacking all manner of targets, including Hannah More, and trying to breathe new life into the Blagdon controversy.[62] A section on 'Female Agency' insists anew on the linking of enthusiasm, sexual crime, radical politics and female power:

Thus is female agency degraded into an engine of fanaticism. It is scarcely more degraded when we see it the instrument of rebellion. '*Female Reforming Societies*,' we observe, have been just established at Blackburn, at Stockport, and at

Manchester. At a late meeting of Reformers at Blackburn, 'a most enchanting scene occurred' – (so says their own *Oracle*) – 'The Female Committee, making their way through immense crowds, ascended the hustings! "Liberty or death!" was vociferated from every mouth: – the tear of sympathy seemed to start from every eye!' – 'The banner was lowered, crowned by the cap of Liberty!' – 'This novel expression of public sentiment would have struck Castlereagh dead to the ground!' – It is notorious that our Reforming Women are, in several places, the most abandoned of the sex. Admitting that they are not so, surely we must see and regret, that they have deserted their proper station.[63]

Given the hostility that Blake displays to the 'Female Will' his work might seem to belong with Polwhele's attacks on 'Female Agency'; but to make such a link would be to miss the consistency of Blake's defence of female agency and of the disruptive power of sexuality. Polwhele recycles old images from Lavington's 1749 attack on the Moravians that appeared in Hogarth's satires in the 1760s and that John Ireland warned over in 1798.

Deriving from the same historical circumstances as Hannah More's, Blake's imagination produces parallels that invert meanings. The entry of Ololon into Blake's garden offers an ironic reversal of a scene in More's 1808 *Coelebs* in which Coelebs, the hero and narrator, leaves the gentry house in which he is staying and wanders into a cottage in the nearby village. Knowingly or not, More replays the primal scene of voyeurism that is common to pornography, mythography and satire in this period, adapting the scenes of pagan ritual that Warburton attempted to cleanse of danger but that still fired the imaginations of Lavington and Hogarth. Ann Stott suggests that this episode shows how More eroticised the work of philanthropy and 'might explain why so many middle-class young women eagerly devoured a book almost entirely void of incident'.[64] But More was baffled and distressed by the accusation of indecency in an unidentified passage from a reviewer in the *Christian Observer*.[65] For More, the cottage location contains the sexual charge, offering the 'site of an idealized, private, domestic life' that, as John Barrell shows, 'was far more widely invoked in the 1790s than in the 1770s or 1780s', and clearly continues to carry ideological meaning in the nineteenth century.[66] The cottage is an emblem of the happiness possible for the lower ranks:

At the distance of a quarter of a mile from the Park-Gate, on a little common, I observed, for the first time, the smallest and neatest cottage I ever beheld. There was a flourishing young orchard behind it, and a little court full of flowers in front. But I was particularly attracted by a beautiful rose tree in full blossom which grew against the house, and almost covered the clean white walls.[67]

Although the 'beautiful rose tree in full blossom' hints at love the cottage is also safe: 'smallest', 'neatest', 'beautiful', 'little' and 'clean'. The narrative replays the familiar story of the loss of innocence with Coelebs, the narrator, in the role of Satan:

I opened the low wicket which led into the little court, and looked about for some living creature of whom I might have begged the flowers. But seeing no one, I ventured to gather a branch of the roses, and the door being opened, walked into the house, in order to acknowledge my theft, and make my compensation.[68]

Desire, in this story, is male and femininity is cleared of the charge of desire since the passive construction allows us to read the opened door either as already opened or as opened by Coelebs. As Anne Mellor comments, 'it is clear that this Eve-like woman must and does arouse his erotic desires as well as his moral approbation'.[69] The rules of this paradisiacal scene are also determined by class. Even though Coelebs asserts the economic probity of the exchange, his entry into the privacy of the cottage is 'Impelled by a curiosity which, considering the rank of the inhabitants, I did not feel it necessary to resist'. Imagined as feminine space, the privacy of the lower-class cottage can be entered uninvited, an assumption that Blake resisted in his confrontation with the soldier Schofield.

If Coelebs is worryingly like Satan creeping into Eden, the words 'softly' and 'gently' (that Hayley used to win over the female reader) seek to make his entry acceptable: 'I softly stole up the narrow stairs, cautiously stooping as I ascended, the lowness of the ceiling not allowing me to walk upright. I stood still at the door of a little chamber, which was left half open to admit the air. I gently put my head through.' The scene he witnesses is a philanthropic pornutopia: the male viewpoint allowing a full exploration of the (here female) fantasy of being discovered doing good, and the power of the scene to arouse Coelebs is striking:

What were my emotions when I saw Lucilla Stanley kneeling by the side of a little clean bed, a large old Bible spread open on the bed before her, out of which she was reading one of the penitential Psalms to a pale emaciated female figure, who lifted up her failing eyes, and clasped her feeble hands in solemn attention! (II, pp. 280–2)

The cottager is a mere adjunct of the scene, herself deprived of sexual power, 'a pale emaciated female figure'. The sexual charge of this undeniably sexual scene is that of the gentry visitors not that of the poor whom they visit.

At the centre of the scene (appropriately for an evangelical) is the revelation of the book: instead of the 'membrum virile' that Lavington imagines as the climax of the Eleusinian mysteries, these rustic mysteries climax in the revelation of the book 'spread open on the bed before her'. Watching this scene provokes Coelebs to a loss of control:

Neither the poor woman nor myself could hold out any longer. She was overcome by her gratitude, and I by my admiration, and we both at the same moment involuntarily exclaimed, Amen! I sprang forward with a motion which I could no longer control. Lucilla saw me, started up in confusion,

> 'and blush'd
> Celestial rosy red.'   (II, p. 283)

The quotation identifies Lucilla as angelic, since More quotes Raphael's response in *Paradise Lost* when Adam asks him how angels express love: 'To whom the angel with a smile that glowed/ Celestial rose red, love's proper hue' (VIII. ll.618–9). Raphael answers that angelic bodies are air not flesh:

> Easier than air with air, if spirits embrace,
> Total they mix, union of pure with pure
> Desiring; nor restrained conveyance need
> As flesh to mix with flesh, or soul with soul.   (VIII, ll.626–9)

More draws on Milton to enforce the distinction between the spiritual and the corporeal that the reviewers saw Blake's illustrations to *The Grave* as dissolving. More thus maintains the distinction between 'the two realms' that Essick sees as typical of the nineteenth century. Whereas Milton represents heavenly sex as the incorporeal mingling of ungendered angelic spirits, More translates this scene into the visual pleasure of Coelebs as he watches Lucilla engaged in the work of philanthropy (and of Lucilla as she sees her own virtuous action mirrored in Coelebs' glance). Blake in *Jerusalem* instead revises Raphael's words from *Paradise Lost* to insist on the continued existence of ungendered bodies in eternity where 'Embraces are Cominglings: from the Head even to the Feet;/ And not a pompous High Priest entering by a Secret Place' (E223). In doing so, he also rejects the framing of sexuality within the contemporary evangelical imagination where, in More's cottage heaven, the 'pompous High Priest' is the watching gentleman.

Lucilla's blush locates her sexuality as unfallen: philanthropy replaces sexuality since all she has to conceal is the Bible: 'Then eagerly endeavouring to conceal the Bible, by drawing her hat over it, "Phoebe," said she

with all the composure she could assume, "is the broth ready?"' (II, p. 284).
From the plucking of the rose unbidden to Lucilla's blush and question
about the broth, desire suffuses the scene, desire legitimated and rendered
safe by the presence of the hidden Bible. Control is located exclusively
within the figure of Coelebs and the poor are doubly distanced from
pleasure in this spectacle. As the third party in a scene of mutual admiration, however, the 'poor woman' also surely represents the role of the
celibate Hannah More: she is the spectator who implicitly admits the
voyeurism inherent in the philanthropic project and the passage, like
Oothoon's imagined offer in *Visions*, acts as a meditation on the problem
of viewing another's pleasure.

More's scene of philanthropy in action seems designed to materialise
the ethical consequences of a philosophy of sensibility in which feeling for
the Other results in practical action. Nevertheless, the scene reveals a
disturbing sense that rather than a meeting with the object of charity the
driving force is a contemplation of the virtue of the self reflected in the
other: Coelebs sees his own goodness manifested in Lucilla. Badiou argues
that in an ethical system based on sympathy 'what I cherish is that me-
myself-at-a-distance which, precisely because it is "objectified" for my
consciousness, founds me as a stable construction, as an interiority accessible in its exteriority'.[70] In the series of mergings that take place at the end
of *Milton* the Other disappears as Ololon joins with Milton.

It would be too easy to argue that Blake celebrates 'happy copulation'
in the 1790s because sex really was about to go out of fashion, threatened
by the regulatory discourses of bourgeois culture, evangelical moralism
and the ideology of the asexual woman. For the regulatory discourse, of
course, is in itself sexual; as Foucault argued, the regulation of sexuality
produces a pervasive sexual discourse.[71] The sexual reading of Hannah
More is the work of my hostile criticism just as the 'libidinousness' of the
illustrations to *The Grave* is created in the reviews of the *Examiner* and
the *Anti-Jacobin*. In Lavington's work it is the bishop who is the pornographer. Cowper's work is pervasively sexual. In Blake's work, however, it
is only rarely that sexuality is a discrete subject.

The conditions of Blake's production process (domestic) and sales
(limited and private) to a few known collectors would have been perfect
for the manufacture and distribution of upmarket pornography.[72] But
with the possible exception of the *Allegory of a Dream of Love*, Blake's
illustrations lack crucial features of contemporary pornography: they
eschew the representation of the isolated (visually castrated) sexual organs
present in the phallic images that fascinated Payne Knight and they avoid

the focus on penetration of other forms of visual pornography. They lack the seductive framing of the female body through loose and slipping clothes which titillate in polite erotica of the period. Karen Harvey shows how 'Erotic culture did not constitute an "impolite" world; rather, it had politeness at its heart, both as something to mock and as something to aspire to'.[73] Sex in Blake's art and writing is not the hidden secret to be revealed in a scene of darkness and fear, nor is sexuality associated exclusively with the viewing of the genitals, the revelation of the *membrum virile* that so horrifies and amuses Lavington. The scene of rapturous reintegration in *The Reunion of the Soul and the Body* is just one of the series of extraordinary forms of penetration in Blake's writing. If this one occurs through the eyes, nose and mouth, reintegration is also imagined via the feet. In Blake's now most famous lyric an intensely eroticised rhetoric describes the longing of 'England's green and pleasant land' for the feet of her lover. In *Milton*, penetration is again via the feet, both in the falling stars that land on the feet of William and Robert Blake, and in the entry of Milton to Blake, Los to Blake and Ololon to Milton.[74] Rather than the contained meeting via hygienic virtual selves in the economy of sentiment described by Adam Smith, or the entry of a 'Pompous high priest by a secret place', Blake's art and writing describe forms of reorganisation that exceed the modern understanding of sexuality.

Notes

INTRODUCTION

1 See in particular Robert Essick's summary of recent critical discussion in 'William Blake's "Female Will" and its biographical context', *Studies in English Literature, 1500–1900*, vol. 31, no. 4, *Nineteenth Century* (autumn 1991), pp. 615–30, 617.

2 S. Foster Damon, *A Blake Dictionary: the Ideas and Symbols of William Blake* (London: Thames and Hudson, 1973, 1979), p. 43.

3 Erdman points out (E813) that the two surviving reissues of 'For the Sexes' are on paper dated 1818 and 1825. *The Complete Poetry and Prose of William Blake*, ed. David E. Erdman, rev. edn (New York: Doubleday, 1998).

4 Quoted Katherine Binhammer, 'Thinking gender with sexuality in 1790s' feminist thought', *Feminist Studies*, vol. 28, no. 3 (autumn 2002), pp. 667–90, 675.

5 Bruce R. Smith, 'Premodern sexualities', *PMLA*, vol. 115, no. 3 (May 2000), pp. 318–29, 318.

6 Gail Bederman, 'Sex, scandal, satire, and population in 1798: revisiting Malthus's first essay', *The Journal of British Studies*, vol. 47, no. 4 (October 2008), pp. 768–95, 769 fn.

7 See Christopher Z. Hobson's 'Blake and the evolution of same-sex subjectivity', in Helen P. Bruder and Tristanne Connolly, eds., *Queer Blake* (Basingstoke: Palgrave Macmillan, 2010), pp. 23–39, 24 for the case against Foucault.

8 Helen P. Bruder, *William Blake and the Daughters of Albion* (Basingstoke: Macmillan, 1997); Christopher Z. Hobson, *Blake and Homosexuality* (New York and Basingstoke: Palgrave, 2000); Andrew Elfenbein, *Romantic Genius: the Prehistory of a Homosexual Role* (New York: Columbia University Press, 1999).

9 Hobson, *Blake and Homosexuality*, p. 34.

10 Binhammer, 'Thinking gender with sexuality in 1790s' feminist thought', p. 668.

11 Anne K. Mellor, 'Blake, gender and imperial ideology: a response', in Jackie DiSalvo, G. A. Rosso and Christopher Z. Hobson, eds., *Blake, Politics, and History* (New York: Garland, 1998), pp. 350–3, 350, 351.

12 See James Grantham Turner, *One Flesh: Paradisal Marriage and Sexual Relations in the Age of Milton* (Oxford: Clarendon Press, 1987), esp. p. 39.

13 'Sexual' to mean 'sexed, sexuate; capable of sexual reproduction' is not cited before 1830 although the sense of 'Designating those organs or anatomical structures concerned in sexual reproduction' is said to exist from 1753: 'Leachery is such a monster, as ... to be no less than a strong inclination to transform the whole bodily frame into sexual organs.'

14 Binhammer, 'Thinking gender with sexuality in 1790s' feminist thought', p. 669. On new constructions of gender see Dror Wahrman, *The Making of the Modern Self: Identity and Culture in Eighteenth-Century England* (New Haven and London: Yale University Press, 2004), esp. pp. 8–70.

15 Tristanne Connolly, *William Blake and the Body* (Basingstoke and New York: Palgrave Macmillan, 2002), p. 211.

16 See, for instance, Christopher Hobson's discussion of the sex of figures in *The Marriage*: *Blake and Homosexuality*, p. 27. Hobson's project is driven, however, by the aim of challenging what is perceived as heterosexual bias within readings of Blake.

17 See Nicholas M. Williams, *Ideology and Utopia in the Poetry of William Blake* (Cambridge University Press, 1998).

18 Alain Badiou, *Ethics: an Essay on the Understanding of Evil*, trans. Peter Hallward (London: Verso, 2002), p. 26.

19 See, for example, Jon Mee, 'Blake's politics in history', in Morris Eaves, ed., *The Cambridge Companion to William Blake* (Cambridge University Press, 2003), pp. 133–49, 146; Saree Makdisi, *William Blake and the Impossible History of the 1790s* (Chicago University Press, 2003), p. 181.

20 Williams, *Ideology and Utopia in the Poetry of William Blake*, p. 78.

21 E. J. Clery, *The Feminization Debate in Eighteenth Century England: Literature, Commerce and Luxury* (Basingstoke: Palgrave Macmillan, 2004), p. 103.

22 Thomas Laqueur, *Making Sex: Body and Gender from the Greeks to Freud,* (Cambridge, MA: Harvard University Press, 1990), pp. 1–3.

23 E. P. Thompson, *Witness Against the Beast: William Blake and the Moral Law* (Cambridge University Press, 1993), p. xv.

24 Makdisi, *Blake and the Impossible History of the 1790s*, p. 3.

25 Marsha Keith Schuchard, *Why Mrs Blake Cried: William Blake and the Sexual Basis of Spritual Vision* (London: Century, 2006), p. 14.

26 Jon Mee, *Dangerous Enthusiasm: William Blake and the Culture of Radicalism in the 1790s* (Oxford: Clarendon Press, 1992, rpt 2002), p. 214.

27 Martin Myrone, *The Blake Book* (London: Tate Publishing, 2007), p. 8.

28 Schuchard, *Why Mrs Blake Cried*; Robert Rix, *William Blake and the Cultures of Radical Christianity* (Aldershot: Ashgate, 2007).

29 Peter Otto, 'A pompous high priest: Urizen's ancient phallic religion in 'The Four Zoas', *Blake: an Illustrated Quarterly*, vol. 35, no. 1 (summer 2001), pp. 4–22, 9. Otto argues persuasively that 'the phallus is created by Urizen as a privileged image of the absolute (god the father/ Heaven), the ultimate

source and guarantor of the Law used to discipline the wayward bodies of the fallen world': p. 5.

30 Northrop Frye, *Fearful Symmetry: a Study of William Blake* (Princeton University Press, 1947, 1969), pp. 167, 313.

31 Makdisi, *William Blake and the Impossible History of the 1790s*, p. 35.

32 See Jon Mee's discussion in *Dangerous Enthusiasm*, pp. 218–23. In contrast to John Howard, Marilyn Butler and Paul Mann, Mee argues that 'Blake's vulgar enthusiasm functioned as the mark of an unrespectability which excluded him from this emergent public sphere' (p. 220). He also points out that Fuseli's support of Blake had 'the air of patronage about it' (p. 221).

33 See Robert N. Essick and Morton D. Paley, '"Dear Generous Cumberland": a newly discovered letter and poem by William Blake', *Blake: an Illustrated Quarterly*, vol. 32, no. 1, (summer 1998), pp. 4–13, 4.

34 See Helen P. Bruder, ed., *Women Reading William Blake* (Basingstoke: Palgrave Macmillan, 2007), esp. Tristanne Connolly's 'Transgender juvenilia: Blake's and Cristall's poetical sketches', pp. 26–34 and Harriet Kramer Linkin's 'William Blake and Romantic women poets: "Then what have I to do with thee?"', pp. 127–36.

35 Myrone, *The Blake Book*, p. 12.

36 Anna Clark, *Desire: a History of European Sexuality* (New York: Routledge, 2008), p. 10.

37 *Ibid.*, p. 7.

38 Angela Carter, *The Sadeian Woman* (London: Virago, 1979, 2000), p. 9.

39 Katherine Binhammer, 'The sex panic of the 1790s', *Journal of the History of Sexuality*, vol. 6, no. 3 (January 1996), pp. 409–34, 410.

40 Clark, *Desire*, p. 10.

41 Robert N. Essick, 'Erin, Ireland, and the emanation in Blake's *Jerusalem*', in Steve Clark and David Worrall, eds., *Blake, Nation and Empire* (Basingstoke: Palgrave Macmillan, 2006), pp. 201–13, 203.

42 Frye, *Fearful Symmetry*, p. 167.

43 Alicia Ostriker, 'Desire gratified and ungratified: William Blake and sexuality', *Blake: an Illustrated Quarterly*, vol. 16 (1982–3), pp. 156–65, 161.

44 Badiou, *Ethics*, p. 21.

45 *Ibid.*, pp. 9ff.

46 Susan Fox, 'The female as metaphor in William Blake's poetry', *Critical Inquiry*, vol. 3 (1977), pp. 507–19.

47 Binhammer, 'The sex panic of the 1790s' p. 410.

1 'HAPPY COPULATION': VISUAL ENTHUSIASM AND THE SEXUAL GAZE

1 Many critics have shown how verbal language behaves strangely in Blake's illuminated poetry. Angela Esterhammer sees copula verbs as crucial to the language of the last plates of *Jerusalem* where the Eternal speakers show 'the performative power of "is"' and thus 'the possibility of creating a new reality through language'. 'Blake and language', in Nicholas M. Williams, ed.,

Palgrave Advances in William Blake Studies (Basingstoke: Palgrave Macmillan, 2006), p. 79. Compare Nicholas Williams, who notes that 'the progress to utopia in Blake is not effected by the elimination of any element in the fallen world, whether sexuality, labor, or war, but instead by the "copula" which will join fallen signifiers to their utopian meanings'. Nicholas M. Williams, *Ideology and Utopia in the Poetry of William Blake* (Cambridge University Press, 1998), p. 88.

2 Josephine Miles, 'Blake's frame of language', in Morton D. Paley and Michael Phillips, eds., *William Blake: Essays in Honour of Geoffrey Keynes* (Oxford: Clarendon Press, 1973), pp. 86–95, 90.

3 Dustin Griffin, *Regaining Paradise: Milton and the Eighteenth Century* (Cambridge University Press, 1986), pp. 75–6. I discuss Blake's use of Bysshe's *Art of Poetry* in chapter 6.

4 According to Eighteenth Century Collections Online which includes only *Poetical Sketches* and *The Book of Thel* by Blake.

5 Quoted, G. E. Bentley, Jr, *A Bibliography of George Cumberland (1754–1848)* (New York and London: Garland Publishing, 1975), p. xliv.

6 Helen P. Bruder, *William Blake and the Daughters of Albion* (Basingstoke: Macmillan, 1997), p. 82.

7 Marcus Wood, *Slavery, Empathy and Pornography* (Oxford University Press, 2002), p. 183.

8 Adam Smith, *The Theory of Moral Sentiments*, ed. Knud Haakonssen (Cambridge University Press, 2002), p. 12.

9 Jonathan Lamb, 'Horrid sympathy', in Michael T. Davis and Paul A. Pickering, eds., *Unrespectable Radicals: Popular Politics in the Age of Reform* (Aldershot: Ashgate, 2008), pp. 91–105, 95.

10 Smith, *Theory of Moral Sentiments*, p. 34.

11 *Ibid.*

12 James Grantham Turner argues that Milton's 'Protestant worship of marital sexuality comes into conflict, potentially, with his iconoclastic suspicion of "imaginations"'. *One Flesh: Paradisal Marriage and Sexual Relations in the Age of Milton* (Oxford: Clarendon Press, 1987), p. 12. Oothoon's demonstration that sexuality is dependent on imagination therefore attacks a problem within Milton's positive view of sexuality.

13 On the lack of a radical visual culture in the 1790s see John Barrell, 'Radicalism, visual culture, and spectacle in the 1790s', *Romanticism on the Net*, no. 46 (May 2007), p. 2, www.erudit.org/revue/ron/2007/v/n46/016131ar.html, accessed 7 October 2010. On the use of anti-Eastern discourse by radicals in the 1790s see David Fallon, '"That angel who rides on the whirlwind": William Blake's oriental apotheosis of William Pitt', *Eighteenth-Century Life*, vol. 31, no. 2 (2007), pp. 1–28, 9.

14 John Barrell, 'The dangerous goddess: masculinity, prestige and the aesthetic in early eighteenth-century Britain', in *The Birth of Pandora and the Division of Knowledge* (Philadelphia, PA: University of Pennsylvania Press, 1992), pp. 63–87, 65.

15 See John Barrell's review of Paulson's Hogarth for a clear exposition of the debate both between Paulson and Solkin, and between Hogarth and Shaftesbury: 'The view from the street: review of *Hogarth*. Vol. i: *The "Modern Moral Subject" 1697–1732*, by Ronald Paulson', *London Review of Books*, vol. 16, no. 7 (1994), p. 18.

16 John Ireland, *Hogarth Illustrated*, 3 vols. (London: J. Boydell, 1791–8), iii, pp. 233–6.

17 On Tom Cooke's engravings see Morris Eaves, *The Counter-Arts Conspiracy: Art and Industry in the Age of Blake* (Ithaca and London: Cornell University Press, 1992), and Morton D. Paley, 'Blake's poems on art and artists', in Sarah Haggarty and Jon Mee, eds., *Blake and Conflict* (Basingstoke, Palgrave Macmillan, 2009), p. 224. Eaves provides a rich account of the 'English school debate' about the visual culture of the nation but misses the significance of enthusiasm in visual culture. Enthusiasm is best explored by Jon Mee, *Romanticism, Enthusiasm and Regulation: Poetics and the Policing of Culture in the Romantic Period* (Oxford University Press, 2003).

18 See David Solkin, 'Exhibitions of sympathy', in *Painting for Money: the Visual Arts and the Public Sphere in Eighteenth Century England* (New Haven and London: Yale University Press, 1992). The exhibitions at the Foundling Hospital are discussed by Ireland, iii, p. 95.

19 Ireland, *Hogarth Illustrated*, iii, p. xvii.

20 *Ibid.*, p. 240.

21 *Ibid.*, p. 235.

22 Ronald Paulson, *Hogarth Vol. iii: Art and Politics 1750–1764* (Cambridge: The Lutterworth Press, 1993), p. 258.

23 Ireland, *Hogarth Illustrated*, iii, p. 75.

24 *Ibid.*, p. 234.

25 *Ibid.*, pp. 75, 77.

26 James Barry, *An Inquiry into the Real and Imaginary Obstructions to the Acquisitions of the Arts in England* (London: T. Becket, 1775), p. 214; quoted by Ireland, iii, p. 33.

27 Barry, *An Inquiry*, p. 64.

28 Quoted G. E. Bentley, Jr, *Blake Records*, 2nd edn (New Haven and London: Yale University Press, 2001), p. 58.

29 Barry, *An Inquiry*, p. 75.

30 *Ibid.*, p. 76.

31 Paulson, *Art and Politics*, pp. 307, 316.

32 *A Tale of a Tub*, sect. viii, quoted from Robert Demaria, Jr, ed., *British Literature 1640–1789: an Anthology*, 2nd edn (Oxford: Blackwell, 1996, 2001), p. 408.

33 *A Tale of a Tub*, sect. viii, from Demaria, p. 408.

34 Colin Podmore, *The Moravian Church in England, 1728–1760* (Oxford: Clarendon Press, 1998), p. 248.

35 *Ibid.*, p. 17.

36 Keri Davies, 'William Blake's mother: a new identification', *Blake: an Illustrated Quarterly*, vol. 33 (1999), pp. 36–50; Keri Davies and Marsha Keith Schuchard, 'Recovering the lost Moravian history of William Blake's family', *Blake: an Illustrated Quarterly*, vol. 38 (2004), pp. 36–57. For Barrell's argument see 'The view from the street', p. 18.

37 [George Lavington, Bishop of Exeter], *The Enthusiasm of Methodists and Papists Compared*, 3rd edn, 2 vols. (London, J. and P. Knapton, 1752), II, pp. 310–11.

38 Quoted by Podmore, *The Moravian Church*, pp. 279–80.

39 [Lavington], *Enthusiasm of Methodists*, II, p. 335. Warburton claimed 'That the *errors of polytheism* were detected, and the *doctrine of the unity* taught and explained in the *mysteries*'. William Warburton, *The Divine Legation of Moses*, 4th edn, 2 vols. (London: J. and P. Knapton, 1755), I, p. 157.

40 [Lavington], *Enthusiasm of Methodists*, II, pp. 308–9.

41 Edmund Burke, *A Philosophical Enquiry into the Origin of our Ideas of the Sublime and Beautiful*, 5th edn (Berwick: R. and J. Taylor, 1772), p. 58.

42 Peter Otto, 'The regeneration of the body: sex, religion and the sublime in James Graham's Temple of Health and Hymen', *Romanticism On the Net*, vol. 23 (August 2001), www.erudit.org/revue/ron/2001/v/n23/005991ar.html, accessed 7 October 2010.

2 FUSELI AND THE 'FEMALE DREAM' OF 'EUROPE'

1 Markman Ellis, *The History of Gothic Fiction* (Edinburgh University Press, 2000, rpt 2003), pp. 6–8, Bond quoted p. 8.

2 [Erasmus Darwin], *The Botanic Garden, A Poem in Two Parts* (London: J. Johnson, 1791), p. 169 fn.

3 Ellis, *The History of Gothic Fiction*, p. 8.

4 Andrew Lincoln, 'From America to the Four Zoas', in Morris Eaves, ed., *The Cambridge Companion to William Blake* (Cambridge University Press, 2003), pp. 210–30.

5 See D. H. Weinglass, 'Fuseli, Henry (1741–1825)', *Oxford Dictionary of National Biography* (Oxford University Press, 2004).

6 See Helen P. Bruder, *William Blake and the Daughters of Albion* (Basingstoke: Macmillan, 1997), p. 69.

7 See Frederick Antal, *Fuseli Studies* (London: Routledge and Kegan Paul, 1956), p. 79.

8 *The Life and Writings of Henry Fuseli*, ed. John Knowles, 3 vols. (London: Colburn and Bentley, 1871), III, p. 47.

9 See Martin Myrone, 'Fuseli to Frankenstein', in *Gothic Nightmares: Fuseli, Blake and the Romantic Imagination* (London: Tate Publishing, 2006), p. 34.

10 Nancy L. Pressly, *The Fuseli Circle in Rome: Early Romantic Art of the 1770s* (New Haven: Yale Center for British Art, 1979), p. vii.

11 John Barrell, 'The dangerous goddess: masculinity, prestige and the aesthetic in early eighteenth-century Britain', *The Birth of Pandora and the Division of*

Knowledge (Philadelphia, PA: University of Pennsylvania Press, 1992), pp. 63–87, 65. John Barrell, *The Political Theory of Painting from Reynolds to Hazlitt: 'The Body of the Public'* (New Haven and London: Yale University Press, 1986), offers the most important account of the role of civic humanism in art theory of the period.

12 See in particular Christopher Z. Hobson, *Blake and Homosexuality* (New York and Basingstoke: Palgrave, 2000), pp. 23–4; David Fallon, '"She cuts his heart out at his side": Blake, Christianity and political virtue', in Sarah Haggarty and Jon Mee, eds., *Blake and Conflict* (Basingstoke: Palgrave Macmillan, 2009), pp. 84–104, 84.

13 Fallon, '"She cuts his heart out at his side"', p. 84.

14 J. J. Winckelmann, *Reflections on the Painting and Sculpture of the Greeks*, trans. Henry Fuseli (London: A. Millar, 1765); Henry Fuseli, *Remarks on the Writings and Conduct of J. J. Rousseau* (London: T. Cadell, J. Johnson and B. Davenport, 1767).

15 Adam Smith, *The Theory of Moral Sentiments*, ed. Knud Haakonssen (Cambridge University Press, 2002), p. 33. For discussions of the role of Smith's *Theory of Moral Sentiments* in relation to Blake see essays by Jon Mee, 'Bloody Blake: nation and circulation', pp. 63–82 and by James Chandler, 'Blake and the syntax of sentiment', pp. 102–18; in Steve Clark and David Worrall eds., *Blake, Nation and Empire* (Basingstoke: Palgrave, 2006).

16 Winckelmann, *Reflections*, p. 30. See Nancy Pressly's account of Fuseli's reading of Winckelmann, *The Fuseli Circle in Rome*, pp. vi–ix.

17 Julia Wright, *Blake, Nationalism, and the Politics of Alienation* (Athens, OH: Ohio University Press), pp. 6–7, argues for Blake's knowledge of both Winckelmann's and Lessing's writing on the *Laocoon* through his contact with Fuseli. Wright's focus is on Blake's rejection of chronological notions of progress.

18 Smith, *Theory of Moral Sentiments*, p. 13.

19 Knowles, *The Life and Writings of Henry Fuseli*, II, pp. 71–2.

20 *Ibid.*

21 *Ibid.*, II, p. 90.

22 *The Political Register and Impartial Review of New Books*, quoted Carol Louise Hall, *Blake and Fuseli: a Study in the Transmission of Ideas* (New York and London: Garland, 1985), pp. 44–5.

23 'Remarks on the Writings and Conduct of J. J. Rousseau', *The Critical Review: or Annals of Literature by a Society of Gentlemen*, vol. 23 (London: A. Hamilton, May 1767), pp. 374–6.

24 *The Letters of Hannah More*, ed. R. Brimley Johnson (London: Bodley Head, 1925), p. 33.

25 *The Critical Review*, p. 375.

26 Hall, *Blake and Fuseli*, p. 44.

27 On the role of Hume in the creation of a feminine public sphere, see Gary Kelly, 'Bluestocking feminism', in Elizabeth Eger, Charlotte Grant, Clíona Ó Gallchoir and Penny Warburton, eds., *Women, Writing and the Public*

Sphere, 1700–1830 (Cambridge University Press, 2001), p. 165 and Harriet Guest, *Small Change: Women, Learning, Patriotism, 1750–1810* (Chicago University Press, 2000), p. 23.

28 E. J. Clery, *The Feminization Debate in Eighteenth-Century England: Literature, Commerce and Luxury* (Basingstoke: Palgrave Macmillan, 2004), p. 1 and on Hume, pp. 171–8.

29 G. J. Barker-Benfield, *The Culture of Sensibility: Sex and Society in Eighteenth-Century Britain* (Chicago University Press, 1992), pp. 326–7.

30 Fuseli, *Remarks on Rousseau*, pp. 37–8.

31 Matthew Lewis, *The Monk*, ed. Howard Anderson (Oxford University Press, 1973), p. 65.

32 M. D. T. Bienville, *Nymphomania, or a Dissertation concerning the Furor Uterinus*, trans. Edward Sloane Wilmot (London: J. Bew, 1775), pp. 171–2.

33 Barker-Benfield, *The Culture of Sensibility*, p. 330.

34 See Jonah Siegel, *Desire and Excess: the Nineteenth Century Culture of Art* (Princeton and Oxford: Princeton University Press, 2000), pp. 40–72.

35 On the importance of the biological theory of culture to Fuseli see Matthew Craske, *Art in Europe 1700–1830* (Oxford University Press, 1997), pp. 239–44.

36 See Lewis M. Knapp, 'Dr John Armstrong, littérateur, and associate of Smollett, Thomson, Wilkes, and Other Celebrities', *PMLA*, vol. 59, no. 4 (December 1944), pp. 1019–58 and Susan Matthews, 'The surprising success of Dr Armstrong: love and economy in the eighteenth century', in Steve Clark and Tristanne Connolly, eds., *Liberating Medicine 1720–1835* (London: Pickering and Chatto, 2009), pp. 193–208.

37 John Armstrong, *The Oeconomy of Love* (London: M. Cooper, 1758), p. 2.

38 Lucretius, *Of the Nature of Things*, trans. Thomas Creech, 2 vols. (London: T. Warner, 1722), I, pp. 3–5. On the influence of Lucretius, see Martin Priestman, *Romantic Atheism: Poetry and Freethought, 1780–1830* (Cambridge University Press, 1999), p. 44.

39 Lancelot Temple [John Armstrong], *A Short Ramble through some parts of France and Italy* (London: Cadell, 1771), pp. 15–17.

40 *Ibid.*, pp. 34–7.

41 Henry Fuseli, *Satirische Selbstkarikatur*, 1778. Zurich, Kunsthaus. Reproduced in Siegel, *Desire and Excess*, p. 46. Siegel reads the image as a lament for the artist, overwhelmed by the art of the past, pp. 47–9.

42 Fuseli lecture XII: 'On the Present State of Art, and the causes which check its progress', Knowles, *The Life and Writings of Henry Fuseli*, III, p. 48.

43 Quoted in *Henry Fuseli 1741–1825* (London: Tate Gallery, 1975), p. 42.

44 Knowles, *The Life and Writings of Henry Fuseli*, III, p. 145.

45 James Barry, *A Letter to the ... President, Vice-Presidents, and the rest of the Noblemen and Gentlemen, of the Society for the Encouragement of Arts, Manufactures and Commerce* (London: Thomas Davison, 1793), p. 2.

46 [J. Boydell], *A Catalogue of the Pictures in the Shakspeare Gallery* (London: Sold at the Place of Exhibition, 1789), p. xii.

47 On the complex range of references in *The Nightmare*, see Christopher Grayling, 'Fuseli's *The Nightmare:* somewhere between the sublime and the ridiculous', in Myrone, ed., *Gothic Nightmares*, p. 14.

48 Knowles, *The Life and Writings of Henry Fuseli*, I, p. 297.

49 Nicholas Williams rightly sees the late concept of the 'Female Will' as an extension of Enitharmon's dominion in *Europe*. See *Ideology and Utopia in the Poetry of William Blake* (Cambridge University Press, 1998), p. 72.

50 Robert Bromley, *A Philosophical and Critical History of the Fine Arts*, 2 vols. (London, T. Cadell, 1793), I, p. 36.

51 *Ibid.*, p. 37.

52 Quoted by Knowles, *The Life and Writings of Henry Fuseli*, I, pp. 182–3.

53 *Ibid.*, p. 183.

54 John Howard, *Infernal Poetics: Poetic Structures in Blake's Lambeth Prophecies* (Cranbury, NJ and London: Associated University Presses, 1984), pp. 149–50.

55 [Boydell], *A Catalogue*, p. x.

56 See Nicola Bown, *Fairies in Nineteenth-Century Art and Literature* (Cambridge University Press, 2001), p. 22. My reading is indebted to Bown's account of the gendering of the painting and the varied sizes of the figures, pp. 21–4.

57 Knowles, *The Life and Writings of Henry Fuseli*, III, p. 144.

58 William Hayley, *A Philosophical, Historical, and Moral Essay on Old Maids*, 3 vols. (London: T. Cadell, 1785), III, p. 137.

59 Mary Wollstonecraft, *A Vindication of the Rights of Woman*, ed. Miriam Brody (Harmondsworth: Penguin, 1975, rev. 1992), p. 151.

60 Charles Allen, *A New and Improved History of England* (London: J. Johnson, 1798), p. 224, quoted D. H. Weinglass, *Prints and Engraved Illustrations By and After Henry Fuseli* (Aldershot: Scolar Press, 2000), p. 186.

61 On Enitharmon and Marie Antoinette, see Bruder, *William Blake and the Daughters of Albion*, pp. 145–64.

62 See David V. Erdman *Prophet against Empire*, 3rd edn (Guildford, Surrey: Princeton University Press, 1954, rpt 1977), p. 221.

63 *The Rape of the Lock, [...] Adorned with Plates* (London: F. J. du Roveray, 1801), p. 46.

64 Knowles, *The Life and Writings of Henry Fuseli*, III, p. 144.

65 On Blake's covert reshaping of the pictorial language of miniature as a form of resistance to Hayley, see Mark Crosby, 'A minute skirmish: Blake, Hayley and the art of miniature painting', in Sarah Haggarty and Jon Mee, eds., *Blake and Conflict* (Basingstoke: Palgrave Macmillan, 2009), pp. 164–84.

66 Bromley, *A Philosophical and Critical History*, I, p. 42.

67 Winckelmann, *Reflections*, p. 8.

68 Humphry Repton, *The Bee* (London [1789]), p. 34.

69 *Ibid.*, p. 48.

70 [Boydell], *A Catalogue*, p. 2.

71 George Cumberland, *Thoughts on Outline* (London: Wilson, Robinson and Egerton, 1796), p. 6.

72 Siegel, *Desire and Excess*, p. 52.

73 *The Analytical Review, or History of Literature, Domestic and Foreign, on an Enlarged Plan* IV (May to August 1789) (London: J. Johnson, 1789), p. 110.

74 Martin Priestman, *Romantic Atheism*, pp. 96–7. The argument that Blake shares Taylor's neoplatonic mistrust of the body derives from Kathleen Raine, *Blake and Tradition*, 2 vols. (London: Routledge, 1969), I, p. 219.

75 David Bindman, *The Complete Graphic Works of William Blake* (Bath: Thames and Hudson, 1978, 1986), pp. 469–70.

76 *Virgil's Aeneid tr. John Dryden*, ed. Frederick M. Keener (London: Penguin, 1997), p. 180.

77 Urania Molyviati-Toptsis, 'Sed falsa ad caelum mittunt insomnia manes (*Aeneid* VI.896)', *The American Journal of Philology*, vol. 116, no. 4 (winter 1995), p. 642.

78 William Warburton, *The Divine Legation of Moses*, 4th edn, 2 vols. (London: J. and P. Knapton, 1755), I, p. 284.

79 [Darwin], *The Botanic Garden*, p. 53 (the notes are separately paginated).

80 See Jon Mee's discussion of Darwin's reading of the story in *Dangerous Enthusiasm: William Blake and the Culture of Radicalism in the 1790s* (Oxford: Clarendon Press, 1992), p. 151.

81 Thomas Taylor, *A Dissertation on the Eleusinian and Bacchic Mysteries* (Amsterdam: J. Weinstein, 1792), advertisement.

82 *Ibid.*, p. 5.

83 Weinglass, *Prints and Engraved Illustrations*, pp. 121–2.

84 See Myrone, *Gothic Nightmares*, p. 166, no. 122.

85 Marina Warner, 'Invented plots: the enchanted puppets and fairy doubles of Henry Fuseli', in Myrone, *Gothic Nightmares*, p. 27.

86 See Hobson, *Blake and Homosexuality*, pp. 36–9.

87 On Blake's knowledge of Hindu culture see David Weir, *Brahma in the West: William Blake and the Oriental Renaissance* (New York: State University of New York Press, 2003) esp. pp. 31–44. Weir points out Blake's 1795 *Song of Los* appears to share the belief of a 1794 *Analytical Review* author that the Hindu religion derives from Egypt (p. 42). Tristanne Connolly in '"The authority of the ancients": Blake and Wilkins' translation of the *Bhagvad-Geeta*', in Steve Clark and Masashi Suzuki, eds., *Blake in the Orient* (London: Continuum, 2006), pp. 145–58, argues that Blake reproduces orientalist assumptions in his view of Hindu culture; Marsha Keith Schuchard, *Why Mrs Blake Cried: William Blake and the Sexual Basis of Spiritual Vision* (London: Century, 2006), pp. 294–300 sees Blake as seeking out detailed knowledge of sexual techniques in Eastern writings.

88 Quoted Weir, *Brahma in the West*, p. 39.

89 Marilyn Butler, *Jane Austen and the War of Ideas* (Oxford: Clarendon Press, 1976), p. 45.

90 See Cora Kaplan, 'Wild nights: pleasure/sexuality/feminism', in Nancy Armstrong and Leonard Tennenhouse, eds., *The Ideology of Conduct: Essays*

in Literature and the History of Sexuality (London and New York: Methuen, 1987), pp. 160–84.

91 Bruder, *William Blake and the Daughters of Albion*, p. 86.

92 Jane Moore, 'Wollstonecraft's secrets', *Women's Writing*, vol. 4, no. 2 (July 1997), pp. 247–62, 249. I find Moore's article by far the most persuasive account of Wollstonecraft on sexuality. See also Adriana Craciun, 'Violence against difference: Mary Wollstonecraft and Mary Robinson', in Greg Clingham, ed., *Making History: Textuality and the Forms of Eighteenth-Century Culture* (Lewisburg, PA: Bucknell University Press, 1998), pp. 111–41. While Craciun takes for granted Wollstonecraft's hostility to sexuality as the basis of women's oppression, she rethinks Wollstonecraft's account of corporeality to stress her concern with female strength.

93 Mary Wollstonecraft, *Political Writings*, ed. Janet Todd (Oxford University Press, 1994), p. 146.

94 *Ibid.*

95 Harriet Guest, *Small Change: Women, Learning, Patriotism, 1750–1810* (University of Chicago Press, 2000), p. 278.

96 On Wollstonecraft's insistent linking of body and mind, see Katherine Binhammer, 'Thinking gender with sexuality in 1790s' feminist thought', *Feminist Studies*, vol. 28, no. 3 (Autumn 2002), pp. 667–90: 'Wollstonecraft achieves the interdependence of the body and mind, in part, through the compounding effect of the repeated phrase "body and mind"' (p. 676).

97 Knowles, *The Life and Writings of Henry Fuseli*, I, p. 402.

3 A HISTORY OF SOFTNESS: WILLIAM HAYLEY
AND 'THE TRIUMPHS OF TEMPER'

1 William Hayley, *The Triumphs of Temper; a poem in six cantos*, 2nd edn (London, for J. Dodsley, 1781), p. viii.

2 John Milton, *Paradise Lost*, ed. Alastair Fowler, 2nd edn (Harlow, London: Longman, 2007).

3 *The Cambridge History of English Literature*, ed. Sir A. W. Ward and A. R. Waller (Cambridge University Press, 1914), XI, p. 176. Saintsbury continues: 'That puerility and anility which were presently to find, for the time, final expression in the Della Cruscan school, displayed themselves in Hayley with less extravagance, with less sentimentality and with less hopelessly bad taste than the revolutionary school were to impart, but still unmistakably' (p. 176).

4 Mary Wollstonecraft, *A Vindication of the Rights of Woman, Political Writings*, ed. Janet Todd (Oxford University Press, 1994), p. 169.

5 G. E. Bentley, Jr, *The Stranger from Paradise: a Biography of William Blake* (New Haven and London: Yale University Press, 2001), pp. 240–1.

6 Blake annotated his copy of *Aphorisms on Man, Translated* [by J. H. Fuseli] *from the Original Manuscript of the Rev. John Caspar Lavater, Citizen of Zuric* (London: J. Johnson, 1788). See *The Complete Poetry and Prose of William Blake*, ed. David E. Erdman, rev. edn (New York: Doubleday, 1988), p. 599.

7 Jon Mee, *Romanticism, Enthusiasm and Regulation: Poetics and the Policing of Culture in the Romantic Period* (Oxford University Press, 2003), p. 257.

8 Jon Mee points out that Blake only uses this term in his later writing, and links its appearance to the hostile reviews of Leigh Hunt: *Romanticism, Enthusiasm and Regulation*, pp. 264–73. Shaun Irlam in *Elations: the Poetics of Enthusiasm in Eighteenth-Century Britain* (Stanford University Press, 1999), describes 'a gradual aestheticization of enthusiasm' in the work of John Dennis, Shaftesbury and Joseph Addison: 'They inaugurated changes in poetic priorities that profoundly altered poetic practice between about 1730 and 1776, between the time of Thomson and Young, and the time of Blake and Cowper' (p. 37).

9 William Hayley, *The Life of Milton, in 3 parts* (London: Cadell and Davis, 1796), p. 132; William Hayley, *Memoirs of the Life and Writings of William Hayley*, ed. John Johnson, 2 vols. (London: Henry Colburn and Simpkin and Marshall, 1823), I, p. 450.

10 Holger Hoock, *The King's Artists: the Royal Academy of Arts and the Politics of British Culture 1760–1840* (Oxford: Clarendon Press, 2003), p. 180.

11 Wollstonecraft, *Political Writings*, p. 89.

12 *Ibid.*, p. 128.

13 Hayley, *Memoirs*, II, p. 217.

14 On the importance of the metaphor of conversation, see Clifford Siskin, *The Work of Writing: Literature and Social Change in Britain 1700–1830* (Baltimore and London: Johns Hopkins University Press, 1998), pp. 164–5.

15 William Hayley, *The Triumphs of Temper; a poem: in six cantos*, 6th edn (London: T. Cadell, 1788).

16 *The Speeches of Edmund Burke*, 4 vols. (London: Longman, Hurst, Rees and Orme, 1816), II, pp. 178–9.

17 *The Works of Hannah More*, 8 vols. (London: Cadell and Davis, 1801), *The Slave Trade*, I, pp. 98–9.

18 Elizabeth Kowaleski-Wallace, *Their Father's Daughters: Hannah More, Maria Edgeworth and Patriarchal Complicity* (New York and Oxford: Oxford University Press, 1991), p. 36.

19 See Anne K. Mellor, *Mothers of the Nation: Women's Political Writing in England, 1780–1830* (Bloomington and Indianapolis: Indiana University Press, 2000); Kevin Gilmartin, '"Study to be quiet": Hannah More and the invention of conservative culture in Britain', *ELH* vol. 70, no. 2 (2003), pp. 493–540.

20 William Cowper, *Poems*, 2nd edn, 2 vols. (London: J. Johnson, 1786), I, p. 17.

21 Samuel Johnson, *Prefaces, Biographical and Critical, to the Works of the English Poets*, 6 vols. (London: J. Nichols, 1779), II, p. 117.

22 Hayley, *Memoirs*, I, p. 312.

23 Harriet Guest, *Small Change: Women, Learning, Patriotism, 1750–1810* (University of Chicago Press, 2000), p. 183.

24 Hayley, *The Triumphs of Temper*, 2nd edn, pp. 2–3.

25 Hannah More, *Sacred dramas ... To which is added, sensibility, a poem* (London: T. Cadell, 1782), p. 289.
26 Cowper, *Poems*, I, p. 142.
27 Roger Lonsdale, ed., *Eighteenth-Century Women Poets* (Oxford University Press, 1989), p. xxxv.
28 Imoinda, 'Stanzas occasion'd by reading the Triumphs of Temper, a Poem by Mr. Hayley', *Town and Country Magazine*, vol. 14 (August 1782), p. 437.
29 Anonymous, 'Bas-Bleu Intelligence', *The Argus* (10 March 1790).
30 Adam Smith, *The Theory of Moral Sentiments*, ed. Knud Haakonssen (Cambridge University Press, 2002), p. 28.
31 Hayley, *Memoirs*, II, pp. 17–19.
32 *Ibid.*, I, p. 22.
33 See William St Clair, *The Reading Nation in the Romantic Period* (Cambridge University Press, 2004), p. 563.
34 Harriet Guest, 'Suspicious minds: spies and surveillance in Charlotte Smith's novels of the 1790s', in Peter de Bolla, Nigel Leask and David Simpson, eds. *Land, Nation and Culture, 1740–1840* (Basingstoke: Palgrave Macmillan, 2005), p. 172.
35 Bentley, *Stranger from Paradise*, pp. 76–7.
36 Flaxman, *Lectures on Sculpture* (London: John Murray, 1829), quoted by Bentley, *Stranger from Paradise*, p. 74, fn.
37 See Michael Phillips's account of attempts to identify the characters in William Blake, *An Island in the Moon: a Facsimile of the Manuscript*, ed. Michael Phillips (Cambridge University Press, 1986), p. 7.
38 Jon Mee, '"A little less conversation, a little more action": mutuality converse and mental fight', in Sarah Haggarty and Jon Mee, eds., *Blake and Conflict* (Basingstoke: Palgrave Macmillan, 2009), pp. 132–3.
39 Mary Wollstonecraft, *A Short Residence in Collected Novels and Memoirs of William Godwin*, ed. Mark Philp, 8 vols. (London: Pickering, 1992), I, p. 113.
40 See Robert N. Essick, *William Blake's Commercial Book Illustrations* (Oxford: Clarendon Press, 1991), pp. 36–8.
41 *Ibid.*, p. 37.
42 OED entry for 'feminization' quoting *Blackwood's Magazine* article from 1844.
43 On characters and caricaturas, see Tim Batchelor, Cedar Lewisohn and Martin Myrone, *Rude Britannia* (London: Tate Publishing, 2010), p. 18.
44 On Blake and the Bakhtinian carnivalesque see David Fallon's '"Creating new flesh on the Demon cold": Blake's *Milton* and the apotheoses of a poet', Blackwell, *Literature Compass*, vol. 2, no. 1 (2005). On the *Four Zoas* marginalia see Peter Otto, *Blake's Critique of Transcendence* (Oxford University Press, 2000), esp. pp. 225–31.
45 For Tristanne Connolly, *The Book of Urizen* is evidence of Blake's view of the body as a grotesque form; see *William Blake and the Body* (Basingstoke and New York: Palgrave Macmillan, 2002), pp. 73–94.
46 *Ibid.*, p. 73.

47 *Ibid.*, p. 93.
48 *The Temple of Folly, in four cantos,* Theophilus Swift (London: J. Johnson, 1787), Frontispiece by Fuseli: see David Weinglass, *Prints and Engraved Illustrations By and After Henry Fuseli* (Aldershot: Scolar Press, 1994), no. 76, p. 84.
49 *The Temple of Folly,* 1.67–70, p. 9.
50 Sarah Scott, *Millenium Hall,* ed. Gary Kelly (Ontario: Broadview, 1995, 1999), p. 71.
51 Swift, *The Temple of Folly.*
52 Wollstonecraft, *Political Writings,* p. 147.
53 Tobias Smollett, *The Expedition of Humphry Clinker,* ed. Angus Ross (Harmondsworth: Penguin, 1967), p. 72.
54 Phillips, 'Introduction', Blake, *An Island in the Moon,* p. 10.
55 Martin Myrone, *The Blake Book* (London: Tate Publishing, 2007), p. 72.
56 William Hayley, *A Philosophical, Historical, and Moral Essay on Old Maids, by a Friend to the Sisterhood,* 3 vols. (London: T. Cadell, 1785), I, p. 158.
57 Hayley, *Memoirs,* I, pp. 239–40.
58 Quoted Morchard Bishop, *Blake's Hayley: the Life, Works and Friendships of William Hayley* (London: Victor Gollancz, 1951), p. 68.
59 More, *Works,* VIII, pp. 219–20.
60 John Armstrong, *The Art of Preserving Health,* introd. J. Aikin (London: T. Cadell and W. Davies, 1795), p. 25.
61 See John Armstrong, *The Art of Preserving Health … to which is prefixed a short account of the author* (Edinburgh: Constable and Hill, 1811): 'The subject of politics divided Armstrong and Wilkes, though in the epistle above mentioned [i.e. *Day*] he concludes a pleasant letter with "ever, ever yours;" but it required a stronger friendship than theirs to resist the men-struum of party-politics' (pp. iii–iv).
62 Hayley, *The Triumphs of Temper,* 2nd edn, p. 119.
63 *Memoirs,* I, p. 210.
64 Letter to Sadleir quoted in the *Memoirs,* I, p. 342.
65 *The Diary of Joseph Farington,* ed. Kenneth Garlick and Angus Macintyre, 17 vols. (New Haven and London: Yale University Press, 1979), IV, p. 1126.
66 Saree Makdisi, *William Blake and the Impossible History of the 1790s* (University of Chicago Press, 2003), p. 79.
67 Quoted by Bishop, *Blake's Hayley,* pp. 64–5.
68 [John Armstrong] *The Oeconomy of Love* (London: M. Cooper, 1758), p. 1.
69 See my 'The surprising success of Dr Armstrong: love and economy in the eighteenth century', in Steve Clark and Tristanne Connolly, eds., *Liberating Medicine* (London: Pickering and Chatto, 2009), pp. 193–208, 204–5.
70 On fears about women's reading see G. J. Barker-Benfield, *The Culture of Sensibility: Sex and Society in Eighteenth-Century Britain* (London: University of Chicago Press, 1992), pp. 326–33.
71 On More's refusal to join in the evangelical campaign against Shakespeare, see Ann Stott, *Hannah More: the First Victorian* (Oxford University Press, 2003), p. 273. Thanks to Philippa Simpson for pointing out this Blake image.

72 Cowper, *Poems*, I, pp. 56–7, 'The Progress of Error'.
73 Anonymous, 'Hayley's Memoirs', *Blackwood's Magazine*, vol. 14 (September 1823), p. 308.
74 Page references are to the second edition, William Hayley, *The Triumphs of Temper; a poem in six cantos* (London: J. Dodsley, 1781) and the twelfth edition William Hayley, *The Triumphs of Temper. A poem in six cantos*, with new original designs by Maria Flaxman (Chichester: J. Seagrave and London: T. Cadell and W. Davies, 1803).
75 Hannah More, *Coelebs in Search of a Wife*, 4th edn, 2 vols. (London: Cadell and Davies, 1809), II, p. 40.
76 *Ibid.*, p. 69.
77 Quoted Iona and Peter Opie, eds., *The Oxford Dictionary of Nursery Rhymes* (Oxford University Press, 1951, 1977), pp. 100–1.
78 David V. Erdman, *Prophet against Empire*, 3rd edn (Guildford, Surrey: Princeton University Press, 1954, rpt 1977), p. 368.
79 Richard Polwhele, *The Unsex'd Females* (New York; republished by Wm Cobbett, 1800) (From Ecco 1800 New York edition as BL 1798 edition missing), p. 6, fn.
80 Polwhele uses the same test as William Gifford in *The Baviad* (London: R. Faulder, 1791), p. 47, who writes that Pope protects against the 'vile infection' of Della Cruscan poetry. Order and hierarchy survive 'if yet there be/ One bosom from this vile infection free' who

> Canst hang enamour'd o'er the magic page,
> Where desperate ladies desperate lords engage,
> While gnomes and sylphs the fierce contention share,
> And heaven and earth hang trembling on a hair …

81 I explore this question in 'Blake, Hayley and the history of sexuality', in Steve Clark and David Worrall, eds., *Blake, Nation and Empire* (Basingstoke: Palgrave Macmillan, 2006), pp. 83–101, 85–9.
82 See Saree Makdisi, 'Blake's metropolitan radicalism', in James Chandler and Kevin Gilmartin, eds., *Romantic Metropolis* (Cambridge University Press, 2005), p. 119.
83 In the Erdman edition words or letters that Blake deleted, erased or wrote over are indicated by italics in square brackets.
84 Scott, *Millenium Hall*, p. 184.
85 *Ibid.*, p. 193.
86 Jane Moore, 'Wollstonecraft's secrets', *Women's Writing*, vol. 4, no. 2 (July 1997), pp. 247–62, 254.

4 THE 'ESSAY ON OLD MAIDS' AND THE LEARNED LADY

1 See A. N. L. Munby, ed., *Sale Catalogues of Libraries of Eminent Persons. Vol. II: Poets and Men of Letters* (London: Mansell, Sotheby, 1971).
2 See John Barrell, *The Spirit of Despotism: Invasions of Privacy in the 1790s* (Oxford University Press, 2006), p. 213.

3 Christopher Z. Hobson, '"What is Liberty without Universal Toleration":
  Blake, homosexuality, and the cooperative commonwealth', in Steve Clark
  and David Worrall, eds., *Blake, Nation and Empire* (Basingstoke: Palgrave
  Macmillan, 2006), pp. 136–52, 152 fn.

4 Andrew Lincoln, 'Restoring the nation to Christianity: Blake and the
  aftermyth of revolution', in Clark and Worrall, *Blake, Nation and Empire*,
  pp. 153–66, 163.

5 William Hayley, *A Philosophical, Historical, and Moral Essay on Old Maids by
  a Friend to the Sisterhood*, 3 vols. (London: T. Cadell, 1785), I, p. xviii.

6 Munby, *Sale Catalogues*, p. 130.

7 Bernard Mandeville, *The Virgin Unmask'd: or Female Dialogues Betwixt an
  Elderly Maiden Lady, and her Niece on Several Diverting Discourses*, 4th edn
  (London: T. Cooper, 1742), pp. 38–9.

8 For an alternative account of the role of circulation in the *Book of Urizen* see
  Jon Mee, 'Bloody Blake: nation and circulation', in Clark and Worrall,
  Blake, Nation and Empire, pp. 63–82, esp. pp. 74–80.

9 Mary Hays, *Memoirs of Emma Courtney*, 2 vols. (London: G. G. and
  J. Robinson, 1796), II, p. 77.

10 Anna Clark, *Desire: a History of European Sexuality* (New York and London:
  Routledge, 2008), p. 2.

11 Sarah Scott, *Millenium Hall*, ed. Gary Kelly (Ontario: Broadview, 1995,
  1999), p. 202. For an extensive discussion of the polypus in Blake and in
  the period which focuses on nature rather than sexuality, see Kevin Hutchings, *Imagining Nature: Blake's Environmental Poetics* (Montreal and Kingston: McGill-Queen's University Press, 2002), pp. 188–204.

12 Erasmus Darwin, *Zoonomia, or the Laws of Organic Life*, 2 vols. (London,
  1794–6), I, p. 488.

13 Martin Madan, *Thelyphthora; or a Treatise on Female Ruin*, 2 vols. (London:
  J. Dodsley, 1780), I.

14 Felicity Nussbaum, 'Polygamy, *Pamela*, and the prerogative of empire',
  in Ann Bermingham and John Brewer, eds., *The Consumption of Culture
  1600–1800: Image, Object, Text* (London and New York: Routledge, 1995),
  pp. 217–36, 224.

15 See E. B. Murray, 'Thel, Thelyphthora, and the Daughters of Albion',
  Studies in Romanticism, vol. 20 (1981), pp. 275–97; David Worrall, 'Thel
  in Africa: William Blake and the post-colonial, post-Swedenborgian
  female subject', in Steve Clark and Masashi Suzuki, eds., *The Reception
  of Blake in the Orient* (London and New York: Continuum, 2006),
  pp. 17–28.

16 Conrad Brunström, *William Cowper: Religion, Satire, Society* (Lewisburg:
  Bucknell University Press, 2004), p. 70.

17 Richard Hill, *The Blessings of Polygamy Displayed* (London: Mathews, Dilly
  and Eddowes, 1781), pp. 39, 48.

18 *The Poems of William Cowper*, ed. John Baird and Charles Ryskamp
  (Oxford: Clarendon Press, 1980), I, p. 232.

19 See my 'Impurity of diction: the 'Harlots Curse' and dirty words', in Sarah Haggarty and Jon Mee, eds., *Blake and Conflict* (Basingstoke: Palgrave Macmillan, 2009) for a longer version of this argument.

20 On the relation of religion and sexuality in *The Monk* see George E. Haggerty, *Queer Gothic* (Urbana and Chicago: University of Illinois Press, 2006), pp. 64–70.

21 Madan, *Thelyphthora*, I, p. 177.

22 On the continuing belief that Protestant Christianity contributed to raising the status of women see Leonore Davidoff and Catherine Hall, *Family Fortunes: Men and Women of the English Middle Classes 1780–1850*, rev. edn (London and New York, 1987, 2002), p. 115.

23 [Kinnaird], *A Letter to the Rev. Mr. Madan* (London: Fielding and Walker, 1780), p. 21.

24 James Grantham Turner, *One Flesh: Paradisal Marriage and Sexual Relations in the Age of Milton* (Oxford: Clarendon Press, 1987), p. 7.

25 John Duncombe, *The Feminiad* (London: M. Cooper, 1754), p. 8, ll.43–8.

26 Cora Kaplan, 'Wild Nights: pleasure/sexuality/feminism', in Nancy Armstrong and Leonard Tennenhouse, eds., *The Ideology of Conduct: Essays in Literature and the History of Sexuality* (London: and New York: Methuen, 1987), p. 163.

27 Madan, *Thelyphthora*, I, pp. vii–viii.

28 *The Poems of William Cowper*, I, pp. 232–8.

29 See Deirdre Coleman, *Romantic Colonization and British Anti-Slavery* (Cambridge University Press, 2005) and my discussion in 'Africa and Utopia: refusing a local habitation', in Clark and Suzuki, pp. 104–20.

30 Nussbaum, 'Polygamy, Pamela, and the prerogative of empire', pp. 224–5.

31 Madan, *Thelypththora*, I, pp. 105–6.

32 Mary Wollstonecraft, *Political Writings*, ed. Janet Todd (Oxford University Press, 1994), p. 142.

33 William Hayley, *The Life of Milton, in three parts, to which are added Conjectures on the origin of Paradise Lost* (London: Cadell and Davis, 1796). In the 1794 edition published by Boydell, Hayley was persuaded to cut references to Milton's republicanism. These sections were replaced for the 1796 Cadell and Davis edition from which I quote.

34 Hayley, *The Life of Milton*, p. 84.

35 John Locke, *Two Treatises of Government*, 17th edn (London: W. Whiston, J. Strahan and F. Rivington, 1722), ch. 7, pp. 236–7.

36 Compare George Cumberland's utopia where the Sophians 'do not object to polygamy, as you call the having more than one wife, when all the parties agree; because there may be many reasons which may make such an arrangement in some ways prudent; but it is very uncommon, on account of the necessity of that agreement'. *The Captive of the Castle of Sennaar*, ed. G. E. Bentley, Jr (Montreal and Kingston: McGill-Queen's University Press, 1991), p. 68.

37 On Blake's 1809 image of the *Whore of Babylon* as a critique of Britain's martial culture see Anthony Blunt, *The Art of William Blake* (London: Oxford University Press, 1959), p. 103.

38 See G. E. Bentley, Jr, 'Thomas Butts, white collar Maecenas', *PMLA*, vol. 71, no. 5 (December 1956), p. 1053.

39 Robert Essick, 'William Blake's "Female Will" and its biographical context', *Studies in English Literature, 1500–1900*, vol. 31, no. 4, *Nineteenth Century* (autumn 1991), p. 621.

40 *Ibid.*, pp. 621–2. Joseph Viscomi suggests that the poem 'To the Phoenix' dates from 1800–3. See *Blake: an Illustrated Quarterly*, vol. 29 (summer 1995), pp. 12–15.

41 Mary Lynn Johnson, '*Milton* and its contexts', in Morris Eaves, ed., *The Cambridge Companion to William Blake* (Cambridge University Press, 2003), pp. 231–50, 247.

42 For a reading of Madan's influence on Blake in biographical terms, suggesting that Blake may have drawn on Madan to support concubinage in the case of marital infertility, see Marsha Keith Schuchard, *Why Mrs Blake Cried: William Blake and the Sexual Basis of Spiritual Vision* (London: Century, 2006), pp. 238–9.

43 Turner, *One Flesh*, p. 24.

44 William Alexander, *The History of Women, from the Earliest Antiquity, to the present time*, 3rd edn, 2 vols. (London: Dilly, 1782), pp. 31–2. Hayley owned this edition.

45 Enoch the Patriarch, tr. Lewis, *History of the Angels, and Their Gallantry With the Daughters of Men* (Oxford, 1715).

46 [William Mason], *The Celestial Beds; or, a Review of the Votaries of the Temple of Health, Adelphi, and the Temple of Hymen* (London, Pall-Mall, 1781).

47 Similarities between the book of Enoch and Blake's myth in the 1790s illuminated books have led to repeated attempts to locate a route for the transmission of the story to Blake. While G. E. Bentley assumes that Blake could not have known of the content of Enoch 1 in any detail until 1821 when the first translation by Richard Laurence appeared, John Beer suggests that Blake may have known passages which appeared in the *Monthly Magazine* in 1801. See G. E. Bentley, Jr, 'A jewel in an Ethiop's ear: the book of Enoch as inspiration for William Blake, John Flaxman, Thomas Moore, and Richard Westall', in Robert N. Essick and Donald Pearce, eds., *Blake in his Time* (Bloomington and London: Indiana University Press, 1978), pp. 213–40 and John Beer, 'Blake's changing view of history: the impact of the book of Enoch', in Steve Clark and David Worrall, eds., *Historicizing Blake* (Basingstoke: St Martin's Press, 1994), pp. 159–78.

48 Angus Whitehead, '"A wise tale of the Mahometans": Blake and Islam, 1819–26', in Jon Mee and Sarah Haggarty, eds., *Blake and Conflict* (Basingstoke: Palgrave Macmillan, 2008) p. 46. fn. Saree Makdisi argues that Blake consistently avoids the tropes of orientalism: see the chapter 'Blake and

Romantic imperialism', in his *William Blake and the Impossible History of the 1790s* (University of Chicago Press, 2003).

49 See *Memoirs of the Life and Writings of William Hayley*, ed. John Johnson, 2 vols. (London: Henry Colbum and Simpkin and Marshall, 1823), I, p. 322. Marsha Keith Schuchard argues that Hayley might have known of the manuscript's arrival in England through the Swedenborgian connections of his friend John Flaxman. *Why Mrs Blake Cried*, pp. 269–71. This account wrongly claims that Hayley knew James Bruce.

50 Schuchard, *Why Mrs Blake Cried*, p. 271. John Johnson mentions Hayley's 'totally abstaining from public worship' and discusses a piece in the *Gentleman's Magazine* that speculates that Hayley shared his friend Gibbon's scepticism: *Memoirs*, II, p. 207.

51 James Bruce, *Travels to Discover the Source of the Nile*, 5 vols. (Edinburgh: J. Ruthven, London: G. G. J. and J. Robinson, 1790); Hayley, *Memoirs*.

52 James Bruce, *Travels to Discover the Source of the Nile*, I.

53 *Ibid.*, I, p. 283.

54 Jane Moore, 'Wollstonecraft's secrets', *Women's Writing*, vol. 4, no. 2 (July 1997), pp. 247–62, 254.

55 Helen P. Bruder, 'The sins of the fathers: patriarchal criticism and the Book of Thel', in *William Blake and the Daughters of Albion* (Basingstoke: Palgrave, 1997), pp. 38–54.

56 Worrall, 'Thel in Africa', p. 17.

57 Edward Larrissy, 'Blake's Orient', *Romanticism*, vol. II, no. 1 (2005), pp. 1–13, 10. See Angus Whitehead's careful discussion of the phrase 'a loose Bible' in 'A wise tale of the Mahometans' in Sarah Haggarty and Jon Mee, eds., *Blake and Conflict* (Basingstoke: Palgrave Macmillan, 2008), pp. 29–30.

58 Bruder, *William Blake and the Daughters of Albion*, p. 177. See also Jon Mee, *Dangerous Enthusiasm: William Blake and the Culture of Radicalism in the 1790s* (Oxford: Clarendon Press, 1992), p. 155.

59 See E. J. Clery, *The Feminization Debate in Eighteenth-Century England: Literature, Commerce and Luxury* (Basingstoke: Palgrave Macmillan, 2004), p. 82.

60 *Ibid.*, p. 71.

61 Quoted *ibid.*, p. 82.

62 For Wahrman, the central subject of *An Essay on Old Maids* is motherhood and the work is as a symptom of a new order rather than a relic of the old insofar as it assumes that maternity is the defining experience 'for each and every woman'. See *The Making of the Modern Self: Identity and Culture in Eighteenth-Century England* (New Haven and London: Yale University Press, 2004), p. 13.

63 Madan, *Thelyphthora*, II, p. 87.

64 Harriet Guest, 'Suspicious minds: spies and surveillance in Charlotte Smith's novels of the 1790s', in Peter de Bolla, Nigel Leask and David Simpson, eds., *Land, Nation and Culture, 1740–1840* (Basingstoke: Palgrave Macmillan, 2005), p. 172.

65 *Ibid.*

66 Jerome McGann, *The Poetics of Sensibility: a Revolution in Literary Style* (Oxford: Clarendon Press, 1996), p. 25.

67 See my 'Hayley on his toilette': Blake, Hayley and homophobia', in Helen P. Bruder and Tristanne Connolly, eds., *Queer Blake* (Basingstoke: Palgrave Macmillan, 2010), pp. 209–20, esp. p. 213.

68 *Blake's Water-colour Designs for the Poems of Thomas Gray*, introd. Geoffrey Keynes (London: Trianon Press, 1971), p. 43.

69 Hayley, *An Essay on Old Maids*, I, 16.

70 Samuel Richardson, *Sir Charles Grandison*, ed. Jocelyn Harris (Oxford University Press, 1986), vol. II, letter II, pp. 231–2.

71 Discussions of Wollstonecraft's use of misogyny include, notably, Susan Gubar, 'Feminist misogyny: Mary Wollstonecraft and the paradox of "it takes one to know one"', *Feminist Studies*, vol. 20 (1994), pp. 452–73. For a recent refutation see Barbara Taylor, *Mary Wollstonecraft and the Feminist Imagination* (Cambridge University Press, 2004).

72 Scott, *Millenium Hall*, pp. 132, 133.

73 *Ibid.*, p. 167.

74 *Ibid.*, p. 18.

75 Clery, *The Feminization Debate*, p. 68.

76 Hayley, *A Philosophical, Historical, and Moral Essay on Old Maids. By a Friend to the Sisterhood*, 3rd edn, 3 vols. with corrections and additions (London: T. Cadell, 1793), III, p. 205.

77 See Joan K. Kinnaird, 'Mary Astell and the conservative contribution to English feminism', *The Journal of British Studies*, vol. 19, no. 1 (autumn 1979), pp. 53–75.

78 See the discussion of this painting and engraving by Lucy Peltz, 'Constructing and celebrating the professional woman in literature and the arts', in Elizabeth Eger and Lucy Peltz, *Brilliant Women: Eighteenth Century Bluestockings* (London: National Portrait Gallery, 2008), pp. 56–93, 59–64.

79 [Hayley] *An Essay on Old Maids*, III, 166.

80 G. A. Rosso, 'The religion of empire: Blake's Rahab in its biblical contexts', in Alexander S. Gourlay, ed., *Prophetic Character: Essays on William Blake in Honor of John E. Grant* (West Cornwall, CT: Locust Hill Press, 2002), pp. 287–326, 299.

81 Catherine L. McClenahan, 'Albion and the sexual machine: Blake, gender and politics 1780–1795', in Jackie DiSalvo, G. A. Rosso and Christopher Z. Hobson, eds., *Blake, Politics and History* (New York and London: Garland Publishing, 1998), pp. 301–24, 301.

82 Quoted by Karen O'Brien, *Women and Enlightenment in Eighteenth-Century Britain* (Cambridge University Press, 2009), p. 228. See O'Brien's whole section on Malthus and women writers, pp. 226–36.

83 Cumberland, *Captive of the Castle of Sennaar*, p. 67.

84 O'Brien, *Women and Enlightenment*, p. 228.

5 COWPER'S FEAR: NATURE, POPULATION, APOCALYPSE

1 Marshall Brown, *Preromanticism* (Stanford University Press, 1991), p. 63.

2 Hannah More, *Strictures on the Modern System of Female Education*, 2 vols., 2nd edn corrected (London: Cadell and Davies, 1799), I.

3 Quoted by Morchard Bishop, *Blake's Hayley: the Life, Works and Friendships of William Hayley* (London: Victor Gollancz, 1951), pp. 99–100.

4 On the importance of Cowper to middle-class evangelical readers see Leonore Davidoff and Catherine Hall, *Family Fortunes: Men and Women of the English Middle Class 1780–1850*, rev. edn (London and New York: Routledge, 1987, 2002), pp. 162–72.

5 Martin Priestman, *Romantic Atheism: Poetry and Freethought, 1780–1830* (Cambridge University Press, 1999), p. 121.

6 Christopher Z. Hobson, *Blake and Homosexuality* (New York and Basingstoke: Palgrave, 2000).

7 See Morton D. Paley, 'Cowper as Blake's spectre', *Eighteenth Century Studies*, vol. I, no. 3 (spring 1968), pp. 236–52, esp pp. 240–1 on Blake's likely knowledge of Cowper's madness.

8 William Hayley, *The Life and Posthumous Writings of William Cowper*, 3 vols. (London: J. Johnson, 1804), I, 135.

9 James Lind, *A Treatise of the Scurvy, in Three Parts*, 2nd edn (London: A. Millar, 1757), p. 135.

10 William Hayley, *A Philosophical, Historical, and Moral Essay on Old Maids, by a Friend to the Sisterhood*, 3 vols. (London: T. Cadell, 1785), I, p. 10.

11 *The Life and Posthumous Writings of William Cowper*, I, 38.

12 Andrew Elfenbein rightly points out that Davidoff and Hall overlook the fact that Cowper was a bachelor, but at the same time fails to see that Hayley presents Cowper as sharing a domestic relationship with Mrs Unwin; see Andrew Elfenbein, *Romantic Genius: the Prehistory of a Homosexual Role* (New York: Colombia University Press, 1999), p. 73.

13 Helen P. Bruder, '"The Bread of sweet Thought & the Wine of Delight": gender, aesthetics and Blake's "dear Friend Mrs Anna Flaxman" (E709)', in Helen P. Bruder, *Women Reading William Blake* (Basingstoke: Palgrave Macmillan, 2007), p. 7.

14 I owe this suggestion to Luisa Calè's paper, delivered 22 September 2006 at the Oxford, 'Blake and Conflict' conference. For an account of Grangerisation see Marcia Pointon, *Hanging the Head: Portraiture and Social Formation in Eighteenth-Century England* (New Haven and London: Yale University Press, 1993), p. 69.

15 Hayley, *The Life and Posthumous Writings of William Cowper*, III, p. viii.

16 William Cowper, *Poems*, 2 vols., 2nd edn (London: J. Johnson, 1786), I, p. 215. Hayley singles out this poem for praise in his 1803 *Life of Cowper*, I, p. 113, using it to end the first section.

17 See Elfenbein, *Romantic Genius*, pp. 63–86.

18 *Ibid.*, p. 84.

19 Quoted *ibid.*, p. 83. Francis Jeffrey, 'Hayley's Life of Cowper', *Edinburgh Review*, vol. 2 (1803), pp. 64–86.

20 Hobson, *Blake and Homosexuality*, p. 18.

21 See my '"Hayley on his toilette"': Blake, Hayley and homophobia', in Helen P. Bruder and Tristanne Connolly, eds., *Queer Blake* (Basingstoke: Palgrave Macmillan, 2010), pp. 209–20.

22 Claude Prosper Jolyot de Crébillon, *The Sopha: a Moral Tale*, trans. anon (London: T. Cooper, 1781), 2 vols.

23 A. N. L. Munby, ed., *Sale Catalogues of Libraries of Eminent Persons*. Vol. II: *Poets and Men of Letters* (London: Mansell, Sotheby, 1971), pp. 83–172.

24 Bishop, *Blake's Hayley*, p. 130.

25 William Hayley, *Two Dialogues; Containing a Comparative View of the Lives, Characters, and Writings, of Philip, the late Earl of Chesterfield, and of Dr. Samuel Johnson* (London: T. Cadell, 1787).

26 William Hayley, *The Triumphs of Temper*, 2nd edn (London: J. Dodsley, 1781), p. 99.

27 George Cumberland, *The Captive of the Castle of Sennaar*, ed. G. E. Bentley, Jr (McGill-Queen's University Press, Montreal and Kingston, 1991), p. 39.

28 Jean-Jacques Rousseau, *Emilius and Sophia; or, a New System of Education*, trans. from the French, 4 vols. (London: T. Beckett and R. Baldwin, 1783), I, p. 361.

29 John Brown, *An Estimate of the Manners and Principles of the Times*, 7th edn (London and Boston: Green and Russell, 1758), p. 18.

30 *Ibid.*, p. 27.

31 *Ibid.*

32 Hayley, *The Life and Writings of William Cowper*, I, p. 12.

33 On the academic uses of the word 'sexuality' see Bruce R. Smith, 'Premodern sexualities', *PMLA*, vol. 115, no. 3 (May 2000), pp. 318–29. The new edition of the OED places the first use three years earlier when J. Walker writes that ('*Elem. Geogr.* (ed. 3) vii. 125 The Linnaean system is founded on the sexuality of plants').

34 William Blake, *Annotations to Richard Watson*, ed. and introd. G. Ingli James (University College Cardiff Press, 1984), p. 7.

35 See Kevis Goodman's account of Cowper reading the newspapers: *Georgic Modernity and British Romanticism: Poetry and the Mediation of History* (Cambridge University Press, 2004), p. 68 onwards.

36 Sir William Hamilton, 'An Account of the late earthquakes in Calabria, Sicily, etc, Communicated to the Royal Society by Sir William Hamilton', *General Evening Post*, September 1783.

37 Hobson, *Blake and Homosexuality*, p. 27.

38 Diana Donald, *The Age of Caricature: Satirical Prints in the Reign of George III* (New Haven and London: Yale University Press, 1996), p. 76. David Bindman sees an echo of the print in *Jerusalem* plate 76: 'William Blake and popular religious imagery', *Burlington Magazine*, vol. 128, no. 1003 (October 1986), pp. 712–18, 714; and D. Bindman, 'The English Apocalypse', in

Francis Carey, ed., *The Apocalypse and the Shape of Things to Come* (London: British Museum Press, 1999), pp. 208–31.

39 S. Whitchurch, *Another Witness! Of Further Testimony in Favor of Richard Brothers*, pp. 4–5, quoted by James K. Hopkins, *A Woman to Deliver her People: Joanna Southcott and English Millenarianism in an Era of Revolution* (Austin, TX: University of Texas Press, 1982), p. xii.

40 Blake, *Annotations to Richard Watson*, p. 14.

41 See David Fallon, '"Creating new flesh on the Demon cold": Blake's Milton and the apotheoses of a poet', *Literature Compass*, vol. 2 no. 1 (2005), pp. 1–17, 5.

42 See Geoffrey Keynes, *The Tempera Paintings of William Blake* (London: Arts Council, 1951), pp. 14–15.

43 S. Foster Damon, *A Blake Dictionary: the Ideas and Symbols of William Blake*, with a new index by Morris Eaves (London: Thames and Hudson, 1965, 1973, 1979), p. 7.

44 See David Worrall, ed., *William Blake: the Urizen Books* (London: The William Blake Trust/The Tate Gallery, 1995), p. 185.

45 See Kazuya Okada's discussion in '"Typhon, the lower nature": Blake and Egypt as the Orient', in Steve Clark and Masashi Suzuki, eds., *The Reception of Blake in the Orient* (London and New York: Continuum, 2006), p. 30.

46 'Love Abused' is included by Hayley in an appendix of original poems; *Life of Cowper*, II, p. 293.

47 Bemard Mandeville, *A Modest Defence of Publick Stews: or an Essay Upon Whoring, as it is Now Practis'd in these Kingdoms. Written by a Layman* (London: A. Moore, 1724), p. 1.

48 *Poems*, II, p. 86.

49 Anne K. Mellor, 'Blake, the Apocalypse and Romantic women writers', in Tim Fulford, ed., *Romanticism and Millenarianism* (New York and Basingstoke: Palgrave, 2002), pp. 139–52.

50 Martha Nussbaum, 'Polygamy, *Pamela*, and the prerogative of empire', in Ann Bermingham and John Brewer, eds., *The Consumption of Culture 1600–1800: Image, Object, Text* (London and New York: Routledge, 1995), pp. 217–36, 224.

51 Hayley, *Memoirs*, I, p. 10.

52 On the separation of sexuality and breastfeeding in the period see also Ruth Perry, 'Colonizing the breast: sexuality and maternity in eighteenth century England', in John C. Font, ed., *Forbidden History: the State, Society and the Regulation of Sexuality in Modern Europe* (Chicago and London: University of Chicago Press, 1992).

53 Cowper, *Poems*, II, p. 38.

54 See Vincent Newey, 'Cowper prospects: self, nature, society', in Gavin Hopps and Jane Stabler, eds., *Romanticism and Religion from William Cowper to Wallace Stevens* (Aldershot: Ashgate, 2006), pp. 41–56.

55 The attribution is suggested by Martin Butlin, *William Blake* (London: Tate Gallery, 1978), p. 82 and discussed by Essick, 'William Blake's "Female Will"

and its biographical context', *Studies in English Literature, 1500–1900*, vol. 31, no. 4 (autumn 1991), pp. 615–30.

56 Hayley, *An Essay on Old Maids*, 1785, I, p. 36.

57 Laurence Sterne, *The life and opinions of Tristram Shandy, gentleman*, 9th edn, 6 vols. (London: J. Dodsley, 1772–3), VI, p. 36.

58 Johann Wolfgang von Goethe, *The Sorrows of Werter*, trans. Daniel Malthus (Oxford and New York: Woodstock Books, 1991), p. 63.

59 Cowper, *Poems*, II, 141–2.

60 *Poems of William Cowper, a New Edition with Plates after Fuseli* (London: J. Johnson, 1806).

61 Joseph Farington, *The Diary of Joseph Farington*, ed. Kenneth Garlick and Angus Mcintyre, 17 vols. (New Haven and London: Yale University Press, 1979), VI, p. 2040; 28 May 1803, quoted D. H. Weinglass, *Prints and Engraved Illustrations By and After Henry Fuseli* (Aldershot: Scolar Press, 2000), p. 313.

62 Quoted *The Life and Writings of Henry Fuseli*, ed. John Knowles, 3 vols. (London: Colburn and Bentley, 1831), I, p. 82.

63 Quoted *ibid.*, pp. 82–3.

64 Quoted *ibid.*, II, p. 88.

65 *Poems by the late William Cowper, illustrated with engravings from the designs of Richard Westall*, 2 vols. (London: John Sharp, 1810).

6 BLAKE READS RICHARDSON: ANTHOLOGIES, ANNOTATION AND CULTURES OF READING

1 See James Chandler, 'Blake and the syntax of sentiment: an essay on "Blaking" understanding', in Steve Clark and David Worrall, eds., *Blake, Nation and Empire* (Basingstoke: Palgrave Macmillan, 2006), pp. 102–18, 105. Chandler comments: 'There is probably another paper entirely in the topic of Blake's relation to Richardson' (p. 104).

2 *The Life and Writings of Henry Fuseli*, ed. John Knowles, 3 vols. (London: Colburn and Bentley, 1831), I, p. 13.

3 David Fallon, '"Creating new flesh on the Demon cold": Blake's Milton and the apotheoses of a poet', *Literature Compass*, vol. 2, no. 1 (2005); John Milton, *Paradise Lost*, ed. Alastair Fowler, 2nd edn (Harlow, London: Longman, 2007), XI, 1.453.

4 The full annotation is quoted by Tom Keymer, *Richardson's Clarissa and the Eighteenth-Century Reader* (Cambridge University Press, 1992), p. 142.

5 Quoted by Jacqueline Pearson, *Women's Reading in Britain 1750–1835: a Dangerous Recreation* (Cambridge University Press, 1999), p. 29. See especially pp. 24–9.

6 Keymer, *Richardson's Clarissa*, pp. 190–1; but see Keymer's whole section on the 'Lovelace controversy', pp. 189–98.

7 On the work of Richardson's *Clarissa* in the transformation of sexual culture see E. J. Clery, *The Feminization Debate in Eighteenth-Century England: Literature, Commerce and Luxury* (Basingstoke: Palgrave Macmillan, 2004), esp. pp. 95–131.

8 *The Correspondence of Samuel Richardson*, ed. Anna Laetitia Barbauld, 6 vols. (London: Richard Phillips, 1804).

9 See Claudia Johnson's account of Barbauld's *The British Novelists* in '"Let me make the novels of a country": Barbauld's The British Novelists (1810/1820)', *Novel*, vol. 34, no. 2 (spring 2001), pp. 163–79.

10 'Introduction' in Samuel Richardson, *Sir Charles Grandison*, ed. Jocelyn Harris (Oxford University Press, 1986), p. iii.

11 Francis Jeffrey, *Samuel Richardson* (London: Longman, Brown, Green, 1853), p. 23.

12 John Barrell, *The Spirit of Despotism: Invasions of Privacy in the 1790s* (Oxford University Press, 2006), pp. 210–28.

13 See *ibid.*

14 John Thelwall, *Poems Chiefly Written in Retirement* (London: R. Phillips, 1801), p. xxix.

15 William Hayley, *The Life and Posthumous Writings of William Cowper*, 3 vols. (London: J. Johnson, 1804), III, p. iv.

16 Margaret Anne Doody, 'Samuel Richardson: fiction and knowledge', in John Richetti, ed., *The Cambridge Companion to the Eighteenth Century Novel* (Cambridge University Press, 1996), p. 109.

17 Henry Boyd, *A Translation of the Inferno of Dante Alighieri in English Verse. With Historical Notes and the Life of Dante*, 2 vols. (London: C. Dilly, 1785), I, p. 40. Blake's annotations are reproduced E633–5.

18 Boyd, *Inferno*, I, p. 40.

19 Samuel Richardson, *Clarissa, or the History of a Young Lady*, 6th edn, 8 vols. (London: J. Rivington, 1768), VII, p. 4.

20 See Robert N. Essick, 'William Blake's "female will" and its biographical content', *Studies in English Literature, 1500–1900*, vol. 31, no. 4, *Nineteenth Century* (autumn 1991), pp. 615–30; Anne K. Mellor, 'Blake, gender and imperial ideology: a response', in Jackie DiSalvo, G. A. Rosso and Christopher Z. Hobson, eds., *Blake, Politics, and History* (New York: Garland, 1998), pp. 350–3.

21 See for instance John Howard, *Infernal Poetics: Poetic Structures in Blake's Lambeth Prophecies* (Cranbury, NJ and London: Associated University Presses, 1984).

22 George Cumberland, *The Captive of the Castle of Sennaar: an African Tale*, ed. G. E. Bentley, Jr (Montreal and Kingston: McGill-Queen's University Press, 1991).

23 Nicholas M. Williams, *Ideology and Utopia in the Poetry of William Blake* (Cambridge University Press, 1998), p. 86.

24 Martin Priestman, *Romantic Atheism: Poetry and Freethought, 1780–1830* (Cambridge University Press, 1999), p. 116.

25 Marcus Wood, *Slavery, Empathy and Pornography* (Oxford University Press, 2002), p. 184.

26 See Melissa M. Matthes, *The Rape of Lucretia and the Founding of Republics: Readings in Livy, Machiavelli and Rousseau* (University Park, PA: Penn State

University, 2000). On the image of rape in the politics of the period, see Ronald Paulson, *Representations of Revolution 1789–1820* (New Haven and London: Yale University Press, 1983), p. 61.

27 See Sylvana Tomaselli in Sylvana Tomaselli and Roy Porter, eds., *Rape: an Historical and Social Enquiry* (London: Basil Blackwell, 1986), p. 2.

28 Martin Myrone, 'Fuseli and Gothic spectacle', *Huntington Library Quarterly*, vol. 70, no. 2 (June 2007), pp. 289–310.

29 William Hayley, *A Philosophical, Historical, and Moral Essay on Old Maids, by a Friend to the Sisterhood*, 3 vols. (London, T. Cadell, 1785), I, p. 84.

30 [Hugh Blair], *A Critical Dissertation on the Poems of Ossian, the Son of Fingal* (London: T. Becket and P. A. De Hondt, 1763), p. 18.

31 Christopher Z. Hobson, *Blake and Homosexuality* (New York and Basingstoke: Palgrave, 2000), p. 29.

32 Alain Badiou, *Ethics: an Essay on the Understanding of Evil*, trans. Peter Hallward (London: Verso, 2002), p. 10.

33 Hobson, *Blake and Homosexuality*, p. 25.

34 Assuming that the Preludium describes rape, most critics focus instead on the identification of a historical referent: for an excellent recent reading see Saree Makdisi, *William Blake and the Impossible History of the 1790s* (Chicago University Press, 2003), pp. 45–52. Makdisi takes the violence of the Preludium to *America* as a reflection of Blake's critique of the limits of the bourgeois revolution of the Americans (who ignored the issue of slavery). Andrew Lincoln reads the Preludium as a prequel to the events of the main poem – a story of the colonisation of America which draws on images of the rape of women of the New World. See Andrew Lincoln, 'From America to the Four Zoas', in Morris Eaves, ed., *The Cambridge Companion to William Blake* (Cambridge University Press, 2003), pp. 210–30, 211.

35 Chandler, 'The syntax of sentiment', p. 110.

36 This section revisits issues discussed in my 'Blake, Hayley and the history of sexuality', in Steve Clark and David Worrall, eds., *Blake, Nation and Empire* (Basingstoke: Palgrave Macmillan, 2006), pp. 83–96.

37 Clery, *The Feminization Debate*, p. 122.

38 *Ibid.*

39 Ian Watt, *The Rise of the Novel* (London: Pirnlico, 1957, 2000), p. 228.

40 *Memoirs of the Life and Writings of William Hayley*, ed. John Johnson, 2 vols. (London: Henry Colburn and Simpkin and Marshall, 1823), II, p. III.

41 *The Correspondence of Samuel Richardson*, ed. Anna Laetitia Barbauld, 6 vols. (London: Richard Phillips, 1804), I, p. c.

42 William Cowper, *Poems*, 2nd edn, 2 vols. (London: J. Johnson, 1786), I, pp. 89–90.

43 Kevin Gilmartin, ' "Study to be quiet": Hannah More and the invention of conservative culture in Britain', *ELH*, vol. 70, no. 2 (2003), pp. 493–540, 517.

44 *The Works of Hannah More*, 8 vols. (London: T. Cadell and W. Davies, 1801), V, p. 46.

45 Quoted by Anne Stott, *Hannah More: the First Victorian* (Oxford University Press, 2003), p. 288.

46 Quoted by Stott, *Hannah More*, p. 319, fn.

47 See Jon Mee, *Dangerous Enthusiasm: William Blake and the Culture of Radicalism in the 1790s* (Oxford University Press, 1992), pp. 161–170, esp. 165.

48 Barbauld, *The Correspondence of Samuel Richardson*, I, p. xxxiv.

49 Paul Baines, 'Bysshe, Edward (fl.1702–1714)', *Oxford Dictionary of National Biography* (Oxford University Press, 2004).

50 William Gifford, *The Baviad* (London: R. Faulder, 1791), p. 27.

51 Edward Bysshe, *The Art of English Poetry*, 9th edn, 2 vols. (London: Hitch and Hawes, 1762), I, p. 236.

52 Elizabeth Bronfen, *Over Her Dead Body: Death, Femininity and the Aesthetic* (Manchester University Press, 1992), pp. 145–6.

53 Leopold Damrosch, Jr, 'Burns, Blake, and the recovery of lyric', *Studies in Romanticism*, vol. 21 (winter 1982), pp. 637–60, 657–8. See also Chandler, 'The syntax of sentiment', p. 105.

54 Mary Wollstonecraft, *Political Writings*, ed. Janet Todd (Oxford University Press, 1994), pp. 122–3.

55 *Ibid.*, p. 181.

56 See my discussion above of secrecy and of Jane Moore's article 'Wollstonecraft's secrets', *Women's Writing*, vol. 4, no. 2 (July 1997), pp. 247–62.

57 Luisa Calè, *Fuseli's Milton Gallery: Turning Readers into Spectators* (Oxford: Clarendon Press, 2006), p. 83.

58 *Ibid.*, p. 111.

59 See William Blake, *The Continental Prophecies*, with introduction and notes by D. W. Dorrbecker (London Millbank: The Tate Gallery/William Blake Trust, 1995), p. 208.

60 H. J. Jackson, *Romantic Readers: the Evidence of Marginalia* (New Haven and London: Yale University Press, 2005), p. 170.

61 On Fuseli's illustrations of similes from *Paradise Lost*, see Calè, *Fuseli's Milton Gallery*, pp. 84–7.

62 For a nuanced version of this debate see Makdisi, *William Blake and the Impossible History of the 1790s*, pp. 171–5.

63 G. E. Bentley, Jr, *A Bibliography of George Cumberland (1754–1848)* (New York and London: Garland Publishing, 1975), p. 57.

64 David V. Erdman, *Prophet against Empire*, 3rd edn (Guildford, Surrey: Princeton University Press, 1954, rpt 1977), pp. 153–4.

65 *Ibid.*, p. 267, fn.

66 William Blake, *The Continental Prophecies*, ed. with introduction and notes by D. W. Dorrbecker (London: Tate Gallery/William Blake Trust 1995), pp. 208–10.

67 *Ibid.*, p. 210

68 Aphra Behn, *Oroonoko and Other Writings*, ed. Paul Salzmann (Oxford University Press, 1994), pp. 211–14. Although there were editions of Behn's

plays and novels early in the eighteenth century, her poems were hard to obtain except through the extracts in Bysshe.

69 Marsha Keith Schuchard, *Why Mrs Blake Cried: William Blake and the Sexual Basis of Spiritual Vision* (London: Century, 2006), p. 314 describes Catherine as reading a poem called 'Enjoyment', but the title is the section in Bysshe, which comprises extracts from many writers.

70 See G. E. Bentley, Jr, *The Stranger from Paradise: a Biography of William Blake* (New Haven and London: Yale University Press, 2001) p. 485, n. 106.

71 Edward Young, *Conjectures on original composition. In a letter to the author of Sir Charles Grandison* (London: Millar and Dodsley, 1759), pp. 20–1.

72 *The Correspondence of Samuel Richardson*, I, p. xix.

73 Bysshe, *The Art of English Poetry*, I, pp. 194–5.

74 Shaun Irlam, *Elations: the Poetics of Enthusiasm in Eighteenth-Century Britain* (Stanford University Press, 1999), p. 49. On the 'detortion' of scripture, see 'Religio Laici', ed. Keith Walker, *John Dryden: the Major Works* (Oxford University Press, 1987), p. 222.

75 *Dryden*, pp. 400–3.

76 *Ibid.*, p. 227.

77 Steven Connor, *Dumbstruck: a Cultural History of Ventriloquism* (Oxford University Press, 2000), p. 61.

78 Mary Shelley, *The Last Man*, ed. Morton D. Paley (Oxford University Press, 1994), pp. 5–6.

79 Adam Clark, *A Letter to a Methodist Preacher* (London: Butterworth and Baynes, 1800), p. 28.

80 [George Lavington, Bishop of Exeter] *The Enthusiasm of Methodists and Papists Compared*, 3rd edn, 2 vols. (London: J. and P. Knapton, 1752), I, p. 69.

81 Pearson, *Women's Reading in Britain*, p. 94.

82 Mary Wollstonecraft, *Political Writings*, ed. Janet Todd (Oxford University Press, 1994), p. 81.

83 Andrew Lincoln, 'Blake and the history of radicalism', in Nicholas M. Williams, ed., *William Blake Studies* (Basingstoke: Palgrave Macmillan, 2006), pp. 214–34, 228.

84 Makdisi, *William Blake and the Impossible History of the 1790s*, p. 169; see also pp. 162–88.

85 Frances Ferguson, 'Rape and the rise of the novel', in *Representations*, pp. 88–112, 101. See also Neil Hertz, 'Two extravagant teachings', *Yale French Studies*, no. 63 (1982), pp. 59–71. Hertz suggests that the academic parade of contextual meanings disguises the extent to which the text reveals its own meaning, lending a spurious authority to the teacher.

86 Keri Davies, 'Mrs Bliss: a Blake collector of 1794', in Steve Clark and David Worrall, eds., *Blake in the Nineties* (Basingstoke: Macmillan Press, 1999), pp. 212–30.

87 Michael Phillips, 'Blake and the Terror, 1792–1793', *The Library* sixth series, vol. 16, no. 4 (December 1994), pp. 263–97.

7 A 'BLANK IN NATURE': BLAKE AND CULTURES OF MOURNING

1 Quoted G. E. Bentley, Jr, *A Bibliography of George Cumberland (1754–1848)* (New York and London: Garland Publishing, 1975), p. 92, from whom this account derives.

2 Quoted *ibid.*

3 Masashi Suzuki links this gesture to Ruth 4:7 where the taking off of a shoe signifies the transfer of property rights at marriage; see *Journal of English and Germanic Philology*, vol. 100 (2001), pp. 40–56. More usefully for my purposes, Robert N. Essick and Joseph Viscomi's edition of *Milton a Poem* (London: Tate Gallery William Blake Trust, 1993), p. 126 argues that 'Los's odd gesture … suggests a basic confusion in the relationship between thought and physical action, conception and execution, similar to Los giving the harrow to Satan'.

4 *The Odyssey of Homer Translated into English Blank Verse by William Cowper*, 2nd edn (London: J. Johnson, 1802), p. 26.

5 On Horne Tooke's language theory in *The Diversions of Purley* see Olivia Smith, *The Politics of Language 1791–1819* (Oxford: Clarendon Press, 1984), esp. pp. 118–21.

6 Joseph Viscomi, 'Blake after Blake: a nation discovers genius', in Steve Clark and David Worrall, eds., *Blake, Nation and Empire* (Basingstoke: Palgrave Macmillan, 2006), p. 217.

7 On copies of *Poetical Sketches* see G. E. Bentley, Jr, *Blake Books* (Oxford: Clarendon Press, 1971), p. 352.

8 Philippe Ariès, *Western Attitudes towards Death from the Middle Ages to the Present*, trans. Patricia M. Ranum (Baltimore, MD: Johns Hopkins University Press, 1974); Colleen McDannell and Bernhard Lang, *Heaven, a History* (New Haven and London: Yale University Press, 1988, 2001), esp. p. 183.

9 Hannah More, *Hints towards Forming the Character of a Young Princess*, 2 vols. (London: Cadell and Davis, 1805).

10 William Godwin, *Collected Novels and Memoirs*, ed. Mark Philp (London: Pickering, 1992), I, p. 87.

11 Benjamin Heath Malkin, *Essays on Subjects Connected with Civilization* (London: E. Hodson for C. Dilly, 1795), advertisement.

12 Benjamin Heath Malkin, *A Father's Memoirs of his Child* (London: Longman, Hurst, Rees and Orme, 1806), p. iii.

13 G. E. Bentley, Jr, *The Stranger from Paradise: a Biography of William Blake* (New Haven and London: Yale University Press, 2001), p. 286, fn. Bentley describes it as 'a frankly vanity publication'.

14 Esther Schor, *Bearing the Dead: the British Culture of Mourning from the Enlightenment to Victoria* (Princeton University Press, 1994), p. 4.

15 Adam Smith, *The Theory of Moral Sentiments*, ed. Knud Haakonssen (Cambridge University Press, 2002), p. 27.

16 Memoir by Charlotte Malkin, British Library, MS Add. 83197.

17 John Locke, *An Essay Concerning Human Understanding*, ed. P. H. Nidditch (Oxford: Clarendon Press, 1975, 1984) I, pp. 369–370.
18 Smith, *Theory of Moral Sentiments*, p. 16.
19 Nicholas Dames, *Amnesiac Selves: Nostalgia, Forgetting, and British Fiction, 1810–1870* (New York and Oxford: Oxford University Press, 2003), p. 9.
20 *Ibid.*, p. 26.
21 See *A Vindication of the Rights of Woman* in Mary Wollstonecraft, *Political Writings*, ed. Janet Todd (Oxford University Press, 1994), p. 123.
22 Malkin, *A Father's Memoirs*, p. xiii.
23 Ann Batten Cristall, *Poetical Sketches* (London: J. Johnson, 1795), p. 157. For discussion of Cristall and Blake, see in particular two essays in Helen P. Bruder, ed., *Women Reading William Blake* (Basingstoke: Palgrave Macmillan, 2006): Tristanne Connolly's 'Transgender juvenilia: Blake's and Cristall's poetical sketches' pp. 26–34 and Harriet Kramer Linkin's 'William Blake and Romantic women poets: "Then what have I to do with thee?"', pp. 127–36. The possibility that Cristall echoes Blake is raised by Duncan Wu, though put down to a shared Ossianic inheritance and assumed by Stuart Curran who describes Cristall as 'that rarest of Romantic poets, a follower of William Blake' (quoted by Linkin, p. 127).
24 Cristall, *Poetical Sketches*, p. 159.
25 Malkin, *A Father's Memoirs*, p. xxiii. The reviewer in the *Literary Journal* called it an 'irrelevant panegyric' (BR229, fn).
26 Mary Wollstonecraft, *Mary and the Wrongs of Woman*, ed. Gary Kelly (London: Oxford University Press, 1976), p. 68.
27 William Hayley, *The Life and Posthumous Writings of William Cowper*, 3 vols. (London: J. Johnson, 1804), I, pp. 44, 47.
28 On Godwin's and Wollstonecraft's evolving views on marriage see Mark Philp, *Godwin's Political Justice* (London: Duckworth, 1986), pp. 180–92.
29 Malkin, *Essays on Subjects Connected with Civilisation*, quoted by [T. J. Mathias], *The Pursuits of Literature* (London: T. Becket, 1797), p. 97 fn.
30 Malkin, *Essays on Civilisation*, p. 257.
31 *A Vindication of the Rights of Woman*, p. 126.
32 Malkin, *Essays on Civilisation*, pp. 261 (quoting Wollstonecraft) and 262.
33 See Robert N. Essick and Morton D. Paley, *Robert Blair's The Grave Illustrated by William Blake: A Study with Facsimile* (London: Scolar Press, 1982), p. 27 and Jon Mee, *Romanticism, Enthusiasm and Regulation: Poetics and the Policing of Culture in the Romantic Period* (Oxford University Press, 2003), pp. 270–1.
34 Anne Button 'Ariel', in Michael Dobson and Stanley Wells, eds., *The Oxford Companion to Shakespeare* (Oxford University Press, 2001).
35 Essick and Paley, *Robert Blair's The Grave*, p. 27.
36 Marcia B. Hall, Introduction in *Michelangelo's Last Judgment* (Cambridge University Press, 2005), p. 20.
37 Essick and Paley, *Robert Blair's The Grave*, p. 20.

38 Philip McEvansoneya, 'Lord Egremont and Flaxman's 'St Michael Overcoming Satan', *The Burlington Magazine*, vol. 143, no. 1179 (June 2001), p. 351.

39 Morton D. Paley, *The Traveller in the Evening: the Last Works of William Blake* (Oxford University Press, 2003), pp. 6–7, suggests that one of the illustrations to Thornton's *Virgil*, no. 13, is a 'graceful compliment to the Egremonts' which acknowledges the earl's 'almost legendary' benefactions to the poor.

40 Steven Goldsmith, *Unbuilding Jerusalem: Apocalypse and Romantic Representation* (Ithaca and London: Cornell University Press, 1993), pp. 146–7.

41 For instance Morton D. Paley, *The Apocalyptic Sublime* (New Haven and London: Yale University Press, 1986), p. 97 refers to 'the even more ambitious version commissioned by the Earl of Egremont'.

42 H. A. Wyndham, *A Family History 1688–1837* (London, New York: Oxford University Press, 1950), p. 223.

43 *The Diary of Joseph Farington*, ed. Kenneth Garlick and Angus Macintyre (New Haven and London: Yale University Press, 1979), III, pp. 1113–14 (18 December 1798).

44 *Ibid.*, p. 1115.

45 McEvansoneya, 'Lord Egremont and Flaxman's "St Michael Overcoming Satan"', p. 352, fn.

46 Christopher Rowell, 'Turner's Petworth', in Christopher Rowell, Ian Warrell and David Blayney Brown, eds., *Turner at Petworth* (London Millbank: National Trust/Tate Publishing, 2002), pp. 15–27, 23.

47 Farington, *Diaries*, VI, p. 2281 (27 March 1804).

48 *Ibid.*

49 On aristocratic sexual mores in the period, see Philp, *Godwin's Political Justice*, p. 177.

50 *The Life and Writings of Henry Fuseli*, ed. John Knowles, 3 vols. (London: Colburn and Bentley, 1831), III, pp. 163–4.

51 On Fuseli's view of Raphael see John Barrell, *The Political Theory of Painting from Reynolds to Hazlitt: 'The Body of the Public'* (New Haven and London: Yale University Press, 1986), pp. 294–300.

52 On Bonasone see Frances Carey, ed., *The Apocalypse and the Shape of Things to Come* (London: British Museum Press, 1999), pp. 186–7.

53 On Michelangelo's *Last Judgment* see Hall, 'Introduction', p. 25. Morton Paley comments on the presence of 'a naked couple embracing' in Signorelli's *Resurrection of the Flesh* and Blake's Last Judgment design for *The Grave*. See Paley, *The Apocalyptic Sublime*, p. 95.

54 Goldsmith, *Unbuilding Jerusalem*, pp. 147–8.

55 *Ibid.*, p. 148.

56 *Ibid.*

57 *Ibid.* quoting Damrosch, *Symbol and Truth in Blake's Myth*.

58 Damrosch, *Symbol and Truth in Blake's Myth*, p. 238.

59 On the 'multiple iterations' of this male figure in Blake's work, from *The Marriage*, to *America* to *The Grave*, see Saree Makdisi, 'The political

aesthetic of Blake's images', in Morris Eaves, ed., The *Cambridge Companion to William Blake* (Cambridge University Press, 2003), pp. 118–26.

8 WOLLSTONECRAFT AND THE ADULTEROUS WOMAN

1 On the publication of Godwin's *Memoirs of the Author of a Vindication of the Rights of Woman* see *Collected Novels and Memoirs of William Godwin*, ed. Mark Philp (London: Pickering, 1992), I, p. 87.

2 On prostitution in the eighteenth century see Laura Rosenthal, *Infamous Commerce: Prostitution in Eighteenth-Century British Literature and Culture* (Ithaca, NY: Cornell University Press, 2006). For a historical account of prostitution, see T. Henderson, *Disorderly Women in Eighteenth-Century London: Prostitution and Control in the Metropolis 1730–1830* (Harlow: Pearson Education, 1999). On anti-adultery literature see Katherine Binhammer, 'The sex panic of the 1790s', *Journal of the History of Sexuality*, vol. 6 (1996), pp. 409–34; Donna T. Andrew, '"Adultery à-la-mode": privilege, the law and attitudes to adultery, 1770–1809', *History*, vol. 82 (1997), pp. 5–23.

3 See Binhammer, 'The sex panic of the 1790s', pp. 409–34.

4 *Memoirs illustrating the History of Jacobinism, translated from the French of the Abbé Barruel*, 4 vols. (London: T. Burton, 1797), I, p. iv.

5 Gail Bederman, 'Sex, scandal, satire, and population in 1798: revisiting Malthus's first essay', *The Journal of British Studies*, vol. 47, no. 4 (October 2008), pp. 768–95, 769.

6 Binhammer, 'The sex panic of the 1790s', p. 421.

7 See Gillian Russell, 'The theatre of crim.con.: Thomas Erskine, adultery and radical politics in the 1790s', in Michael T. Davis and Paul A. Pickering, eds., *Unrespectable Radicals? Popular Politics in the Age of Reform* (Aldershot: Ashgate, 2008), pp. 57–89, 59.

8 Binhammer, 'The sex panic of the 1790s', p. 422.

9 Hannah More, *Strictures on the Modern System of Female Education*, 2 vols. (London: Cadell and Davies, 1799), I, p. 48.

10 Mary Wollstonecraft, *Political Writings*, ed. Janet Todd (Oxford University Press, 1994), p. 199.

11 I explore James Barry's response to the Wollstonecraft scandal, and Blake's praise of Barry's memory, in 'An alternative national gallery: Blake's 1809 exhibition and the attack on evangelical culture', *Tate Papers* (January 2011).

12 Andrew Lincoln, 'Restoring the nation to Christianity: Blake and the after-myth of revolution', in Steve Clark and David Worrall, eds., *Blake, Nation and Empire* (Basingstoke: Palgrave Macmillan, 2006), pp. 153–66 esp. pp. 154–5, 162. Lincoln cites my 1992 essay '*Jerusalem* and nationalism', p. 166 fn., reading this to justify the claim that Blake moves towards the 'language of empire'. My aim was rather to suggest the dirtiness of Blake's language, an argument which I have since developed in 'Impurity of diction: the "Harlots curse" and dirty words', in Sarah Haggarty and John Mee, eds., *Blake and Conflict* (Basingstoke: Palgrave Macmillan, 2009), pp. 65–83.

13 George Cumberland is not mentioned in Godwin's diary, although Horne Tooke was a mutual friend. Godwin records dining at Horne Tooke's on 21 June 1797.

14 Quoted G. E. Bentley, Jr, introduction to George Cumberland, *The Captive of the Castle of Sennaar: an African Tale* (Montreal and Kingston: McGill-Queen's University Press, 1991), p. xliii.

15 Francis Greenacre, 'George Cumberland (1754–1848) writer on art and watercolour painter', *Oxford Dictionary of National Biography*; Sarah Symmons, 'Flaxman, John (1755–1826)', *Oxford Dictionary of National Biography* (Oxford University Press, September 2004).

16 *The Life and Writings of Henry Fuseli*, ed. John Knowles, 3 vols. (London: Colburn and Bentley, 1831), III, p. 103.

17 Mary Wollstonecraft, *Mary and the Wrongs of Woman*, ed. Gary Kelly (London: Oxford University Press, 1976), p. 28.

18 *Ibid.*

19 *Ibid.*, p. 33.

20 *Ibid.*, pp. 33–4.

21 George Cumberland, *Thoughts on Outline* (London: Wilson, Robinson and Egerton, 1796), pp. 44–5.

22 Helen P. Bruder, '"The Bread of sweet Thought & the Wine of Delight": gender, aesthetics and Blake's "dear Friend Mrs Anna Flaxman"', in Helen P. Bruder, ed., *Women Reading William Blake* (Basingstoke: Palgrave Macmillan, 2007), p. 7.

23 *Ibid.*, pp. 44–5.

24 Wollstonecraft, *Political Writings*, p. 200.

25 Cumberland's 'Petwin' is a quotation from 'letter xiv' from John Petvin, *Letters Concerning Mind* (London: John and James Rivington, 1750), p. 81. He omits 'to use the Poet's Expression' before '*in some measure what we behold*'.

26 Cumberland, *Thoughts on Outline*, p. i.

27 See Jonathan Lamb, 'Horrid sympathy', in Davis and Pickering, eds., *Unrespectable Radicals*, pp. 95–6.

28 Richard Polwhele, *The Unsex'd Females* (New York; republished by Wm Cobbett, 1800), p. 11 fn.

29 Katherine Binhammer, 'Thinking gender with sexuality in 1790s' Feminist Thought', *Feminist Studies*, vol. 28, no. 3 (autumn 2002), pp. 667–90. See especially p. 673: 'By modesty, Hays does not mean a denial of sexual feelings'.

30 For the connection between Cumberland and Cagliostro, see G. E. Bentley, Jr, 'Mainaduc, magic and madness: George Cumberland and the Blake connection', *Notes and Queries*, vol. 236 (September 1991), pp. 294–6. Cumberland both collected books about Cagliostro and visited him in prison in Rome. Iain McCalman suggests that Blake represents Cagliostro in *The French Revolution*. See *The Last Alchemist: Count Cagliostro, Master of Magic in the Age of Reason* (London: HarperCollins Perennial, 2004), p. 238.

31 Cumberland, *The Captive of the Castle of Sennaar*, p. 8.
32 *Ibid.*, p. 65.
33 More, *Strictures on the Modern System of Female Education*, I, pp. 85–6.
34 Hannah More, *Coelebs in Search of a Wife*, 4th edn, 2 vols. (London: Cadell and Davies, 1809), p. 404.
35 More quotes here from Nicholas Rowe's *The Fair Penitent* where Sciolto describes his daughter Calista: 'Amidst the general wreck, see where she stands/ Like Helen, in the night when Troy was sack'd/, Spectatress of the mischief which she made.'
36 Cumberland, *Thoughts on Outline*, p. 7.
37 Quoted by Bentley, Jr, 'Introduction', in Cumberland, *Captive*, p. xliv.
38 See in particular Steve Clark, 'Jerusalem as imperial prophecy', in Steve Clark and David Worrall, eds., *Blake, Nation and Empire* (Basingstoke: Palgrave Macmillan, 2006), pp. 175–82.
39 See David Solkin and Philippa Simpson, 'Turner and the North', in David Solkin, ed., *Turner and the Masters* (London: Tate Publishing, 2009), quoting Farington, diary, vol. VIII, 10 June 1807, p. 3,064.
40 Benjamin Heath Malkin, *A Father's Memoirs of his Child* (London: Longman, Hurst, Rees and Orme, 1806); G. E. Bentley, Jr, *Blake Records*, 2nd edn (New Haven and London: Yale University Press), p. 564 and fn.
41 Paul Rapin de Thoyras, *The History of England as well ecclesiastical as civil*, trans N. Tindal, 15 vols. (London: James and John Knapton, 1729), VI, p. 156.
42 Nicholas Rowe, *The Tragedy of Jane Shore*, 15th edn (Dublin: P. Wogan, 1792), p. 48.
43 Malkin's publisher for the 1806 *Father's Memoirs of his Child* is Longman and Rees, the same publisher that Robinson used for the 1799 *Letter to the Women of England.*
44 See Mary Robinson, *A Letter to the Women of England, on the Injustice of Mental Subordination* [1799], ed. Adriana Craciun, Anne Irmen Close, Megan Musgrave, Orianne Smith, A Romantic Circles Electronic Edition http://www.rc.umd.edu/editions/robinson/contents.htm (accessed 14 December 2009).
45 David Fallon, '"That angel who rides on the whirlwind": William Blake's oriental apotheosis of William Pitt', *Eighteenth-Century Life*, vol. 31, no. 2 (2007), pp. 1–28, 18.
46 See Jonathan Lamb, 'Fantasies of paradise', in Martin Fitzpatrick, Peter Jones, Christa Knewllwolf and Iain McCalman, eds., *The Enlightenment World* (Abingdon: Routledge, 2007), pp. 522–3.
47 *A Missionary Voyage to the Southern Pacific Ocean* (London: T. Chapman, 1799), p. 129.
48 See Francis Haskell and Nicholas Penny, *Taste and the Antique: the Lure of Classical Sculpture 1500–1900* (New Haven and London: Yale University Press, 1981), pp. 272–3.
49 *Ibid.*, p. 273.

50 James Barry, *An Account of a Series of Pictures in the Great Room of the Society of Arts, Manufactures, and Commerce, at the Adelphi* (London: Cadell and Walter, 1783), pp. 60–1.

51 *A Missionary Voyage*, pp. 129–30

52 My account of the Thames bathing bills derives from Vic Gatrell's *City of Laughter: Sex and Satire in Eighteenth Century London* (London: Atlantic Books, 2006) and uses his quotations, p. 456.

53 Barry, *An Account of a Series of Pictures*, p. 191.

54 Cumberland, *The Captive of the Castle of Sennaar*, p. 85.

55 James Barry, *An Inquiry into the Real and Imaginary Obstructions to the Acquisitions of the Arts in England* (London: T. Becket, 1775), p. 106.

56 Fallon, "'That angel who rides on the whirlwind'", p. 18.

57 See Morton D. Paley, 'Blake's poems on art and artists', in Sarah Haggarty and Jon Mee, eds., *Blake and Conflict* (Basingstoke: Palgrave Macmillan: 2009), pp. 210–27, esp. p. 224. On Tom Cook's engravings of Hogarth see Morris Eaves, *The Counter-Arts Conspiracy: Art and Industry in the Age of Blake* (Ithaca and London: Cornell University Press, 1992), pp. 221–2.

58 G. E. Bentley, Jr, uses rhyme in the notebook verses to discuss Blake's pronunciation in 'Blake's pronunciation', *Studies in Philology*, vol. 107, no. 1 (winter 2010), pp. 114–29. He concludes that 'Blake's pronunciation defies genteel conventions, both his own and ours' (p. 121). Perhaps equally significant is that Blake uses poetry to record a defiance of genteel convention.

59 William Cowper, *Poems*, 2nd edn, 2 vols. (London: J. Johnson, 1786), II, p. 6.

60 R. Polwhele, *Anecdotes of Methodism* (London: Cadell and Davies, 1800), p. 6.

61 *Ibid.*, p. 35.

62 Anne Stott, *Hannah More, the First Victorian* (Oxford University Press, 2003), pp. 232–57.

63 [George Lavington], *The Enthusiasm of Methodists and Papists Considered, with Notes, Introduction and Appendix* by Rev. R. Polwhele (London: G. and W. B. Whittaker, Sherwood and Co., 1820), p. ccxliii.

64 Stott, *More*, p. 277.

65 *Ibid.*, pp. 279–80.

66 John Barrell, *The Spirit of Despotism: Invasions of Privacy in the 1790s* (Oxford University Press, 2006), p. 214.

67 More, *Coelebs in Search of a Wife*, II, pp. 280–1.

68 *Ibid.*

69 Ann K. Mellor, *Mothers of the Nation: Women's Political Writing in England, 1780–1830* (Bloomington and Indianapolis: Indiana University Press, 2000), p. 30: Mellor emphasises that 'More did not urge women to deny their sexual desires, but only to channel them into marriage with a morally as well as sexually desirable partner' (p. 30).

70 Alain Badiou, *Ethics: an Essay on the Understanding of Evil*, trans. Peter Hallward (London: Verso, 2002), p. 21.

71 Michel Foucault, *The Will to Knowledge: The History of Sexuality*, vol. 1, trans. Robert Hurley (London: Penguin, 1976, 1998), p. 11.
72 See in particular Keri Davies, 'Mrs Bliss: a Blake collector of 1794', in Steve Clark and David Worrall, eds., *Blake in the Nineties* (Basingstoke: Macmillan, 1999), pp. 212–30.
73 Karen Harvey, *Reading Sex in the Eighteenth Century: Bodies and Gender in English Erotic Culture* (Cambridge University Press, 2004), p. 75.
74 See David Fallon, '"My left foot", Milton and Blake', *Blake Journal*, vol. 9 (2007), pp. 20–35.

Bibliography

BLAKE EDITIONS

Blake's Water-colour Designs for the Poems of Thomas Gray, introd. Geoffrey Keynes (London: Trianon Press, 1971).

William Blake, *Annotations to Richard Watson*, ed. and introd. G. Ingli James (University College Cardiff Press, 1984).

An Island in the Moon: a Facsimile of the Manuscript, ed. Michael Phillips (Cambridge University Press, 1986).

The Complete Poetry and Prose of William Blake, ed. David E. Erdman, rev. edn (New York, Doubleday, 1988).

Milton a Poem, ed. Robert N. Essick and Joseph Viscomi (London: Tate Gallery/William Blake Trust, 1993).

The Continental Prophecies ed. with introduction and notes by D. W. Dorrbecker (London Millbank: The Tate Gallery/William Blake Trust, 1995).

The Urizen Books, ed. David Worrall (London: Tate Gallery/William Blake Trust, 1995).

The William Blake Archive, ed. Morris Eaves, Robert N. Essick and Joseph Viscomi, http://www.blakearchive.org/.

MANUSCRIPT

Memoir by Charlotte Malkin. British Library, MS Add. 83197.

WORKS CITED

PRIMARY

Alexander, William, *The History of Women, from the Earliest Antiquity, to the present time*, 3rd edn, 2 vols. (London: Dilly, 1782).

Allen, Charles, *A New and Improved History of England* (London: J. Johnson, 1798).

The Analytical Review, or History of Literature, Domestic and Foreign, on an Enlarged Plan IV (May to August 1789) (London: J. Johnson, 1789).

Anonymous, 'Bas-Bleu Intelligence', *The Argus*, 10 March 1790.

Anonymous, 'Hayley's Memoirs', *Blackwood's Magazine,* vol. 14 (September 1823), pp. 303–8.

Anonymous, *A Missionary Voyage to the Southern Pacific Ocean* (London: T. Chapman, 1799).

Armstrong, John, *The Oeconomy of Love* (London: M. Cooper, 1758).

    The Art of Preserving Health, introd. J. Aikin (London: T. Cadell and W. Davies, 1795).

    The Art of Preserving Health … to which is prefixed a short account of the author (Edinburgh: Constable and Hill, 1811).

[John Armstrong] Lancelot Temple, *A Short Ramble through some parts of France and Italy* (London: Cadell, 1771).

Barruel, Abbé Augustin, *Memoirs illustrating the History of Jacobinism translated from the French of the Abbé Barruel,* 4 vols. (London: T. Burton, 1797).

Barry, James, *An Inquiry into the Real and Imaginary Obstructions to the Acquisitions of the Arts in England* (London: T. Becket, 1775).

    An Account of a Series of Pictures in the Great Room of the Society of Arts, Manufactures, and Commerce, at the Adelphi (London: Cadell and Walter, 1783).

    A Letter to the … President, Vice-Presidents, and the rest of the Noblemen and Gentlemen, of the Society for the Encouragement of Arts, Manufactures and Commerce (London: Thomas Davison, 1793).

Behn, Aphra, *Oroonoko and Other Writings,* ed. Paul Salzmann (Oxford University Press, 1994).

Bienville, M. D. T., *Nymphomania, or a Dissertation concerning the Furor Uterinus,* trans. Edward Sloane Wilmot (London: J. Bew, 1775).

[Blair, Hugh], *A Critical Dissertation on the Poems of Ossian, the Son of Fingal* (London: T. Becket and P. A. De Hondt, 1763).

Boyd, Henry, *A Translation of the Inferno of Dante Alighieri, in English Verse. With Historical Notes, and the Life of Dante* (London: C. Dilly, 1785).

[Boydell, J.], *A Catalogue of the Pictures in the Shakspeare Gallery* (London: Sold at the Place of Exhibition, 1789).

Bromley, Robert, *A Philosophical and Critical History of the Fine Arts,* 2 vols. (London, T. Cadell, 1793).

Brown, John, *An Estimate of the Manners and Principles of the Times,* 7th edn (London and Boston: Green and Russell, 1758).

Bruce, James, *Travels to Discover the Source of the Nile,* 5 vols. (Edinburgh: J. Ruthven London: G. G. J. and J. Robinson, 1790).

Burke, Edmund, *A Philosophical Enquiry into the Origin of our Ideas of the Sublime and Beautiful,* 5th edn (Berwick: R. and J. Taylor, 1772).

    The Speeches of Edmund Burke, 4 vols. (London: Longman, Hurst, Rees and Orme, 1816).

Bysshe, Edward, *The Art of English Poetry,* 9th edition, 2 vols. (London: Hitch and Hawes, 1762).

Clark, Adam, *A Letter to a Methodist Preacher* (London: Butterworth and Baynes, 1800).

Cowper, William, *Poems*, 2nd edn, 2 vols. (London: J. Johnson, 1786).

The Odyssey of Homer Translated into English Blank Verse, 2nd edn (London: J. Johnson, 1802).

Poems of William Cowper, a New Edition with Plates after Fuseli (London: J. Johnson, 1806).

Poems by the Late William Cowper, illustrated with engravings from the designs of Richard Westall, 2 vols. (London: John Sharp, 1810).

The Poems of William Cowper, ed. John D. Baird and Charles Ryskamp, (Oxford: Clarendon Press, 1980).

Crébillon, Claude Prosper Jolyot de, *The Sopha: a Moral Tale*, trans. anon, 2 vols. (London: T. Cooper, 1781).

Cumberland, George, *Thoughts on Outline* (London: Wilson, Robinson and Egerton, 1796).

The Captive of the Castle of Sennaar: an African Tale, ed. G. E. Bentley, Jr (Montreal and Kingston: McGill-Queen's University Press, 1991).

[Darwin, Erasmus], *The Botanic Garden, A Poem in Two Parts* (London: J. Johnson, 1791).

Darwin, Erasmus, *Zoonomia, or the Laws of Organic Life*, 2 vols. (London, 1794–6).

Dryden, John, *The Major Works*, ed. Keith Walker (Oxford University Press, 1987).

trans., *Virgil's Aeneid*, ed. Frederick M. Keener (London: Penguin, 1997).

Duncombe, John *The Feminiad* (London: M. Cooper, 1754).

Enoch the Patriarch, trans. Lewis, *History of the Angels, and Their Gallantry With the Daughters of Men* (Oxford, 1715).

Farington, Joseph, *The Diary of Joseph Farington*, ed. Kenneth Garlick and Angus Macintyre, 17 vols. (New Haven and London: Yale University Press, 1979).

Fuseli, Henry 'Remarks on the Writings and Conduct of J. J. Rousseau', *The Critical Review: or Annals of Literature by a Society of Gentlemen*, vol. 23 (London: A. Hamilton) (May 1767), pp. 374–6.

Remarks on the Writings and Conduct of J. J. Rousseau (London: T. Cadell, J. Johnson and B. Davenport, 1768).

The Life and Writings of Henry Fuseli, ed. John Knowles, 3 vols. (London: Colburn and Bentley, 1831).

Gifford, William, *The Baviad* (London: R. Faulder, 1791).

Godwin, William, *Collected Novels and Memoirs*, ed. Mark Philp (London: Pickering, 1992).

Goethe, Johan Wolfgang von, *The Sorrows of Werter*, trans. Daniel Malthus (Oxford and New York: Woodstock Books, 1991).

Hamilton, William, 'An Account of the late earthquakes in Calabria, Sicily, etc', Communicated to the Royal Society by Sir William Hamilton, *General Evening Post*, September 1783.

Hayley, William, *The Triumphs of Temper; a poem in six cantos*, 2nd edn (London: for J. Dodsley, 1781).

A Philosophical, Historical, and Moral Essay on Old Maids by a Friend to the Sisterhood, 3 vols. (London: T. Cadell, 1785).

Two Dialogues; Containing a Comparative View of the Lives, Characters, and Writings, of Philip, the late Earl of Chesterfield, and of Dr. Samuel Johnson (London: T. Cadell, 1787).

The Triumphs of Temper; a poem: in six cantos, 6th edn (London: T. Cadell, 1788).

A Philosophical, Historical, and Moral Essay on Old Maids. By a Friend to the Sisterhood, 3rd edn, 3 vols., with corrections and additions (London: T. Cadell, 1793).

The Life of Milton, in three parts, to which are added Conjectures on the origin of Paradise Lost (London: Cadell and Davis, 1796).

The Triumphs of Temper, 12th edn, designs by Maria Flaxman (London: Cadell and Davies, 1803).

The Life and Posthumous Writings of William Cowper, 3 vols. (London: J. Johnson, 1804).

Memoirs of the Life and Writings of William Hayley, ed. John Johnson, 2 vols. (London: Henry Colburn and Simpkin and Marshall, 1823).

Hays, Mary, *Memoirs of Emma Courtney*, 2 vols. (London: G. G. and J. Robinson, 1796).

Hill, Richard, *The Blessings of Polygamy Displayed* (London: Mathews, Dilly and Eddowes, 1781).

Imoinda, 'Stanzas occasion'd by reading the Triumphs of Temper, a Poem by Mr. Hayley', *Town and Country Magazine*, vol. 14 (August 1782).

Ireland, John, *Hogarth Illustrated*, 3 vols. (London: J. Boydell, 1791–8).

Jeffrey, Francis, *Samuel Richardson* (London: Longman, Brown, Green, 1853).

Johnson, Samuel, *Prefaces, Biographical and Critical, to the Works of the English Poets*, 6 vols. (London: J. Nichols, 1779).

[Kinnaird], *A Letter to the Rev. Mr. Madan* (London: Fielding and Walker, 1780).

Lavater, John Caspar, *Aphorisms on Man, Translated* [by J. H. Fuseli] *from the Original Manuscript of the Rev. John Caspar Lavater, Citizen of Zuric* (London: J. Johnson, 1788).

[Lavington, George], *The Enthusiasm of Methodists and Papists Compared*, 3rd edn, 2 vols. (London: J. and P. Knapton, 1752).

The Enthusiasm of Methodists and Papists Considered, with Notes, Introduction and Appendix by Rev. R. Polwhele (London: G. and W. B. Whittaker, Sherwood and Co: 1820).

Lewis, Matthew, *The Monk*, ed. Howard Anderson (Oxford University Press, 1973).

Lind, James, *A Treatise of the Scurvy, in Three Parts*, 2nd edn (London: A. Millar, 1757).

Locke, John, *Two Treatises of Government*, 17th edn (London: W. Whiston, J. Strahan and F. Rivington, 1772).

An Essay Concerning Human Understanding ed. P. H. Nidditch (Oxford: Clarendon Press, 1975, 1984).

Lucretius, *Of the Nature of Things*, trans. Thomas Creech, 2 vols. (London: T. Warner, 1722).

Madan, Martin, *Thelyphthora; or a treatise on Female Ruin*, 2 vols. (London: J. Dodsley, 1780).

Malkin, Benjamin Heath, *Essays on Subjects Connected with Civilisation* (London: E. Hodson for C. Dilly, 1795).

A Father's Memoirs of his Child (London: Longman, Hurst, Rees and Orme, 1806).

Mandeville, Bernard *A Modest Defence of Publick Stews: or an Essay Upon Whoring, as it is Now Practis'd in These Kingdoms. Written by a Layman* (London: A. Moore, 1724).

The Virgin Unmask'd: or Female Dialogues Betwixt an Elderly Maiden Lady, and her Niece on Several Diverting Discourses, 4th edn (London: T. Cooper, 1742).

[Mason, William], *The Celestial Beds; or, a Review of the Votaries of the Temple of Health, Adelphi, and the Temple of Hymen* (London, Pall-Mall, 1781).

Mathias, T. J., *The Pursuits of Literature* (London: T. Becket, 1797).

Milton, John, *Paradise Lost*, ed. Alastair Fowler, 2nd edn (Harlow, London: Longman, 2007).

More, Hannah, *Sacred dramas ... To which is added, sensibility, a poem* (London: T. Cadell, 1782).

Strictures on the Modern System of Female Education, 2nd edn corrected, 2 vols. (London: Cadell and Davies, 1799).

The Works of Hannah More, 8 vols. (London: Cadell and Davis, 1801).

Hints towards Forming the Character of a Young Princess, 2 vols. (London: Cadell and Davis, 1805).

Coelebs in Search of a Wife, 4th edn, 2 vols. (London, Cadell and Davies, 1809).

The Letters of Hannah More, ed. R. Brimley Johnson (London: Bodley Head, 1925).

Petvin, John, *Letters Concerning Mind* (London: John and James Rivington, 1750).

Polwhele, Richard, *The Unsex'd Females* (New York; republished by Wm Cobbett, 1800).

Anecdotes of Methodism (London: Cadell and Davies, 1800).

Pope, Alexander, *The Rape of the Lock, ... Adorned with Plates* (London: F. J. du Roveray, 1801).

Rapin de Thoyras, Paul, *The History of England as well ecclesiastical as civil*, trans. N. Tindal, 15 vols. (London: James and John Knapton, 1729), vi.

Repton, Humphry, *The Bee* (London [1789]).

Richardson, Samuel, *Clarissa, or the History of a Young Lady*, 6th edn, 8 vols. (London: J. Rivington, 1768).

The Correspondence of Samuel Richardson, ed. Anna Laetitia Barbauld, 6 vols. (London: Richard Phillips, 1804).

Sir Charles Grandison, ed. Jocelyn Harris (Oxford University Press, 1986).

Robinson, Mary, *A Letter to the Women of England, on the Injustice of Mental Subordination* [1799], ed. Adriana Craciun, Anne Irmen Close, Megan

Musgrave, Orianne Smith, A Romantic Circles Electronic Edition http://www.rc.umd.edu/editions/robinson/contents.htm (accessed 14 December 2009).

Rousseau, Jean-Jacques, *Emilius and Sophia; or, a New System of Education, tr. from the French*, 4 vols. (London: T. Becket and R. Baldwin, 1783).

Rowe, Nicholas, *The Tragedy of Jane Shore*, 15th edn (Dublin: P. Wogan, 1792).

Scott, Sarah, *Millenium Hall*, ed. Gary Kelly (Ontario: Broadview, 1995, 1999).

Shelley, Mary, *The Last Man*, ed. Morton D. Paley (Oxford University Press, 1994), pp. 5–6.

Smith, Adam, *The Theory of Moral Sentiments*, ed. Knud Haakonssen (Cambridge University Press, 2002).

Smollett, Tobias, *The Expedition of Humphry Clinker*, ed. Angus Ross (Harmondsworth: Penguin, 1967).

Sterne, Laurence, *The life and opinions of Tristram Shandy, gentleman*, 9th edn, 6 vols. (London: J. Dodsley, 1772–3).

Swift, Jonathan, *A Tale of a Tub*, Sect. VIII, quoted from Robert Demaria, Jr, ed., *British Literature 1640–1789: an Anthology*, 2nd edn (Oxford: Blackwell, 1996, 2001).

Swift, Theophilus, *The Temple of Folly, in four cantos* (London: J. Johnson, 1787).

Taylor, Thomas, *A Dissertation on the Eleusinian and Bacchic Mysteries* (Amsterdam: J. Weinstein, 1792).

Thelwall, John, *Poems Chiefly Written in Retirement* (London: R. Phillips, 1801).

Warburton, William, *The Divine Legation of Moses*, 4th edn, 2 vols. (London: J. and P. Knapton, 1755).

Winckelmann, J. J., *Reflections on the Painting and Sculpture of the Greeks*, trans. Henry Fuseli (London: A. Millar, 1765).

Wollstonecraft, Mary, *Mary and the Wrongs of Woman*, ed. Gary Kelly (London: Oxford University Press, 1976).

Political Writings, ed. Janet Todd (Oxford University Press, 1994).

Young, Edward, *Conjectures on original composition. In a letter to the author of Sir Charles Grandison* (London: Millar and Dodsley, 1759), pp. 20–1.

SECONDARY

Andrew, Donna T., '"Adultery à-la-mode": privilege, the law and attitudes to adultery, 1770–1809', *History*, vol. 82 (1997), pp. 5–23.

Anonymous, *Henry Fuseli 1741–1825* (London: Tate Gallery, 1975).

Antal, Frederick, *Fuseli Studies* (London: Routledge and Kegan Paul, 1956).

Ariès, Philippe, *Western Attitudes towards Death from the Middle Ages to the Present*, trans. Patricia M. Ranum (Baltimore, MD: Johns Hopkins University Press, 1974).

Badiou, Alain, *Ethics: an Essay on the Understanding of Evil*, trans. Peter Hallward (London: Verso, 2002).

Barker-Benfield, G. J., *The Culture of Sensibility: Sex and Society in Eighteenth-Century Britain* (Chicago University Press, 1992).

Barrell, John *The Political Theory of Painting from Reynolds to Hazlitt: 'The Body of the Public'* (New Haven and London: Yale University Press, 1986).

'The dangerous goddess: masculinity, prestige and the aesthetic in early eighteenth-century Britain', *The Birth of Pandora and the Division of Knowledge* (Philadelphia, PA: University of Pennsylvania Press, 1992), pp. 63–87.

'The view from the street: review of *Hogarth*, Vol. 1: *The "Modern Moral Subject" 1697–1732*, by Ronald Paulson' *London Review of Books*, vol. 16, no. 7 (1994).

The Spirit of Despotism: Invasions of Privacy in the 1790s (Oxford University Press, 2006).

'Radicalism, visual culture, and spectacle in the 1790s', *Romanticism on the Net*, no. 46 (May 2007).

Batchelor, Tim, Cedar Lewisohn and Martin Myrone, *Rude Britannia* (London: Tate Publishing, 2010).

Bederman, Gail, 'Sex, scandal, satire, and population in 1798: revisiting Malthus's first essay', *The Journal of British Studies*, vol. 47, no. 4 (October 2008), pp. 768–95.

Beer, John, 'Blake's changing view of history: the impact of the book of Enoch', in Steve Clark and David Worrall, eds., *Historicizing Blake* (Basingstoke: St Martin's Press, 1994), pp. 159–78.

Bentley, G. E., Jr, 'Thomas Butts, white collar Maecenas', *PMLA*, vol. 71, no. 5 (December 1956), pp. 1052–66.

Blake Books (Oxford: Clarendon Press, 1971).

A Bibliography of George Cumberland (1754–1848) (New York and London: Garland Publishing, 1975).

'A jewel in an Ethiop's ear: the book of Enoch as inspiration for William Blake, John Flaxman, Thomas Moore, and Richard Westall', in Robert N. Essick and Donald Pearce, eds., *Blake in his Time* (Bloomington and London: Indiana University Press 1978), pp. 213–40.

'Mainaduc, magic and madness: George Cumberland and the Blake connection', *Notes and Queries*, vol. 38 (September 1991), pp. 294–6.

The Stranger from Paradise: a Biography of William Blake (New Haven and London: Yale University Press, 2001).

Blake Records, 2nd edn (New Haven and London: Yale University Press, 2004).

Bindman, David, *The Complete Graphic Works of William Blake* (Bath: Thames and Hudson, 1978, 1986).

'William Blake and popular religious imagery', *Burlington Magazine*, vol. 128, no. 1003 (October 1986), pp. 712–18.

'The English Apocalypse', in Francis Carey, ed., *The Apocalypse and the Shape of Things to Come* (London: British Museum Press, 1999), pp. 208–31.

'Blake as a painter', in Morris Eaves, ed., *The Cambridge Companion to William Blake* (Cambridge University Press, 2003), pp. 85–109.

Binhammer, Katherine, 'The sex panic of the 1790s', *Journal of the History of Sexuality*, vol. 6 (1996), pp. 409–34.

'Thinking gender with sexuality in 1790s' feminist thought', *Feminist Studies*, vol. 28, no. 3 (autumn 2002), pp. 667–90.

Bishop, Morchard, *Blake's Hayley: the Life, Works and Friendships of William Hayley* (London: Victor Gollancz, 1951).

Blunt, Anthony, *The Art of William Blake* (London: Oxford University Press, 1959).

Bown, Nicola, *Fairies in Nineteenth-Century Art and Literature* (Cambridge University Press, 2001).

Brewer, John, *The Pleasures of the Imagination: English Culture in the Eighteenth Century* (London: HarperCollins, 1997).

Bronfen, Elizabeth, *Over Her Dead Body: Death, Femininity and the Aesthetic* (Manchester University Press, 1992).

Brown, Marshall, *Preromanticism* (Stanford University Press, 1991).

Bruder, P. Helen, *William Blake and the Daughters of Albion* (Basingstoke: Macmillan, 1997).

' "The bread of sweet thought & the wine of delight": gender, aesthetics and Blake's "dear Friend Mrs Anna Flaxman"', in Helen P. Bruder, ed., *Women Reading William Blake* (Basingstoke: Palgrave Macmillan, 2007), pp. 1–11.

ed., *Women Reading William Blake* (Basingstoke: Palgrave Macmillan, 2007).

Brunström, Conrad, *William Cowper: Religion, Satire, Society* (Lewisburg: Bucknell University Press, 2004).

Butler, Marilyn, *Jane Austen and the War of Ideas* (Oxford: Clarendon Press, 1976).

Butlin, Martin, *William Blake* (London: Tate Gallery, 1978).

Button, Anne, 'Ariel', in Michael Dobson and Stanley Wells, eds., *The Oxford Companion to Shakespeare* (Oxford University Press, 2001).

Calè, Luisa, *Fuseli's Milton Gallery: Turning Readers into Spectators* (Oxford: Clarendon Press, 2006).

Carey, Frances, ed., *The Apocalypse and the Shape of Things to Come* (London: British Museum Press, 1999).

Carter, Angela. *The Sadeian Woman* (London: Virago, 1979, 2000).

Castle, Terry, *The Female Thermometer: Eighteenth-Century Culture and the Invention of the Uncanny* (New York and Oxford: Oxford University Press, 1995).

Chandler, James, 'Blake and the syntax of sentiment: an essay on "Blaking" understanding', in Steve Clark and David Worrall, eds., *Blake, Nation and Empire* (Basingstoke: Palgrave, 2006), pp. 102–18.

Clark, Anna, *Desire: a History of European Sexuality* (New York: Routledge, 2008)

Clark, Steve, 'Jerusalem as imperial prophecy', in Steve Clark and David Worrall, eds., *Blake, Nation and Empire* (Basingstoke: Palgrave Macmillan, 2006), pp. 102–18.

Clery, E. J., *The Feminization Debate in Eighteenth-Century England: Literature, Commerce and Luxury* (Basingstoke: Palgrave Macmillan, 2004).

Coleman, Deirdre, *Romantic Colonization and British Anti-Slavery* (Cambridge University Press, 2005).

Connolly, Tristanne, *William Blake and the Body* (Basingstoke and New York: Palgrave Macmillan, 2002).

'"The authority of the ancients": Blake and Wilkins' translation of the *Bhagvad-Geeta*', in Steve Clark and Masashi Suzuki, eds., *Blake in the Orient* (London: Continuum, 2006), pp. 145–58.

'Transgender juvenilia: Blake's and Cristall's poetical sketches', in Helen P. Bruder, ed., *Women Reading William Blake* (Basingstoke: Palgrave Macmillan, 2007), pp. 26–34.

Connor, Steven, *Dumbstruck: a Cultural History of Ventriloquism* (Oxford University Press, 2000).

Cott, Nancy, 'Passionlessness: an interpretation of Victorian sexual ideology, 1790–1850', *Signs: Journal of Women in Culture and Society*, vol. 4, no. 2 (1978), pp. 219–36.

Craciun, Adriana, 'Violence against difference: Mary Wollstonecraft and Mary Robinson', in Greg Clingham, ed., *Making History: Textuality and the Forms of Eighteenth-Century Culture* (Lewisburg, PA: Bucknell University Press, 1998), pp. 111–41.

Craske, Matthew, *Art in Europe 1700–1830* (Oxford University Press, 1997).

Crosby, Mark, 'A minute skirmish: Blake, Hayley and the art of miniature painting', in Sarah Haggarty and Jon Mee, eds., *Blake and Conflict* (Basingstoke: Palgrave Macmillan, 2009), pp. 164–84.

Dames, Nicholas, *Amnesiac Selves: Nostalgia, Forgetting, and British Fiction, 1810–1870* (New York and Oxford: Oxford University Press, 2003).

Damon, S. Foster, *A Blake Dictionary: the Ideas and Symbols of William Blake*, with a new index by Morris Eaves (London: Thames and Hudson, 1965, 1973, 1979).

Damrosch, Leopold, 'Burns, Blake, and the recovery of lyric', *Studies in Romanticism*, vol. 21 (winter 1982), pp. 637–60.

Davidoff, Leonore and Catherine Hall, *Family Fortunes: Men and Women of the English Middle Classes 1780–1850*, rev. edn (London and New York: Routledge, 1987, 2002).

Davies, Keri. 'William Blake's mother: a new identification', *Blake: An Illustrated Quarterly*, vol. 33 (1999), pp. 36–50.

'Mrs Bliss: a Blake collector of 1794', in Steve Clark and David Worrall, eds., *Blake in the Nineties* (Basingstoke: Macmillan Press, 1999), pp. 212–30.

Davies, Keri and Marsha Keith Schuchard, 'Recovering the lost Moravian history of William Blake's family', *Blake: An Illustrated Quarterly*, vol. 38 (2004), pp. 36–57.

DiSalvo, Jackie, G. A. Rosso and Christopher Z. Hobson, eds., 'Albion and the sexual machine: Blake, gender and politics 1780–1795', in *Blake, Politics and History* (New York and London: Garland Publishing, 1998), pp. 301–24.

Donald, Diana, *The Age of Caricature: Satirical Prints in the Reign of George III* (New Haven and London, Yale University Press, 1996).

Doody, Margaret Anne, 'Samuel Richardson: fiction and knowledge', in John Richetti, ed., *The Cambridge Companion to the Eighteenth Century Novel* (Cambridge University Press, 1996).

Eaves, Morris, *The Counter-Arts Conspiracy: Art and Industry in the Age of Blake* (Ithaca and London: Cornell University Press, 1992).

Elfenbein, Andrew, *Romantic Genius: the Prehistory of a Homosexual Role* (New York: Columbia University Press, 1999).

Ellis, Markman, *The History of Gothic Fiction* (Edinburgh University Press, 2000, rpt 2003).

Erdman, David V., *Prophet against Empire*, 3rd edn (Guildford, Surrey: Princeton University Press, 1954, rpt 1977).

Essick, Robert N., *William Blake's Commercial Book Illustrations* (Oxford: Clarendon Press, 1991).

'William Blake's "Female Will" and its biographical context', *Studies in English Literature, 1500–1900*, vol. 31, no. 4, *Nineteenth Century* (autumn 1991), pp. 615–30.

'Erin, Ireland, and the emanation in Blake's *Jerusalem*', in Steve Clark and David Worrall, eds., *Blake, Nation and Empire* (Basingstoke: Palgrave Macmillan, 2006), pp. 201–13.

Essick, Robert N. and Morton D. Paley, *Robert Blair's The Grave Illustrated by William Blake: a Study with Facsimile* (London: Scolar Press, 1982).

'"Dear Generous Cumberland": a newly disovered letter and poem by William Blake', *Blake: An Illustrated Quarterly*, vol. 32, no. 1 (summer 1998), pp. 4–13.

Esterhammer, Angela, "Blake and language", in Nicholas M. Williams, ed., *Palgrave Advances in William Blake Studies* (Basingstoke: Palgrave Macmillan, 2006).

Fallon, David '"Creating new flesh on the Demon cold": Blake's Milton and the apotheoses of a poet', *Blackwell Literature Compass*, vol. 2, no. 1 (2005), pp. 1–17.

'"That angel who rides on the whirlwind": William Blake's oriental apotheosis of William Pitt', *Eighteenth-Century Life*, vol. 31, no. 2 (2007), pp. 1–28.

'"My left foot", Milton and Blake', *Blake Journal*, vol. 9 (2007), pp. 20–35.

' "She cuts his heart out at his side": Blake, Christianity and political virtue', in Sarah Haggarty and Jon Mee, eds., *Blake and Conflict* (Basingstoke: Palgrave Macmillan, 2009).

Ferguson, Frances, *'Rape and the Rise of the Novel'*, in *Representations*, vol. 20 (fall 1987), pp. 88–112.

Foucault, Michel, *The Will to Knowledge: the History of Sexuality*, vol. 1, trans. Robert Hurley (London: Penguin, 1976, 1998).

Fox, Susan, 'The female as metaphor in William Blake's poetry', *Critical Inquiry*, vol. 3 (1977), pp. 507–19.

Frye, Northrop, *Fearful Symmetry: a Study of William Blake* (Princeton University Press, 1947, 1969).

Gatrell, Vic, *City of Laughter: Sex and Satire in Eighteenth Century London* (London: Atlantic, 2006).

Gilmartin, Kevin, '"Study to be quiet": Hannah More and the invention of conservative culture in Britain', *ELH*, vol. 70, no. 2 (2003), pp. 493–540.

Goldsmith, Steven, *Unbuilding Jerusalem: Apocalypse and Romantic Representation* (Ithaca and London: Cornell University Press, 1993).

Goodman, Kevis, *Georgic Modernity and British Romanticism: Poetry and the Mediation of History* (Cambridge University Press, 2004).

Grayling, Christopher, 'Fuseli's *The Nightmare*: somewhere between the sublime and the ridiculous', in Martin Myrone, *Gothic Nightmares: Fuseli, Blake and the Romantic Imagination* (London: Tate Publishing, 2006).

Greenacre, Francis, 'George Cumberland (1754–1848) writer on art and watercolour painter', *Oxford Dictionary of National Biography* (Oxford University Press: September 2004).

Griffin, Dustin, *Regaining Paradise: Milton and the Eighteenth Century* (Cambridge University Press, 1986).

Gubar, Susan, 'Feminist misogyny: Mary Wollstonecraft and the paradox of "it takes one to know one"', *Feminist Studies*, vol. 20 (1994), pp. 231–2.

Guest, Harriet, *Small Change: Women, Learning, Patriotism, 1750–1810* (Chicago University Press, 2000).

'Suspicious minds: spies and surveillance in Charlotte Smith's novels of the 1790s', in Peter de Bolla, Nigel Leask and David Simpson, eds., *Land, Nation and Culture, 1740–1840* (Basingstoke: Palgrave Macmillan, 2005), pp. 169–87.

Haggerty, George E., *Queer Gothic* (Urbana and Chicago: University of Illinois Press, 2006).

Hall, Carol Louise, *Blake and Fuseli: a Study in the Transmission of Ideas* (New York and London: Garland, 1985).

Hall, Marcia B., Introduction in Marcia B. Hall, ed., *Michelangelo's Last Judgment* (Cambridge University Press, 2005).

Harvey, Karen, *Reading Sex in the Eighteenth Century: Bodies and Gender in English Erotic Culture* (Cambridge University Press, 2004).

Haskell, Francis and Nicholas Penny, *Taste and the Antique: the Lure of Classical Sculpture 1500–1900* (New Haven and London: Yale University Press, 1981).

Henderson, T., *Disorderly Women in Eighteenth-Century London: Prostitution and Control in the Metropolis 1730–1830* (Harlow: Pearson Education, 1999).

Hertz, Neil, 'Two extravagant teachings', *Yale French Studies*, no. 63 (1982), pp. 59–71.

Hobson, Christopher Z., *Blake and Homosexuality* (New York and Basingstoke: Palgrave, 2000).

'"What is liberty without universal toleration?": Blake, homosexuality, and the cooperative commonwealth', in Steve Clark and David Worrall, eds., *Blake, Nation and Empire* (Basingstoke: Palgrave Macmillan, 2006), pp. 136–52.

'Blake and the evolution of same-sex subjectivity', in Helen P. Bruder and Tristanne Connolly, eds., *Queer Blake* (Basingstoke: Palgrave Macmillan, 2010), pp. 23–39.

Hoock, Holger, *The King's Artists: the Royal Academy of Arts and the Politics of British Culture 1760–1840* (Oxford: Clarendon Press, 2003).

Hopkins, James K., *A Woman to Deliver Her People: Joanna Southcott and English Millenarianism in an Era of Revolution* (Austin: University of Texas Press, 1982).

Howard, John, *Infernal Poetics: Poetic Structures in Blake's Lambeth Prophecies* (Cranbury, NJ and London: Associated University Presses, 1984).

Hutchings, Kevin, *Imagining Nature: Blake's Environmental Poetics* (Montreal and Kingston: McGill-Queen's University Press, 2002).

Irlam, Shaun, *Elations: the Poetics of Enthusiasm in Eighteenth-Century Britain* (Stanford University Press, 1999).

Jackson, H. J., *Romantic Readers: the Evidence of Marginalia* (New Haven and London: Yale University Press, 2005).

Johnson, Claudia, '"Let me make the novels of a country": Barbauld's The British Novelists (1810/1820)', *Novel*, vol. 34, no. 2 (spring 2001).

Johnson, Mary Lynn, '*Milton* and its contexts', in Morris Eaves, ed., *The Cambridge Companion to William Blake* (Cambridge University Press, 2003), pp. 231–50.

Kaplan, Cora, 'Wild Nights: pleasure/sexuality/feminism', in Nancy Armstrong and Leonard Tennenhouse, eds., *The Ideology of Conduct: Essays in Literature and the History of Sexuality* (London and New York: Methuen, 1987), pp. 160–84.

Kelly, Gary, 'Bluestocking feminism', in Elizabeth Eger, Charlotte Grant, Clíona Ó Gallchoir and Penny Warburton, eds., *Women, Writing and the Public Sphere, 1700–1830* (Cambridge University Press, 2001), pp. 163–80.

Keymer, Tom, *Richardson's Clarissa and the Eighteenth-Century Reader* (Cambridge University Press, 1992).

Keynes, Geoffrey, *The Tempera Paintings of William Blake* (London: Arts Council, 1951).

Kinnaird, Joan K., 'Mary Astell and the conservative contribution to English feminism', *The Journal of British Studies*, vol. 19, no. 1 (autumn 1979), pp. 53–75.

Klein, Lawrence, *Shaftesbury and the Culture of Politeness: Moral Discourse and Cultural Politics in Early Eighteenth-Century England* (Cambridge University Press, 1994).

Knapp, Lewis M., 'Dr John Armstrong, littérateur, and associate of Smollett, Thomson, Wilkes, and Other Celebrities', *PMLA*, vol. 59, no. 4 (December 1944), pp. 1019–58.

Kowaleski-Wallace, Elizabeth, *Their Father's Daughters: Hannah More, Maria Edgeworth and Patriarchal Complicity* (New York and Oxford: Oxford University Press, 1991).

Lamb, Jonathan, 'Fantasies of paradise', in Martin Fitzpatrick, Peter Jones, Christa Knellwolf and Iain McCalman, eds., *The Enlightenment World* (Abingdon: Routledge, 2007), pp. 522–3.

  'Horrid sympathy', in Michael T. Davis and Paul A. Pickering, eds., *Unrespectable Radicals: Popular Politics in the Age of Reform* (Aldershot: Ashgate, 2008), pp. 91–106.

Laqueur, Thomas, *Making Sex: Body and Gender from the Greeks to Freud* (Cambridge, MA: Harvard University Press, 1990, 1999).

Larrissy, Edward, 'Blake's Orient', *Romanticism*, vol. 11, no. 1 (2005).

Lincoln, Andrew, 'From America to the Four Zoas', in Morris Eaves, ed., *The Cambridge Companion to William Blake* (Cambridge University Press, 2003), pp. 210–30.

'Restoring the nation to Christianity: Blake and the aftermyth of revolution', in Steve Clark and David Worrall, eds., *Blake, Nation and Empire* (Basingstoke: Palgrave Macmillan, 2006), pp. 153–66.

'Blake and the history of radicalism', in Nicholas M. Williams, ed., *William Blake Studies* (Basingstoke: Palgrave Macmillan, 2006), pp. 214–34.

Linkin, Harriet Kramer, 'William Blake and Romantic women poets: "Then what have I to do with thee?"', in Helen P. Bruder, ed., *Women Reading William Blake* (Basingstoke: Palgrave Macmillan, 2007), pp. 127–36.

Lonsdale, Roger, ed., *Eighteenth-Century Women Poets* (Oxford University Press, 1989).

McCalman, Iain, 'Mad Lord George and Madame La Motte: riot and sexuality in the genesis of Burke's Reflections on the Revolution in France', *The Journal of British Studies*, vol. 35, no. 3 (July 1996), pp. 343–67.

The Last Alchemist: Count Cagliostro, Master of Magic in the Age of Reason (London: HarperCollins Perennial, 2004).

McClenahan, Catherine L., 'Albion and the sexual machine: Blake, gender and politics 1780–1795', in Jackie DiSalvo, G. A. Rosso and Christopher Z. Hobson, eds., *Blake, Politics and History* (New York and London: Garland Publishing, 1998), pp. 301–24.

McDannell, Colleen and Bernhard Lang, *Heaven, a History* (New Haven and London: Yale University Press, 1988, 2001).

McEvansoneya, Philip, 'Lord Egremont and Flaxman's "St Michael Overcoming Satan"', *The Burlington Magazine*, vol. 143, no. 1179 (June 2001), pp. 351–9.

McGann, Jerome, *The Poetics of Sensibility: a Revolution in Literary Style* (Oxford: Clarendon Press, 1996).

Makdisi, Saree, *William Blake and the Impossible History of the 1790s* (Chicago University Press, 2003).

'Blake's metropolitan radicalism', in James Chandler and Kevin Gilmartin, eds., *Romantic Metropolis* (Cambridge University Press, 2005), pp. 113–31.

Matthes, Melissa M., *The Rape of Lucretia and the Founding of Republics: Readings in Livy, Machiavelli and Rousseau* (University Park, PA: Penn State University, 2000).

Matthews, Susan, 'Jerusalem and nationalism', in Stephen Copley and John Whale, eds., *Beyond Romanticism: New Approaches to Texts and Contexts 1780–1832* (London: Routledge, 1992).

'Blake, Hayley and the history of sexuality', in Steve Clark and David Worrall eds., *Blake, Nation and Empire* (London: Palgrave Macmillan, 2006), pp. 83–101.

'Africa and Utopia: refusing a local habitation', in Steve Clark and Masashi Suzuki, eds., *The Reception of Blake in the Orient* (London: Continuum, 2006), pp. 104–20.

'Impurity of diction: the "Harlots curse" and dirty words', in Sarah Haggarty and Jon Mee, eds., *Blake and Conflict* (London: Palgrave Macmillan, 2009), pp. 65–83.

'The surprising success of Dr Armstrong: love and economy in the eighteenth century', in Steve Clark and Tristanne Connolly, eds., *Liberating Medicine 1720–1835* (London: Pickering and Chatto, 2009), pp. 193–208.

'Hayley on his toilette': Blake, Hayley and homophobia', in Helen P. Bruder and Tristanne Connolly, eds., *Queer Blake* (Basingstoke: Palgrave Macmillan, 2010), pp. 209–20.

'An alternative national gallery: Blake's 1809 exhibition and the attack on Evangelical Culture', *Tate Papers* (January 2011).

Mee, Jon, *Dangerous Enthusiasm: William Blake and the Culture of Radicalism in the 1790s* (Oxford University Press, 1992).

Romanticism, Enthusiasm and Regulation: Poetics and the Policing of Culture in the Romantic Period (Oxford University Press, 2003).

'Blake's politics in history', in Morris Eaves, ed., *The Cambridge Companion to William Blake* (Cambridge University Press, 2003), pp. 133–49.

'Bloody Blake: nation and circulation', in Steve Clark and David Worrall, eds., *Blake, Nation and Empire* (London: Palgrave Macmillan, 2006), pp. 63–82.

'"A little less conversation, a little more action": mutuality, converse and mental fight', in Sarah Haggarty and Jon Mee, eds., *Blake and Conflict* (London: Palgrave Macmillan: 2009), pp. 126–43.

Mellor, Anne K., 'Blake, gender and imperial ideology: a response', in Jackie Disalvo, G. A. Rosso and Christopher Z. Hobson, eds., *Blake, Politics, and History* (New York: Garland, 1998) pp. 350–3.

Mothers of the Nation: Women's Political Writing in England, 1780–1830 (Bloomington and Indianapolis: Indiana University Press, 2000).

'Blake, the Apocalypse and Romantic women writers', in Tim Fulford, ed., *Romanticism and Millenarianism*, (New York and Basingstoke: Palgrave, 2002), pp. 139–52.

Miles, Josephine, 'Blake's frame of language', in Morton D. Paley and Michael Phillips, eds., *William Blake: Essays in Honour of Geoffrey Keynes* (Oxford: Clarendon Press, 1973), pp. 86–95.

Mitchell, W. J. T., 'Dangerous Blake', *Studies in Romanticism*, vol. 21, no. 3 (fall 1982), pp. 410–16.

Molyviati-Toptsis, Urania, 'Sed falsa ad caelum mittunt insomnia manes (*Aeneid* 6.896)', *The American Journal of Philology*, vol. 116, no. 4 (winter 1995), pp. 639–52.

Moore, Jane, 'Wollstonecraft's secrets', *Women's Writing*, vol. 4, no. 2 (July 1997), pp. 247–62.

Munby, A. N. L., ed., *Sale Catalogues of Libraries of Eminent Persons*. Vol. II: *Poets and Men of Letters* (London: Mansell, Sotheby, 1971).

Murray, E. B. 'Thel, Thelyphthora, and the Daughters of Albion', *Studies in Romanticism*, vol. 20 (1981), pp. 275–97.

Myrone, Martin, *Bodybuilding: Reforming Masculinities in British Art 1750–1810* (New Haven and London: Yale University Press, 2005).

'Fuseli to Frankenstein', in Martin Myrone *et al.*, *Gothic Nightmares: Fuseli, Blake and the Romantic Imagination* (London: Tate Publishing, 2006).

The Blake Book (London: Tate Publishing, 2007).

'Fuseli and gothic spectacle', *Huntington Library Quarterly*, vol. 70, no. 2 (June 2007), pp. 289–310.

Newey, Vincent, 'Cowper prospects: self, nature, society', in Gavin Hopps and Jane Stabler, eds., *Romanticism and Religion from William Cowper to Wallace Stevens* (Aldershot: Ashgate, 2006), pp. 41–56.

Nussbaum, Felicity, 'Polygamy, *Pamela*, and the prerogative of empire', in Ann Bermingham and John Brewer, eds., *The Consumption of Culture 1600–1800: Image, Object, Text* (London & New York: Routledge, 1995), pp. 217–36.

O'Brien, Karen, *Women and Enlightenment in Eighteenth-Century Britain* (Cambridge University Press, 2009).

Okada, Kazuya, '"Typhon, the lower nature": Blake and Egypt as the Orient', in Steve Clark and Masashi Suzuki, eds., *The Reception of Blake in the Orient* (London and New York: Continuum, 2006), pp. 29–37.

Opie, Iona and Peter, eds., *The Oxford Dictionary of Nursery Rhymes* (Oxford University Press, 1951, 1977).

Ostriker, Alicia, 'Desire gratified and ungratified: William Blake and sexuality', *Blake: an Illustrated Quarterly*, vol. 16 (1982–3), pp. 156–65.

Otto, Peter, *Blake's Critique of Transcendence* (Oxford University Press, 2000).

'A pompous high priest: Urizen's ancient phallic religion in "The Four Zoas"', *Blake: an Illustrated Quarterly*, vol. 35, no. 1 (summer 2001), pp. 4–22.

'The regeneration of the body: sex, religion and the sublime in James Graham's Temple of Health and Hymen', *Romanticism On the Net*, 23 (August 2001).

Paley, Morton D., 'Cowper as Blake's spectre', *Eighteenth Century Studies*, vol. 1, no. 3 (spring 1968), pp. 236–52.

The Traveller in the Evening: the Last Works of William Blake (Oxford University Press, 2003).

'Blake's poems on art and artists', in Sarah Haggarty and Jon Mee, eds., *Blake and Conflict* (Basingstoke: Palgrave Macmillan, 2009), pp. 210–27.

Paulson, Ronald, *Representations of Revolution 1789–1820* (New Haven and London: Yale University Press, 1983).

Hogarth Vol. III: *Art and Politics, 1750–1764* (Cambridge: The Lutterworth Press, 1993).

Pearson, Jacqueline, *Women's Reading in Britain 1750–1835: a Dangerous Recreation* (Cambridge University Press, 1999).

'Mothering the novel: Frances Burney and the next generations of women novelists', *CW3: Corvey Women Writers on the Web*.

Peltz, Lucy. 'Constructing and celebrating the professional woman in literature and the arts', in Elizabeth Eger and Lucy Peltz, eds., *Brilliant Women: Eighteenth Century Bluestockings* (London: National Portrait Gallery, 2008), pp. 56–93.

Perry, Ruth, 'Colonizing the breast: sexuality and maternity in eighteenth century England', in John C. Font, ed., *Forbidden History: the State, Society and the Regulation of Sexuality in Modern Europe* (Chicago and London: University of Chicago Press, 1992), pp. 107–38.

Phillips, Michael, 'Blake and the Terror, 1792–1793', *The Library*, sixth series, vol. 16, no. 4 (December 1994), pp. 263–97.

Philp, Mark, *Godwin's Political Justice* (London: Duckworth, 1986).

Podmore, Colin, *The Moravian Church in England, 1728–1760* (Oxford: Clarendon Press, 1998).

Pointon, Marcia, *Hanging the Head: Portraiture and Social Formation in Eighteenth-Century England* (New Haven and London: Yale University Press, 1993).

Porter, Roy and Lesley Hall, *The Facts of Life: the Creation of Sexual Knowledge in Britain, 1650–1950* (New Haven and London: Yale University Press, 1995).

Pressly, Nancy L., *The Fuseli Circle in Rome: Early Romantic Art of the 1770s* (New Haven: Yale Center for British Art, 1979).

Priestman, Martin, *Romantic Atheism: Poetry and Freethought, 1780–1830* (Cambridge University Press, 1999).

Raine, Kathleen, *Blake and Tradition*, 2 vols. (London: Routledge, 1969).

Reisner, M. E., 'Effigies of power: Pitt and Fox as Canterbury Pilgrims', *Eighteenth-Century Studies*, vol. 12, no. 4 (summer 1979), pp. 481–503.

Rix, Robert, *William Blake and the Cultures of Radical Christianity* (Aldershot: Ashgate, 2007).

Rosenthal, Laura, *Infamous Commerce: Prostitution in Eighteenth-Century British Literature and Culture* (Ithaca, NY: Cornell University Press, 2006).

Rosso, G. A., 'The religion of empire: Blake's Rahab in its biblical contexts', in Alexander S. Gourlay, ed., *Prophetic Character: Essays on William Blake in Honor of John E. Grant* (West Cornwall, CT: Locust Hill Press, 2002), pp. 287–326.

Rowell, Christopher, 'Turner's Petworth', in Christopher Rowell, Ian Warrell and David Blayney Brown, *Turner at Petworth* (London Millbank: National Trust/ Tate publishing, 2002), pp. 15–27.

Russell, Gillian, 'The Theatre of Crim.Con.: Thomas Erskine, Adultery and Radical Politics in the 1790s', in Michael T. Davis and Paul A. Pickering, eds., *Unrespectable Radicals? Popular Politics in the Age of Reform* (Aldershot: Ashgate, 2008), pp. 57–89.

St Clair, William, *The Reading Nation in the Romantic Period* (Cambridge University Press, 2004).

Schor, Esther, *Bearing the Dead: the British Culture of Mourning from the Enlightenment to Victoria* (Princeton University Press, 1994).

Schuchard, Marsha Keith, *Why Mrs Blake Cried: William Blake and the Sexual Basis of Spiritual Vision* (London: Century, 2006).

Shaw, Jane, *Miracles in Enlightenment England* (New Haven and London: Yale University Press, 2006).

Siegel, Jonah, *Desire and Excess: the Nineteenth Century Culture of Art* (Princeton and Oxford: Princeton University Press, 2000).

Siskin, Clifford, *The Work of Writing: Literature and Social Change in Britain 1700–1830* (Baltimore and London: Johns Hopkins University Press, 1998).

Smith, Bruce R., 'Premodern sexualities', *PMLA*, vol. 115, no. 3 (May 2000), pp. 318–29.

Smith, Olivia, *The Politics of Language 1791–1819* (Oxford: Clarendon Press, 1984).

Solkin, David, 'Exhibitions of sympathy', in *Painting for Money: the Visual Arts and the Public Sphere in Eighteenth Century England* (New Haven and London: Yale University Press, 1992).

Solkin, David and Philippa Simpson, 'Turner and the North', in David Solkin, ed., *Turner and the Masters* (London: Tate Publishing, 2009).

Stott, Anne, *Hannah More: the First Victorian* (Oxford University Press, 2003).

Taylor, Barbara, *Mary Wollstonecraft and the Feminist Imagination* (Cambridge University Press, 2004).

Thompson, E. P., *Witness Against the Beast: William Blake and the Moral Law* (Cambridge University Press, 1993).

Tomaselli, Sylvana and Roy Porter, eds., *Rape: an Historical and Social Enquiry* (London: Basil Blackwell, 1986).

Turner, James Grantham, *One Flesh: Paradisal Marriage and Sexual Relations in the Age of Milton* (Oxford: Clarendon Press, 1987).

Viscomi, Joseph, 'Blake after Blake: a nation discovers genius', in Steve Clark and David Worrall, eds., *Blake, Nation and Empire* (Basingstoke: Palgrave Macmillan, 2006), pp. 214–50.

Wahrman, Dror, *The Making of the Modern Self: Identity and Culture in Eighteenth-Century England* (New Haven and London: Yale University Press, 2004).

Warner, Marina, 'Invented plots: the enchanted puppets and fairy doubles of Henry Fuseli', in Martin Myrone et al., *Gothic Nightmares: Fuseli, Blake and the Romantic Imagination* (London: Tate Publishing, 2006).

Watt, Ian, *The Rise of the Novel* (London: Pimlico, 1957, 2000).

Weinglass, D. H., *Prints and Engraved Illustrations By and After Henry Fuseli* (Aldershot: Scolar Press, 2000).

'Fuseli, Henry (1741–1825)', *Oxford Dictionary of National Biography* (Oxford University Press, September 2004).

Weir, David, *Brahma in the West: William Blake and the Oriental Renaissance* (New York: State University of New York Press, 2003).

Whitehead, Angus, '"A wise tale of the Mahometans": Blake and Islam, 1819–26', in Jon Mee and Sarah Haggarty, eds., *Blake and Conflict* (Basingstoke: Palgrave Macmillan, 2008), pp. 27–47.

Williams, Nicholas M., *Ideology and Utopia in the Poetry of William Blake* (Cambridge University Press, 1998).

'Introduction' in Nicholas M. Williams, ed., *Palgrave Advances in William Blake Studies* (Basingstoke: Palgrave Macmillan, 2006).

Wood, Marcus, *Slavery, Empathy and Pornography* (Oxford University Press, 2002).

Worrall, David, 'Thel in Africa: William Blake and the post-colonial, post-Swedenborgian female subject', in Steve Clark and Masashi Suzuki, eds., *The Reception of Blake in the Orient* (London: Continuum, 2006), pp. 17–28.

Wright, Julia, *Blake, Nationalism, and the Politics of Alienation* (Ohio University Press, 2004).

Wyndham, H. A., *A Family History 1688–1837* (London and New York: Oxford University Press, 1950).

Index

Africa 91, 98, 100, 118
Armstrong, John 38–9

Badiou, Alain 7, 15, 209
Banks, Thomas 201
Barbauld, Anna Laetitia 35, 66, 151–2, 156, 161
Barker-Benfield, G. J. 37
Barrell, John 21, 32, 215
Barruel, Abbé Augustin 84, 91, 189
Barry, James 40
  and Blake's 1809 exhibition 202
  Commerce 200
  on enthusiasm and visual culture 25–6
  An Inquiry 25
  Jupiter and Juno on Mount Ida, etching 180
Bederman, Gail 5, 189
Behn, Aphra 160
Beulah 1, 6, 14, 80, 86, 106–7, 187
  Daughters of 2, 54, 57, 83, 118
  and *A Midsummer Night's Dream* 55
  Songs of 92, 94
Bible, the 20, 132, 207
  bibliomancy 164
  British and Foreign Bible Society 153
  'Fragment Hypothesis' 154
  a 'loose Bible' 101
  Old Testament polygamy 88
  reading 152
Bienville, M. T. D., *Nymphomania* 36
Bindman, David 50
Binhammer, Katherine 4, 5, 6, 189
Blair, Robert, *The Grave* 14, 177–80
Blake, William
  1809 exhibition 45, 171
  All Religions are One 7
  The Ancient Britons 202
  commercial work 10
  Europe 163; the 'female dream' 30;
    copy D 157
  Everlasting Gospel 112, 191

Felpham 58, 59, 60, 80, 83, 87, 115, 143
'Female Will', 41
The French Revolution 19
The Goats 199
'Imitation of Pope' 203
An Island in the Moon 40
Milton 2
Oberon and Titania 48
Pity, colour print 19
'Some Questions Answered' 9
Spiritual Form of Nelson 202
Spiritual Form of Pitt 202
'To Tirzah' 14
Visions of the Daughters of Albion 5, 12, 16–21,
    28, 52, 124, 147, 149
Whore of Babylon 92, 93, 182, 185
bluestockings 5, 64, 71
Boyd, Henry 141, 144–5
Boydell, John 21, 42, 139
  Shakespeare gallery 40, 47
Bromley, Robert 41
Bruder, Helen P. 5, 18, 53, 100, 102, 149, 193
Butts, Thomas 40–1, 45, 59, 60, 92
Bysshe, Edward, *The Art of English Poetry*
    17, 154, 160–4

caricature 39, 67, 148, 198
Carter, Elizabeth 63, 65, 106
Catholicism 25, 36, 88
circulation 60, 85, 153, 157
civic humanism 32, 217
Clark, Anna 12, 13, 86
Clery, E. J. 8, 35, 105
commerce 37, 119, 201
Connolly, Tristanne 7, 14
convents 41
Cooke, Tom 21
coquette, the figure of the 45, 53, 86
Cowper, William 4, 59, 76, 87, 110
  the 'adult'ress' 190
  Anti-Thelyphthora 90

Cowper, William (cont.)
  the cottager 153
  Gordon riots, the 62
  letters 144
  Odyssey translation 169
  Omai 202
  the poor 64
  reaction to *Thelyphthora* 87
  view of heaven 176
Crébillon, Claude Prosper Solyot de 82,
  97, 116
Cristall, Ann Batten 11, 175, 190
Cumberland, George 6, 8, 11, 19, 30, 60, 109, 118,
  146, 169, 190
  Europe copy D 157–60
  looking at art 192–5
  nakedness 202
  Thoughts on Outline 49
Cupid 39, 52, 194

Darwin, Erasmus 3, 4, 30, 79, 137
  Botanic Garden 51
  Fertilization of Egypt 45
  Linnaean taxonomy 120
  polypus 86
  Rosicrucian machinery 80
domestic, the 20, 30, 60, 72, 87, 113, 177,
  184, 209
domestic affections 119
domestic happiness 110
domestic ideology 13, 170, 189, 200, 206
domestic intimacy 144
domestic, the masculine 180
domestic memoirs 171
domestic privacy 196
Dryden, John 51, 145, 154, 159, 161
Duncombe, John 90, 142

earthquake 121–5
Egremont, Countess of 182–3
Egremont, Lord 181
  as patron 184
Eleusinian mysteries 27, 28, 48, 51, 208
Elfenbein, Andrew 5
Elizabeth I 44
Ellis, Markman 30
embroidery 72; *see also* Wollstonecraft, Mary
enthusiasm 14
  and bereavement 58, 174
  as bourgeois category 59
  controlled by sentiment 59
  danger to women 175
  feminised 174
  and hot countries 47
  and madness 111

and pictures 25
and sexual licence 26
and the Sibyl 161
visual 23, 25, 31
and women 27
Erdman, David 78, 158
Essick, Robert N. 1, 13, 93, 178
Esterhammer, Angela 213
exhibition culture 21–9, 31, 49

fairies 46, 48, 80, 88, 92
Fallon, David 32
fashion 40
feminist critique 1, 5
  limitations of androgyny 7
  Second Wave feminism 6
Flaxman, Ann 113, 168, 193
Flaxman, John 59, 60, 66, 74, 75, 170, 176, 181,
  182, 184, 186, 192, 203
Flaxman, Maria 60
Foucault, Michel 4, 5, 37, 209
Fox, Charles James 196
Fox, Susan 15
Frye, Northrop 10
Fuseli, Henry 6, 11, 14, 30
  Aphorisms on Art 39
  and William Blake, *Allegory of a Dream
    of Love* 50
  on *Clarissa* 141
  on Cowper's *Iliad* 137
  The Danish King Poisoned While He Sleeps 49
  dreams as subject matter 41
  illustrating Cowper's *Poems* 137
  knowledge of Hindu mythology 52
  on the Last Judgment 183
  *The Mighty Mother Sails Through
    the Air* 69
  Milton gallery 157, 176
  The Nightmare 30, 42, 93, 138
  Prospectus to *The Grave* 177
  Remarks on Rousseau 34–6
  sexuality of the ancient world 38
  Titania and Bottom 43–8, 186

Gatrell, Vic 201
Gordon riots, the 61, 62, 160, 188
Graham, James 28, 96
Gray, Thomas 10, 104, 113, 168, 180
  the cottage 113

Hayley, William 3, 6, 11, 12, 182, 204
  the book of Enoch 95–8
  celibacy 82–6
  child memoirs 171
  on Elizabeth I 44

Essay on Old Maids 44, 82–5, 105, 129
The Life of Cowper 112–15
Life of Milton 59
reception 77–9
and sensibility 73–7
The Triumphs of Temper 56–66
women writers 144
heaven 2, 18, 35, 55, 95, 107, 115, 125, 170, 171,
    175, 180, 185, 204; *see also* Cowper,
    William; Milton, John; Wollstonecraft,
    Mary
  as bourgeois family 171
  corporeality of 178
  Hannah More on 203
  of sensibility 65
  sex in 208
Hindu mythology 52
Hobson, Christopher 5, 32, 52, 111, 116, 149
Hogarth, William 133
  Analysis of Beauty 21
  The Distrest Poet 154
  Enthusiasm Delineated 21–7
  The Harlot's Progress 125
  Marriage à la Mode 116
  Satan, Sin and Death 125
  The Sleeping Congregation 205
Horne Tooke, John 11, 66, 169

identity politics 7, 8, 18
Islam 97, 98

Johnson, John 59, 60, 129, 151
Johnson, Joseph 11, 52, 53, 67, 70, 71, 80, 106,
    137, 140, 176, 188, 190
Johnson, Samuel 16, 34, 62, 69, 107, 117

Kaplan, Cora 4, 53, 90

Lamb, Jonathan 20, 131, 194
Laqueur, Thomas 8, 96, 151, 188
Lavater, John Casper 58, 208
Lavington, George 27–8, 165, 205
Lewis, Matthew *The Monk* 17, 36
libertine enlightenment 82
libertinism 31, 32, 34, 49, 50, 53, 88, 94, 96,
    98, 145, 189, 204
looking 9, 16, 19, 21, 24, 27, 136;
    see also voyeurism
  the innocence of 192–4
  London spectacle 32
Lucretius, *De Rerum Natura* 38
luxury 32, 38, 39, 45, 78, 119–20

Madan, Martin 86–92, 120
Makdisi, Saree 8, 9, 74, 80, 167

Malkin, Benjamin Heath 11
  child memoirs 171
  on enthusiasm 174, 175
  on Wollstonecraft 176
Malkin, Charlotte 171
  memoir 172
Malthus, Daniel 136
Malthus, Thomas 108
Mandeville, Bernard 82, 84, 105, 132
marriage 2, 31, 74, 88, 89, 91, 105, 109, 115, 124,
    125, 176, 188, 189
masturbation 37, 52
Mee, Jon 8, 67
  bricolage 166
  vulgar enthusiasm 213
Mellor, Anne K. 5, 133, 207
memory 173
metaphor 19
Milton, John 6
  allegory of Satan, Sin and Death 62
  on divorce 89
  domestic relations 62
  Nativity Ode 30
  Paradise Lost 20
  Protestant sexuality 88
  sex in heaven 208
miniature 40, 45, 93, 180
misogyny 1, 12, 14, 102–5, 111, 121, 182
missionary work 197, 199
Moravian church 27
  casting lots 165
Moravian culture 164
  of sexuality 9
  visual 27
More, Hannah 5, 13, 34, 62, 106
  on the arts 195
  the Blagdon controversy 205
  monarchy as bourgeois family 171
  on reading the Bible 153
  quoting Cowper 110
  Sensibility, an Ode 63
  Strictures 73, 91
  on Wollstonecraft 189
mourning 169–74
Muses, the 38, 54, 106, 175
Myrone, Martin 9, 11, 31, 72

ornament 118, 137, 143, 195
Ostriker, Alicia 14
Otaheite *see* Tahiti
Otto, Peter 10

passions 20, 32, 36, 44, 54, 55, 60, 63, 115,
    162, 175, 183, 185
phallic religion 213

pity 15, 33, 78, 88, 129, 170, 172
Polwhele, Richard
  Anecdotes of Methodism 205
  on Hayley 79
  The Unsex'd Females 4
  on Wollstonecraft, Mary 194
polygamy 88, 91, 95, 98, 101, 133, 146
polypus, the 57, 86, 113
Pope, Alexander 79, 92, 116, 137, 166, 178, 202
  The Dunciad 102
  Epistle to a Lady 35, 56, 69
  Essay on Man 99
  The Iliad 158, 204
  The Rape of the Lock 56
pornography 19, 50–3, 139, 180, 206, 209
preaching 72, 205
Priestman, Martin 50, 111, 147
prints 21, 39, 67
prostitution 18, 92, 132, 188, 201
Protestant visual culture 39
Protestantism 25, 84
  and sexuality 88
public
  as Blake's audience 10
  and censorship 34
  cultural power of women 6
  and education 146
  and enthusiasm 72
  female influence in 12
  and libertinism 145
  women's contribution to 63
public art
  civic emancipation from sexuality 32
  and the domestic 39
  and fantasy 42
  and fresco 45
public art exhibitions 21, 197
  first public art exhibition 26
public hospitals
  and prostitution 103
public mourning 171
public patronage 41
public sphere, the
  and domestic affections 119
public, the death of the 171
puppets and puppet shows 24, 45

queer theory 5

rape 12, 17, 20, 96, 129, 144, 146, 147, 148–51, 152, 155
Raphael 24, 42, 184
raree-shew box 136
republicanism
  and domestic relations 62
rhyme 137, 159, 204

Richardson, Samuel 65
  category of 'woman' 8
  Clarissa as novel of feeling 141
  the English cottage 143
  as impolite author 143
  and letters 144
  Lovelace as Satan 142
  and rape 148–51
  use of Bysshe 154–6
Robinson, Mary 198
Rome 31, 38, 52
Rosicrucian machinery 79, 80, 156
Rowe, Nicholas
  The Fair Penitent 158, 198
  The Tragedy of Jane Shore 198–9
Royal Academy 25, 41
  exhibitions 28

Schuchard, Marsha Keith 9, 10
Sensibility, Age of 12
sex panic 13
sexual fantasy 18
sexuality
  adultery panic 13
  phallic religion 10
  polygamy debate 13
  and secrecy 10
  semantic change 3–5, 212
sexuality of plants 3
Shakespeare 34, 39, 42, 75
  in Bysshe's *Art of Poetry* 160
  Macbeth 19, 35
  A Midsummer Night's Dream 42–3, 55
  as original genius 143
  sex of Ariel 178
Smith, Adam 19–22, 32, 44
  on conversation 65
  imagining death 173
  on mourning 172
Smith, Bruce R. 4
Society of Arts, Manufactures and
  Commerce 200
softness 38, 49, 56, 57, 58, 61, 67, 73, 77,
  118, 160, 203, 204
Southcott, Joanna 156, 159, 165
Sterne, Laurence 34, 67, 77, 195
sublime, the 25, 28, 39, 44
  and Dante 144
  and religious enthusiasm 59
Swedenborg 9, 24, 107, 171
  conjugal love 100
Swift, Jonathan 27, 63, 67
  attack on Astell 105
  A Tale of a Tub 27, 62
Swift, Theophilus 69, 98

sympathy 19–22
  'horrid sympathy' 20

Tahiti 202
Taylor, Thomas 17, 50
  Dissertation on the Eleusinian and Bacchic Mysteries 51
  on Wollstonecraft, Mary 191
Thompson, E. P. 9
Thomson, James 38, 75, 129
Turner, James 214

Virgil, *Aeneid* 51, 162
virginity 35, 82, 83, 84, 95, 96, 99, 102, 108, 150, 152, 156
  early Christian cult of 89
voyeurism 12, 161, 206
  and philanthropy 209

Wahrman, Dror 7, 102

Warburton, William 27, 51
Williams, Nicholas M. 7, 8, 147, 214
Winckelmann, Johann Joachim 32–4
Wollstonecraft, Mary 57, 165, 189, 190, 191
  on conversation 60
  the distinction of sex 176
  heaven 81
  history painting 192
  on passion 53–4
  polygamy 91
  secrecy 156
  on sewing 72
  on temper 77
  A Vindication of the Rights of Woman 6
women readers 12, 213
Worrall, David 9

Young, Edward 40, 143

CAMBRIDGE STUDIES IN ROMANTICISM

General Editor
JAMES CHANDLER, *University of Chicago*

1. *Romantic Correspondence: Women, Politics and the Fiction of Letters*
   MARY A. FAVRET

2. *British Romantic Writers and the East: Anxieties of Empire*
   NIGEL LEASK

3. *Poetry as an Occupation and an Art in Britain, 1760–1830*
   PETER MURPHY

4. *Edmund Burke's Aesthetic Ideology: Language, Gender and Political Economy in Revolution*
   TOM FURNISS

5. *In the Theatre of Romanticism: Coleridge, Nationalism, Women*
   JULIE A. CARLSON

6. *Keats, Narrative and Audience*
   ANDREW BENNETT

7. *Romance and Revolution: Shelley and the Politics of a Genre*
   DAVID DUFF

8. *Literature, Education, and Romanticism: Reading as Social Practice, 1780–1832*
   ALAN RICHARDSON

9. *Women Writing about Money: Women's Fiction in England, 1790–1820*
   EDWARD COPELAND

10. *Shelley and the Revolution in Taste: The Body and the Natural World*
    TIMOTHY MORTON

11. *William Cobbett: The Politics of Style*
    LEONORA NATTRASS

12. *The Rise of Supernatural Fiction, 1762–1800*
    E. J. CLERY

13. *Women Travel Writers and the Language of Aesthetics, 1716–1818*
    ELIZABETH A. BOHLS

14. *Napoleon and English Romanticism*
    SIMON BAINBRIDGE

15. *Romantic Vagrancy: Wordsworth and the Simulation of Freedom*
    CELESTE LANGAN

16. *Wordsworth and the Geologists*
    JOHN WYATT

17. *Wordsworth's Pope: A Study in Literary Historiography*
ROBERT J. GRIFFIN

18. *The Politics of Sensibility: Race, Gender and Commerce in the Sentimental Novel*
MARKMAN ELLIS

19. *Reading Daughters' Fictions, 1709–1834: Novels and Society from Manley to Edgeworth*
CAROLINE GONDA

20. *Romantic Identities: Varieties of Subjectivity, 1774–1830*
ANDREA K. HENDERSON

21. *Print Politics: The Press and Radical Opposition in Early Nineteenth-Century England*
KEVIN GILMARTIN

22. *Reinventing Allegory*
THERESA M. KELLEY

23. *British Satire and the Politics of Style, 1789–1832*
GARY DYER

24. *The Romantic Reformation: Religious Politics in English Literature, 1789–1824*
ROBERT M. RYAN

25. *De Quincey's Romanticism: Canonical Minority and the Forms of Transmission*
MARGARET RUSSETT

26. *Coleridge on Dreaming: Romanticism, Dreams and the Medical Imagination*
JENNIFER FORD

27. *Romantic Imperialism: Universal Empire and the Culture of Modernity*
SAREE MAKDISI

28. *Ideology and Utopia in the Poetry of William Blake*
NICHOLAS M. WILLIAMS

29. *Sexual Politics and the Romantic Author*
SONIA HOFKOSH

30. *Lyric and Labour in the Romantic Tradition*
ANNE JANOWITZ

31. *Poetry and Politics in the Cockney School: Keats, Shelley, Hunt and their Circle*
JEFFREY N. COX

32. *Rousseau, Robespierre and English Romanticism*
GREGORY DART

33. *Contesting the Gothic: Fiction, Genre and Cultural Conflict, 1764–1832*
JAMES WATT

34. *Romanticism, Aesthetics, and Nationalism*
DAVID ARAM KAISER

35. *Romantic Poets and the Culture of Posterity*
ANDREW BENNETT

36. *The Crisis of Literature in the 1790s: Print Culture and the Public Sphere*
PAUL KEEN

37. *Romantic Atheism: Poetry and Freethought, 1780–1830*
MARTIN PRIESTMAN

38. *Romanticism and Slave Narratives: Transatlantic Testimonies*
HELEN THOMAS

39. *Imagination under Pressure, 1789–1832: Aesthetics, Politics, and Utility*
JOHN WHALE

40. *Romanticism and the Gothic: Genre, Reception, and Canon Formation, 1790–1820*
MICHAEL GAMER

41. *Romanticism and the Human Sciences: Poetry, Population, and the Discourse of the Species*
MAUREEN N. MCLANE

42. *The Poetics of Spice: Romantic Consumerism and the Exotic*
TIMOTHY MORTON

43. *British Fiction and the Production of Social Order, 1740–1830*
MIRANDA J. BURGESS

44. *Women Writers and the English Nation in the 1790s*
ANGELA KEANE

45. *Literary Magazines and British Romanticism*
MARK PARKER

46. *Women, Nationalism and the Romantic Stage: Theatre and Politics in Britain, 1780–1800*
BETSY BOLTON

47. *British Romanticism and the Science of the Mind*
ALAN RICHARDSON

48. *The Anti-Jacobin Novel: British Conservatism and the French Revolution*
M. O. GRENBY

49. *Romantic Austen: Sexual Politics and the Literary Canon*
CLARA TUITE

50. *Byron and Romanticism*
JEROME MCGANN AND JAMES SODERHOLM

51. *The Romantic National Tale and the Question of Ireland*
    INA FERRIS

52. *Byron, Poetics and History*
    JANE STABLER

53. *Religion, Toleration, and British Writing, 1790–1830*
    MARK CANUEL

54. *Fatal Women of Romanticism*
    ADRIANA CRACIUN

55. *Knowledge and Indifference in English Romantic Prose*
    TIM MILNES

56. *Mary Wollstonecraft and the Feminist Imagination*
    BARBARA TAYLOR

57. *Romanticism, Maternity and the Body Politic*
    JULIE KIPP

58. *Romanticism and Animal Rights*
    DAVID PERKINS

59. *Georgic Modernity and British Romanticism: Poetry and the
    Mediation of History*
    KEVIS GOODMAN

60. *Literature, Science and Exploration in the Romantic Era: Bodies
    of Knowledge*
    TIMOTHY FULFORD, DEBBIE LEE, AND PETER J. KITSON

61. *Romantic Colonization and British Anti-Slavery*
    DEIRDRE COLEMAN

62. *Anger, Revolution, and Romanticism*
    ANDREW M. STAUFFER

63. *Shelley and the Revolutionary Sublime*
    CIAN DUFFY

64. *Fictions and Fakes: Forging Romantic Authenticity, 1760–1845*
    MARGARET RUSSETT

65. *Early Romanticism and Religious Dissent*
    DANIEL E. WHITE

66. *The Invention of Evening: Perception and Time in Romantic Poetry*
    CHRISTOPHER R. MILLER

67. *Wordsworth's Philosophic Song*
    SIMON JARVIS

68. *Romanticism and the Rise of the Mass Public*
    ANDREW FRANTA

69. *Writing against Revolution: Literary Conservatism in Britain, 1790–1832*
KEVIN GILMARTIN

70. *Women, Sociability and Theatre in Georgian London*
GILLIAN RUSSELL

71. *The Lake Poets and Professional Identity*
BRIAN GOLDBERG

72. *Wordsworth Writing*
ANDREW BENNETT

73. *Science and Sensation in Romantic Poetry*
NOEL JACKSON

74. *Advertising and Satirical Culture in the Romantic Period*
JOHN STRACHAN

75. *Romanticism and the Painful Pleasures of Modern Life*
ANDREA K. HENDERSON

76. *Balladeering, Minstrelsy, and the Making of British Romantic Poetry*
MAUREEN N. MCLANE

77. *Romanticism and Improvisation, 1750–1850*
ANGELA ESTERHAMMER

78. *Scotland and the Fictions of Geography: North Britain, 1760–1830*
PENNY FIELDING

79. *Wordsworth, Commodification and Social Concern: The Poetics of Modernity*
DAVID SIMPSON

80. *Sentimental Masculinity and the Rise of History, 1790–1890*
MIKE GOODE

81. *Fracture and Fragmentation in British Romanticism*
ALEXANDER REGIER

82. *Romanticism and Music Culture in Britain, 1770–1840: Virtue and Virtuosity*
GILLEN D'ARCY WOOD

83. *The Truth about Romanticism: Pragmatism and Idealism in Keats, Shelley, Coleridge*
TIMOTHY MILNES

84. *Blake's Gifts: Poetry and the Politics of Exchange*
SARAH HAGGARTY

85. *Real Money and Romanticism*
MATTHEW ROWLINSON

86. *Sentimental Literature and Anglo-Scottish Identity, 1745–1820*
     JULIET SHIELDS

87. *Romantic Tragedies: The Dark Employments of Wordsworth,*
     Coleridge, and Shelley
     REEVE PARKER

88. *Blake, Sexuality and Bourgeois Politeness*
     SUSAN MATTHEWS

For EU product safety concerns, contact us at Calle de José Abascal, 56–1°,
28003 Madrid, Spain or eugpsr@cambridge.org.

www.ingramcontent.com/pod-product-compliance
Ingram Content Group UK Ltd.
Pitfield, Milton Keynes, MK11 3LW, UK
UKHW020335140625